Healthy Young Children
A Manual for Programs

Healthy Young Children
A Manual for Programs

Editors
Abby Shapiro Kendrick, Roxane Kaufmann, and Katherine P. Messenger

Consulting Editors
Francine H. Jacobs and Serena Mailloux, M.D.

A cooperative effort of

Administration for Children, Youth and Families

American Academy of Pediatrics

Division of Maternal and Child Health, U.S. Department of Health and Human Services

Georgetown University Child Development Center

Massachusetts Department of Public Health

National Association for the Education of Young Children

National Association for the Education of Young Children
Washington, D.C.

This manual was originally funded through an intra-agency agreement between the Administration for Children, Youth and Families; the Division of Maternal and Child Health, U.S. Department of Health and Human Services; and the Massachusetts Department of Public Health, through federal Maternal and Child Health Block Grant funds to the Commonwealth of Massachusetts and to Georgetown University Child Development Center, 3800 Reservoir Road, N.W., Washington, DC 20007.

Photographs

Hildegard Adler, cover
Nancy P. Alexander, 12, 38, 86, 99, 128, 161
Dena Bawinkel, 191
Robert J. Bennett, 137
Marja Bergen, 25
Faith Bowlus, 6
Jim Bradshaw, cover, 166
Judy Burr, 19
Rose Engel, 164
Ginger Howard, 31
Robert Koenig, 148
Lois Main, 129

Merrie L. Murray, 80
Katherine Nell, 195
Wendy Press, 60
Rick Reinhard, 259
Paul M. Schrock Photos, 175
Michael Siluk, 74
Steve & Mary Skjold Photographs, 118
Michaelyn Straub, 75
Subjects & Predicates, 32, 78, 165, 205
Dave Swan, 61
Bob Taylor, 68
James A. Tuck, cover

Production coordinator and designer—Melanie Rose White
Illustrations—Dilworth Design

The information in this manual complements, but is not a substitute for, the advice of a child's or program's health care provider. It reflects current research and standards in the fields of health and early childhood education. However, in such rapidly changing fields, new information and regulations are constantly emerging. You are reminded to be alert to such changes and to always check with your local department of public health for the most current recommendations.

Published by the National Association for the Education of Young Children
1509 16th Street, N.W.
Washington, DC 20036-1426

Library of Congress Catalog Card Number: 88-060739
ISBN Catalog Number: 0-935989-69-2
NAEYC #704

Printed in the United States of America

Preface

As program directors and teachers, you must protect and promote the health and well-being of the young children, staff, and families in your care. This manual was developed as a reference and resource guide to help you meet your health and safety responsibilities. You can achieve major health gains by taking several simple steps. Washing hands, for example, is the single best thing people can do to prevent the spread of infectious disease. When you include toothbrushing in the daily routine, children learn good habits for life. You may prevent a tragic injury by conducting frequent site safety checks. Your careful, regular observations of children may reveal health problems that can respond to early treatment. Specific information, procedures, and recommendations on each of these topics, as well as on many others, are provided here.

This manual has been reviewed by both health and early childhood professionals and describes very high standards for health policies. None of the recommendations was made lightly or without good evidence that it is important to protect the health of children and staff. You may find it impossible to meet some of these standards in your program. Implement as many of these recommendations as you can, but don't expect to change everything overnight. Plan carefully and thoroughly before you make any changes.

You may find that some of our recommendations differ from materials you have received from the Centers for Disease Control and Prevention (CDC), *National Health and Safety Performance Standards: Guidelines for Out-of-Home Child Care Programs* of the American Public Health Association/American Academy of Pediatrics, or from your own health consultants. Because there is not complete agreement within the medical community about specific procedures and treatments, you will have to make the best decision you can after hearing many points of view. Your state or local department of public health can serve as a valuable resource for information and guidance.

Healthy Young Children was designed as a reference document and contains a great deal of information. To use it effectively, you should read it through at least one time to become familiar with the contents and to complete information for your program.

You may copy any part of the manual for staff, parents, your health consultant, or community agencies, but be sure to acknowledge the source of the material when you reuse it.

Acknowledgments

Hundreds of people have been involved in the preparation of this document. The need for a comprehensive guide about health in programs for young children has been acute. The Preschool Health Program, Division of Family Health Services, Massachusetts Department of Public Health, first tackled the enormous task of pulling together material for child care workers in that state.

At the same time, the Georgetown University Child Development Center and the National Association for the Education of Young Children were also seeking to publish material on child care health. A grant from the Administration for Children, Youth and Families and the Division of Maternal and Child Health of the U.S. Department of Health and Human Services was awarded to Georgetown to develop materials on the topic. Georgetown and NAEYC were fortunate to learn of the work from Massachusetts and collaborated with Abby Shapiro Kendrick to adapt the original material, written especially for Massachusetts, for a national audience. In addition to the Massachusetts edition, a limited edition was made available through Georgetown University Child Development Center. Since those volumes were released, the material has been revised further and updated by the National Association for the Education of Young Children, with special assistance from Karen Sokal-Gutierrez, M.D., in reviewing the 1995 edition with the standards of the American Public Health Association and the American Academy of Pediatrics as published in *Caring for Our Children— National Health and Safety Performance Standards: Guidelines for Out-of-Home Child Care Programs*.

NAEYC gratefully acknowledges the American Academy of Pediatrics for their cooperative efforts during each of the revisions of this publication— with special thanks to the Academy's Committee on Early Childhood, Adoption, and Dependent Care.

Any undertaking of this magnitude necessarily involves many people with expertise in different areas. Some wrote major sections of the book, other served as reviewers, and still others were consultants. Several provided editorial and word processing services. We gratefully acknowledge the contributions of the many people and organizations whose untiring efforts made this publication a reality and a current source of information.

Primary author

Abby Shapiro Kendrick

Contributing authors

Susan S. Aronson, M.D.
Mary Jean Brown
Elba Crespo
Margaret Dyke
Kathleen Gallagher
Ellie Goldberg
Jo-Ann S. Harris, M.D.
Kim Hesse
Marilyn Hoy-Youngblood
Paul Hunter
Francine Jacobs
Mary Renck Jalongo
Roxane Kaufmann
Susan Lett, M.D.
Serena Mailloux, M.D.
Massachusetts Department of Social Services
Michelle Miclette
Janice Mirabassi
Lynne Mofenson, M.D.
Ruth Palombo
Barbara Polhamus
Preschool Enrichment Team staff
Melissa Ann Renck
Diane Ricciotti
Cindy Rogers
Karen Sokal-Gutierrez, M.D.
Mary Terrell
Esther Wender, M.D.
Howard Wensley
Patricia Wise

Consulting editors

Francine H. Jacobs
Serena Mailloux, M.D.

Primary reviewers

Susan S. Aronson, M.D., (1990, 1991, 1995 editions)
Karen Sokal-Gutierrez, M.D., (1995 edition)

Reviewers

American Academy of
    Pediatrics
American Red Cross
Jenny Austin
Phil Baimas
Fran Barrett
Helene Bednarsch
Connie Brown
Mary Jean Brown
Linda Burbank
Nancy Carrey-Beaver
Peggy Casey
Lisa Cole
Gregory Connolly
Pamela Coughlin
Elba Crespo
Donna Deardorff
Betty Donovan
Joan Doyle
Margaret Dyke
Beverly Edgehill
Bess Emanuel
Martin Favero, M.D.
Gail Fenton
Sally Fogerty
Karen Frederick
Beth Fredericks
Donna Haig Friedman
Gerri Norris Funke
Susan Gallagher
Ellie Goldberg
George Grady
Mary Greene
Bernard Guyer
Dorothy Hall
Jo-Ann S. Harris, M.D.
Cathy Hess
Patti Hills
Marilyn Hoy-
    Youngblood
Lily Hsu
Paul Hunter
Francine Jacobs
Mary Renck Jalongo
Karl Kastorf
Marie Keefe
Nancy Kloczko
Beverly Larson
Mary Leary
Linette Liebling
Anne Long

Phyllis Magrab
Marion Malinowski
Massachusetts
    Department of Social
    Services
Bernadine McQueeney
Michelle Miclette
Janice Mirabassi
Lynne Mofenson, M.D.
New England
    Association for the
    Education of Young
    Children
Jean Collins Norris
Mary O'Connor
Ruth Palombo
Fran Patch
Rea Pfeiffer
Judith Pokorni
Barbara Polhamus
Preschool Enrichment
    Team staff
Elizabeth Pressman
Virginia Rail
Melissa Ann Renck
Cindy Rodgers
Pamela Romanow
Dennis Rosen
Tanya Ryden
Nancy Schirmer
Ken Schulman
Joyce Sebian
Jack Shonkoff
Benjamin Siegel
Barbara Silverstein
Havi Stander
Mary Terrell
Linda Truitt
Deborah Klein Walker
Deborah A. Waring
Michael Weitzman
Howard Wensley
Jack Wertheimer
Becky Wilson
Patricia Wise
Suzi Wojdyslawski
Linda Yeomans
Marian Zeitlin
Deborah A. Ziegler
David Zuccolo

Contents

Preface, v

List of figures, xiii

Section A—Promoting health in programs for young children

1—The basics: Policies, providers, and records, 3
Health policies, 3
Staff responsibilities for health, 3
Communicating with health providers, 7
Talking to the child's physician: Thoughts for the child care provider, 8
Keeping health records, 10

2—Health education in programs for young children, 11
Health curriculum for children, 11
Health education for staff and parents, 12

Section B—Healthful environment

3—Creating a healthy environment, 16
Keeping clean, 17
Handwashing, 17
Disposable gloves, 19
Space, 22
Air quality, 22
Indoor pollution, 23
Food handling, 25
Handling contaminated items, 25
Turnover and health issues, 26

4—Sanitation standards, 29
Housekeeping, 29
Handwashing, 32
Kitchen facilities, 32
Storage and disposal of garbage, 34
Laundry, 34
Toilet facilities, 35
Plumbing, 35
Ventilation, light, and heat, 35

5—Diapering and toilet learning
  Diapering, 37
  Toilet learning, 38

Section C—Safety and first aid

6—Safety, 47
  Creating a safe facility, 47
  Times when children get hurt, 47
  Indoor safety, 47
  Safety beyond the classrooms, 64
  Special safety tips for infants and children, 69
  Safety education, 74

7—Transportation safety, 75
  Child safety restraints, 75
  Preparation for emergencies, 78
  Field trips/car pools, 79
  Passenger safety education, 80

8—Emergencies and first aid, 81
  Preparing for emergencies, 81
  Getting help, 86
  Emergency evacuation plans, 86
  First-aid procedures, 88
  First-aid education, 89
  Choking/CPR, 90
  First aid for common situations, 92

Section D—Preventive health care

9—Preventive health care for children, 97
  Why preventive care is important, 97
  Health histories, 101
  Observations, 101
  Major health screenings, 105
  Medical examinations, 119

10—Adult health, 121
  Ways to promote good health, 121
  Your adult health plan, 121

11—Dental health, 127
  Healthy foods for teeth, 127
  Fluoride, 127
  Brushing teeth, 127
  Dental health education, 128
  Dental care, 128
  Special dental problems, 130

Section E—Nutrition

12—Nutrition in programs for young children, 133
Feeding infants, 133
Weaning, 138
Feeding toddlers, 138
Common nutritional concerns, 142
Special nutritional problems, 144
Feeding children who have special needs, 147
Special nutritional concerns for children with disabilities, 147
Nutrition education, 148
Dietary guidelines for all ages, 148
Nutrition education with children, 149
Community nutrition resources, 151
Running a food service, 152

Section F—Special health issues

13—Children with special needs, 161
Inclusion, 164
Staff's feelings and attitudes toward children with special needs, 166
Resources and support, 167
Modifying your program, 167
Types of disabilities, 172

14—Child abuse and neglect, 175
Identification of abused and neglected children, 175
Physical abuse, 176
Emotional abuse, 176
Sexual abuse, 177
Physical and emotional neglect, 177
Characteristics of families at risk for child abuse, 177
How early childhood educators can help abused children and stressed families, 178
Reporting procedures, 179
Preventing abuse and neglect in programs for young children, 179

15—Lead poisoning, 185
Sources of lead, 185
Lead screening, 185
Treatment and follow-up, 185
Environmental management, 186
Measures to protect children, 186

16—Chronic health conditions, 189
Allergy, 189
Asthma, 191
Heart problems, 195
Epilepsy/seizure disorder, 196
Sickle-cell anemia, 197
Diabetes, 198
Review of emergency planning considerations, 200

Section G—Managing illnesses

17—Infectious diseases, 203
The five commandments of infectious disease control, 203
Diseases spread through the intestinal tract, 206
Diseases spread through the respiratory tract, 217
Diseases spread through direct contact, 232
Infectious diseases spread through blood, 247
Vaccine-preventable diseases, 251
Noncontagious infectious diseases, 255

18—Care of the mildly ill child, 259
Basic issues for decision making, 260
Know what to do when a child appears ill, 261
Common minor illnesses, 264
Guidelines for heat exhaustion and dehydration, 270
How to give medication, 270
Tips for giving medicine safely, 273

19—Models for the care of mildly ill children, 275
General guidelines, 275
Care for mildly ill children in group programs, 275
Care for mildly ill children in family child care programs, 276
Sick care services at home, 276

References, 277

Appendix 1—National resources for health and safety information, 283

Appendix 2—Children's picture books about health, nutrition, and safety, 289

Index, 291

Information about NAEYC, 297

List of figures

1.1. Topics to include in health policies, 4

2.1. Sample integrated health education objectives: Mental/family health, 13

3.1. Bleach solution, 18

3.2. Handwashing poster, 20

3.3. Alternative to running water, 21

4.1. Cleaning guidelines, 30

4.2. Handwashing procedure, 33

5.1. How to change a diaper, 39

6.1. Site safety checklist, 48

6.2. Playground safety checklist, 56

6.3. How to choose art supplies, 62

6.4. Poisonous plants, 63

6.5. Safe playground habits, 65

6.6. Loose-fill playground surfacing materials: Depth needed, 66

6.7. How to select safe infant furniture and equipment, 70

6.8. Safe toys for children younger than age 3, 73

7.1. Transportation safety rules, 76

7.2. How to use car safety seats and safety restraints, 77

8.1. Emergency procedures, 82

8.2. Inventory for the first-aid kit, 82

8.3. Emergency telephone kit, 83

8.4. Child care emergency contact information, 84

8.5. Incident report form, 85

9.1. Recommendations for preventive pediatric health care, 98

9.2. Potential health team members, 100

9.3. Developmental health history, 102

9.4. Developmental red flags for children age 3 to 5, 106

9.5. Physical growth NCHS percentiles, 114

9.6. Child health assessment, 120

10.1. Suggestions on how to protect your back, 122

10.2.   Child care staff health assessment, 124

11.1.   Dental referral criteria, 129

12.1.   Developmental sequence of feeding skills, 134

12.2.   Food components for infants, 136

12.3.   Food components for toddlers, preschoolers, and school-age children, 139

12.4.   Ideas for nutritious snacks, 140

12.5.   Types of vegetarian snacks, 143

12.6.   Dietary sources of calcium, 144

12.7.   Ideas for nutrition education, 150

12.8   Menu planning and sample menus, 154

12.9   Menu planning worksheet, 156

13.1.   The ADA: "A New Way of Thinking" Title III: Public Accommodations, 162

13.2.   National resources for children with special needs, 168

14.1.   Considerations when examining materials on child sexual abuse/personal safety for young children, 182

14.2.   National resources for information on child abuse and neglect, 183

16.1.   Special care plan, 190

16.2.   Asthma record, 193

17.1.   Recommended childhood immunization schedule—United States—January, 1995, 204

17.2.   Criteria for excluding an ill or infected child from an early childhood program, 207

17.3.   Letter to parents about diarrheal diseases, 210

17.4.   Letter to parents about pinworms, 214

17.5.   Letter to parents about hepatitis A, 216

17.6.   Letter to parents about hand, foot, and mouth syndrome (coxsackievirus), 218

17.7.   Letter to parents about strep throat, 221

17.8.   Letter to parents about chicken pox, 223

17.9.   Letter to parents about fifth disease, 225

17.10. Letter to parents about meningococcal illnesses, 227

17.11. Letter to parents about Hib disease, 230

17.12. Letter to parents about impetigo, 234

17.13. Letter to parents about ringworm, 236

17.14. Letter to parents about conjunctivitis, 237

17.15. Letter to parents about scabies, 239

17.16. Letter to parents about head lice, 241

17.17. Symptoms/diagnosis/treatment of major sexually transmitted diseases, 245

18.1.   Symptom record, 262

18.2.   Daily health check instructions, 263

18.3.   How to take a child's temperature, 266

18.4.   Medication consent and log, 272

Section A
Promoting health in programs for young children

Major concepts

- The health program must be carefully planned and carried out through comprehensive health policies that integrate community resources.

- All staff and parents must be aware of and fully understand your program's health policies.

- The experiences of children and families in your program can lay the foundation for future health practices.

- Early childhood educators promote better child health by encouraging appropriate health care and offering some preventive health services.

1
The basics: Policies, providers, and records

Health policies

Health care policies are the blueprint for thinking about health issues and how they relate to other aspects of your program. They should bring together the recommendations of staff, parents, health experts, and especially your health consultant. You should review and revise the policies each year in response to program experiences and new medical recommendations. (*Model Child Care Health Policies* is a resource designed to facilitate the process of rewriting health policies. See page 277.)

Tips on writing policies

Write specific and detailed policies. Keep in mind the following questions. WHO (is responsible)? WHAT? WHERE? WHEN? WHY? HOW? Be sure responsibilities are clearly defined. For example, policies about the first-aid kit might be

> The director will purchase all items for the first-aid kit and review its contents every month to be sure all supplies are available. The kit shall at all times contain. . . . The first-aid kit will be stored out of children's reach on the top shelf in the bathroom above the sink. Any teacher who administers first aid to a child must report the incident on the injury report on the day it occurs. The report shall be filed in the child's folder and the center incident log. Parents shall receive a copy as well.

Include parents, staff, and your health consultant in a small committee to write or review/revise your policies. Send the draft to staff, parents, and medical experts for review. Be sure the policies are understood and that all groups are willing to carry them out.

Figure 1.1 outlines topics to include when you write or revise your policies. You should develop policies that work well in your program and that suit your needs. Organize the policies under topics so that they can be easily referenced. You may want to color code or index sections for fast access in an emergency.

Be sure to give copies of your health care policies to all staff, parents, and health consultants. Post a reference copy in your center. Make sure everyone is told about policy revisions.

Staff responsibilities for health

Health policies are an excellent means to protect and promote children's health. Through them you create a healthful and safe environment; practice preventive measures such as washing hands and monitoring the safety of the playground; and educate staff, parents, and children about health issues.

Daily observation of children during a long period plays a critical role in identifying potential health problems. While staff members are not expected to diagnose medical problems, they can add to the information used to make the diagnosis.

One of the services early childhood programs provide is to act as a switchboard for health data—receiver, collector, and distributor of health information. The administrator should obtain a medical record and a detailed developmental health history for each child in the program. Both the administrator and teaching staff should become familiar with this information. It is easy to assume a child who appears very healthy has no outstanding health needs. However, if you do not know he is allergic to bee stings, you could be confronted with a shocking and life-threatening emergency if he is stung. Or, knowing that a child has had an extended early hospitalization may help you to understand her separation difficulties or her reluctance to become attached to staff.

Figure 1.1. Topics to include in health policies

Answer the following questions for each section:
What should be done?
Why should it be done (rationale)?
Who is responsible?
What is the process? (How will it be done?)

Health records for children
Contents of health record (include forms used)
Results of screenings, etc.
Review/update of health record (with physician and parent as necessary, e.g., HIV/AIDS)
Review/update immunization record
Communication system among health providers, staff, parents
Protecting confidentiality and distribution of records, including procedures for disclosure of HIV/AIDS status and "need to know"

Health care for staff
Requirements for pre-employment and periodic health exams (including who pays)
Contents of health record
Staff exclusion policies
Plan for sick leave, breaks, and substitutes

Health care consultant
Tasks of the consultant
Back-up resources for special situations, e.g., outbreak of infectious disease
Free arrangements, if any
Lines of communication

Daily admissions
Greeting child/observation of possible health problems
Communications system between staff and parents (e.g., nap, food intake, bowel movements, mood)

Injury prevention
Monitoring the environment daily to remove hazards
Procedure to perform in-depth monthly checks
Maintaining a central log or file of injuries and monitoring safety record
First-aid certification of all direct care staff
CPR certification for at least one staff person at all times

Prohibition of smoking in child areas during child care hours
Supervision required to prevent injuries indoors, outdoors, and on trips
Safe storage of poisonous and hazardous materials
Purchase and maintenance of safe toys, equipment, and materials

Managing injuries and first aid
Who is responsible for giving first aid
Assessment of injuries
First-aid procedures
Type and location of first-aid supplies
Method for using and maintaining first-aid equipment
Notifying parents or other emergency contacts
Method for emergency transportation
Writing/filing injury report
Special field trip procedures (e.g., portable first-aid supplies, copies of emergency forms, etc.)
Reviewing injury reports to identify hazards

Emergency preparedness (evacuation)
Posting emergency plan near all telephones and exits
Contacting parents or other emergency contact persons
Evacuation procedures including special considerations for infants and toddlers and nonwalking persons
Staff responsibilities
Conducting regularly scheduled and unscheduled evacuation drills at least once a month
Management of injuries, if necessary
Alternate facility to use when necessary until parents arrive

Management of infectious diseases
Care of mildly ill children, including special precautions for intestinal, respiratory, direct contact, and bloodborne illnesses
Criteria for signs and symptoms of illness to determine inclusion/exclusion
Method for evaluating symptoms
Procedure for care of the ill child at the center who develops symptoms of an excludable disease until child can be taken home or suitably cared for elsewhere or until evaluated by a health

Figure 1.1 *continued*

professional and considered to pose no health risk to self or others

Plans for management of outbreaks—communication with health care consultant and involved children's health providers

Criteria for safe return of child who has been excluded

Procedure for written and/or verbal notification of parents regarding exposure to a communicable disease

Procedure to notify local board of health of reportable disease

Procedures for preventing and responding to exposures to bloodborne pathogens

Procedure for getting medical advice, if needed

Maintaining and reviewing surveillance records

Implementation and monitoring compliance with infection control procedures

Handwashing

Disinfecting

Personal hygiene

Diapering and toileting

Disposal

Laundering

Giving medications

Getting written parent permission and prescription of standing doctor's order, as appropriate

Storage

Giving medications

Recording medicines given (log)

Parent/staff communication (e.g., side effects, child's reactions)

Meeting individual needs

Plan to meet specific health care needs, including identification of and protection from allergic substances

Procedure for referrals for screening, diagnosis, treatment, or supportive services

Resources commonly used for training, curriculum development, screening, treatment, supportive services, medical consultation, financial assistance, etc.

Child abuse/neglect

Recognizing the signs of abuse/neglect

Documentation of observations

Procedures for filing reports of suspected abuse or neglect

Procedures for handling accusations of abuse/neglect by program staff

Procedures/resources for children who have been abused/neglected

Transportation

Requirements for safety restraints for children and adults

Safety procedures for field trips

Safety procedures for safe arrival and departure, including escorting children to and from vehicles

Who is allowed to drive for the program

Driver training

Late arrival/pickup

Vehicle maintenance

Vehicle attendants

Nutrition/food preparation and handling

Getting and using information about child's usual feeding schedule, food habits, vitamin or mineral supplements, food allergies, cultural eating habits

Managing food services, including food ordering, menu planning, food preparation, and food storage

Transporting/storing perishable foods sent from home to center

Special food procedures for infants

Dental

Daily teeth/gum cleaning procedure

Storage of toothbrushes

Dental first-aid procedures

Fluoridation program, if appropriate

Health curriculum for children

Concepts/topics to be taught

Methods for integrating health into overall curriculum

Staff/parent health training

Methods (e.g., workshops, newsletters)

Process for assessing needs

Possible topics to be covered

Teachers must be trained in first aid, rescue breathing, and choke-saving techniques, and learn to recognize common childhood illnesses. In addition to obtaining health data for individual children, child care staff must learn how to deal with their specific needs. For instance, asthma is very common in early childhood. If you have a child with asthma in your program, review the history of treatment and current medications. Use reference material to read about asthma's triggers and signs of distress. Ask the parents how the child responds best during the attack. Ask your health consultant or the child's health provider to give you appropriate information. Know what *you* need to do in the event of an attack. With adequate information, you and the child will be able to manage the situation with confidence.

Each staff member must be sensitive, conscientious, and systematic in addressing a child's health needs on a daily basis. Most teachers greet the child in the morning and notice such things as a new haircut or outfit. Look at the child's appearance. Is there any significant change? Through daily observation, you learn a great deal about the child as an individual: typical coloring and appearance, moods and temperament, response to pain and sickness, activity level, and patterns of behavior. Each of these is a vital clue to health.

While you are expected to be observant, you are not expected to be an expert on health. Observe the child, record relevant data, and then report anything unusual to the appropriate person on your staff and to the parents. You cannot and should not offer diagnoses or treatment plans. But health professionals will be able to make better judgments using the information you have provided. Health observation is an important first step before screening, diagnosis, or treatment. These topics are discussed in greater detail in Chapter 9.

Role of the director or administrator

The administrator is responsible for overseeing all health services, policies, and procedures in your program. The administrator should

- develop and carry out health policies to protect the health of children and staff
- insure that staff have first-aid training (some states specify the type of first-aid training). The American Academy of Pediatrics recommends that all staff should be certified in pediatric first aid including rescue breathing and first aid for choking.
- organize the center, equipment, and materials to prevent injuries and the spread of infectious diseases
- exchange health information with parents at children's enrollment
- collect and monitor information for individual health files, including permissions and releases
- be sure children receive immunizations and screenings on schedule
- take appropriate action when children are injured or sick, including contacting parents and emergency personnel when necessary
- maintain a working relationship with a health consultant and community health resources

Your program's health care consultant should be aware of early childhood and parenting issues, be knowledgeable about infectious diseases in group settings, and be able to promote health among children and adults.

- supervise caregivers to be sure they follow your health policies
- assist families to arrange health care, as requested
- coordinate health education for children, staff, and parents
- maintain a quality food service program
- report suspected child abuse or neglect to the appropriate agency

Role of the teaching staff

Staff who work directly with children must

- maintain a clean, safe, risk-controlled, and healthful environment
- observe children for signs of illness or potential health problems and report any concerns to the appropriate person
- administer medications according to center policy and local health regulations
- assure appropriate care is given to mildly ill children who remain in the program
- provide health education to children, including daily health routines
- supervise children to insure safety
- report suspected child abuse or neglect to the appropriate agency

Communicating with health providers

Your health care consultant

Qualifications and role. Your program's health care consultant should be a physician, nurse, or nurse practitioner who has pediatric experience and regularly deals with children. It is very important that this individual be familiar with the specific medical and developmental needs of children from birth to 5 years. Look for a consultant who is aware of early childhood and parenting issues, has knowledge of infectious diseases in group settings, and can promote health among children and adults. Ideally, the consultant should be involved in the local community and familiar with community resources for referral, support, and educational materials. The consultant should be able to develop positive relationships with children, families, staff, other health providers, and the community.

As a minimum, your health consultant should perform three major tasks:

- approve and aid in developing health care policies

- approve the plan for first-aid and health training of staff
- be available for consultations and brokering differences of opinion among the children's health providers

In addition, she or he should

- provide information about specific medical issues
- provide advice about group issues such as outbreaks of infectious disease, integration of children with special needs, or general health
- explain and advocate for the program's health policies with parents and/or family health care provider
- review the overall plan for staff and parent training on health issues and provide training when appropriate
- have access to other medical resources to assist in areas beyond her or his expertise
- be available for site visits, especially if your program serves infants and/or toddlers

While it is tempting to seek the consultant's advice about individual cases, it is better to use her or his services for broad issues and policies that affect the group or program.

Communicating with your consultant. Ideally, your consultant should be in regular contact with your program, not just for emergencies. Invite your consultant to visit often to learn more about the program and your children so as to make the most effective suggestions on such topics as safety issues, child interactions, or sanitation procedures. The relationship with your consultant should be flexible so that needs can be addressed as they arise. Be sure to share this manual with your health consultant.

Where to find a consultant. It is not always an easy task to find a qualified health consultant. If you are looking for a consultant, this resource list may be a good starting point:

- neighborhood or community health centers
- local health clinics or hospital pediatric departments
- public health nurses
- visiting nurse associations or other home health agencies
- private health providers (e.g., pediatricians, pediatric nurse practitioners, family doctors, health maintenance organizations)

- regional pediatric societies or state chapter of the American Academy of Pediatrics (AAP)

Remember to be clear from the beginning about your needs, expectations, and ability to pay for services.

Children's health care providers

In providing health care for the child, each family's health care provider has learned about the child's medical status and personality as well as family strengths. This wealth of information should be shared with your program. Likewise, health care providers can learn more about the child's growth and development from your extensive observations.

To encourage good communication about the children, set up a system to exchange information. One system might be to mail each child's periodic reports (with parental permission) to the family's health care provider to keep her or him up to date on the child's development from your perspective. You might also suggest that the health form provided to your program include developmental information or identify health issues. (See Chapter 9, Preventive health care for children, for more information.)

The American Academy of Pediatrics (1984) has outlined these common topics for communication between physicians and early childhood educators:

- current state of health and nutrition, including management of colds, diarrhea, bruises, chronic illness, disabilities, and appetite
- growth patterns and their significance
- hearing and vision (e.g., the child with frequent ear infections or the child who needs glasses but doesn't wear them)
- patterns of development, fine-motor skills, communications, self-care, interaction with adults and children, and types of play
- family involvement to maintain positive parent-child relationships
- child's initial and current adjustment to the program

All communication with health care providers concerning individual children must be done only with parents' permission.

Talking to the child's physician: Thoughts for the child care provider
(Dixon 1990)

1. Understand the physician's constraints: The physician can only discuss issues concerning *a particular child* if the parents or legal guardian have given permission. In other than emergencies, the physician will expect that to be a written consent form. In any case, the child care worker will have discussed permission with the family. Therefore, formalize that permission with the parents through a simple form, copy it for your records, and send the original to the physician. Do this ahead of time if possible.

2. Find out the office operating procedures. Most pediatricians have a "call hour." Find out when it is and call then for non-emergency situations. If the issue will take more than 5 to 8 minutes to discuss, set up a separate phone appointment with the physician. Ask the office staff to pull the child's chart (and permission slip) and have it on the physician's desk at the time of your call. Don't expect the physician to remember the child without a refresher (i.e., the chart). Also don't expect the physician to

- come out of a room to pick up your call if it's not an emergency
- try more than twice to return your call if you are unavailable
- discuss a child without the parent's approval

3. Format your call. Orient the physician.
- "I'm calling about *(child's name)*. I'm *(your name)*, his child care provider for *(a week, a year)*."

Say your topic sentence *first* with the appropriate level of urgency or worry.
- "She's fallen from the slide and appears badly hurt. I think she needs to be seen *now*."
- "He has gone back to wetting after full toileting training. Today he seems to be mildly uncomfortable when urinating."
- "I've been concerned about her language development for at least 6 months; she isn't up to her peers at all and isn't picking up."

Physicians like to hear the main point *first* with

substantiating material afterward. In my experience, educators and child care providers like to tell the story from the beginning with descriptive detail. Physicians get distracted and lost with that approach. Hit them with the main point first, and do not add information that is not focused on this issue unless you clearly change subjects (e.g., "A second issue concerning Elizabeth is. . . .").

4. Clearly state what you would like of the physician; don't make her guess (e.g., "I'd like you to see this child now," or "Please consider a hearing test next week during your planned visit.").

5. Repeat plans or recommendations concisely to ensure that you understand each other, particularly regarding which of you will convey this information to the parents. Listing these is a style physicians can understand.

6. When discussing a case, convey observation data as separate from opinion (e.g., "David appears ill: He doesn't play actively, clings to the teacher, and is refusing foods."). These clear observations have been shown to be highly reliable indicators of illness—better in many cases than the child's temperature, although that is important too. Take it before you call about an ill child; "the child feels warm" does not provide enough information.

7. Don't ask a physician about the health issue of a child who is not his patient. This puts him in a bind: The physician cannot ethically or legally be involved unless the child is under direct care, and yet most physicians want to be advocates for children.

8. If you are concerned about the medical care or treatment of a child, share your concerns with the parents and provide them with the names of *several* other physicians in your community for a second opinion. Beware of *single* referral suggestions as this practice alienates the local professional community, making other physicians disinclined to help and support your center.

9. If you need help with health policies, ask a local pediatrician to serve as a consultant to your center. To best use your consultant, do your homework first, using resources from NAEYC, the American Academy of Pediatrics, the Red Cross, and your local public health department to develop drafts of policies or at least an outline of concerns or issues. Your consultant will bring greater enthusiasm and longevity to the project if she or he doesn't have to start from scratch on your health policies, procedures, or staff education. Always separate this role from that of health management of individual children in the center.

Child care providers and the child's physician share a common commitment to advocacy for children. A close working alliance is natural. Speaking the same language and understanding each other's needs facilitate clear communication. Ultimately this should result in better care for children.

What if medical experts disagree?

Some information about the health of young children in groups is so new that many health care providers have not yet been trained in current recommendations. Some research is so new or limited that it remains controversial. Therefore, this manual presents some recommendations that may differ from what you have been told by your health consultant. This may be confusing and frustrating. As with all policy decisions, you will have to weigh the facts and rationale and make the best decision for your setting at that time. If you receive conflicting opinions, follow this advice:

1. Try to work out your policies with your health consultant before difficult situations arise (e.g., how to handle Hib disease or diarrhea before an outbreak occurs). Share these policies with parents.

2. When difficult questions about health or infection arise, ask your health consultant for help. If individual health care providers disagree with your program's health policy, ask your consultant to broker differences of opinion for you.

3. If you have additional questions or conflicts, (e.g., between your health consultant and a child's pediatrician) contact your local board of health or your state department of public health. They have the legal responsibility to make decisions about health issues for groups of people.

Other community resources
Identify the agencies and individuals in your area who can assist the children, staff, and families in your program. You may want to keep a resource file for handy reference when you want additional information, training, and referral services. The following list will help you get your file started.
- child protective agencies
- colleges and universities
- community health centers
- community mental health centers/state department of mental health
- county extension service
- department of public health/regional public health offices
- department of social services
- food stamp program
- hospital and health clinics
- local board of health or health department
- library
- medical or dental society
- physicians and other health specialists
- poison control centers
- public schools
- voluntary and service organizations
- Women, Infants and Children program (WIC)

Keeping health records
Maintain a complete, up-to-date health record for each child enrolled in the program. Make this health record available to the child's parents in case the child leaves the program or the program closes. Establish clear policies about confidentiality. No information may be released by the program without specific permission from the parent or guardian.

Contents
The health record should contain at least the following information:
- telephone numbers where parents and at least two emergency contacts can be reached at all times (Figure 8.3)
- the name of the child's regular health care provider, address, and telephone number
- child's pre-admission medical examination form, including immunization status
- developmental health history (Figure 9.3)
- results of all screenings and assessments

- notations about allergies, special diet, chronic illness, or other special health concerns
- emergency transportation permission slip (Figure 8.3)
- all permission slips authorizing non-emergency health care and giving medications
- reports of all injuries or illnesses that occur while child is present in program
- medication logs
- reports of referrals and follow-up action
- notes about any health communication with parents or health providers
- written correspondence about the child's health
- health observations of staff

The record should be reviewed periodically to be sure that it is up-to-date and that staff are familiar with its contents.

Confidentiality
Confidentiality of health records must be maintained to protect the child and family. Use the following guidelines when developing or reviewing your confidentiality policy.
- Health records must be kept away from public access and unauthorized review.
- Information may not be shared with anyone inside or outside the facility without parental review and consent.
- Telephone requests for information are not acceptable unless the parent has previously instructed you in writing to release information or given witnessed telephone consent (by use of an extension line).
- Information collected by others and forwarded to you with parental consent becomes part of your record and thus the responsibility of the program.
- All releases of information should be properly logged.
- Parents have a right to see all information in their child's file.
- Parents must be made aware of the nature and type of all information collected and how it will be used.
- Though parents may ask to speak to you in confidence, you must receive this information in a responsible manner. This is particularly true in relationship to child abuse. Your primary responsibility is to protect the child.

2

Health education in programs for young children

During the early childhood years, children form habits and attitudes that can last a lifetime. We know that health education can help establish good habits such as eating low sugar snacks, exercising regularly, avoiding poisons, and choosing other positive lifetime health behaviors.

Health education works best in the framework of a healthy environment and healthy adult behavior. Your program should follow healthy routines such as frequent handwashing and toothbrushing. It should be safe and organized so that children feel secure and cared for. All people, adults and children, must respect other people and materials. Your health education program will not make sense otherwise.

To create a healthy environment, all staff should be models of good behavior. If adults talk about how we need to take care of our bodies, but sit in the kitchen smoking, drinking soda, and munching candy, children will recognize the contradiction. Adult behavior, attitudes, and appearance all affect children's learning.

Your program can promote good health by providing information and activities for children, staff, and parents, addressing the same topic with all three groups at the same time. The child health curriculum will be more successful if adults are involved in the process and can reinforce the ideas and practices being taught. In addition, adults themselves will also gain valuable health and child development information.

Health curriculum for children

How to include health learning

Health activities should fit into the natural flow of the program throughout the year. Routines such as brushing teeth, handwashing, careful food handling, and good nutrition should happen everyday. An occasional puppet show or filmstrip is not enough.

When you know what you want to teach, you can capture the teachable moments when children are most likely to learn. For example, when a child is sitting in your lap with the sniffles, talk about taking good care of your body when sick (rest, drink liquids). When a child is going into the hospital, that is a perfect time to set up a hospital corner and to read hospital books. Spring is a natural time to talk about growing foods and which foods are good to eat—plant a garden if you can. Talk about sticky and sweet foods while you're brushing teeth.

Learning always has more meaning when it

- is concrete
- is geared toward the skills and interests of the children
- fits into the rest of the children's learning and understanding
- is presented in many different ways—books, discussions, free play, group activities, field trips, films
- is tied into all areas of the curriculum—science (growing food), cooking, dramatic play (hospital play), art (making a collage of pictures of ways to exercise)
- is strengthened through practice

What to include

Health education should be interpreted in the broadest sense—teaching children about well-being. Your health education program should focus not only on physical health and safety, but also on topics such as emotional health, growing and changing, and the environment. You should provide children with an opportunity to learn about personal health, the health of those around them, and their world. Ideally, your health education plan should draw upon the resources of teachers, parents, nutritionists, mental health specialists, special needs staff, and others, including community agencies and resources. Many groups have materials and teaching ideas especially for young children.

Following are some broad topic areas that can be included in your health curriculum:
- growth and development
- similarities and differences
- families (including cultural heritage and pride)
- expression of feelings (verbal and physical)
- nutrition
- dental health
- personal hygiene

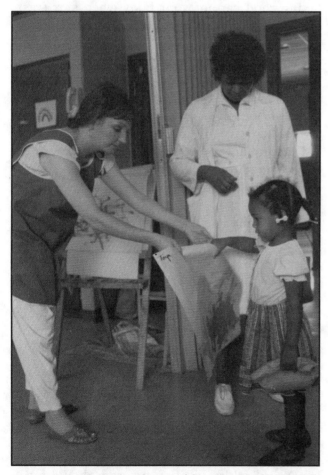

Parents need to develop stable relationships with their child's program and community health care providers.

- safety
- physical health
- awareness of disabilities
- environmental health

Health education for staff and parents

Knowledge is power

Having good information is one of the best ways to feel confident and in control. When you know what to do—whether it is taking a temperature, giving first aid, or keeping a child relaxed during an asthma attack—both you and the child are going to benefit from your knowledge. You can provide the necessary care, remain calm, and maintain control. Lack of information often leads to panic in emergencies or to improper care, such as spreading disease by not washing hands when necessary.

Keys to getting the message across

Some basic ways for program administrators to teach staff, parents, and volunteers about health include
- *Model* good health behaviors—practice what you preach!
- Establish good health routines such as toothbrushing, serving only healthy foods, handwashing.
- Post routines and suggestions as reminders—emergency plans, handwashing techniques, diapering instructions.
- Teach children good habits and they will remind you!
- Use a variety of media and training techniques such as staff meeting discussions, workshops/guest speakers, newsletters, site visits (e.g., hospital emergency room), newspaper and magazine clippings, posters, pamphlets, and other audiovisual materials.

Topics

How do you know what to plan for staff/parent health training? Many state licensing agencies require specific training in topics such as approved first-aid procedures, CPR, and treatment of convulsions and choking. Beyond that, decide what is most important for your group this year. Here are some ideas to help you plan:

- Ask your administrator or health consultant to observe the program, consider families' needs and strengths, and suggest topics for immediate and long-term concern.
- Ask staff and parents about their needs and interests. It is usually helpful to present a list of suggested topics. You might ask them to set priorities for their choices.
- Find out the most convenient time to meet with parents.
- Try to get a sense of the learning style of the parents and staff. Plan something for everyone—speakers, written materials, hands-on experience, films.
- Plan a yearly training schedule based on the priority topics. Revise and update your schedule each year. Some suggested topics are
  —orientation to your health policies
  —preventive health practices
  —nutritional needs of children
  —safety/injury prevention, including transportation safety and site surveys
  —first aid
  —management of minor illness
  —child growth and development
  —observing and recording health signs
  —child abuse/neglect
  —cultural views of health
  —how to be a good consumer of health services/ health advocacy
  —health education for young children
  —the meaning of health screenings
  —chronic illness/special needs
  —parenting
  —discipline, talking with children

Figure 2.1 will also help you identify objectives to integrate your health program for children, staff, and parents.

Figure 2.1. Sample integrated health education objectives: Mental/family health

For children
- Know that it is healthy and normal to express feelings.
- Know that feelings are to be expressed in ways that are not dangerous or traumatic to themselves or others.
- Know that everyone has feelings and everyone needs to have opportunities to express them.
- Understand *same* and *different* (both physical and role), and learn to function with all kinds of people.
- Learn they have abilities by experiencing success in daily activities and thereby develop self-confidence.
- Learn they are part of a family and group.
- Be aware of their bodies and respond appropriately.

For staff
- Provide effective developmental assessment of children.
- Recognize and support importance of children's secure home base.
- Recognize children's normal reactions to strange situation.
- Provide psychologically safe environment for children, staff, and parents.
- Model positivism and acceptance.
- Be aware of own attitudes concerning family, emotional expression, cultural differences, sexual curiosity of children.
- Develop partnership with parents, using resources of home and community.

For parents
- Develop skills in observing children's feelings and needs.
- Recognize importance of secure home base for children.
- Develop stable relationship with children's program and community health care providers.
- Develop self-confidence through participation.

Section B
Healthful environment

Major concepts

- Good handwashing and cleaning of the materials and facility will help to prevent the spread of disease.

- Good air quality (proper temperature, ventilation, and humidity) and open space help prevent illness and injury.

- Some play activities and materials carry health risks that must be considered.

- Food handling requires special sanitation precautions.

- Specific sanitation procedures are necessary during diapering and toileting to prevent the spread of disease.

- Monitor staff health practices and the environment regularly.

3
Creating a healthy environment

Many programs for young children cannot totally control their environments. Some spaces are rented and were not designed to meet children's needs in the first place. Even so, there are ways you can improve your space. As you work toward ideal conditions, you can establish policies that will control the spread of infectious diseases and maintain a healthier environment.

Keeping clean

Throughout this manual, the importance of sanitizing surfaces and objects with a recommended bleach solution will be mentioned (see Figure 3.1).

The standard recommended bleach solution is a ¼ cup bleach to 1 gallon of water (1 tablespoon per quart).

Use this solution to disinfect items and surfaces (diaper changing surfaces, table tops, toys, eating utensils) after they have been cleaned with soap and water. The concentration of bleach recommended for disinfection varies with the type of application (i.e., spray versus dunk/soak); the type of surface (porous versus hard surfaces); and the time that the object and the bleach solution are in contact.

Generally, disinfection can be accomplished if you start with a clean, rinsed surface and spray it until it is glistening with a fresh solution of 1 tablespoon of bleach to 1 quart of water, leave the bleach solution on the surface for at least 2 minutes before drying with a paper towel or allowing the surface to air dry. If you use the soaking method, you will need a more concentrated solution because each object can introduce germs into the solution. The recommended solution of household bleach for soaking to disinfect toys is ¾ cup of bleach to 1 gallon of water. Put toys into a net bag, soak them for 5 minutes, rinse them with clean water, and hang the bag to air dry.

You need to make fresh bleach solution *each day* because bleach loses its strength when it is exposed to air. Bleach is quite inexpensive and readily available. However, acceptable commercial alternatives can be used by those who prefer other sanitizing agents. If you purchase commercial products, select those that are EPA chemical germicides registered as hospital disinfectants.

Handwashing

Handwashing is the first line of defense against infectious disease. Numerous studies have shown that unwashed or improperly washed hands are the primary carriers of infections. When you wash and how often you wash are more important than what you wash with.

Always wash your hands at least
- before eating or handling food
- before feeding a child
- after diapering and toileting
- after handling or cleaning body fluids (blood, mucus, vomitus) and after wiping noses, mouths, bottoms, sores
- after handling or feeding pets
- after playing in dirt/sand outdoors

The five most important concepts to remember about handwashing are
- You must use running water that drains—not a stoppered sink or container. A common container of water spreads germs!
- You must use soap, preferably liquid.
- You must rub your hands together for at least 10 seconds. This friction helps remove the germs. Rinse hands well under running water until all the soil and soap are gone.

Figure 3.1. Bleach solution

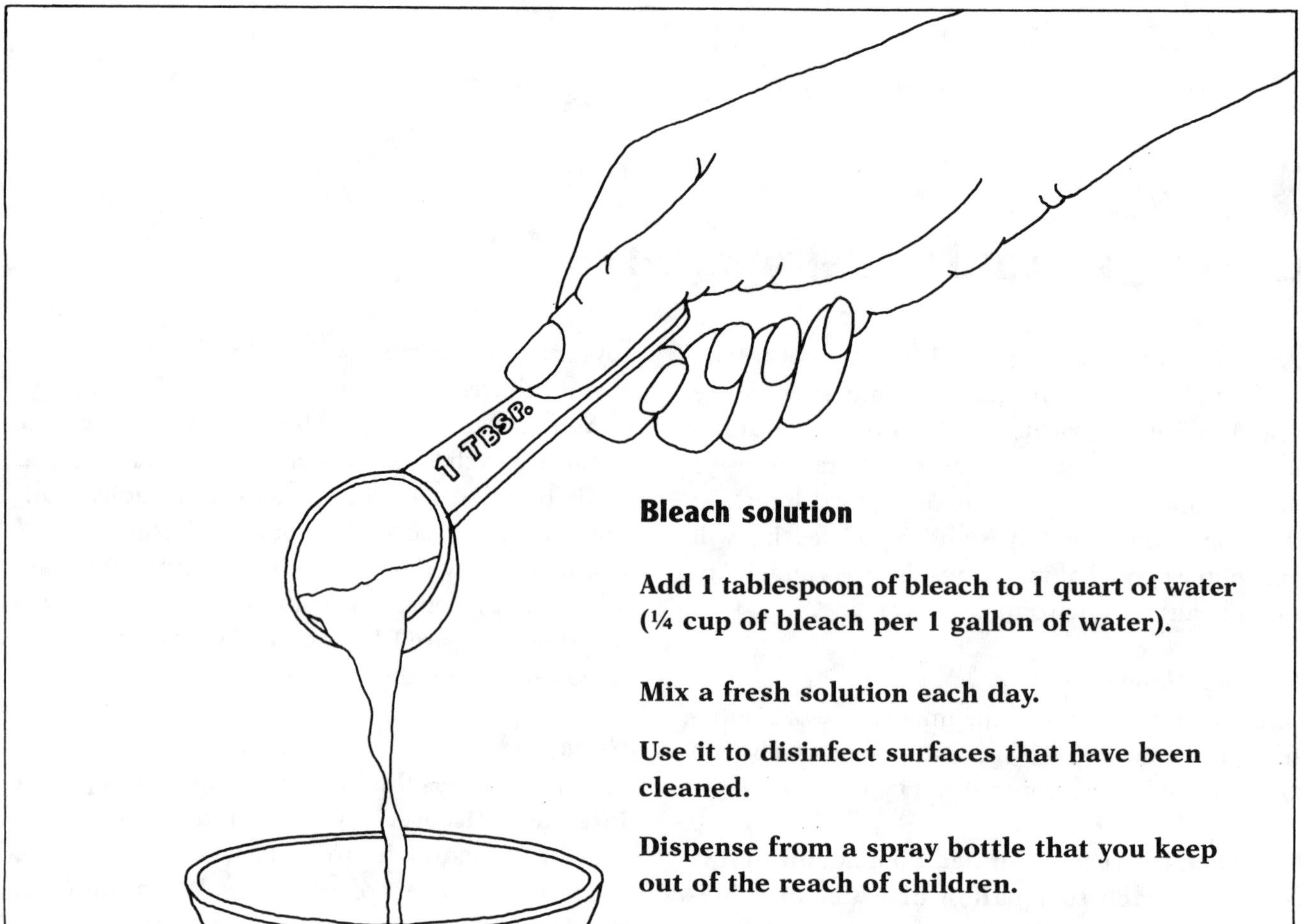

Bleach solution

Add 1 tablespoon of bleach to 1 quart of water (¼ cup of bleach per 1 gallon of water).

Mix a fresh solution each day.

Use it to disinfect surfaces that have been cleaned.

Dispense from a spray bottle that you keep out of the reach of children.

Wet the entire surface until glistening, and leave solution on the surface at least 2 minutes. Dry with a paper towel or allow to air dry.

- You must turn off the faucet with a paper towel. Because you use your dirty hands to turn on the faucet, the faucet is considered dirty at all times. If you touch it with clean hands you will be recontaminated. Ideally, the paper towel should be thrown into a lined, covered trash container that has a foot pedal.
- Hand lotion should be available for staff to prevent dry or cracked skin.

Post the handwashing poster (Figure 3.2) above every sink. Refer, also, to Figure 4.2 for detailed procedures for handwashing.

Ideally, sinks should be located near all diapering, toileting, and food areas. If you are renovating or building new space, consider installing a sink with a knee or elbow faucet handle to avoid the concerns of recontaminating hands. Electric-eye faucets are another more sanitary option to consider for new installations; they are not much more expensive than conventional faucets. Even where new plumbing for sinks is not possible, you might develop some creative alternatives. One interesting example using a portable water tank bubbler is described in Figure 3.3. Portable water alternatives such as these are fine for handwashing as long as

- there is *running* water—not a common basin
- the water temperature is not higher than 120° F.
- the container of contaminated water is out of the children's reach
- the system is safe for children (do *not* use a hot coffee urn for water)
- soap is available

When handwashing is impossible, such as on a field trip, use disposable wet wipes with an alcohol base. (These are better than nothing, but are not as effective as washing with running water.)

Disposable items such as paper towels, diapering covers, and wet wipes are expensive. Consider buying in bulk from medical or paper supply companies. Use centralized buying whenever possible; if you are not part of a system or large agency, ask other programs near you to join in bulk purchases. It is worth it!

Disposable gloves

Gloves can provide a protective barrier against germs that cause infections. Gloves should be disposable latex (reusable rubber for those allergic to latex) and removed and disposed of properly after contact with each child. **Gloves should never be used as a substitute for handwashing.** Hands and other skin surfaces should be washed immediately and thoroughly if contaminated with blood and/or other body fluids. Hands should be washed immediately after gloves are removed.

Disposable gloves should be worn in the following situations:

- when contact with blood or blood-containing fluids from a child is likely, particularly if the caregiver's hands open cuts or sores (e.g., when using first aid for a child's cut or changing a diaper with bloody diarrhea)
- when cleaning surfaces that have been contaminated with blood or gross contamination with body fluids, such as large amounts of vomitus or feces

For added protection, disposable gloves can be worn when changing the diaper of a child with diarrhea or a diagnosed gastrointestinal disease.

Children should play outside every day except in extreme weather conditions.

Figure 3.2. Handwashing poster

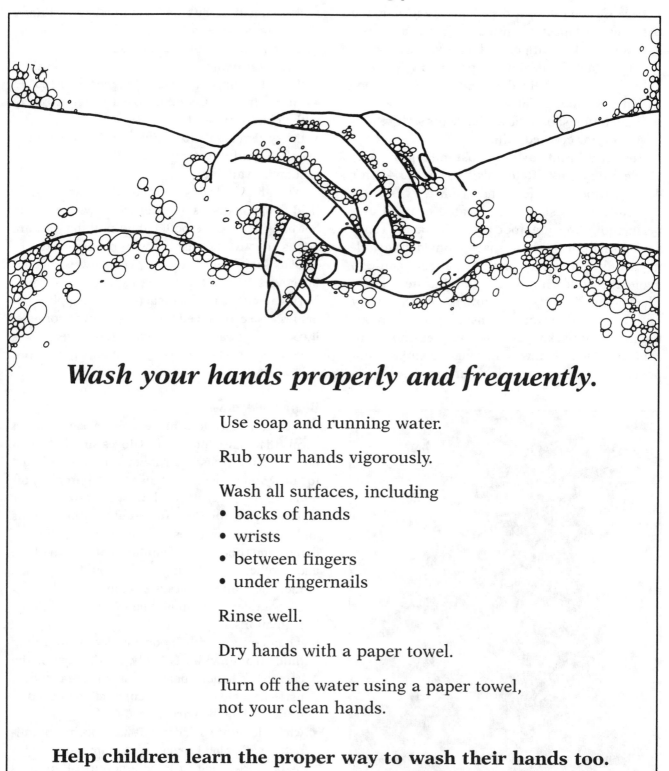

Wash your hands properly and frequently.

Use soap and running water.

Rub your hands vigorously.

Wash all surfaces, including
- backs of hands
- wrists
- between fingers
- under fingernails

Rinse well.

Dry hands with a paper towel.

Turn off the water using a paper towel,
not your clean hands.

Help children learn the proper way to wash their hands too.

Figure 3.3. Alternative to running water

Use a portable water (bubbler) tank, a sink top, and a cabinet that can be locked to create a place for handwashing, even if plumbing is not available. The tank will be very heavy when filled with water.

Setup

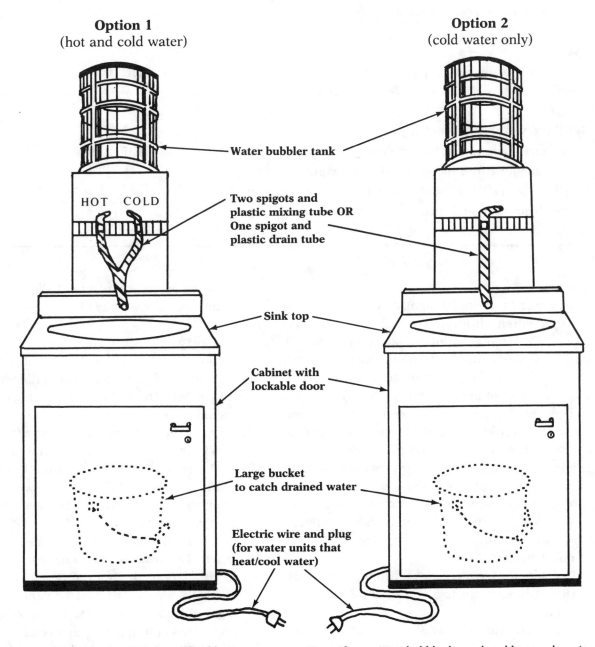

Option 1
(hot and cold water)

Option 2
(cold water only)

Water bubbler tank

Two spigots and plastic mixing tube OR One spigot and plastic drain tube

Sink top

Cabinet with lockable door

Large bucket to catch drained water

Electric wire and plug (for water units that heat/cool water)

Caution: If your water bubbler has both hot and cold spigots, **you MUST use plastic tubing to mix the water before it reaches the sink.** Hot water can cause severe burns.

Note: If your water bubbler has only cold water, keep it unplugged so the water will remain at room temperature.

Figure 3.3 *continued*

Shop at a discount hardware store if possible to find the items needed to set up your bubbler unit. Select a spigot that locks in the ON position (similar to that on a large coffee urn) so that hands can be washed together. If water flow control is important, use a screw-type faucet. Tubing should be either 3/8" or ½" in diameter. Connect the apparatus as shown in the diagram.

Place a very large bucket inside the cabinet under the drainpipe for the sink. Keep the cabinet door locked so children cannot reach the bucket.

Use

Wash hands using running water from the spigot(s) and liquid soap. Check the waste-water bucket frequently, and empty it into a toilet as needed.

Refilling water/disinfecting

- If you **replace the water bubbler tank,** remember to disinfect the plastic tubing with bleach solution periodically. Rinse thoroughly before using.
- When you **refill** the water bubbler tank, be sure to disinfect both the tank and plastic tubing with bleach solution and rinse thoroughly before refilling.

Space

Infections pass more frequently from one child to another when children are confined in small spaces. Children need lots of space to roam, for both developmental and health reasons. Open space and good ventilation decrease the opportunity for germs to pass among children.

The best big space available is the outdoors! **Children should play outside every day** except in extreme weather conditions. Outdoor play is healthy on many levels—it provides open space to decrease spread of infections, a variety of opportunities for gross-motor development, and balance in the children's play and routine. Some children who have particularly high energy levels need lots of outdoor play.

Consider these suggestions for your use of space.
- Do not concentrate toys and equipment in small areas.
- Place cots/cribs at least 3' from each other and alternating foot to head so that air circulates freely and children do not breathe directly on each other.
- Take children outdoors as often as possible.
- If you group infants and toddlers with preschoolers, be sure to keep the group small to limit the spread of infectious diseases. (Diseases are spread easily by children in diapers.)

Air quality

Adequate ventilation, humidity, and temperature control increase our resistance to illness and ability to get well after sickness. In winter, dry, hot air takes moisture from skin and mucous membranes. In summer, hot and humid air prevents children's bodies from cooling off well, and they tend to overheat. Therefore, pay specific attention to the air around you, and try to do the following.
- Keep the air temperature between 65° and 75° F. in winter and between 68° and 82° F. in summer if at all possible.
- **Open the windows in every room every day** to circulate fresh air, even in winter (except in centrally air-conditioned or ventilated buildings). Windows must be screened to prevent insects from entering and children from exiting.
- Offer more liquids and sponge bathing in extremely hot weather to prevent overheating and dehydration. Use sprinklers outside for toddlers and preschoolers. Young children, especially infants, become dehydrated more easily than adults.

- Provide extra clothing during cold weather to maintain body heat. Ask parents to leave extra clothing or develop your own supply. (Shared clothing must be washed between uses by different children.) Hats should never be shared.
- Use a humidifier or cool air vaporizer to add moisture to dry air. Do not use a steam vaporizer. Wash and sanitize the humidifier regularly according to the manufacturer's instructions. Otherwise, germs can collect in the water and be spewed back into the air.
- If you use an air conditioner, be sure that it is cleaned and serviced regularly. Air conditioners can build up molds and dust that are harmful allergens for some children and adults.
- Avoid strong odors. Some people, including children, have allergic responses to smoke, perfume, and room deodorizers.
- **Do not allow cigarette smoking in any spaces that children will use. An even better policy would be to prohibit smoking in the child care facility at any time.**

Indoor pollution

(Modified from Noyes 1987)

Indoor pollutants can pose major environmental hazards to children and staff in early childhood programs. These hazards may exist in many forms and some of them are not easily observed or found. Hazards may lurk in cleaning agents; art supplies with formaldehyde; pesticides; building materials (asbestos, insulation, lead paint); fuel by-products (from heaters, wood stoves, or gas cooking equipment); cigarette smoke; and radon gas.

Children are more sensitive to environmental hazards than most healthy adults for these reasons:

1. Their organs and systems are still developing, and disruption—particularly at critical developmental periods—may result in permanent damage.

2. Their immune (defense) system may not be able to repair damage.

3. Their central nervous systems are more fragile than adults'.

4. Immature liver and kidneys are less able to break down and get rid of toxins.

5. Their bodies can potentially keep in toxins for long periods of time.

6. They inhale, ingest, and absorb through their more sensitive skin more pollutants per unit of body weight than most adults do.

7. Their exposure to certain hazards (habits such as putting everything in their mouths) may be greater.

There may be immediate and/or long-term effects from exposure to poisonous substances. Immediate illnesses may include nausea, vomiting, diarrhea, lightheadedness, difficult breathing, blurred vision, watering of the eyes, and skin reactions. Long-term conditions may include damage to organs and systems of the body such as the kidney, liver, lungs, bone marrow, digestive system, reproductive system, and nervous system. Children may develop learning difficulties, developmental delays, and behavioral problems. Serious health conditions such as emphysema and increased risk of infection and cancer may result from chemical exposure as well.

While some products have been designated as "nontoxic" for adults by the American Society for Testing and Materials, they cannot be considered safe for children. Unfortunately, there is no current standard of toxicity of products to children. If any label reads, "Harmful if swallowed," "Use only with proper ventilation," "Avoid skin contact," or contains another similar warning, do NOT use the product with young children. Store any such item in a locked cabinet out of children's reach.

There are some basic important steps to take to reduce indoor air pollution in general.

Employers should provide child care staff with hazard information as required by the Occupational Safety and Health Administration (OSHA) about the presence of toxic substances such as asbestos or formaldehyde insulation. Ingredients of art and cleaning supplies should be identified. Since the Environmental Protection Agency (EPA) regards indoor pollution as a greater risk than outdoor air pollution, poor air quality poses a potential health risk for child care staff.

Important steps to reduce indoor air pollution

1. Eliminate cigarette smoking at home and in programs for children.

2. Properly vent heating and cooking equipment.

3. Check the safety of building and insulating materials for formaldehyde and asbestos.

4. Reduce the use of toxic pesticides, cleaners,

polishes, carpet shampoos, bleaches, and other household chemicals and personal care products. Avoid aerosols where possible. Do not use any chemical product in higher concentrations than necessary.

5. Look for lead in toys and furniture for young children. Check art, craft, and hobby materials for lead content.

6. Proceed with caution when choosing paints, fabrics, carpeting, etc., for redecorating; watch out for hazardous ingredients.

7. Never leave a car or mower engine running in an attached shed or garage. Shut off the engine and leave the garage door open for a moment or two before opening the door into the house. Keep the door to the house closed and sealed at all times.

8. Regularly clean air conditioners and air filters as well as humidifiers and dehumidifiers.

9. Store paints, varnishes, and pesticides outdoors in a locked shed.

10. Open windows and let pollutants out often.

11. Check the radon situation in your locale with your health department or environmental agency.

12. Control dampness.

13. Control dust.

Pesticides

Chemical poisons are typically used against insects, rodents, weeds, and molds. Since chemicals used against pests often pose more hazards than the pests themselves, the risk of any pest controls should be balanced against the risk of the pest. In fact, only some pests are actually harmful; others are just annoying. Any pest control program should be based on the least toxic, most effective, and most permanent solution to the problem. Sometimes these measures include simple sanitation improvements and installing structures or barriers to prevent pests from entering or breeding in the building.

Try doing the following as first steps before you begin a chemical control program:

- Use pest-resistant containers for storage of food, supplies, trash, and garbage.
- Clean carefully to remove spilled food and beverages.
- Reduce clutter to improve ability to clean and reduce nesting and hiding places.
- Repair the facility as needed to fix water leaks; gutters; holes in windows, screens, and walls.

- Install thresholds at bottoms of doors and caulk cracks and crevices.

If you need to use a chemical pesticide approach, be sure that you use **only** certified pest control operators to apply the chemicals. Find out what chemicals will be used and talk to your regional certified poison control center to learn where and how the chemical can be safely used. **Always** go with the pest control operator to monitor where the chemicals are used. Pesticides should never be applied while children are present in the facility. Following the application of a pesticide, the area should be ventilated for the period of time that is recommended on the manufacturer's label or by the local poison control center. Before reoccupying the facility, the pesticide levels should be tested as recommended by the Environmental Protection Agency, 401 M Street, N.W., Washington, DC 20460, to ensure safety. Consult your regional office of the EPA for information and technical assistance.

The safest and most effective chemical approach to control roaches is the use of 99% concentration boric acid powder.

Radon

Radon is a dangerous, colorless, and odorless gas that seeps naturally from the ground into buildings. As radon gas breaks down it makes small particles of harmful chemicals. Radiation and these chemical particles pose a severe threat of cancer, especially lung cancer.

Buildings that are "airtight" without outdoor ventilation are particularly at risk. Concentrations of radon are highest on the basement and first-floor levels. If you use lower levels of your building, and if you have little fresh air circulation, your space should be tested for radon. There are inexpensive kits that can measure radon levels. Contact your regional office of the EPA for more information.

Building materials and carpeting

Insulation seals in many pollutants from wood, coal, and kerosene, and may itself pose a risk from formaldehyde. Formaldehyde is often used in particle board, chipboard, and other building materials. If you repair, renovate, or newly build any part of your facility, be sure to check the composition of all building materials you choose.

It is always a good idea to open windows to air out your space **at least** once a day. This practice has the benefit of not only reducing air pollutants but also the concentration of germs in the air.

Carpets should be made of cotton or polypropylene. Nylon, orlon, wool, and silk give off toxic fumes when they burn. Areas that have been recently carpeted or paneled using an adhesive that may contain toxic materials should be well ventilated and should not be used for at least 7 days after installation or until there is no odor.

Mothballs, moth crystals, incense, and chemical air fresheners should not be used in child care environments.

Other pollutants

Lead and art supplies are sources of pollutants in child care. For more information about lead poisoning, please read Chapter 15 (page 185–187). Poisoning from art supplies is addressed in Chapter 6 on page 61 and 62. Please refer to Figure 6.3 for information about choosing safe art supplies.

Asbestos

Asbestos is the name given to material that separates into fibers. If the fibers from these products are inhaled, they can cause cancer or lung disease.

Asbestos is a common insulation material on heating pipes, boilers, and furnaces. **If asbestos insulation is cracked, torn, or crumbling, it can release harmful asbestos fibers.** In most cases, the material can be repaired to prevent fiber release. However, when the material is beyond repair, it should be removed. Because the repair or removal process can release very dangerous fibers into the air, repair and/or removal methods must be approved according to state and local regulations.

If you are concerned that there may be exposed or crumbling asbestos in your facility, contact your board of health.

Food handling

Improper food handling is one sure way to spread infection! Specific information on sanitary food handling appears in Chapters 4 and 12. Please refer to them and remember these basic concepts for food handling.

- Always wash hands before handling food.
- Never allow children to share food unless individual portions are made (do not lick the same ice cream cone, or put two spoons into the same serving).
- Always keep food far away from a diapering area.
- Whenever possible, adults who change diapers should not prepare food on the same day.
- Keep food and food utensils separate from classroom items.
- Provide drinking fountains that are the approved jet-angle type with a mouth guard above the rim.

Handling contaminated items

Contact with heavily contaminated materials such as tissues, toilet paper, soiled diapers, bandages, soiled clothing, and vomitus encourages the spread of disease. **Be sure that as few people as possible handle contaminated items and that**

*All toys used by infants carry the risk of spreading disease because they are mouthed frequently and passed around. All infant toys should be **washable** as well as safe.*

cleanup areas are completely separated from food handling areas.

- Use disposable gloves to clean up blood and blood spills. If possible, use them when cleaning up other types of potentially contaminated surfaces.
- Dispose of soiled items immediately into covered containers.
- **Wash hands immediately!**
- Do **not** rinse or wash soiled cloth diapers or clothing. Place it in a plastic bag, label with the child's name, close it tight, and keep it out of the reach of children. Ask the parent to take the items home for laundering. Changes of clothing should be kept handy.
- Soiled diapers should be disposed of in a tightly covered, foot-pedal-operated container that is lined with a disposable plastic bag.
- Wash, rinse, and disinfect all mouthed toys before they pass from one child to another and frequently enough to keep them from gathering dirt and growing germs. One easy way to do this is to keep a dishpan labeled "soiled" on a counter into which you put toys when they have been mouthed and put down by a child. Use a dilute solution of dishwashing detergent and water to soak mouthed toys. These toys should be thoroughly cleaned and disinfected by the end of the day. If toys are dishwasher safe, use a dishwasher approved to sanitize dishes with hot water that reaches 170° F. and heat dries the objects in it. Other toys can be washed by hand, rinsed, and disinfected by spraying them with or soaking them in a bleach solution. If you use a soaking method to disinfect, you will need a more concentrated bleach solution (¾ cup of bleach to 1 gallon of water) because each object can introduce germs into the solution. (See page 17.) Anything not washable in a dishwasher, by hand, or in a laundry machine should not be owned by the program. Allow such an item only if it is a child's personal belonging that is not shared. Adequate numbers of toys should be available to correspond with the washing frequency.
- Wash and disinfect daily all frequently used surfaces with the bleach solution. (See Figure 3.1, page 18.)
- Wash and disinfect the changing surface and any potty-chairs with bleach solution after each use.

Consider whether the time and risk of spread of disease involved in potty-chair cleanup makes them undesirable in child care.

- Label toothbrushes and personal items. Make sure they are used **only by their owners.**
- Vacuum any carpeted areas on a daily basis, and shampoo at least every 6 months and when soiled.

Turnover and health issues

Aside from the obvious emotional benefits of low turnover of staff and children, there are health benefits too. High turnover constantly introduces new infections. New children and staff may not be immune to the infections already there and may become sick more often. Of course, turnover is a most difficult problem to solve. It is mentioned here so you will be aware of the health risks involved.

Because of the number of comings and goings, large programs (with 50 or more children) open more than 10 hours a day appear to be at greater risk for spreading infectious diseases. Such centers should be particularly careful about preventive health routines.

Do not admit new children into your program during an outbreak of a serious infectious disease (for example, hepatitis A). With your health consultant, decide upon an appropriate waiting period for each infectious disease.

Consider limiting the mixing of children in diapers with older children when possible, although this also may inhibit developmental learning opportunities. If you can, avoid having staff care for different groups of children during the same day.

Risks from play materials and activities

Some materials and activities for young children can carry specific health risks. You should be aware of the potential risks and know how to handle them. Try to create an environment that is both challenging *and* safe for children and staff.

Water play

A container of water that is shared by many children carries the risks of spreading germs through the water and the toys. Germs grow in warm and wet environments. If you decide to keep a water table you should

- be sure the water table is cleaned and disinfected

with the bleach solution and filled with fresh water at least daily

- have children wash their hands *before* playing at the table
- wash and disinfect all water toys daily (Wash with soap and water and spray with bleach solution, or put in the dishwasher.)
- consider using *individual basins* within the water table. The basins can be cleaned and disinfected more easily between use by children and the water table catches the splashes so cleanup around the table is much easier.

Dress-up clothes

Sharing clothing generates the risk of spreading disease, particularly head lice and certain skin infections. Any clothing soiled by stool or other body fluids should be removed immediately and not returned until laundered. Hats should NEVER be shared. Wash them in hot water in a washing machine and dry in a hot dryer before they are worn by another child. If there is an outbreak of head lice or scabies you should

- take away all play clothing until the outbreak has stopped
- launder and clean all items according to directions listed in Chapter 17 or store in airtight plastic bags for 2 weeks.

Infant/toddler toys

All toys used by infants carry the risk of spreading disease because they are mouthed frequently and passed around. All infant toys should be **washable** as well as **safe.**

- Mouth toys (that *must* be used in the mouth such as bubble pipes, horns, tubing for water tables, and toy thermometers) **should not be allowed** unless you are prepared to supervise the use to be sure that the toy is washed, rinsed, and disinfected with the bleach solution between users.
- Toys with hard plastic, rubber, or other cleanable surfaces should be washed and disinfected with the bleach solution at least once daily. Some toys are dishwasher safe.
- Stuffed toys should be machine washable, individually assigned if mouthed, and should be washed at least weekly or more often, if soiled.

Toys that cannot be washed according to these guidelines should not be used. See Chapter 6 regarding choking hazards also.

Pools (including wading pools)

Pools carry the double risk of spreading disease and possible drowning. Because of these clear health risks, the use of wading pools in early childhood programs is not recommended. Sprinklers are a safe alternative to wading pools.

Any container of water (bucket, bathtub, swimming pool) is considered a possible hazard and must be supervised by an adult at **all** times. The adult should be *directly* beside the water. Supervision from a nearby area of the playground is **not** acceptable. Use these guidelines whenever young children are near water.

- Be sure your swimming pool meets the requirements of and is licensed by your board of health.
- **Supervise children at all times.**
- Be sure that at least one person trained in water safety and certified in infant and child CPR is in attendance when the pool is in use.
- Do not use disposable diapers in pools with filters because the diapers can clog the filters. Use cloth diapers and/or rubber pants.
- Fence and lock swimming pools in accordance with accepted safety practice to prevent accidental drownings or chance access by children or others.
- Post safety rules for the use of pools in a conspicuous location and be sure the rules are reviewed by staff.

Sand

The care of play sand is a significant maintenance task. Sand should be washed and free of organic materials. If your sand area is accessible to animals, it should be kept covered when not in use. Animal feces can spread infectious diseases. The cover should allow light and air to reach the sand.

Sandboxes should be tightly covered when not in use to keep sand dry and free from animal feces which can spread infection. Children should not be allowed to play in sand that is not in a protected sandbox. In addition, at least once a year, the sand should be turned over to a depth of 18 inches and at least every 2 years completely replaced.

4
Sanitation standards

The standards presented in this chapter will help you create a sanitary, healthful environment for children. Careful practices can limit the spread of infectious disease. These recommended standards are based on federal and typical state health regulations, recommended standards from the American Academy of Pediatrics, and *Accreditation Criteria & Procedures of the National Academy of Early Childhood Programs* (National Association for the Education of Young Children 1991).

Housekeeping

Early childhood programs should have written policies and procedures for the routine cleaning and maintenance of the facility. Such written policies and procedures should specify the type of cleaning and disinfecting agents used and the method and schedule for cleaning and disinfecting. They should also name the person responsible for supervising and monitoring cleaning and other maintenance activities.

Figure 4.1 provides a chart as a highly visible reminder of which items/surfaces should be cleaned and disinfected, how frequently, and by whom.

Standard I—The facility is neat, clean, and free of rubbish.
- Clean the facility in a way that avoids contamination of food and food-contact surfaces.
- Keep soiled linens or aprons in laundry bags or other suitable containers.
- Wash all windows inside and outside at least twice a year.
- Do not use deodorizers to cover up odors caused by unsanitary conditions or poor housekeeping. Ventilate bad smells away.

- Keep storage areas, attics, and cellars free from refuse, furniture, old newspapers, and other paper goods.
- Keep flammable cleaning rags or solutions in closed metal containers in locked cabinets.
- Wash surfaces with soap and water until you can not see any soil. Rinse with water.
- Use a standard bleach solution consisting of a ¼ cup bleach to 1 gallon of water (1 tablespoon of bleach to 1 quart of water) to disinfect clean surfaces. Dispense the solution, made up fresh daily, from a spray bottle, and leave solution in contact with surface for at least 2 minutes. Dry with a paper towel or allow to air dry.
- Wash plastic mats, toys, and commonly used surfaces at least once a day and disinfect with bleach solution. See page 27 for specific information on cleaning and disinfecting mouthed toys.

Standard II—Maintain adequate housekeeping and maintenance equipment and cleaning supplies. The equipment is kept clean, in good working condition, and stored safely.
- Provide adequate housekeeping equipment and cleaning supplies including wet and dry mops, mop pails, brooms, cleaning cloths, and at least one vacuum cleaner.
- Store housekeeping equipment in a separate, locked space such as a closet or cabinet. Do not store it in bathrooms, halls, on stairs, or near food.
- When possible, use a separate sink (not used for food preparation) with hot and cold running water for cleaning purposes only.
- Launder wet mops, dusting and cleaning cloths, and sponges **daily** and dry mops **twice a week.** Store sponges in bleach solution between uses.
- Wash kitchen and bathroom floors daily. Spot-

Figure 4.1. Cleaning guidelines

Use the guidelines in these charts to determine which surfaces should be cleaned and how frequently they should be cleaned. **Clean** means to remove visible soils by using a product suitable for the surface being cleaned. **Disinfect** means to kill germs by using a disinfectant cleaner, chlorine bleach solution, or other disinfectant and air dry.

Classroom	Clean	Disinfect	Frequency	Who is responsible:
Countertops/tabletops	X	X	When soiled or at least once daily.	
Tabletops/counters used for food	X	X	Before & after food is served daily.	
Food preparation area	X	X	Before & after preparing foods.	
Floors	X	X	Daily or when soiled.	
Carpet	X		Daily vacuum. When obviously soiled, use carpet cleaner.	
Small rugs	X		Daily vacuum. Weekly launder.	
Utensils	X	X	After each use.	
Toilet Area	Clean	Disinfect	Frequency	Who is responsible:
Handwashing sinks	X	X	Daily & when soiled.	
Faucets and handles	X	X	Daily & when soiled.	
Surrounding counters	X	X	Daily & when soiled.	
Toilet bowls	X	X	Daily.	
Seats	X	X	Daily or immediately if obviously soiled.	
Flushing handle	X	X		
Door knobs	X	X		
Floors	X	X		
Changing table	X	X	After each use & daily.	
Potty chairs	X	X	After each use. Discourage use.	
Toys	Clean	Disinfect	Frequency	Who is responsible:
Small toys that can go into mouth	X	X	After each use & daily.	
Larger toys	X		Weekly.	
Dress-up clothes	X		After each use or at least weekly.	
Hats	X		After each use or at least weekly.	
Cubbies	X		After each use or at least weekly.	
Cribs	X		After each use or at least weekly.	

Clean Immediately:
If a surface is contaminated with body fluids: saliva, mucus, vomitus, urine or stools:
   Use a multi-purpose cleaner, then a disinfectant or use a disinfectant cleaner and air dry.
If a surface is contaminated by blood:
   Wear disposable gloves. Clean the surface with a multi-purpose cleaner, then disinfectant and air dry.

Adapted with permission from *The ABCs of Clean* Teachers' Guide. The Soap and Detergent Association, 475 Park Avenue, South, New York, NY 10016.

clean walls and carpets monthly and deep-clean them every 6 months.

- If potty-chairs are used, use a separate sink to wash, rinse, and disinfect the potty-chair bowl. This sink should not be used for handwashing or any other purpose.

Standard III—There is a pest control program for the facility.

- Provide screens for exterior windows and doors.
- Store pesticides away from child activity areas and in non-food service and storage areas. Lock all storage areas. Store only in original containers.
- Post instructions on the safe and proper use of these chemicals in a highly visible location.
- Be sure that all extensive extermination is provided **only** by a certified/licensed pest control operator with chemicals and in a manner approved by the EPA. Be sure a qualified staff member accompanies the pest control operator to be sure no chemical is applied to surfaces that children can touch. The insects are much less harmful than the pesticide. The treated area must be ventilated for the recommended time before being used again.
- Do not use over-the-counter products for crawling insects such as roaches, ants, and spiders. You may use over-the-counter products for flying insects such as bees, wasps, and hornets. Read directions carefully, wash your hands after use, and store the product safely out of the reach of children.
- Be sure that bait for catching pests is kept out of children's reach and in tamper-proof boxes.
- Do not use no-pest strips in food service or sleeping areas. Fly paper is acceptable if it is changed regularly.

Standard IV—Animals housed as pets are adequately fed, sheltered, and clean.

- Do not allow any animals in areas used for preparing, eating, or storing food.
- Do not allow turtles, birds of parrot family, ferrets, or any wild or dangerous animal.
- Be sure that no child is allergic to the animals in your program. Since it may be traumatic to remove an animal after an allergy is discovered, you should think about whether you truly need

an animal likely to cause such problems (rabbits, guinea pigs, and other furry animals).

- Be sure that animals are friendly and have an appropriate temperament to be around children.
- Use only animal cages that are of an approved type with false bottoms.
- Clean animal areas frequently. Do not use food service facilities. Wash hands afterward. To protect children from contamination, do not let them assist with pet cleaning or maintenance.
- Be sure animals are healthy and appropriately immunized and licensed. Dogs and cats should be maintained on a flea, tick, and worm control program. Check pet health and care requirements with a veterinarian before bringing the pet into child care. Some pets need to be protected from abuse by children.
- Be sure children and staff wash their hands after handling or feeding animals.
- Separate animal food and cleaning supplies from food service supplies.

All programs need a written policy specifying when handwashing is required for personnel and children.

- Keep all animal litter boxes away from children's reach.
- Teach children safe practices around animals (e.g., do not provoke or startle animals, remove their food, etc.).

Handwashing

Standard V—The program has a written policy that specifies when handwashing is required for personnel and children, defines the handwashing procedure, and provides continuing monitoring to assure that the handwashing procedure is carried out according to criteria in Figure 4.2.

Kitchen facilities

Standard VI—Programs that provide meals and snacks to children maintain a clean kitchen with adequate equipment and space for food preparation, serving, and storage.
- Make sure food is handled and used properly by doing the following:

Programs that provide meals and snacks to children must maintain a clean kitchen with adequate equipment and space for food preparation, serving, and storage. If you do not have adequate facilities for cleaning and disinfecting dishes and utensils, use only **disposable** *items.*

—Limit direct handling of food by using utensils such as forks, knives, trays, spoons, and scoops.
—Wash raw fruits and vegetables before use.
—Cover foods that are stored in the refrigerator and on shelves.
—Throw away handled leftovers and food left in serving bowls.
—Pay close attention to expiration dates, especially on foods that spoil easily (dairy products, mayonnaise, processed meats, and all dated products, etc.).
—Take special care when handling raw meat, chicken, and eggs. After contact with these raw foods, the food preparer should wash her or his hands well and clean and disinfect contaminated cutting boards, dishes, bowls, and utensils.
—Do not use the kitchen area as a traffic way or meeting room while food is being prepared.
(Also refer to Chapter 12 for more information about food preparation and service.)
- Require that staff who prepare food follow these hygiene procedures.
  —Wear clean clothes, maintain a high standard of personal cleanliness, and carry out strict hygiene procedures during working hours.
  —Wash hands according to prescribed handwashing procedures before preparing and serving food and as necessary to remove soil contamination.
  —Keep hands clean while handling food contact surfaces, dishes, and utensils.
  —Do not prepare or serve food while ill with a communicable disease or with uncovered hand or skin lesions. A staff person with lesions on her or his hands should use gloves while preparing food.
  —If possible, do not diaper children or assist with toileting on the same day as food preparation.
  —Keep hair covered with a hairnet or cap while preparing food.
- Provide easy-to-clean equipment and utensils.
  —Use food contact surfaces and utensils that are easy to clean, nontoxic, corrosion resistant, and nonabsorbent. (Do not use wood utensils or cutting boards.)
  —If you use disposable articles, be sure they are made of nontoxic materials. Do not reuse disposable articles.

Figure 4.2. Handwashing procedure

Adults
- Wash hands upon arrival.
- Wash hands **before** preparing food, eating, or feeding a child.
- Wash hands **after**
  —toileting self or a child
  —handling body secretions (e.g., changing diapers, cleaning up a child who has vomited or spit up, wiping a child's nose, handling soiled clothing or other contaminated items)
- Post signs to remind staff and children to wash their hands in the toilet room, the kitchen, and the area where diapers are changed.
- Be sure that the hot water supplied to fixtures accessible to children does not exceed a maximum temperature of 120° F.

How to wash hands
- Check to be sure a paper towel is available. Turn on water to a comfortable temperature.
- Moisten hands with water and apply heavy lather of *liquid* soap.
- Wash well under running water for at least 10 seconds.
- Pay particular attention to areas between fingers, around nail beds, under fingernails, and backs of hands.

- Rinse well under running water until free of soap and dirt. Hold hands so that water flows from wrist to fingertips.
- Dry hands with paper towel.
- Use paper towel to turn off faucet; then discard towel.
- Use hand lotion, if desired.

Infants/toddlers
Use soap and water at a sink if you can. If a baby is too heavy to hold for handwashing at the sink, use disposable wipes or follow this procedure:
- Wipe the child's hands with a damp paper towel moistened with a drop of liquid soap.
- Wipe the child's hands with a paper towel wet with clear water.
- Dry the child's hands with a paper towel.

Older children
- Squirt a drop of liquid soap on children's hands.
- Wash and rinse their hands in running water, directing flow from wrist to fingertips.
- Dry hands with paper towel.
- Turn off faucet with paper towel and discard.
- Teach older children to carry out the procedure themselves. Supervise younger children in carrying out this handwashing procedure.

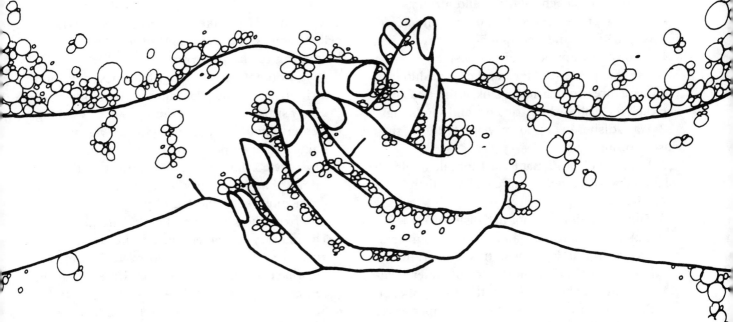

—Install appliances so that they, and areas around them, can be cleaned easily.

—Be sure food contact surfaces are free of cracks and crevices; pots and pans are free of pits and dents; and plates are free of chips and cracks. Cracks in any surface can harbor germs.

- Make sure that food contact surfaces and utensils are kept clean.

—Clean and disinfect all eating and drinking utensils, tableware, kitchenware, and food contact surfaces after use.

—Do not use cloths used for wiping food contact surfaces for anything else.

—Wash a spoon or other utensil used to test food before using again.

—Wash food contact surfaces with soap and water, rinse, disinfect with bleach solution, and sun or air dry.

—Clean kitchenware and food contact surfaces that have come in contact with spoiled food or raw meat, chicken, or eggs; disinfect the kitchenware and surfaces with the bleach solution; and let them air dry.

—Scrape and presoak dishes, pots and pans, and utensils, if necessary, to remove food particles before washing.

—Wash high chair trays, bottles, and nipples in a dishwasher, if available. If the trays do not fit in dishwasher, wash in detergent, rinse, spray with bleach solution, and air dry.

—Use the proper concentration of suitable detergent for hand and machine dishwashing, according to package directions.

—Use this procedure for hand dishwashing:

1. Use a three-compartment sink or three basins— one each for dishwashing, rinsing, and sanitizing.

2. Wash dishes in hot, soapy water (120° F.), then rinse thoroughly.

3. Immerse dishes for at least 1 minute in bleach solution that is at a temperature no lower than 75° F.

4. Rinse dishes.

5. Sun or air dry. (Do not use dish towels.)

—Make sure that the water used in your dishwasher is 170° F. Because this temperature is higher than that allowed for hot water heaters, you may have to adjust the dishwasher so that the water will reach this temperature. Periodically check the temperature of the hot water in the dishwasher by using special test strips on a thermometer made for this purpose that is held by a rubber band to a glass or cup.

—Pick up and touch clean spoons, knives, and forks only by handles, not by any part that will be in contact with food.

—Handle clean cups, glasses, and bowls so that fingers and thumbs do not touch the inside or the lip contact surfaces.

Note: If you do not have adequate facilities for cleaning and sanitizing dishes and utensils, use only **disposable** items.

Storage and disposal of garbage

Standard VII—The facility is kept free of accumulated garbage.

- Store garbage in water- and rodent-proof containers with tight lids. Remove such containers from children's areas daily.
- Put out garbage for pick up on the day of collection.
- After the garbage is removed, clean the containers, room, and areas.
- Use plastic bags to line covered containers. These may be put out for collection unless prohibited by the board of health. (Store plastic bags out of children's reach.)

Laundry

Standard VIII—Make arrangements to wash crib sheets, cot covers, and other items belonging to the program.

- If you do not have laundry facilities, develop a written policy and procedure for handling emergency situations and for doing routine washing.
- Centers should have a mechanical washing machine and dryer on site or a contract with a laundry service. Large or small family child care homes that do laundry for children in the program must keep the laundry equipment separate from the kitchen and child care areas.
- The laundry equipment must either wash or dry at above 140° F., or an approved disinfectant must be used in the rinse cycle. Dryers must be vented to the outside.
- Soaps, bleaches, and other laundry supplies should be stored in locked cabinets.

Toilet facilities

Standard IX—The toilet room is kept clean and sanitized, and the fixtures are in good working condition.

- Provide toilet fixtures designed to be easily cleaned and disinfected. If potty-chairs are used, select those with as few cracks and crevices as possible to make cleaning easier. After each use of a potty

   —Empty contents into the toilet.

   —Rinse potty-chair with water in a sink never used for food preparation purposes and empty into toilet.

   —Wash all parts of the potty with soap and water. Consider using paper towels or disposable mop. Empty soapy water into toilet.

   —Rinse again. Empty into toilet.

   —Spray with bleach solution.

   —Air dry.

   —Wash and disinfect sink.

   —Wash hands.

   Now that you know what is necessary if you use potties, you may want to reconsider whether you really want to use them! Suggest that each child have her or his own potty-chair sent from home if parents wish a child to use a potty rather than the toilet, but you will still have to follow the procedure listed above.

- Provide toilet paper and holders, towels, and soap dispensers with liquid soap where they can be easily reached by all users.
- Label toothbrushes and make sure they are not shared. Store them brush up, not touching each other, and away from contamination to air dry thoroughly. Egg cartons and shoe-box lids are easily adapted, disposable toothbrush holders.
- Empty and disinfect trash containers regularly, using the bleach solution.
- Wash with soap and water, rinse, and disinfect bathroom fixtures with bleach solution at least daily or when contaminated by feces or vomitus.

Plumbing

Standard X—Plumbing is in compliance with the regulations and codes for your state and county or city.

Ventilation, light, and heat

Standard XI—All rooms are well lighted, ventilated, and sufficiently heated.

- Be sure that adequate light is available in rooms, halls, and stairways. Supplement natural light with properly diffused and distributed artificial light.
- Maintain adequate ventilation by using windows that can be opened, air conditioning, or a ventilating system.
- Have the heating and ventilation systems checked at least once a year by a certified (licensed) heating and ventilation contractor to be sure the air flow and exchange are adequate. Names of licensed contractors can be obtained from the local building inspector authority.

5
Diapering and toilet learning

Diapering and toileting carry distinct health risks to children and adults. You need to handle both of these activities with extreme care from both sanitation and child development viewpoints.

Toileting is one of the most basic physical needs of young children. The way that you handle the process of toileting can have major emotional effects as well. The entire process from diapering infants to teaching toddlers and preschoolers about using the toilet should be a **positive** one. At diapering time you have a chance to engage in special individual communication with a child. It is a time to show extra caring and support.

Often the process of toilet learning for toddlers becomes an unnecessary struggle for control between adults and children. You can join forces with the part of the child that wants to learn and grow. You help a child gain her or his **own** control with your patience and understanding. This chapter will provide ways to meet the physical **and** emotional needs of young children.

Diapering

Diapering area
Follow these very important rules about the diapering area.
- Use the area only for diapering.
- Set up the diapering area as far away as possible from any food handling area.
- Provide running water within an arm's reach to clean and disinfect the diapering area and for appropriate handwashing.
- Construct a diapering surface that is flat, safe, and at a comfortable height for the caregiver to work without bending the back. Diapers should

not be changed on the floor because of the greater risk for contamination of the floor and other children that may come along.
- Be sure this surface is clean, waterproof, and free of cracks, tape, and crevices. Cover it with a relatively nonabsorbent, disposable cover. Use inexpensive materials such as shelf paper, freezer paper, butcher paper, or buy disposable squares from discount medical supply companies. Paper towels are not a good choice because they are so absorbent.
- Keep all creams, lotions, and cleaning items out of the reach of children. Never give a child any of these to play with while being diapered since she or he could be poisoned.
- Add a guardrail or recessed area to the diapering surface as a good extra safety measure. Always keep a hand on the child. **Never leave the child, even for a second.** *Do not* use safety straps.

How to change a diaper
To correctly change a diaper, follow the steps in Figure 5.1. Please copy and post this information above your diapering area.

Cloth or paper diapers?
There is considerable controversy about the use of disposable versus cloth diapers in early childhood programs. The American Public Health Association/American Academy of Pediatrics Standards (1992) state that
- All diapers must be able to contain urine and stool, thereby minimizing fecal contamination of children, staff, and the environment.
- The diaper must have an inner absorbent lining *attached* to an outer waterproof covering that prevents the escape of feces and urine.

- The outer and inner linings must be changed as a unit and should not be reused unless both parts are cleaned and disinfected.

Only modern disposable paper diapers with absorbent gelling material fully meet these criteria. Reusable cloth diapers worn either without a covering or with removable, *unattached* pants or wrap do not meet these criteria. At this time there are insufficient data to determine whether reusable diaper systems (with an outer waterproof covering and *attached* inner cotton lining *changed as a unit*) are an acceptable alternative to disposable paper diapers in child care facilities.

When changing a child's diaper, caregivers should follow every step listed in Figure 5.1 and should use the following precautions—
If you use disposable diapers—

- Put the disposable diaper into a lined, covered diaper pail with foot pedal (step can).

The best technique for toilet learning is to wait until the child is ready and to take the cues directly from the child's own pattern.

- Empty the pail at least every day or more often as needed.

If you use a cloth diaper service—

- Use a diaper service that meets the standards for cleaning and sanitizing developed by the National Association of Diaper Services.
- Use only a one-unit diapering system that meets the requirements as outlined.
- Never rinse cloth diapers in the toilet. You may empty bulky stool into the toilet if the diaper service asks you to do so.
- Place the soiled diaper in a disinfecting container provided by the commercial diaper service or a lined diaper step can with a tight fitting lid.
- Arrange for the diaper service to pick up soiled diapers frequently to avoid unpleasant odor.

If you use cloth diapers sent from home—

- Use only a one-unit diapering system that meets the requirements as outlined.
- Never rinse cloth diapers in the toilet. You may empty bulky stool into the toilet.
- Place the unrinsed, soiled diaper in a leakproof container or plastic bag. Label it with the child's name and store it out of reach. Ask the parent to take it home for laundering.

Toilet learning

When is a child ready?

Using the self-mastery approach, children must be ready to participate willingly if the process of toilet learning is to be a positive one. Otherwise, toilet "training" can be a battle of the wills and endless disciplining and disappointments. The purpose of toilet learning is to help children gain control of their body functions. If a child is ready, the process of toilet learning can become a sign of great success and achievement for the child's own sense of growing up. Look for these landmarks that indicate a child is ready for toilet learning.

There is a considerable cultural variation in handling toilet "training." Being sensitive to these differences requires close communication with parents about these issues. Most health care and child care experts recommend the self-mastery approach rather than simply conditioning the child to empty urine or stool when put on the toilet.

Figure 5.1. How to change a diaper

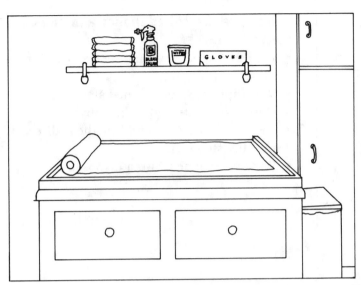

1. Get organized

- Before you bring the child to the diaper changing area, gather what you need: non-absorbent paper, a fresh diaper, wipes, gloves if you use them, a plastic bag for any soiled clothes, and a dab of any diaper cream if the baby uses it. Take the supplies you will need out of the containers and put the containers away.
- Put on the disposable gloves, if you use them.

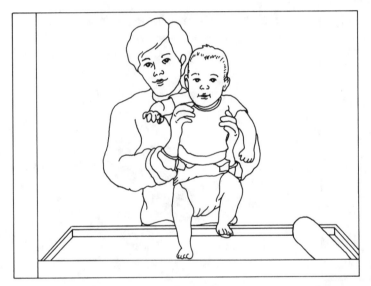

2. Avoid contact with soiled items, and always keep a hand on the baby

Anything that comes in contact with stool or urine is a source of germs.

- Carry the baby to the changing table, keeping soiled clothing away from you.
- Bag soiled clothes and securely tie the plastic bag to send them home.

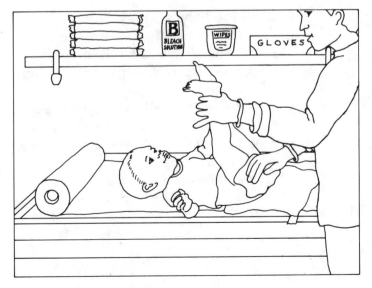

3. Clean the child's diaper area

- Unfasten the diaper, but leave the soiled diaper under the child.
- Use disposable wipes to clean the diaper area. Remove stool and urine from front to back and use a fresh wipe each time. Put the wipes into the soiled diaper.
- Note and report any skin problems such as redness.

Continued on page 40.

Figure 4.1 *continued*

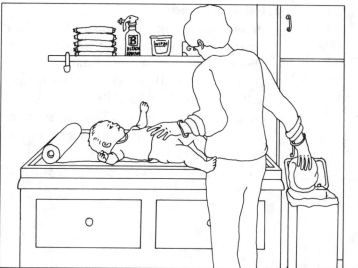

4. Remove the soiled diaper and clean soiled surfaces.

- Fold the diaper over and secure it with the tabs.
- Put it into a covered, lined step can.
- Check for spills under the baby.
- Remove the gloves and put them directly into the step can.
- Wipe your hands with a disposable wipe.

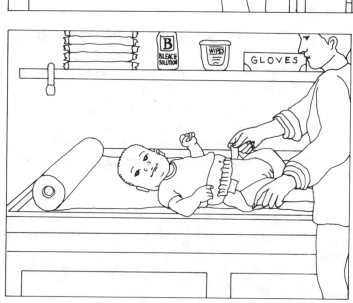

5. Put on a clean diaper

Slide the diaper under the baby, adjust and fasten it.

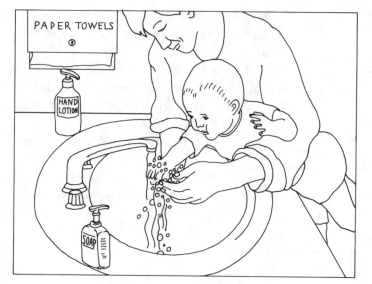

6. Clean the baby's hands

Use soap and water at a sink if you can. If a baby is too heavy to hold for handwashing at the sink, use disposable wipes or follow this procedure:

- Wipe the child's hands with a damp paper towel moistened with a drop of liquid soap.
- Wipe the child's hands with a paper towel wet with clear water.
- Dry the child's hands with a paper towel.

Figure 4.1 *continued*

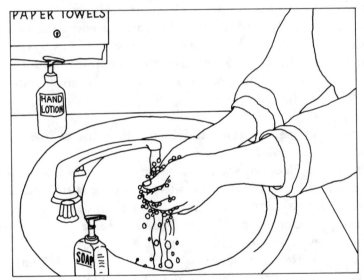

7. Clean and disinfect the diapering area

- Dispose of the table liner.
- Clean any visible soil from the changing table.
- Disinfect the table by spraying it so you wet the entire surface with bleach solution (1 tablespoon household bleach to 1 quart of water. Mix fresh daily.).
- Leave the bleach on the surface for 2 minutes. The surface can then be wiped dry or left to air dry.

8. Wash your hands and record in the child's daily log

- Use soap and running warm water.
- Use a paper towel to turn off faucet.
- Use hand lotion to keep your hands from becoming dry and chapped.
- Record in daily log what was in the diaper and any problems.

Toilet learning *continued*

Muscle control. This child must be able to work the bottom muscles at will. She or he must be able to squeeze the sphincter (bottom) and stomach muscles at the same time. This muscle coordination is automatic in children without physical abnormalities. What is learned with development is the ability to control this process—both to begin and hold back emptying stool and urine. Usually most children do not have this control until around their second birthday. Some are not ready until age 3. They should also be able to undress enough to be able to sit on a toilet or potty without assistance and without fear of falling off.

Communication. The child should be able to use words or consistent gestures to ask for help undressing or getting to the toilet and to communicate the urge "to go." Remember to ask parents about their word preferences for toileting (i.e., *urine, b.m., pee,* or *poop*). *Bowel movement* and *urine* are good words for children to learn because they are part of the child's needed vocabulary as a grown-up.

Desire. Starting before children want to learn about the toilet may set up a lasting power struggle. Children have a natural desire to please those whom they love and trust. Children also love to imitate! Children will eventually become uncomfortable in diapers and may want to wear underwear instead. Never force children to sit on a potty or toilet.

Parents and staff should decide together when the child is ready to begin toilet learning. Develop a plan together that will be consistent and manageable in both settings. Different approaches are confusing and may be upsetting. If possible, you should develop similar schedules and use similar equipment.

The process of toilet learning usually is neither fast nor consistent. For some children, the process may take several years to complete. Commonly, children have accidents when they are sick (especially with urine infections or diarrhea), tired, excited, very involved in play, or stressed (e.g., when a sibling is born or when there is an illness in the family).

Children should not be punished for lapses in using the toilet. If you expect some backslide, you will be more apt to accept a child's behavior. Children need your understanding and patience when they are having difficulty in toileting. Your support should actually shorten the time for children to regain their toileting patterns. Punishment will prolong the struggle.

It is appropriate for adults to indicate their expectation that the child use the toilet appropriately. However, a child's resistance to this expectation should be ignored without the caregiver showing anger or resentment.

Equipment needs

Some children need no special equipment except a good supply of extra underpants and clothing. Wearing overclothes over the diaper also reduces diarrhea problems by further containing stool and urine. Training pants are extra thick and absorbent and may be helpful, although not necessary, in the beginning.

Some children are insecure or frightened on an adult-size toilet and may need one or more of the following:

- **Stool** to step up to the toilet—Use a nonslippery plastic stool, wooden block covered with a washable surface, or any inexpensive step so the children can easily reach the toilet. A step also acts as a firm footrest for pushing. A stool is recommended for all young children who use a toilet.
- **Toilet seat adapter**—This inexpensive adapter fits over the regular seat to make the seat more child-size and secure. Be sure it is washable plastic.
- **Potty-chair**—Potty-chair frames should be made of a continuous surfaced, smooth, nonporous material that is easily cleanable. Wood frames are not recommended. The waste container should be easily removable and fit securely into the chair. **Many medical experts recommend that potty-chairs not be used in groups because of hygiene problems.** If a child truly needs a potty-chair, ask the parents to provide it as a personal item to be used only by that child. If you do use potty-chairs, follow the guidelines for cleaning them described under Standard IX in Chapter 4.

Hygiene when children are learning to use the toilet

- Place any soiled clothes in double, labeled, plastic bags for parents to take home at the end of the day. Washing different children's soiled clothes together can spread disease.
- Help the child use the toilet.
- Help the child wash her or his hands. Tell children that washing their hands will stop germs that might make them sick. When children use the toilet, make sure they wash their hands correctly. Show them how to wash their hands (see Figure 4.2). Watch children wash their hands after they use the toilet, or ask children if they have washed their hands when they return from the bathroom.
- If a potty-chair is used, follow the guidelines for cleaning in Chapter 4, Standard IX.
- Children learning to use the toilet commonly contaminate nearby surfaces such as the toilet seat, paper holder, flushing handle, and nearby walls. These should be washed and disinfected at least daily and when soiled.
- Wash your hands.

Helpful hints

The best technique for toilet learning is to wait until the child is ready and to take cues directly from the child's own pattern. Beyond that, these suggestions may help:

- Choose clothing that is easy to remove in a hurry. A child must be able to act on an urge to toilet immediately. Avoid tight snaps, lots of buttons, etc. Velcro fasteners are especially easy.

- Use the equipment necessary to make the child feel secure. Always explain the equipment and your expectations for its use. In some cases, it may be best if you flush the toilet or remove the waste after the child leaves the room; the noise or disappearance of the waste may frighten some children. Others may enjoy the sound and action.

- Suggest regularly that the child use the toilet. Common toileting times are after meals, before and after naptime, and before trips. Be sure that you do not expect a child to go only on your schedule. Especially in the beginning, children often need/want to go to the toilet frequently.

- Ask the child to sit on the toilet for no more than 5 minutes **unless** the child is upset or uncomfortable. Never insist that the child sit there until "the job is done."

- Always give the child lots of positive feedback and encouragement for success. **Never** punish the child for failures.

Section C
Safety and first aid

Major concepts

- Most injuries can be prevented.

- Regular safety checks of the indoor and outdoor environment should be made and improvements implemented immediately.

- Infants and toddlers require special safety precautions.

- Safety education for staff, children, and parents must be provided.

- Children and adults must be properly restrained while riding in a vehicle, and specific safety rules must be followed.

- All staff must be trained in first aid and prepared to carry out the facility's emergency procedures.

6
Safety

Injuries are the result of problems in the environment, a mismatch between a child's abilities and activities, and/or a lack of adult supervision. Sometimes there are hidden dangers that are seen only after a child or staff member is injured. Injuries can often be prevented by

- being aware of potential hazards
- taking action to eliminate or reduce these hazards
- knowing what to do in an emergency
- teaching children about safety

Creating a safe facility

A safe facility is arranged so that children can play freely without harming themselves or others. A safe environment allows children to learn by taking risks and challenging themselves and, at the same time, protects them from injury. A sterile, risk-free environment and rules that do not let children play and explore are not healthy. Young children do not yet understand the concept of danger. Also, children may not recognize that certain behaviors or actions are likely to cause injuries.

Your program must follow certain safety standards and practices to be licensed. Local building, sanitary, and fire safety codes must also be observed. You can also create a safe environment by carefully following these additional basic guidelines.

- Be alert to hazards both indoors and outdoors and eliminate or avoid them.
- Look at the world through the eyes of a young child—it is colorful, mysterious, and has new places and objects to experiment with and explore. Get down on your hands and knees to see what a child sees. You may be surprised at what you find!
- Conduct regular safety checks. Each room and the outdoor play area should be checked at least

once per month. Use the checklists that begin on page 48 (Figures 6.1 and 6.2).

- Encourage all staff to participate in conducting the checks and planning ways to deal with hazards. Parents and older children can help too.
- Know what you're buying or what is being donated to your program. Read labels and instructions carefully. If you have any questions or complaints about the safety of a product, call the Consumer Product Safety Commission (CPSC) at its toll-free number: **800-638-2772.**

Times when children get hurt

During certain situations and times of day, children are more likely to be injured. Injuries are more likely when

- another child becomes ill or injured and the routine is disrupted (other children become more at risk)
- staff are absent or busy
- children are not involved in the activity that was planned, and they are tired or hungry (for example, immediately before lunch)
- hazards are too attractive
- staff are not up-to-date on children's abilities
- during field trips, when there are new places to explore and safety rules may be forgotten
- late morning and late afternoon, especially in the spring and fall

Indoor safety

Traffic and play areas

- Make sure there is enough space for all furniture and equipment and for traffic around them.
- Bolt top-heavy furniture (e.g., cubbies) to the wall or floor.

Figures 6.1 and 6.2 provide a site safety checklist and a playground safety checklist. No checklist can include **all** potential hazards to children or identify **every** health and safety factor specific to your site. The items included on these checklists represent features to be checked on a regularly scheduled basis to promote the health and safety of children and staff of your program. Use the checklists to find hazards. Whenever a hazard is found, fix it if you can. If you cannot fix it, make a note of it and follow up with plans to get it fixed. Safety checks should be done on a regularly scheduled basis—some features need to be checked daily; others weekly or monthly. Having different people do the safety checks helps find more hazards. The more people are involved in watching for hazards, the more they will help fix hazards. Safety is everyone's business!

Figure 6.1. Site safety checklist

General indoor areas

Yes	No	
❑	❑	Guns, projectile toys, darts, and cap pistols are not kept in the child care setting.
❑	❑	Floors are smooth and have nonskid surfaces. Rugs are skid-proof.
❑	❑	Doors to places that children can enter, such as bathrooms, can be easily opened from the outside by a child or by an adult.
❑	❑	Doors in children's areas have see-through panes so children are visible to anyone opening the door.
❑	❑	Doors have slow-closing devices and/or rubber gaskets on the edges to prevent finger pinching.
❑	❑	Glass doors and full-length windows have decals on them that are at the eye levels of both children and adults.
❑	❑	Windows cannot be opened more than 6" from the bottom.
❑	❑	All windows have closed, permanent screens.
❑	❑	Bottom windows are lockable.
❑	❑	Walls and ceilings have no peeling paint and no cracked or falling plaster.
❑	❑	The child care setting is free of toxic or lead paint and of crumbly asbestos.
❑	❑	Safety covers are on all electrical outlets.
❑	❑	Electrical cords are out of children's reach. Electrical cords are placed away from doorways and traffic paths.
❑	❑	Covers or guards for fans have openings small enough to keep children's fingers out.
❑	❑	Nobody smokes or has lighted cigarettes, matches, or lighters around children.
❑	❑	Freestanding space heaters are not used.

Figure 6.1 *continued*

General indoor areas *continued*

Yes No

❑ ❑ Pipes, radiators, fireplaces, wood burning stoves, and other hot surfaces cannot be reached by children or are covered to prevent burns.

❑ ❑ Tap water temperature is 120° F. or lower.

❑ ❑ Trash is covered at all times and is stored away from heaters or other heat sources.

❑ ❑ Drawers are closed to prevent tripping or bumps.

❑ ❑ Sharp furniture edges are cushioned with cotton and masking tape or with commercial corner guards.

❑ ❑ Emergency lighting equipment works.

❑ ❑ Regular lighting is bright enough for good visibility in each room.

❑ ❑ Enough staff members are always present to exit with children safely and quickly in an emergency.

❑ ❑ All adults can easily view all areas used by children.

❑ ❑ Pets are free from disease, are immunized as appropriate, and are maintained in a sanitary manner.

❑ ❑ Poisonous plants are not present either indoors or outdoors in the child care areas.

❑ ❑ All adult handbags are stored out of children's reach.

❑ ❑ All poisons and other dangerous items are stored in locked cabinets out of children's reach. This includes medicines, paints, cleansers, mothballs, etc.

❑ ❑ Pesticides are applied only to surfaces that children cannot reach and surfaces not in direct contact with food.

❑ ❑ A certified pest control operator applies pesticides while observed by a caregiver.

❑ ❑ Cots are placed in such a way that walkways are clear for emergencies.

❑ ❑ Children are never left alone in infant seats on tables or other high surfaces.

❑ ❑ Teaching aids such as projectors are put away when not in use.

❑ ❑ A well-stocked first-aid kit is accessible to all caregivers.

❑ ❑ Heavy equipment or furniture that may tip over is anchored.

Figure 6.1 *continued*

Toys and equipment

Yes No

☐ ☐ Toys and play equipment have no sharp edges or points, small parts, pinch points, chipped paint, splinters, or loose nuts or bolts.

☐ ☐ All toys are painted with lead-free paint.

☐ ☐ Toys are put away when not in use.

☐ ☐ Toys that are mouthed are washed and disinfected between users.

☐ ☐ Children are not permitted to play with any type of plastic bag or balloon.

☐ ☐ Toys are too large to fit completely into a child's mouth and have no small, detachable parts to cause choking. No coins, safety pins, or marbles for children under 4 years of age.

☐ ☐ Infants and toddlers are not permitted to eat small objects and foods that may easily cause choking, such as hot dogs, hard candy, seeds, nuts, popcorn, and uncut round foods such as whole grapes and olives.

☐ ☐ Toy chests have air holes and a lid support or have no lid. A lid that slams shut can cause head injuries or suffocation.

☐ ☐ Shooting or projectile toys are not present.

☐ ☐ Commercial art materials are stored in their original containers out of children's reach. The word *nontoxic* appears on the manufacturer's label.

☐ ☐ Rugs, curtains, pillows, blankets, and cloth toys are flame resistant.

☐ ☐ Hinges and joints are covered to prevent small fingers from being pinched or caught.

☐ ☐ Cribs, playpens, and high chairs are away from drapery cords and electrical cords.

☐ ☐ Cribs, playpens, and high chairs are used properly and according to the manufacturer's recommendations for age and weight. Cribs have no corner posts.

☐ ☐ Cribs have slats placed 2 3/8" apart or less and have snug-fitting mattresses. Mattresses are set at their lowest settings and sides are locked at their highest settings.

☐ ☐ Toys are not hung across the cribs of infants who can sit up.

☐ ☐ Rattles, pacifiers, or other objects are never hung around an infant's neck.

☐ ☐ Infant walkers are not used.

Figure 6.1 *continued*

Hallways and stairs

Yes	No	
❏	❏	Handrails are securely mounted at child height.
❏	❏	Handrails are attached to walls for right-hand descent, but preferably are attached to the walls on both right and left sides.
❏	❏	Stairway gates are locked in place when infants or toddlers are nearby. Gates should have openings small enough to prevent a child's head from fitting through. No accordion-type gates are used.
❏	❏	Doorways to unsupervised or unsafe areas are closed and locked unless the doors are used for emergency exits.
❏	❏	Emergency exit doors have easy-open latches.
❏	❏	Safety glass is used in all areas of potential impact.
❏	❏	Caregivers can easily monitor all entrances and exits to keep out strangers.
❏	❏	Stairways and hallways are clear of objects that can cause a fall.

Kitchen and food preparation and storage areas

Yes	No	
❏	❏	Caregivers always wash hands before handling food.
❏	❏	Caregivers always wash children's hands before mealtimes.
❏	❏	Trash is always stored away from food preparation and storage areas.
❏	❏	Refrigerator temperature is monitored by thermometer and is kept at or below 40° F.
❏	❏	All perishable foods are stored in covered containers at 40° F. or lower.
❏	❏	Hot foods are kept at 140° F. or higher until ready to be eaten.
❏	❏	Pest strips are not used.
❏	❏	Cleansers and other poisonous products are stored in their original containers, away from food, and out of children's reach.
❏	❏	Nonperishable food is stored in labeled, insect-resistant metal or plastic containers with tight lids.
❏	❏	Five-gallon buckets are not accessible to children.

Figure 6.1 *continued*

Kitchen and food preparation and storage areas *continued*

Yes No

❑ ❑ Refrigerated medicines are kept in closed containers to prevent spills that would contaminate food.

❑ ❑ Food preparation surfaces are clean and are free of cracks and chips.

❑ ❑ Eating utensils and dishes are clean and are free of cracks and chips.

❑ ❑ Appliances and sharp or hazardous cooking utensils are stored out of children's reach.

❑ ❑ Pot handles are always turned toward the back of the stove.

❑ ❑ An ABC-type fire extinguisher is securely mounted on the wall near the stove.

❑ ❑ All caregivers know how to use the fire extinguisher correctly and have seen a demonstration by members of the fire department.

❑ ❑ There is a "danger zone" in front of the stove where the children are not allowed to go.

❑ ❑ A sanitarian has inspected food preparation and service equipment and procedures within the past year.

❑ ❑ Children are taught the meaning of "hot."

❑ ❑ Trash is stored away from the furnace, stove, and hot water heater.

❑ ❑ Kitchen area is not accessible to children without constant adult supervision.

❑ ❑ Caregivers do not cook while holding a child.

❑ ❑ Hot foods and liquids are kept out of children's reach.

❑ ❑ Stable step stools are used to reach high places.

Bathrooms

Yes No

❑ ❑ Stable step stools are available where needed.

❑ ❑ Electrical outlets have safety covers or are modified to prevent shock.

❑ ❑ Electrical equipment is stored away from water.

❑ ❑ Cleaning products and disinfectants are locked in a cabinet out of children's reach.

Figure 6.1 *continued*

Bathrooms *continued*

Yes No

☐ ☐ Toilet paper is located where children can reach it without having to get up from the toilet.

☐ ☐ If potty-chairs are used, they are easy to clean with the bleach solution in a utility sink used only for that purpose, if possible.

☐ ☐ Potty-chairs are not used in the food preparation or dining areas, and potty-chairs cannot be reached by children when they are not in use.

☐ ☐ There are enough toilets so children do not have to stand in line.

☐ ☐ Caregivers and children always wash hands after toileting and diaper changing.

☐ ☐ The changing of diapers or soiled underwear is done in a special, separate area away from food and play.

☐ ☐ The diapering or changing table has rails to keep the child from rolling off.

☐ ☐ Trash cans for diapers, tissues, and other materials that come in contact with body fluids can be opened with a step pedal and are lined with a plastic bag, emptied daily, and kept clean.

☐ ☐ Paper towels and liquid soap are readily available at the sink.

☐ ☐ Thermometers are used to check that the temperature of water that will be in direct contact with children does not exceed 120° F.

☐ ☐ Cosmetics are stored out of children's reach.

☐ ☐ Bathtubs have skid-proof mats or stickers.

☐ ☐ Children take baths only when adults can supervise.

☐ ☐ Children are never left alone on a changing table, bed, or any other elevated surface.

☐ ☐ Children are never left unsupervised in or near water.

Swimming pools

Yes No

☐ ☐ All pools and ponds are enclosed with four-sided fencing that is resistant to climbing, is at least 5' high, comes within 3½" of the ground, and has openings no greater than 3½".

☐ ☐ Fence openings have self-closing latching gates with the latch at least 55" from the ground.

☐ ☐ Walk areas around the pool have a nonskid surface.

Figure 6.1 *continued*

Swimming pools *continued*

Yes No

❑ ❑ The pool and pool maintenance have been inspected and approved by the local health department within the past year.

❑ ❑ Small, portable wading pools are not used for group water play.

❑ ❑ Equipment is available and used every 2 hours while children are in the water to test and maintain the pH of the water between 7.2 and 8.2.

❑ ❑ Water temperatures are maintained between 82° F. and 93° F. while the pool is in use.

Emergency preparedness

Yes No

❑ ❑ All caregivers have roles and responsibilities in case of fires, injury, or other disasters.

❑ ❑ One or more caregivers certified in infant and child first aid, and where children swim or children with disabilities are in care, one or more caregivers certified in infant and child CPR are always present.

❑ ❑ Emergency procedures include the following:
- How to telephone emergency medical services (EMS) system
- Transportation to an emergency facility
- Notification of parents
- Where to meet if the child care setting is evacuated
- Plans for an adult to care for the children while a caregiver stays with injured children. This includes escorting children to emergency medical care.
- Alternate location for care is known to staff and parents and is stocked with essential supplies (formula, diapers, toys, first-aid supplies)

❑ ❑ All first-aid kits have the required supplies. The kits are stored where caregivers can easily reach them in an emergency.

❑ ❑ Caregivers always take a first-aid kit on trips.

❑ ❑ Smoke detectors and other alarms work.

❑ ❑ Each room and hallway has a fire escape route clearly posted.

❑ ❑ Emergency procedures and telephone numbers are clearly posted near each phone.

❑ ❑ Children's emergency telephone numbers are posted near the telephone and can be easily taken along in case of an emergency evacuation.

❑ ❑ All exits are clearly marked and free of clutter.

Figure 6.1 *continued*

Emergency preparedness *continued*

Yes	No	
❏	❏	Doors and gates all open out for easy exit.
❏	❏	Children are taught to tell if they or anyone else is hurt.
❏	❏	Children are taught the words *stop* and *no*. Caregivers avoid using those words unless there is danger.
❏	❏	Children are taught their own telephone number, address, and parents' work numbers.
❏	❏	Children are taught how to telephone EMS (911).
❏	❏	Children are taught how to Stop, Drop, Roll, Cool in case their clothes catch fire.
❏	❏	Children are taught to turn in any matches they find to an adult.

Vehicles

Yes	No	
❏	❏	All vehicles work well.
❏	❏	Everyone, during every ride, uses age-appropriate safety restraints.
❏	❏	Staff help to unbuckle and buckle up children at drop-off and pickup.
❏	❏	Drivers use child-resistant door locks when the vehicle is in motion.
❏	❏	All vehicles are locked when not in use.
❏	❏	A well-stocked first-aid kit is in the vehicle for every ride.
❏	❏	The caregiver has on hand current emergency contact information when driving children.
❏	❏	Trip plans include how to manage emergencies.
❏	❏	Children wear program identification when transported.
❏	❏	Pickup and drop-off points are safe from traffic.
❏	❏	Infant seats are installed correctly, with seats facing the rear of the car until the child exceeds the weight recommended by the manufacturer for facing the rear.
❏	❏	Driver knows where children are before putting vehicle in reverse.
❏	❏	Young bikers know traffic rules.

Figure 6.1 *continued*

Vehicles *continued*

Yes   No

❑   ❑   Children do not horse around while riding bikes and do not ride in the street.

❑   ❑   Bicyles and other riding toys are stable, well balanced, and of the appropriate size. They do not have broken parts.

❑   ❑   Children use helmets approved by ANSI (American National Standards Institute) or Snell Memorial Foundation when riding bikes and other pedal powered riding toys.

❑   ❑   Young children never cross the street without an adult. Children should know rules for crossing the street.

Figure 6.2. Playground safety checklist

Playground

Yes   No

❑   ❑   The playground offers a wide range of parallel and interactive activities.

❑   ❑   All surfaces underneath play equipment are covered with the amount of impact-absorbing material required per CPSC recommendations for the highest possible fall. Material such as sand, wood chips, or pea gravel, or a manufactured energy-absorptive surface is installed under and extends at least 6' beyond all sides of the equipment.

❑   ❑   Surfaces are raked weekly to remove litter, sharp objects, and animal feces.

❑   ❑   Stagnant pools of water are not present.

❑   ❑   All pieces of play equipment are at least 12' apart, except
- Equipment less than 30" high, spring riders, and balance beams are at least 6' apart.
- Swing sets are placed 12' or more from other equipment and at least 6' from walls, fences, walkways, and other play areas. There is a clear space two times the height of the swing beam in front and two times the height of the swing beam in back of the swing.

❑   ❑   Boundaries such as railroad ties, low bushes, benches, or painted lines separate play equipment from walking areas.

❑   ❑   Bike or trike riding areas are separate from other equipment.

❑   ❑   Playgrounds are fenced in.

❑   ❑   Exposed concrete or hard anchoring material is covered.

❑   ❑   Equipment is appropriate to the size and development of the children.

Figure 6.2 *continued*

Playground *continued*

Yes	No	
❑	❑	There are no sharp edges, loose connections, or exposed nails. Bolt ends are less than or equal to two threads and are not a protrusion hazard.
❑	❑	The playground is designed for safety. Caregivers remind children regularly of playground safety rules.
❑	❑	Swings are hung at least 2' apart from one another. There are no more than two swings per bay.
❑	❑	Slides have run-off space that is 4' plus the height of the slide.
❑	❑	Slides are no taller than 6' and have side rims at least 4" high. [Short, spiral slides are suggested for children between 2 to 5 years.]
❑	❑	Slides have an enclosed platform at the top for children to rest on and get into position.
❑	❑	Slide ladders have flat steps and a handrail on each side.
❑	❑	Slides have a flat surface at the bottom to slow children down.
❑	❑	Metal slides are shaded to prevent overheating.
❑	❑	The slide incline is equal to or less than a 30° angle.
❑	❑	Steps and rungs are 7 to 11" apart and are evenly spaced for easy climbing. Steps or rungs between 3½ and 9" are filled in to eliminate an entrapment hazard.
❑	❑	Climbing or swinging bars stay in place when grasped.
❑	❑	The maximum height of play equipment is 6'.
❑	❑	Climbers have regularly spaced footholds from top to bottom.
❑	❑	The tops of climbers have a "safe way out" for children.
❑	❑	Playground equipment has no openings 3½ to 9" to entrap a child's head.
❑	❑	Rungs on climbers are painted in bright or contrasting colors for easy visibility.
❑	❑	Swings with chair seats are available for children under 5. Chair seats are not made of wood, metal, or heavy solid material.
❑	❑	Swings with canvas sling seats are available for children over 5. There are no animal swings present.

Figure 6.2 *continued*

Playground *continued*

Yes	No	
❑	❑	Swings have no open-ended hooks. Any "S" hooks are closed tightly at both ends.
❑	❑	The points at which swing seats and chains meet are enclosed in plastic tubing.
❑	❑	Hanging rings are less than 3½" or more than 10" in diameter (smaller or larger than a child's head).
❑	❑	Seesaw equipment is designed to prevent pinching or crushing. Children between 2 and 5 years use only spring-loaded seesaws.
❑	❑	Shock-absorbing material or parts of a rubber tire are placed beneath the ends of seesaws to prevent feet from getting caught.
❑	❑	Merry-go-rounds are installed so that a child cannot fit head or body beneath the turning platform.
❑	❑	Sandboxes are located in the shade, have smooth frames, and are covered when not in use.
❑	❑	Sandbox sand is raked at least every 2 weeks to remove debris.
❑	❑	Pools are fenced in and closed to trespassers. They have been inspected and their safety equipment, sanitation, procedures, and supervision have been approved.
❑	❑	Play areas are free of trash cans and poisonous plants and berries.
❑	❑	Play areas have clean drinking water and lots of shade.
❑	❑	Caregivers can easily view the entire play area.
❑	❑	Caregivers closely supervise high-risk areas such as climbing equipment.
❑	❑	Adult seating near the high-risk areas is provided to encourage adult observation.
❑	❑	Children learn how to use sports equipment and how to use the proper safety equipment for each sport.
❑	❑	Children learn water safety and they are always watched by adults when they are in or near water.
❑	❑	Children over 3 years of age should know how to swim.
❑	❑	Playgrounds with different-size equipment are provided for children 2 to 5 years and 5 to 12 years in separate areas.

Figure 6.2 *continued*

Playground *continued*

Yes	No	
☐	☐	The caregiver gives specific safety instructions such as "Don't climb the tree" or "Stay inside the fence."
☐	☐	The caregiver looks around the playground for broken glass and other dangerous debris before permitting children to play.

Figure 6.1 and 6.2 are adapted, courtesy of the American Red Cross Child Care Course, Health & Safety Units, 1990, pages 38–44. This checklist is authorized for use by individual child care providers. All other usage is strictly prohibited without the express approval of the American Red Cross.

- Experiment with different arrangements until you find one that best suits the needs of the children and your program.
- Place chairs and other furniture away from windows, cabinets, and shelves to prevent children from climbing or reaching hazards.
- Keep aisles free of toys, furniture, and other tripping hazards such as spilled water. Break up long aisles to discourage children from running.
- Involve the children in setting rules to limit running, pushing, and other such behaviors. Enforce these rules consistently.

Doors

Finger pinch injuries and bumps from doors being opened onto children are common problems in child care. To avoid these problems
- use doors with vision panels at child height and protected edges to prevent finger pinching
- install rubber gaskets to fill a 1" cut-out of the door 2/3 of the way up the door
- install devices that slow door closings

Kitchen and cooking facilities

- Make sure the kitchen is not accessible to children, unless you can provide constant adult supervision.
- Place other cooking facilities or equipment (e.g., hot plates, toaster ovens) out of reach of children.
- Make sure electrical cords and extension cords are not dangling within children's reach.

- Turn handles of pots and pans in toward the back of the stove.
- Do not carry hot foods or liquids when children are near you.
- Do not place hot items at the edge of a counter, table, or on a tablecloth that could be pulled down by a child.
- Prevent scalds by keeping tap water temperature no higher than 120° F.

Electrical wiring

- Cover unused outlets with outlet covers or shock stops. Cover outlets in use with outlet covers, especially near sinks and where young children can reach them. Many types of shock guards and outlet covers are available. Observe the children around the outlets. If they learn to remove the guards, try using a different type that is more difficult to operate.
- Use extension cords only when absolutely necessary. Place extension cords so they run along the wall, behind furniture, to reduce the chance of tripping. Never run any appliance or extension cord underneath a carpet or rug—it may become worn or frayed and cause a fire. Never run cords through doorways or walls. Do not nail extension cords to the wall. Keep extension cords out of the reach of infants and toddlers to prevent mouth burns and electric shock caused by biting. Store extension cords when not in use.

Choking hazards

Young children may choke during meals or during playtime because they use their mouths to explore and experiment with unfamiliar objects. Children should not be allowed to eat while walking, running, playing, lying down, or riding in vehicles.

- Objects smaller than 1¼" in diameter should not be accessible to children who mouth items (Lego pieces, beads, coins, small wads of paper).
- Check toys and equipment regularly for small parts that may break off, such as eyes and noses on stuffed animals, buttons on doll clothes, or plastic hats or shoes on miniature people. Remove or securely attach these items.
- Foods that are round, hard, small, thick and sticky, smooth, or slippery should not be offered to children younger than 4 years of age. Examples of such foods include hot dogs (sliced into rounds), whole grapes, hard candy, nuts, seeds, raw peas, dried fruit, pretzels, chips, peanuts, popcorn, marshmallows, and spoonfuls of peanut butter.
- For infants, foods should be cut in small pieces no larger than ¼" cubes; for toddlers, pieces no larger than ½" cubes.

- Learn proper techniques for helping a choking infant or child.
- Do not allow balloons. Deflated or broken balloons are a choking hazard.
- Plastic bags and Styrofoam should not be accessible to children younger than 4 years of age.

Toys

If you are careful to choose toys that are appropriate for the age and developmental level of the children who will use them, most toys will not be dangerous by themselves. When selecting toys, or when children bring toys from home, be sure to follow the age recommendations on the labels. If, for example, a toy is labeled "For ages 3 to 6 years," it is not safe to allow a younger child to play with that toy. The way they are used or misused by a child can cause injury.

- Carefully examine toys for sharp, splintered, or jagged edges and small pieces that can be easily broken off. Tug at different parts to test for strength. Reject any with such hazards.
- Check toys frequently and do minor repairs whenever necessary.
- Cover hinges and joints to prevent fingers from being pinched or caught.

Teach children how to play correctly and to put toys away immediately after playing.

- Projectile toys, such as darts, are not appropriate for children.
- Bend plastic toys to test for brittleness. Cheap, hard plastic can break easily, leaving sharp edges.
- Look for the nontoxic label on all painted toys and play equipment.
- Keep wooden toys smooth and free of splinters.
- Pull on the heads and limbs of dolls to make sure they won't come off and expose sharp wires.
- Look for the flame retardant label on cloth toys. Check seams regularly for tearing and weak threads.
- Teach children how to play correctly and safely and to put toys away immediately after playing.
- Comment on children's safe play behavior.

Gross-motor equipment

- Be sure riding toys, such as tricycles, are stable and well balanced.
- Provide an impact-absorbing (200 G) surface under indoor climbers. (Double matting DOES NOT provide a safe surface *unless* it passes the 200 G test. It needs to be just as safe as outdoor surfaces—especially if located over a tile, concrete, or wood floor.)
- Do not use trampolines. They can cause very serious injuries.
- Teach children how to use equipment correctly and safely.
- Compliment children on safe play behavior.

Toy chests

Toy chests are not an appropriate way to display toys for groups of children. Use open shelves instead to limit toy breakage and increase children's ease of selection. Toy boxes also are very cluttered. If parents wish to purchase a toy chest for home use, suggest a laundry basket be used instead. If they insist on a toy chest, the Consumer Product Safety Commission offers the following advice:

- When you buy a chest with a hinged lid, be sure that the lid is lightweight, has a flat inner surface, and has a device to hold it open in a raised position so that it will not slam shut from its own weight. Make sure that the device to hold the lid open cannot pinch. You may want to remove the lid to avoid possible danger.
- Check for rough or sharp edges on all metal

components and for splinters and other rough areas on wooden boxes.
- Try to buy toy chests with rounded and padded edges and corners.
- Be sure the toy box or chest is well ventilated with holes or with a lid that cannot close completely.
- Do not buy a toy chest with a lid that locks.

Poisons

You probably think first of cleansers and medicines, but your program has many other things that could be harmful if eaten or sucked. Refer to Chapter 8, Emergencies and first aid, for ways to handle poison emergencies.

Art materials. Watch children closely during art projects for mouthing of paintbrushes, fingers, crayons, or other objects and materials. Some children are attracted to fruit-scented markers and may try to eat them.

Avoid using homemade dough clay that has large amounts of salt; it can be dangerous if much is eaten.

Make sure your art materials have these labels:

- **Nontoxic.** Item will not cause acute (immediate) poisoning.

Make sure your program's art materials are nontoxic. The safest materials have the AP or CP labels.

- **AP: Approved Product.** Item contains no materials in sufficient quantities to be toxic or injurious, even if eaten or swallowed.
- **CP: Certified Product.** Item meets same standards as AP, but also meets specific standards for quality, color, etc.

The Labeling of Hazardous Art Materials Act (1988) requires that (1) all art materials be reviewed to determine the potential for causing a chronic hazard and (2) appropriate warning labels be put on those found to pose such chronic hazards as determined by the American Society for Testing and Materials (ASTM) Standards. Parents and others buying art materials (e.g., crayons, chalk, paint sets, clay, and pencils) should be alert to and only purchase products that are accompanied by the statement "Conforms to ASTM D-4236" or similar wording. Additional tips on purchasing art supplies are given in Figure 6.3. If you have any questions, call the Art Hazards Information Center at 212-227-6231.

Plants. Plants are a leading cause of poisoning of young children. If eaten, some plants can cause a skin rash or stomach upset—others can even cause death. **Many common household plants are poisonous** (see Figure 6.4). Here are some indoor plants that are safe for growing around young children:

Safe indoor plants

- African violet
- aluminum plant
- begonia
- Boston fern
- coleus
- dracaena
- hen and chickens
- jade plant
- peperomia
- prayer plant
- rubber plant
- sensitive plant
- snake plant
- spider plant
- Swedish ivy
- wandering Jew
- wax plant
- weeping fig

Most plant poisonings can be prevented with some simple measures:

- **Learn** which plants are poisonous. Check library books, garden and floral shops, arboretums, or ask your local cooperative extension service.
- **Remove** poisonous plants.
- **Supervise** young children closely around plants. Eating too much of any plant can make a child sick. Label plants so if ingestion occurs accurate information can be given to the poison control center. It is best to locate all plants out of children's reach if not being used in a specific activity.
- **Teach** children not to put plants, fruits, or berries in their mouth without asking a grown-up first.

Figure 6.3. How to choose art supplies

AVOID powdered clay. It contains silica which is easily inhaled and harmful to the lungs.
USE wet clay which cannot be inhaled.

AVOID glazes, paints, or finishes that contain lead.
USE poster paints/water-based products.

AVOID paints that require solvents, such as turpentine, to clean brushes, and materials with fumes.
USE water-based paints, glues, etc.

AVOID cold-water or commercial dyes that contain chemical additives.
USE natural dyes such as vegetables or onion skins.

AVOID permanent markers that may contain toxic solvents.
USE water-based markers.

AVOID instant papier-mâché which may contain lead or asbestos.
AVOID use of color-print newspaper or magazines with water.
USE newspaper (printed with black ink only) and library paste or liquid starch.

AVOID epoxy, instant glues, or other solvent-based glues.
USE water-based white glue or library paste.

AVOID aerosol sprays.
USE water-based materials/pump sprays.

AVOID powdered tempera paints.
USE liquid tempera paint or any nontoxic paint.

For more information contact Art Hazards Information Center, 5 Beekman Street, New York, NY 10038. Telephone 212-227-6231.

Figure 6.4. Poisonous plants

Children are often attracted to the colorful berries, flowers, fruits, and leaves of plants, but more than 700 typical plants in the United States and Canada have been identified as poisonous. Plants are a common cause of poisonings to preschoolers. Most of these poisonings can be prevented, so it's important for parents, grandparents, teachers, and others to keep poisonous plants away from children. If eaten, some plant parts can cause skin rash or stomach upset; others can even cause death. Here is a partial list of plants that are **very dangerous—CHILDREN HAVE DIED FROM EATING THESE PLANTS.**

- autumn crocus
- azalea
- baneberry
- belladonna
- black cherry
- black locust
- buckeye
- caladium
- caper spurge
- castor bean
- cherry
- chinaberry
- daffodil
- daphne
- delphinium
- dieffenbachia (dumbcane)
- duranta
- false hellebore
- foxglove
- golden chain
- hyacinth
- hydrangea
- jequirity bean
- jessamine
- jimson weed
- lantana
- larkspur
- laurel
- lily of the valley
- lupine
- mistletoe
- monkshod
- moonseed
- mountain laurel
- mushrooms
- nightshade
- oleander
- philodendron
- poison hemlock
- pokeweed
- privet
- rhododendron
- rhubarb leaves
- rosary pea
- rubber vine
- sandbox tree
- tansy
- thorn apple
- tobacco
- tung oil tree
- water hemlock
- white snakeroot
- yellow jessamine
- yellow oleander
- yew

If you think a child may have swallowed **any part** of a poisonous plant, first remove any remaining pieces from the child's mouth. Then bring the child and a piece of the plant to the telephone and call your poison control center. Be sure the telephone number of the poison control center nearest you is posted by each telephone. Keep an up-to-date container of syrup of ipecac available in case the poison control center tells you to use it to make the child vomit a poisonous substance. (See the section about first-aid kits in Chapter 8, page 82.)

Telephone number of local poison control center:

(   ) _____
Area code

Batteries. *Small button batteries found in some toys, cameras, and calculators present a choking hazard and can be extremely poisonous if swallowed.* When replacing a button battery, be sure that you discard the old one immediately, away from children's areas.

Cooking and kitchen utensils. Cooking and preparing foods are important for young children. During these activities, observe safety precautions and make sure that children do not mouth or gnaw on cooking utensils. The handles on some utensils are painted with lead-based paint.

Microwave ovens should be inaccessible to children. Food heats unevenly in microwave ovens and can easily reach scalding temperature. It is recommended that microwave ovens *not* be used to warm infant bottles or infant food. Other foods prepared in a microwave should be removed carefully to prevent spilling and stirred thoroughly before serving.

See *More Than Graham Crackers* (National Association for the Education of Young Children 1979) for other safety and health suggestions for cooking activities.

Poisons in diaper-changing area. Staff should be careful about giving items to children to "keep them occupied" during diaper changing. Avoid giving a bottle of lotion or a container of talcum powder. Many of these substances are dangerous if swallowed or inhaled, and a child mouthing a container might eat some of the contents. Talcum powder should not be used on babies at all because some inevitably gets into the air and can be inhaled and damage the lungs. Also, keep the bleach solution used for cleaning well out of reach of children.

Safety beyond the classrooms

Playgrounds

A well-designed and well-managed play environment can provide a wide range of opportunities for children's development, including motor development, decision making, social development, and learning opportunities enhanced by seeing the world from new perspectives. Playgrounds provide the space in which children can challenge themselves physically. While it is important for children to take risks and experiment, they can also get hurt. Many common playground facilities are not appropriate for younger children. In fact, some equipment may have design flaws that make it unsafe and even deadly. Use the Playground Safety Checklist (Figure 6.2) as a guide to checking the safety of your equipment. It is important to recognize the range of developmental differences in children when planning the type, size, accessibility, and layout of playground equipment for children. For suggestions on how to improve children's outdoor play spaces, see Frost (1986 & 1992), Esbensen (1987), Moore (1987), and McCracken (1990).

Whether the playground you use is on your property or down the street, you can reduce the chance that a child will be injured by following these basic playground safety guidelines (Figure 6.5). Many injuries are due to misuse of equipment. The safest equipment is designed to prevent misuse, but there is no substitute for good supervision.

- Supervise children closely at all times to prevent misuse of the equipment such as swinging too high, running close to moving swings, or playing in equipment that is too advanced. If possible, assign extra staff to areas of high risk.
- Check play equipment and its surroundings daily before use. Programs should develop a plan for systematic inspection and maintenance. A

Suggested General Maintenance Checklist is included in the *Handbook for Public Playground Safety* available from the Consumer Product Safety Commission.

- Look for sharp edges, rough surfaces, and loose or broken parts. Remove them or repair equipment immediately.
- Since most playground injuries are due to **falls,** the most important safety feature is an impact-absorbent surface (in accordance with ASTM [American Society for Tests and Measurements standards]). The ground under and around equipment should be covered with the recommended amount of impact-absorbing material. The Consumer Product Safety Commission has conducted tests on the shock-absorbing properties of commonly used loose-fill surfacing materials to develop recommendations of appropriate depths for specific fall heights. (See Figure 6.6.) Loose-fill materials commonly used include wood chips, shredded bark mulch, sand, and pea gravel. Commercially manufactured playground surfacing materials (often described as unitary materials) are also an option. These materials may be expensive to install but may save money in the long run because sand and wood chips need constant maintenance and frequent replacement. If a manufactured surface is used, it should be identified as meeting ASTM standards.
- Recognize that cement, asphalt, grass, and hardpacked or frozen soil are dangerous surfaces underneath or around equipment such as swings, climbers, and slides, even when children are supervised. Rake sand and other loose materials frequently to keep them soft.
- Keep area clean from glass, litter, and large rocks.
- Teach children how to play safely. Involve them in making rules for playground behavior, and enforce these rules consistently. Praise children when they use the playground appropriately.
- Remove a misbehaving child from play and explain how her or his actions could hurt someone.
- Make sure all play areas are protected from streets and traffic to minimize the chance of a child darting into the street.
- If there is any water nearby (stream, pond, drain-

age ditch, etc.) be sure there is adequate fencing to prevent drownings.

- Check the outdoor environment for poisonous plants and remove them, if possible.
- Avoid poisonous wood preservatives. If possible, use pressure-treated wood instead. However, do not use pressure-treated wood with creosote or PCP. For all types of treated wood, use a double coat of nontoxic, non-slippery wood sealer every 2 years.

Playground safety guidelines

Injuries to children may occur from many types of playground equipment and environmental conditions. To address the hazards that resulted in playground-related injuries and deaths, the Con-sumer Product Safety Commission developed extensive playground equipment safety information in the form of guidelines (see the *Handbook for Public Playground Safety* available from CSPC, Washington, DC 20207). The guidelines are not a CPSC standard and are not mandatory requirements. They are *not* intended to apply to home playground equipment, amusement park equipment, or equipment normally intended for sports use. The guidelines do include recommendations related to the potential for falls from and impact with equipment, the need for protective surfacing under and around equipment, openings with the potential for head entrapment, the scale of equipment and other design features related to user age, layout of equipment on a playground, installation

---

Figure 6.5. Safe playground habits

Swings
- Sit in the center of the swing. Never stand or kneel.
- Hold on with **both** hands.
- **Stop** the swing before getting off.
- Stay **far away** from moving swings.
- Be sure only **one** person is on a swing at a time.
- Don't swing empty swings or twist unoccupied rings.
- Keep head and feet out of the exercise rings.

Slides
- Wait your turn. Give the person ahead lots of room.
- Hold on with **both hands** climbing up.
- Before sliding down, make sure no one is in front.
- Slide down feet first, sitting up, one at a time unless the slide is double or triple width.
- After sliding down, **get away from** the front of the slide.

Climbing apparatus
- Only ___ people at a time. (Fill in your limit.)
- Use **both** hands, and use the lock grip (fingers and thumbs).
- Stay away from other climbers.
- Don't use when wet.

Horizontal ladders and bars
- Only ___ people at a time. (Fill in your limit.)
- Everybody starts at the same end and goes in the same direction.
- Use the lock grip (fingers and thumbs).
- Keep a **big space** between you and the person in front.
- Don't use when wet.
- Drop down with knees bent. Try to land on both feet.

Seesaws (older children only)
Seesaws are not recommended in general, but if used the seesaw should be a spring-type, counter-balanced model, or it should be used only by older children.
- Sit up straight and face each other.
- Hold on tight with **both** hands.
- Keep feet out from underneath the board.
- **Tell your partner** when you want to get off. Get off carefully, **and hold your end** so it rises **slowly** until your partner's feet touch the ground.

Adapted from U.S. Consumer Products Safety Commission (1992). "Play Happy, Play Safe." Washington, DC: U.S. Government Printing Office.

and maintenance procedures, and general hazards presented by protrusions, sharp edges, and pinch points. The CPSC guidelines are intended to promote greater safety awareness among those who purchase, install, and maintain playground equipment.

Figure 6.6. Loose-fill playground surfacing materials: Depth needed

Height of equipment	Type and minimum uncompressed (not packed down) **depth at point of impact** (more must be installed to account for scatter)
5'	6" of fine sand 6" of coarse sand 6" of medium gravel
6'	6" of double-shredded bark mulch 6" of uniform wood chips 6" of fine gravel
7'	6" of wood mulch 9" of uniform wood chips 9" of fine gravel
9'	12" of fine sand
10'	9" of wood mulch 9" of double-shredded bark mulch 12" of fine gravel
11'	12" of wood mulch 12" of double-shredded bark mulch

Adapted from "Critical Heights (in feet) of Tested Materials," Table 2, page 21. For characteristics (fall-absorbing characteristics, installation/maintenance, advantages and disadvantages) of organic and inorganic loose-fill materials and of unitary synthetic materials, see Appendix C, page 29–31. Loose-fill surfacing materials in list above are described in Appendix D, page 31. *Handbook for Public Playground Safety*. Pub. No. 325, U.S. Consumer Product Safety Commission, Washington, DC 1994. Used with permission.

The American Society for Testing and Materials (ASTM) has published the *Standard Consumer Safety Performance Specification for Playground Equipment for Public Use* (ASTM, 1916 Race Street, Philadelphia, PA 19103) establishing nationally recognized safety standards for public playground equipment. In addition to safety performance specifications for various types of playground equipment, this publication includes information on playground layout and detailed specifications to make playgrounds and equipment accessible to and usable by persons with disabilities. When selecting playground equipment, check with the manufacturer and/or installer for certification that equipment meets ASTM standards.

Riding toys

Have several sizes of tricycles or other riding toys available for the older toddlers and preschoolers. If a child is too large for the tricycle, it will be unstable. If the child is too small, the tricycle may be difficult to control properly.

- Be sure that children who ride bikes—even those with training wheels—wear properly sized bicycle helmets.
- Use low-slung riding toys with seats close to the ground and a wide wheelbase. They are more stable.
- Avoid vehicles with sharp edges, particularly fenders.
- Look for pedals and handgrips with nonskid surfaces to prevent children's hands and feet from slipping.
- Teach children safe riding habits and check on their performance frequently.
- Do not allow wheeled vehicles on sidewalks or near streets, because low tricycles cannot be seen by cars or trucks.
- Do not allow children to ride double. Carrying a passenger makes the vehicle unstable unless the bike is designed for two.
- Teach children that riding down hills is dangerous. A tricycle can pick up so much speed that it becomes almost impossible to stop.
- Teach children to avoid sharp turns, to make all turns at low speed, and not to ride down steps or over curbs.

- Advise children to keep hands and feet away from moving spokes.
- Keep the vehicles in good condition. Check regularly for missing or damaged pedals and handgrips, loose handlebars and seats, broken parts, and other defects.
- Cover any sharp edges and protrusions with heavy, waterproof tape.
- Don't leave riding toys outdoors overnight. Moisture can cause rust and weaken metal parts.

Pedestrian safety

Children learn by imitation and experience. Walks to the nearby playground are teachable moments that can be used to introduce and practice safe pedestrian behavior. Children and adults should cross the streets only at cross-walks. Most pedestrian/motor vehicle accidents happen when children dart out in the middle of the block. The four basic rules of preschool pedestrian safety are

1. Sidewalks are for people—streets are for cars, trucks, and buses.

2. Cars and trucks can hurt you.

3. Stop at the curb or the edge of the road. Never go into the street without an adult.

4. Keep away from cars in driveways.

- Use a travel rope to keep younger children together. Children can hold onto spaced knots in the rope. Make the walk fun, not confining, by playing Follow the Leader or singing songs.
- Ask staff to explain rules for crossing the streets safely, enforce the rules consistently, and follow these rules themselves.
- Talk about safety often. Encourage children to think and talk about the reason behind the actions.
- During walks, ask children to point out traffic warning signs (stoplights, signs, and crosswalks) and to explain how they help pedestrians and traffic.

Field trips

Pay extra attention to safety during field trips because children may become excited about new and unfamiliar surroundings. Remember that safety rules for indoors may not apply outdoors and that you may need special rules for each field trip. Increase the safety of your field trips by doing the following:

- Recruit parents, volunteers from senior citizen centers, or students from early childhood courses to help supervise field trips.
- Obtain a signed permission slip for **each** excursion, even neighborhood walks, so you are sure parents approve of the child leaving for that particular trip.
- Be a positive role model. Wear safety belts when riding, and cross traffic areas correctly when walking.
- Involve children in making and enforcing rules. Make sure children **understand** the rules **before** you leave.
- Identify children with a label that states the program's name and telephone number. Do **not** use the child's name.
- Prepare for an emergency by bringing a small first-aid kit with you. Include change for a telephone and a list of emergency telephone numbers, a folder with copies of emergency forms, and the signed permission slips.
- If you are traveling by car, be sure in advance that there are enough vehicles so that each child and adult has a safety seat and/or safety belt.
- Make sure that all safety seats and/or safety belts are properly used. See Chapter 7 for more information on transportation safety.
- If possible, check out the field trip site in advance so that staff are familiar with locations, hazards, telephones, water, etc.

Summer safety

Heat and sun. Warm, sunny weather can present additional areas of concern for outdoor play. Children can easily be burned by the hot sun or by contact with hot surfaces such as sand, asphalt, and playground equipment. Dehydration and heatstroke can also occur. Make sure children have access to drinks before and after vigorous play and at least every 2 hours during the day.

If there is no natural shade on your playground, you may want to create some by using tents or canopies. (They add lots of new fun and adventure, too!) During the period when the hot, midday sun shines (10 a.m. to 2 p.m.) limit the amount of time you spend outdoors. Ask parents to authorize the use of sunscreen lotion and to send protective clothing such as hats or visors.

To avoid spreading disease and possible drowning, the use of sprinklers in early childhood programs is a safe alternative to wading pools.

Protect young children's skin which is more sensitive to the sun than the skin of adults. At the beginning of the season, provide gradual exposure, starting with 5 to 15 minutes the first day and increasing 5 to 10 minutes each day. Although children with darker skin generally can spend more time in the sun than those who have light skin, even children who have dark skin can burn. Suntans in childhood and later years are responsible for skin cancer and wrinkles in adulthood. Please refer to the sunburn section in Chapter 18 for treatment.

Drowning. Drowning is still one of the leading causes of death among young children. Most drownings occur in backyard pools, and the young drowning victim is generally "missing" for only a few minutes before the drowning occurs. States with warm climates, such as Florida, Texas, and California have more drownings than average and need to be especially careful. Make sure that entrances to pools have secure locks and latches that are out of children's reach. Fencing needs to surround the pool on all four sides (i.e., the building cannot serve as an enclosure). For more information on drowning prevention, see Appendix 1—National Drowning Prevention Network. There must be constant adult supervision, with at least one adult certified in water safety and infant/child CPR, when children are near water (such as swimming pools, ponds, streams, or salt marshes). Children can drown in less than an inch of water.

Buckets filled with water (or other liquids)—especially the large 5-gallon size—present a drowning hazard to young children. Never leave any bucket of water or other liquid unattended when small children are around. Even a partly filled bucket can be a drowning hazard to curious young children who pull themselves up while learning to walk and may topple into a bucket and be unable to free themselves.

Teach children these basic water safety rules right from the start.

- **NEVER** climb over a fence or go through a gate where there is a swimming pool unless you are with an adult.
- Swim or play in the water only when an adult has agreed to watch you.
- Do not run, push, or dunk in or around water.
- Do not bring glass near the area.
- Do not swim with something in your mouth.
- Yell for help only when you need it.

Teach all adults and older children how to administer mouth-to-mouth resuscitation, the technique to restore breathing.

Preventing insect stings. Bugs like summer, too. Stinging insects are often seen swarming around sugary containers and trash cans. In late summer, insects are busy gathering sugar from ripe fruits. Although most insects will not sting unless provoked, during late summer and early fall it seems to take less to irritate them and their venom is more potent.

To prevent stings, adults and children should

learn to avoid getting excited and moving around rapidly when they see stinging insects. Such activity is more likely to result in a sting. Prevention also includes keeping sugary foods away from children and adults outside. Keep trash cans away from outside play areas. During picnics, avoid sweet foods such as fruits and fruit juices unless water is available to rinse off sticky areas after eating. Sponge off children to keep them cool because perspiration and overheated skin also seem to attract stinging insects.

See the section on first aid for information on how to handle insect and other bites (page 93).

Staff should know if any of the children in their care are allergic to insect stings, and should be prepared to treat them as recommended by the parents and physicians.

Winter outdoor play

Children of all ages enjoy and benefit from playing outdoors in all except the most extreme weather—and that varies according to what you are accustomed to in your climate. In winter, be sure children are dressed warmly. If they are overdressed and play actively, they will get sweaty and then chilled. Staff and children alike will feel refreshed when fresh air is part of the daily routine.

Children should not be allowed to play outdoors when the wind and cold pose a risk for frostbite.

Snow safety. Children should be encouraged to play in and with snow, so take advantage of this wonderful natural resource for daily winter play activities. Remember these snow safety precautions.

- **Snowballs can be dangerous,** especially when the snow is packed hard or when children put rocks or other items in snowballs. Being hit in the face or head with this type of snowball can cause a serious injury.
- Be sure children do not throw snowballs into parking lots, streets, or at moving cars.
- **Encourage children to play in the snow and with the snow—but don't let them eat it.** Although eating snow is fun, it is **not** healthy. Particularly in cities, snow can contain dirt or other atmospheric substances.
- Keep a watchful eye on scarves and hoods. They can get caught on playground equipment and have caused strangulation and other serious injuries.

- Keep children dry. Wet clothing allows rapid cooling and frostbite.

Special safety tips for infants and toddlers

Never assume that a child's motor abilities will remain the same from day to day. One day a baby could not possibly turn over and fall off a changing table; the very next day the child can give a successful push and end up on the floor! An infant or toddler's natural curiosity can be encouraged in a safe environment if you give special consideration to equipment and indoor and outdoor play areas.

Equipment and toys

Keep safety in mind when you buy and use furniture and equipment for children younger than 3 years old. Injuries involving cribs, baby walkers, and high chairs are fairly common and usually preventable. You can reduce the possibility of injury by selecting appropriate equipment (see Figure 6.7), properly maintaining it, and supervising its use. Infant walkers are no longer recommended because so many injuries are associated with them when children fall over, pull objects down on them, or go down steps in them.

A SPECIAL NOTE: If you buy or use old infant cribs, be sure they meet the criteria in Figure 6.7.

Changing surfaces. Even though the floor may seem to be the safest place to change diapers, it is not recommended for use in groups. **Use a changing surface that is at least 3' above the floor** to help prevent the spread of infectious diseases. Keep diapering and play spaces separate. Always keep at least one hand on the baby. Do not use safety straps. Never leave the baby for a moment. Whenever possible, use a table with guardrails or a recessed top. These offer some additional protection against infant falls. Please refer to Chapter 5 for more information about diapering safety.

Toys. General information about toy safety was presented on page 60 and 61 in this chapter. Refer to Figure 6.8 for examples of safe toys for children younger than age 3. Follow these special guidelines for infant and toddler toys.

- Regularly check any toys that babies can find and grab.

Figure 6.7. How to select safe infant furniture and equipment

Look for a label on *all* items that says the item meets the American Society for Testing and Materials (ASTM) standards for juvenile furniture products.

High chairs
Hazards
- unstable chairs that tip easily
- trays that baby can push against and unlatch
- seat belts attached to tray instead of chair
- rough, sharp edges or points
- parts that can pinch

Safety features
- wide, stable base
- no sharp or rough edges or points
- sturdy restraining straps that are attached securely to chair
- tray that locks securely

Supervision and use
- Place high chairs out of the path of opening doors (such as range or refrigerator).
- Be sure child is strapped in securely. Never use the tray as a restrainer without straps. If the high chair has no safety straps, purchase a set and attach them to the chair.
- Never allow a child to stand up in a high chair.
- Put the high chair out of the way when not in use so it can't be knocked over easily.
- Don't let older children hang onto a high chair while a baby is in it.
- Make sure child's hands are out of the way when attaching or detaching the tray.

Walkers
Walkers are not recommended, but, if you use them, look for the following:
Hazards
- walkers that might tip over when baby leans, runs, or reaches
- children can pull objects down on themselves or fall down stairs
- older x-frame walkers that could trap or sever fingers when walker partially collapses

Safety features
- stability—wheelbase wider and longer than frame of walker
- sturdy materials: unbreakable plastic or tough fabric seats with heavy-duty stitching or large, rugged snaps
- protective covers over coil springs and hinges; no sharp points or exposed screws
- a "brake" that prevents walkers from tumbling down stairs

Supervision and use
- Remain with baby while she or he uses the walker.
- Prevent the baby from running or leaning too far.
- Help the child maneuver over thresholds.
- Remove throw rugs and other obstacles.
- Place guards at the top of all stairways and/or keep stairway doors closed to prevent falls.

Baby carrier seats
Hazards
- narrow base, slippery bottom surface
- supporting devices on back that may collapse
- no safety straps

Safety features
- sturdy materials and wide, stable base
- safety straps
- nonskid bottom surface
- supporting device that locks firmly in place

Supervision and use
- Use the carrier only as intended—it is **not** a car safety seat.
- Always stay with baby.
- Place carrier on a **low, nonslip** surface.
- Always use safety straps.
- Attach rough-surfaced adhesive strips to carriers with slippery bases.
- If you must use a carrier on high surfaces, make sure the child is within arm's reach and out of reach of dangerous objects.
- Check supporting device to make sure it is firmly in place.
- Don't leave the baby (even for a second) untended in an infant carrier above floor level.

Figure 6.7 *continued*

Back carriers

Hazards

- unpadded frames near baby's face and head
- leg openings that are too large
- joints that could accidentally close and pinch

Safety features

- padded covering on frame near baby's face
- seat belts
- leg openings small enough to prevent baby from slipping out
- leg openings big enough to avoid chafing baby's legs
- strong stitching and large, heavy-duty snaps to prevent accidental release

Supervision and use

- Do not use back carriers until baby is 4 to 5 months old and can hold her or his head up.
- Buy carrier to match baby's size and weight.
- Always use restraining straps.
- Be sure leg openings do not chafe the baby's legs.
- Avoid sharp points, edges, and rough surfaces.
- Avoid joints that can accidentally close and pinch or cut the baby.
- Bend from knees when leaning or stooping to minimize chance of baby falling out.
- Walk gently to avoid jolting the baby's neck.

Cribs

Hazards

- removable plastic wrapping on mattress
- mattress too small for crib—baby could get stuck between mattress and sides and suffocate
- crib slats too far apart—baby could wriggle through feet-first and strangle when head gets stuck
- crib so small baby could climb out
- large toys, objects, or bumper pads—older baby could climb on and fall out
- dangling strings—baby may get caught in them and strangle
- finials (decorative devices on cornerposts) and cutouts—baby's head may become caught
- cornerposts that extend more than 1/16" above headboard—baby's clothes can become looped

- crib toys—"baby's crib gyms"—that stretch across the crib

Safety features

- **no more than 2 3/8" between slats**
- snug-fitting mattress—if you can fit two adult fingers between mattress and sides, then mattress is too small
- tight-fitting sheets
- crib sides that lock at maximum height
- no rough edges or exposed bolts
- safe materials, such as nonlead paint—particularly important with older or used equipment
- latching device that cannot be released easily
- no finials, cutouts, or decorative knobs
- no cornerposts that extend more than 1/16" above headboard

Supervision and use

- Check latches to make sure they are secure.
- Check slats on all sides for closeness. Do not use a crib if a slat or rail has been broken.
- Until you can replace a mattress that does not fit snugly, roll large towels and place them between mattress and crib sides.
- Check baby's standing height on mattress against side rail. If height of rail is less than ¾ of baby's height when the mattress is in the lowest position, obtain a larger crib or move the baby to a regular bed.
- Remove large toys or any objects an older baby may stack or use for climbing.
- Never hang any stringed object (including toys) on bedpost—a child could become caught in it. Similarly, never put a loop of ribbon or cord around child's neck.
- Remove "crib gyms" and toys that stretch across the crib when child is able to push up on her or his knees OR when the child reaches 5 months of age.
- Place the crib out of reach of drapery and shade cords. Roll up the cords so walking and crawling children cannot reach them.
- Remove and destroy all plastic wrapping materials on crib mattress. Never use plastic cleaner's bags or trash bags as mattress covers.

Figure 6.7 *continued*

Strollers and carriages
Hazards
- inadequate or faulty brakes
- latches that do not hold securely
- sharp edges or exposed hardware, exposed hinges or dangerous scissors-like mechanisms—children's fingers may be pinched or severed
- canopies that don't lock firmly in place

Safety features
- stability safeguards—stroller will not tip over even if child is reclined as far back as possible
- firm, vertical (or nearly vertical) backrest—child's head should be supported
- firmly attached safety belt, waist strap, or harness
- tightly locking brakes—a two-wheel brake provides extra security
- wide base and wheels with large diameters
- canopy that locks in forward horizontal position and rotates to downward position in rear
- shopping basket that can be mounted in front of, or centered above, rear axle for stability
- plastic coverings over exposed hinges

Supervision and use
- Check brakes **before** taking baby for a ride; always use brakes when stroller is not in motion.
- Make sure baby is safely strapped in.
- Check latch devices for security on collapsible models.
- **NEVER** leave infant unattended.
- Do not allow other children to pull or stand in or on the shopping basket.

Playpens
Hazards
- playpens too small for growing children—baby shouldn't be able to crawl over the side or cause pen to tip over by leaning against it
- mesh playpens with large open weaves (more than ¼"). Child can use mesh for climbing or netting may catch buttons and cause child to asphyxiate.
- protruding bolts or rough edges
- hinges that do not lock tightly
- large toys left in playpen—baby could step on them and climb out
- slats that are loose or more than 2 3/8" apart
- weak floors; no padding on floor
- padding that has torn or been chewed or bitten

Safety features
- mesh netting with weave smaller than tiny baby buttons (less than ¼" diameter)
- slats no more than 2 3/8" apart
- firm floors with a foam pad
- hinges that lock tightly; no sharp edges
- vinyl covering on railings and padding thick enough to resist being chewed and bitten off by teething children

Supervision and use
- **Never leave a baby in a playpen with one side down.**
- Bring playpen indoors after use—rain and sun can damage it.
- Remove any objects that could be stacked and used for climbing.
- Never hang any stringed object (including toys) on playpen; a child could become caught in it. Similarly, never put a loop of ribbon or cord around child's neck.
- Keep an eye on baby and be aware of what she or he is doing.

Adapted from U.S. Consumer Products Safety Commission. (1977). "Nursery Furniture and Equipment Can Be Dangerous." Washington, DC: U.S. Government Printing Office.

Figure 6.8. Safe toys for children younger than age 3

- **The first year**

sturdy rattles

shatterproof mirror

bright objects out of reach but hanging in view (mobiles, pictures)

washable dolls and stuffed animals (with riveted eyes)

bright cloth or rubber balls

soft stacking blocks

nesting toys

ring stack sets

squeaky toys (with unremovable squeakers)

cloth, vinyl, or board books

musical instruments to shake (bells)

- **1 to 2 years old** (in addition to above)

pull toys (with strings no longer than 12")

large, lightweight spinning top

books with cloth or cardboard pages

blocks

wooden threading beads (large size)

snap-together beads (large size)

banging musical instruments (xylophone)

toy telephones

large crayons or watercolor markers (nontoxic)

plastic kitchenware (lightweight, without sharp edges)

puzzles with knobs and a few large pieces

steerable riding toy

- **2 to 3 years old** (in addition to above)

puzzles with more large pieces

blocks (lightweight)

size-shape matching toys and games

books with short stories

soft dough clay (nontoxic)

finger or tempera paint (nontoxic)

construction sets with large pieces

puppets

dress-up clothes

For details, see "Toys: Tools for Learning." (National Association for the Education of Young Children 1985).

- Be sure toys are at least 1¼" in diameter so they can't be swallowed.
- Avoid toys that can be taken apart or use only with constant adult supervision.
- Be sure stuffed animals are not so large or heavy that they can suffocate children. Children can also use large toys to climb out.
- Use this CPSC **rattle test** to avoid choking hazards.
  - Trace the oval here (1 3/8" by 2") on a piece of cardboard.
  - Cut out the oval.
  - If a rattle can pass through this hole to a depth of 1 3/16", discard the rattle. Or, send it to the CPSC so they can recall it.

CPSC rattle test

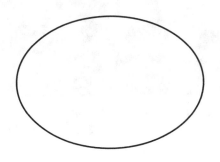

Indoor play areas

Programs with infants and toddlers should make sure that enough floor space is available for crawling and toddling children. **These floors should be clean, free of splinters and cracks, and not highly polished.**

Separate infant and toddler play areas from the general play area for older children. This will encourage the younger children to explore without the danger of the older children knocking them down. Provide a carpeted area for quiet activities and beginning large motor movement by infants. Bolt down top-heavy furniture such as shelving or cubbies to avoid toppling.

Toddlers must be well supervised especially near water tables and in bathrooms near toilets and deep sinks. All these are naturally of great interest to young children and, with the unsteady gait of toddlers, present a potential drowning hazard.

Teach older children to watch out for the younger children to help keep them safe in outdoor play areas.

Sleeping arrangements

Placement of cots and cribs is an important safety issue.

- Leave a clear aisle between cribs. In an emergency, staff must have quick access to each child.
- Place cribs away from open windows, window blinds, and shade cords.
- Do not use stacking cribs.

Outdoor play areas

Because infants and toddlers spend much more time on the ground than older children, **check the playground daily** for items that can be hazardous. Be sure to provide close adult supervision when toddlers and older children are outdoors together. Also, teach older children to watch out for the younger children to help keep them safe in the outdoor play areas.

Safety education

Provide children with the skills to prevent injuries and to help care for themselves and others in case of emergency. Keep in mind that your own attitudes and behaviors toward safety are as important as the physical setup of your facility. Use these different ways to give safety messages to children and staff.

- Be a positive role model.
- Give clear statements when explaining the correct, safe way to do something.
- Compliment children for doing things safely.
- Involve the children in making and enforcing rules. This will increase their safety awareness and help them feel involved. You may also want to involve children in making safety checks.
- Teach children what to do in an emergency and where to get help.
- Use the "teachable moment" to discuss safety (e.g., when a child gets a minor bump or bruise, talk to the children about ways to prevent similar injuries).

In addition to your own ideas, you may wish to use safety curricula from a variety of resources (for example, NAEYC's safety kits: *Walk in Traffic Safely* [WITS] and *Children Riding on Sidewalks Safely* [CROSS]). Select the age-appropriate safety curriculum that best fits the needs and philosophy of your program. Whatever you decide to do, remember that safety education is more than just a one-time activity. Safety concepts should be integrated into all your activities. For example:

- Include poison prevention in nutrition education.
- Children can make a dollhouse from cardboard boxes or hollow blocks. Ask them to use real or paper dolls to act out home hazards such as hot surfaces, poisonous products, toys left on stairs.
- Include messages about clothing into discussions on weather and appropriate dress. Suggest that children wear light colors and reflective clothing at night or on dark, rainy days and dark colors on bright, snowy days.

7
Transportation safety

Transportation is an important aspect of all early childhood programs. Whether you drive the children to and from their homes each day or have only an occasional field trip, the cars or buses that you use form part of your environment. Motor vehicle injuries represent the greatest threat to a child's life. You can reduce the chances of injury to children and staff during transport by being alert to potential dangers, eliminating or avoiding these dangers, and knowing what to do when an emergency occurs.

This chapter offers some ideas for setting up and maintaining a safe transportation system. First, be aware of and follow all state laws and licensing regulations that pertain to your program's transportation.

Next, develop a written policy that clearly states the rules, the responsibilities of staff and children, and the emergency procedures to be followed. Use the rules in Figure 7.1 and the topics in this chapter as a guide to help you develop a policy that fits your program's particular needs.

Finally, make **everyone** including staff, drivers, parents, and children aware of the policies and procedures as well as the reasons for their existence. A written policy will help answer questions and encourage everyone to carry out her or his role.

Child safety restraints

Legal requirements
Whenever motor vehicles are used to transport children, special safety measures are necessary. The driver of any vehicle must assume responsibility for the safety of the passengers and must have a valid license for the vehicle. All states require that children be fastened in a properly adjusted safety seat or seat belt while riding in a motor ve-

hicle. Car injuries are the number one killer of children. Proper child safety seats help prevent death and injury.

Selection of equipment
Passenger safety seats manufactured after January 1981 must meet the Federal Motor Vehicle

All states require that children be fastened in a properly adjusted safety seat or seat belt while riding in a motor vehicle.

Figure 7.1. Transportation safety rules

1. Make sure that all vehicles used to transport children have the most recent federally approved safety seats and/or safety belts. Follow the manufacturer's instructions.

2. Secure each child and adult in her or his own safety seat or safety belt. Never put two or more children in the same safety belt.

3. Every day check vehicles that are used.

4. Before each trip, require the driver to conduct a quick 5-minute check to ensure that the vehicle is working well and contains nothing that could harm the children.

5. Ask drivers to remain alert to changes in the vehicle while driving. Unusual odors, sounds, or vibrations can be warning signals for a breakdown.

6. Never transport children or adults in the cargo area of a station wagon or van.

7. Never leave children alone in a vehicle.

8. Keep sharp or heavy objects in the trunk. They can become deadly projectiles in a sudden stop or accident.

9. Load and unload young children only when the vehicle is pulled up to the curb, side of the road, or in a driveway, releasing them only to an authorized adult.

10. Do not let children put their arms or heads out of the vehicle's windows.

11. There should be no smoking in the vehicle.

12. Drivers should not have used alcohol, drugs, or medications that could impair their judgment within 12 hours of driving.

Safety Standard 213. Select a seat made since that time that will fit securely and properly in your vehicle(s) and will be used correctly on each ride.

Note that some child and infant safety seats have been recalled by the manufacturer due to unsafe features. To obtain information about manufacturer recalls and/or a list of infant, convertible, and booster seats that are certified as meeting the Federal Motor Vehicle Safety Standard contact the National Highway Traffic Safety Administration, NTS-13, 400 Seventh Street, S.W., Washington, DC 20590.

Proper use of restraints

Refer to Figure 7.2 for information on using safety restraints for young children. Report problems with safety seats to the National Highway Traffic Safety Administration at **800-424-9393.**

Protection of child passengers involves more than simply placing them in a safety seat or seat belt. Child restraint devices can be highly effective in preventing death and injury to children **IF** they are properly used. Carefully read instructions for such devices **before** you install and use them. Make an extra copy of the directions to keep on hand.

Train all staff and parent volunteers who will be using safety seats in their proper use. Each person must be able to demonstrate how to properly install and use the seat.

Remember that metal buckles and plastic coverings can get hot and cause serious burns. Cover seats that are not in use with a blanket or towel. Touch all metal pieces to test the temperature before putting a child into a safety seat or safety belt.

Transporting children with special needs

There are automotive safety devices on the market today designed to protect children with special physical and behavioral needs when they are riding in motor vehicles. Devices are available for children of various weights and heights with conditions such as prematurity; muscular and skeletal problems; head and spinal cord injuries; temporary orthopedic conditions, e.g., a fracture; neurological diseases; developmental disabilities; recent surgery; and emotional/behavioral problems that might distract a driver.

Certain principles of passenger safety apply to all children, including children with special needs. A child automotive safety device performs three major roles in a crash. First, it prevents the child from being thrown from the vehicle. Second, it prevents the child from crashing into other passengers and the inside of the vehicle. Third, it absorbs the crash forces and distributes them over the strong parts of the body. Devices should be used only if they have a label attached stating that the device meets Federal Motor Vehicle Safety Standards.

Certain practical considerations need to be kept in mind when choosing a safety device or when

Figure 7.2. How to use car safety seats and safety restraints

There are five essential points to remember about restraining children:
1. The safety seat must be installed and used according to the manufacturer's instructions.
2. The restraint must face in the appropriate direction.
3. The restraint must be correctly installed in the vehicle.
4. The child must be buckled and harnessed properly into the restraint.
5. The safety seat is never used again if it is involved in an auto crash. Replace it with a new seat.

Infant safety seats (birth to 20 lbs.)
- Infants must ride in a rear-facing position. (*Rear facing* means the seat/child faces the rear of the auto.)
- The safety seat should be used in the semi-reclined position.
- The seat belt should be routed through the correct place on the safety seat. Pull the belt tight.
- The harness should be adjusted so it fits snugly over the infant's shoulders and between the baby's legs.
- Rear-facing infant safety seats should **not be used** in the front seats of cars equipped with passenger-side air bags.

Convertible/toddler safety seats (birth to 40 lbs.)
- A convertible seat in the rear-facing position should be used for babies up to 20 lbs.
- A convertible seat in the forward-facing position should be used for children who weigh more than 20 lbs. and who can easily sit up on their own.
- The seat belt should be routed through the safety seat correctly in both forward- and rear-facing positions.
- The child should be secured in the safety seat by a harness or a harness/shield combination. The harness must fit snugly over the shoulders and between the legs.
- The top tether strap must be installed.

Booster seats (40 lbs. to 60 to 70 lbs.)
- Boosters should be used only after children outgrow their convertible seats, at about 40 lbs. (even though most boosters are labeled for use by smaller children).
- Boosters should be used with the vehicle's lap/shoulder belt (instead of a lap belt only) to improve effectiveness.

Safety belts (more than 40 lbs.)
- Safety belts should be used with children who are too tall or too heavy for safety seats. Safety belts are most effective when both the lap belt and the shoulder belt are used together.
- The lap belt should be fastened low and snugly across the child's hips.
- The shoulder belt should be used only if it does not cross the child's face or neck. If the shoulder belt comes across the child's face or neck, a booster or seat belt adapter may be needed to ensure proper positioning of the shoulder belt.
- If the shoulder belt is not used, place it behind the child, not under her or his arm.

Be sure that parents, children, drivers, and other staff all know what to do in an emergency. Emergency situations need to be handled calmly, efficiently, and with constant attention to the children's fears, concerns, and safety.

advising someone who plans to buy a device. Soft padding adds to comfort but *not* to safety. Firm, energy-absorbing materials, that give in a controlled way, are best. The head and neck should be protected from whiplash. Wheelchairs should face forward, not sideways, when being transported in a vehicle. Crash-tested wheelchair tie-downs, *not* homemade devices, should be used to secure wheelchairs in a van. Devices must be easy to use or they will not be used correctly, if at all. Special devices tend to be expensive so it is best to choose one that can be used for a number of years and adjusted as a child grows.

Additional recommendations for safe transportation of children with special needs include (1) training for drivers in issues for children with special needs and in pediatric CPR and (2) equipping vehicles with a two-way radio.

All systems must be crash tested according to federal safety standards and retested even if only a small modification is made. If other equipment, such as an oxygen tank, is required by the passen-

ger it should be secured in the vehicle so that it does not become a missile in a collision.

A child's physician, the public health department, or organizations such as Easter Seals may be helpful resources in the process of trying to locate safety devices.

Preparation for emergencies

To be prepared for transportation emergencies, (1) know what to do (e.g., first aid or evacuation), and (2) have the necessary equipment and information immediately available.

Emergency procedures

Always expect the unexpected, no matter how efficient and safe your transportation system is. Prepare by taking the following steps:

- Be sure that parents, children, driver(s), and other staff all know what to do in an emergency. For each of the following issues, develop a procedure using suggestions from children, parents, and staff. Use discussion groups and/or handouts to inform everyone of these procedures.
- Train drivers in the specific steps to follow under various emergency conditions.
- Make sure that staff who remain at the program know what to do when they are notified of any emergency on the road (e.g., contact parents or provide alternate transportation).
- Each year, remind parents about the center's emergency procedures and collect accurate parent contact information.
- If you use a bus, practice emergency evacuation drills with the children so they will be familiar with what they may be asked to do.

Transportation emergency issues include

- how to evacuate the vehicle
- how to assess injuries and provide first aid
- how to explain the situation to the children and reassure them of their safety
- what staff still in the building are to do
- when to call for emergency support (e.g., police)
- what to do in bad weather
- what to do when a child becomes ill or injured during transport

Emergency situations need to be handled calmly, efficiently, and with constant attention to the children's fears, concerns, and safety.

What to have in the vehicle

The information and equipment listed here is helpful for both daily transportation activities and special field trips.

Information. Keep information about the children and the route in a three-ring notebook in the vehicle. Make sure the driver and other staff can find it easily. In this information notebook

- include a map of the route with estimated mileages and travel times and the names and addresses of children on the route
- include an information/emergency card for each child that describes how to reach parents and emergency contacts and special medical or health information
- provide information on children with special needs so that their ride will be as safe and comfortable as possible. Descriptions of the condition, behavior patterns, and warning signs for medical attention can be helpful in case of an emergency.
- list telephone numbers of emergency services such as local police, fire station, hospital, and ambulance service, and name and telephone number of the program and a contact person there
- provide pen and paper to record information from parents at pickup so this information can be given to child's caregivers

Equipment.
- **First-aid kit**—Use the list of suggested items in Figure 8.2 to assemble your first-aid kit.
- **Emergency toy chest**—Provide songs, books, and toys to help keep children occupied if stuck somewhere.
- **Travel rope**—Use for children to hold onto for easy evacuation of the vehicle or for walks from the vehicle to a safe place.
- **Fire extinguisher,** extra **water,** and appropriate **tools** for minor repairs in case of a breakdown.

Field trips/car pools

A well-organized transportation system is important even if you do not transport children regularly. Special trips mean special circumstances. First of all, drivers may be traveling an unfamiliar route or transporting children who may not ordinarily ride with them. Drivers may be sharing responsibility with volunteers who are themselves in a new situation. Finally, the children may be overly excited or overly tired from a new or long trip or may be frightened because they are going to an unfamiliar place. These suggestions can help staff transport children safely during special trips. Refer also to page 67 for other information about pedestrian safety and field trips.

- When your destination is known in advance, review the route mentally or with a map if the distance is great. Practice the route if you have time and the vehicle is available.
- Make sure you have an authorization for and a list of every child and adult who will be traveling. Each child should have a parent or guardian's permission for each trip. Check your insurance coverage for car pools.
- Make sure both the driver and other adults riding the bus know who is responsible for responding to discipline issues with the children (e.g., parent volunteers, staff, or bus driver). Make sure you tell children who is in charge and what the rules are.
- Make sure that children and all adults are appropriately restrained and/or wearing safety belts when riding in the car.
- Never have more passengers than seat belts.
- Help the driver concentrate by providing soft books or toys, songs, and conversation for the children.
- Use travel time to talk about rules for safe riding or other important concepts.
- If children become unruly or remove their safety restraints, stop and pull off the road to calm them down. **Do not try to drive and discipline at the same time.**
- Make sure that all passengers know when and where they are supposed to return to the vehicle.
- If more than one vehicle is involved in the trip, make sure that all passengers know in which vehicle they are to ride for the return trip.
- On field trips, make sure that no child enters the vehicle alone or plays on the vehicle while the others are visiting the site. **Never leave children alone in the vehicle.**
- Use a trip sheet to record destination, mileage, times of departure and return, and a list of pas-

sengers. For large field trips, the latter is particularly important.

- Be sure that all members of the car pools understand and agree to follow the guidelines you have established for the trip.
- Provide enough staff assistance to be sure every child is buckled up, unbuckled, and removed from all vehicles. Parents who are in a hurry may make unsafe, "just this time" decisions.

Passenger safety education

For children
Preschoolers are old enough to learn simple concepts of auto safety. Consistent use of safe behaviors helps children continue to practice them in later years. There are four major passenger messages to emphasize with children (and parents!).

- Everyone in the car should buckle up—including drivers and passengers in the front and back seats—no matter how short the trip.

Keep parents involved in all educational activities including transportation safety.

- Safety belts go across the hips, not the stomach.
- The back seat is the safest place for child passengers.
- Good passengers buckle up and ride quietly.

The curriculum "We Love You—Buckle Up!" (National Highway Traffic Safety Administration 1984) contains a variety of activities and materials for use with preschool children and parents. You might make pretend cars with cardboard boxes, chairs, or seats, and safety belts from fabric scraps. Play games such as Simon Says, using safety belts, and entering/leaving vehicles correctly. These games are also fun for role-playing and dramatic play activities. Invite the safety officer from your community to come and talk about traffic safety.

For parents
It is important to involve parents in educational activities; they can promote concepts you present in the classroom. Keep them informed of the topics that you cover with letters, parent education meetings, and personal contacts. You can also send activities home that parents and children can work on together (e.g., counting the number of seat belts in the car).

Focus on three main issues when you work with parents:
- The importance of always using child safety seats and safety belts.
- How to select a suitable child safety seat.
- How to use child safety seats and seat belts correctly.

The article "Child Safety Seats—They Work!" (Scott 1985) contains many helpful ideas and an annotated bibliography of resources.

8
Emergencies and first aid

A child falls from the climber on your playground. You suddenly lose your electrical power during a winter storm. You smell gas in the kitchen. A child starts to choke during snack time. Would you know what to do?

No matter how careful and safety conscious you are, there will be times when emergencies occur. If your center has a comprehensive, written emergency policy, you will be better prepared to handle such situations. Your center's policy needs to answer questions such as

- Who will give first aid?
- Who will take the attendance list if the building needs to be evacuated? Where will you go if you cannot go back into the building?
- What will you do if some of the children panic?
- Whom do you call in medical emergencies?
- Whom do you call for electrical, plumbing, gas, or heating emergencies?

Your policy should clearly state the roles and responsibilities of the children and each staff member in an emergency. Parents, too, need to be informed of your emergency policy and their roles in it.

Preparing for emergencies

In the event of an emergency in your program, remember these three important things:

- **KEEP CALM**—if you panic, the children are likely to panic, too.
- **FOLLOW YOUR EMERGENCY PROCEDURES**
- **ACT QUICKLY**

Figure 8.1 outlines emergency procedures you can adapt to fit your program, based on its size, location, and children's ages.

In addition to specifying emergency procedures, you should also take these steps to prepare for potential emergencies.

- **Train all staff in pediatric first aid, including rescue breathing and first aid for choking.** Make sure staff receive training and certification in first aid and renew this certification at least every 3 years.
- If you enroll a child with special needs whose disability may indicate the need for resuscitation, or if you have swimming activities, at least one CPR-certified staff person must be in attendance at all times. CPR certification must be renewed every year.
- **Maintain a first-aid kit.** Figure 8.2 lists the contents for first-aid kits. Pack your kit in any tight-closing container. Keep **at least one** first-aid kit available at all times including neighborhood walks and trips. Keep a first-aid kit near all high-risk areas such as the kitchen or playground. Store your first-aid kits **out of the reach of children** but easily accessible in case of an emergency. Make sure that someone on the staff inspects the kits each month and replaces supplies. Keep a list of contents for the kits, as well as a record of the monthly inspections.
- **Keep information where you need it.** Place a list of emergency telephone numbers (Figure 8.3) and a copy of your emergency procedures near each telephone for quick reference. Keep an extra list with you on field trips, including each child's emergency contact numbers.
- **HAVE IMPORTANT FORMS AVAILABLE**
  Parental permission forms. Hospitals and emergency rooms will not give emergency treatment to any minor child, except in a life-threatening situation, without parental informed consent at the time of treatment. Remind parents that they (or their emergency contacts) must be reachable **at all times** to give consent for medical care. Ask

parents to complete emergency transportation permission forms (Figure 8.4) before enrollment, and keep these on file. Take a copy of all permission forms with you on field trips.

Incident report forms—Your program should develop a standardized form for reporting all injuries or illnesses that require first aid or additional care (Figure 8.5 presents a sample). Give one copy

---

Figure 8.1. Emergency procedures

1. Remain calm. Reassure the victim and others at the scene.

2. Stay at the scene and give help at least until the person assigned to handle emergencies arrives.

3. Send word to the person who handles emergencies for your program. This person will take charge of the emergency, assess the situation, and give any further first aid as needed.

4. Do not move a severely injured or ill person except to save a life.

5. If necessary, telephone for help. Give all the important information slowly and clearly. To make sure that you have given all the necessary information, **wait for the other party to hang up first.** Arrange for transportation of the injured person by ambulance or other such vehicle, if necessary. Do not drive unless accompanied by another adult. Bring your emergency transportation permission form and contact information (Figure 8.4) with you.

6. Do not give any medication unless authorized by your local poison control center (for poisonings) or physician (for other illnesses).

7. Notify parent(s) of the emergency and agree on a course of action with the parent(s).

8. If parent cannot be reached, notify parent's emergency contact person and call the physician shown on the child's emergency transportation permission form.

9. Be sure that a responsible individual from the program stays with the child until parent(s) take charge.

10. Fill out an incident report (Figure 8.5) within 24 hours. File in the child's folder. Give parent(s) a copy, preferably that day. Put a copy in the central injury log.

Figure 8.2. Inventory for the first-aid kit

Every child care setting should have a first-aid kit stocked with items on the list below. You can buy the supplies for the first-aid kit at drugstores or at hospital or medical supply stores.

Each first-aid kit should be large enough to hold all the necessary supplies for first aid in the child care setting. Use a container that will close tightly. It should be stored where adults can reach it easily, but it must be stored out of the reach of children. Arrange the contents so you can reach items easily without emptying the kit. You should be sure that the contents are wrapped tightly and are sanitary. You should restock the kit after each use.

A first-aid kit should contain the following:

*   first-aid cards
*   adhesive strip bandages (½", ¾", 1" strips)
*   gauze bandages (4" x 4", nonstick, sterile)
*   rolled flexible or stretch gauze
*   bandage tape
*   nonstick, sterile pads (different sizes)
*   triangular bandages
*   small splints
*   eye dressing or pad
*   scissors
*   tweezers
*   safety pins
*   thermometer
*   flashlight with fresh batteries
*   disposable latex gloves
*   3 oz. rubber bulb syringe (to rinse out eyes, wounds, etc.)
*   commercial cold pack or plastic bag for ice cubes
*   clean cloth
*   soap
*   small plastic cup
*   sealed packages of antiseptic wipes
*   syrup of ipecac (1-oz. bottle)
*   special items for children with specific health problems (such as a bee sting kit or an inhaler for a child with asthma)
*   emergency telephone guide
*   emergency contact information (telephone numbers of the children's parents)
*   change for pay telephone
*   pen or pencil and notepad

Figure 8.2 courtesy of the American Red Cross

Figure 8.3. Emergency telephone list

Emergency numbers (including area codes)

Emergency medical system (EMS) _____

Poison control center _____

Police _____

Fire _____

Health consultant _____

Hospital _____

Nearest emergency facility _____

Local board of health _____	Water company _____
State dept. public health _____	Heating equipment service _____
Child abuse reporting _____	Electric company _____
Rape crisis center _____	Plumber _____
Battered women's shelter _____	Taxi _____
Suicide prevention hotline _____	Parents Anonymous _____
Gas company _____	Alcoholics Anonymous _____

This telephone is located at _____

Telephone number _____
                     Area code

Program name _____

Description of building _____

Directions for reaching this location from a major road _____

_____

Always provide this information in an emergency:

1. Name
2. Nature of emergency
3. Telephone number
4. Address
5. Easy directions
6. Exact location of injured person(s) (e.g., backyard behind parking lot)
7. Number and age(s) of person(s) involved
8. Condition(s) of person(s) involved

Optional information:

9. Help already given
10. Ways to make it easier to find you (e.g., a staff member will be standing in front of building, waving red flag)

DO NOT HANG UP BEFORE THE OTHER PERSON HANGS UP!

Figure 8-4. Child care emergency contact information

Child's name _____ Birth date _____

Legal guardian #1 name _____

Telephone numbers (home) _____ (work) _____

Legal guardian #2 name _____

Telephone numbers (home) _____ (work) _____

Emergency contacts (to whom child may be released if guardian is unavailable)

Name #1 _____

Telephone numbers (home) _____ (work) _____

Name #2 _____

Telephone numbers (home) _____ (work) _____

Child's usual source of medical care

Name _____

Address _____

Telephone number _____

Child's health insurance

Name of insurance plan _____ ID# _____

Subscriber's name (on insurance card) _____

Special conditions, disabilities, allergies, or medical information for emergency situations

_____

Transport arrangement in an emergency situation

Ambulance service _____ Child will be taken to _____
(Parents/guardians are responsible for all emergency transportation charges.)

Parent/guardian consent and agreement for emergencies

As parent/guardian, I give consent to have my child receive first aid by facility staff, and, if necessary, be transported to receive emergency care. I understand that I will be responsible for all charges not covered by insurance. I give consent for the emergency contact person listed above **to act on my behalf** until I am available. I agree to review and update this information whenever a change occurs and at least every 6 months.

Date _____ Parent/guardian signature _____

Date _____ Parent/guardian signature _____

Reprinted from *Model Child Care Health Policies* with permission of the PA Chapter of the American Academy of Pediatrics.

Figure 8.5. Incident report form

Fill in all blanks and boxes that apply.

Name of program _____ Telephone _____

Address of facility _____

Child's name _____

Sex M F   Birth date _____/_____/_____   Incident date _____/_____/_____

Time of incident _____:_____ a.m./p.m.   Witnesses _____

Parents notified by _____ Time notified _____:_____ a.m./p.m.

Location where incident occurred ❑ playground ❑ classroom ❑ bathroom ❑ hall ❑ kitchen
❑ doorway ❑ large muscle room or gym ❑ office ❑ dining room ❑ stairway ❑ unknown
❑ other (specify) _____
Equipment/product involved ❑ climber ❑ slide ❑ swing ❑ playground surface ❑ sandbox
❑ trike/bike ❑ hand toy (specify) _____
❑ other equipment (specify) _____
Cause of injury (describe) _____
❑ fall to surface; estimated height of fall _____ feet; type of surface _____
❑ fall from running or tripping ❑ bitten by child ❑ motor vehicle ❑ hit or pushed by child
❑ injured by object ❑ eating or choking ❑ insect sting/bite ❑ animal bite
❑ injury from exposure to cold ❑ other (specify) _____
Parts of body injured ❑ eye ❑ ear ❑ nose ❑ mouth ❑ tooth ❑ other face ❑ other part of head
❑ neck ❑ arm/wrist/hand ❑ leg/ankle/foot ❑ trunk ❑ other (specify) _____
Type of injury ❑ cut ❑ bruise or swelling ❑ puncture ❑ scrape ❑ broken bone or dislocation
❑ sprain ❑ crushing injury ❑ burn ❑ loss of consciousness ❑ unknown
❑ other (specify) _____
First aid given at the facility (e.g., pressure, elevation, cold pack, washing, bandage) _____
_____ Treatment provided by _____
❑ no doctor's or dentist's treatment required
❑ treated as an outpatient (e.g., office or emergency room)
❑ hospitalized (overnight) # of days _____

Number of days of limited activity from this incident _____

Follow-up plan for care of the child _____

Corrective action needed to prevent reoccurrence _____

Name of official/agency notified _____ Date _____

Signature of staff member _____ Date _____

Signature of parent _____ Date _____

Reprinted from *Model Child Care Health Policies* with permission of the PA Chapter of the American Academy of Pediatrics.

of the report to the child's parents and keep another copy in the child's folder. Find out which incidents or injuries must be reported to state or local authorities. Maintain one central file of copies of all injury reports so patterns of injury or other incidents can be monitored and safety in your program improved.

Getting help

Most of us assume that we can use a telephone to call for help. Usually we can, but it is important to think about alternatives in case the usual telephone is not available. Know the locations of nearby pay telephones, fire alarm boxes, or places you could go for help. Make sure that the telephone in your program can be reached easily.

Keep a telephone emergency list posted by every telephone (Figure 8.3). Usually you can reach emergency assistance by dialing 911. If 911 is not available in your area, refer to your telephone list for specific numbers for police, fire, and ambu-

Develop a standardized form for reporting all injuries or illnesses that require first aid or additional care.

lance. You can also call the operator, but this is a slower way to get help.

Be sure you know the location of telephones in parks, playgrounds, and other places you visit with the children.

Your telephone list should include your program's address, description of the building, and directions to it from a major road, since these may be hard to remember in a crisis.

Find answers to these questions about your local emergency and medical services.

- Who answers the emergency telephone? (Police, fire, ambulance, dispatcher?)
- What steps does the dispatcher have to take before sending the ambulance? (Call another dispatcher? Call emergency medical technicians?)
- Who provides the ambulance service? (Police, fire, volunteer, private companies, another town?)
- How far do they have to travel to get to your program? Where is the station?
- How long will it usually take them to get to your program?
- Where are the nearest emergency rooms?

Try to visit your local helpers *before* you need them in a crisis. Most ambulance services are happy to show groups of visitors around their office, and some will even come visit you if you ask. Emergency rooms are harder to tour, but you can at least visit the waiting area and become familiar with how to get checked in. Familiarity with helpers now will come in handy when you need them later. These visits will also help reassure children. Be sure your program is well marked so rescue workers can find it easily.

Emergency evacuation plans

Evacuation procedures

Saving lives is the first priority in the event of any emergency. Saving property should be considered **only** when all lives are safe.

Planning, preparation, and practice are the essential ingredients of a successful evacuation plan. Develop a written plan for evacuating and reporting in case of fire, flood, tornado, earthquake, hurricane, blizzard, power failure, or other potential disasters. This plan would include specifics such as routes, assignments for all staff, and location of nearest alarm that alerts the fire department.

When your program has an emergency that requires evacuation, follow these steps.

• Sound alarm—notify everyone in building.
• Evacuate—use exit routes or alternate routes previously marked and practiced in drills.
• Eliminate drafts—close all doors and windows.
• Take a head count—make sure everyone is safely out of the building.
• Call fire department **after** leaving the building—call from the nearest alarm box or telephone if building alarm is not connected to the fire department.

Prepare for emergencies in advance by taking these important actions:

• Maintain a 3-day emergency supply of food (including formula for babies), water, clothes, and diapers.
• Keep up-to-date emergency information for children and staff. Make a specific person responsible for having this information on hand in emergencies, on trips, and in the event of program site evacuation. Ask parents to update emergency contact information every 6 months, and verify it by telephone periodically to be sure emergency numbers reach parents or emergency contacts quickly.
• Know where you are going to stay if the building has to be evacuated. Families must know where to look for their children. Prearrange an emergency shelter where you will stay and inform parents by letter.
• Record daily attendance of staff and children. Designate a staff member to carry the list out of the building so that complete evacuation is assured.
• Post emergency telephone numbers (police, fire, rescue or central emergency code, and poison control) beside every telephone. All individuals using the building should be familiar with these numbers and the procedures to be used in an emergency.
• Plan two exit routes from every area of the building. Post emergency evacuation exit instructions in every room where they can be seen easily.
• Have unannounced evacuation drills at least once a month. Evacuation should include use of alternative exit routes in case of blockage. The time of day should vary to include all activities (naptime too) and when the fewest adults are with the children.
• Maintain logs of evacuation drills for on-site in-spection and review by the building inspector. **For most buildings, evacuation in less than 2 minutes is possible.** Fire-resistant exit routes in large buildings are usually required to provide enough time to exit safely.
• Contact the public education division at your local police and fire departments and ask them to arrange on-site visits to help staff make appropriate emergency plans.

Fire preparedness procedures

• Keep the telephone number of the fire department and heating service company by your telephones (see Figure 8.3).
• Post a diagram showing the main shutoff switches for electricity, gas, and water.
• Test fire and smoke alarms at least once each month to be sure they are working. Have fire extinguishers inspected annually.
• Place fire extinguishers where they can be reached easily.
• Post diagrams of exits and escape routes in each room. Mark exits clearly, and do not block them with furniture or other objects.
• Teach children to stop, drop, and roll and to crawl under smoke.
• Practice leaving the building with the children at least once a month so that they know the sound of the alarm and where to go.
• Include fire and burn prevention in children's curriculum.

Knowing when and when not to use a fire extinguisher is an important part of fire preparedness. Use your extinguisher only if

• you are nearby when a fire starts or the fire is discovered in its early stages
• other staff **get all children out of the building and call the fire department**
• the fire is small (confined to its origin—in a wastepaper basket, cushion, or small appliance)
• you can fight it with your back to an exit
• your extinguisher is in working order, and you
  —stand back about 8'
  —aim at the base of the fire, not the flames or smoke
  —squeeze or press the lever while sweeping from the sides to the middle of the fire
• you can get out fast if your effort is failing

If the fire spreads beyond the spot where it started or if the fire could block your exit, don't try to fight it. **If you have the slightest doubt about whether to fight or not to fight—don't.** Get out and call the fire department.

Helping children during emergency or evacuation procedures

To calm a group of panicked children—Remove them from the scene (if a child has been injured), and reassure them. Explain simply and carefully what has happened and what will happen. Answer their questions truthfully. Then redirect their attention—a game or quiet activity. Most important: **STAY CALM.** If you panic, the children will panic, too. If you need to evacuate the building and children are frightened, have them hold each other's hands. Human touch is very reassuring in scary situations.

To get non-ambulatory children out of the building—Carry two or three infants at the same time. Use a large wagon to quickly transport toddlers or severely disabled children outdoors (if your building has ramps) or at least to the door where someone else can take them.

To get a child who is too scared to move to leave the building—Use your legs to press gently on the back of the child's knees to push him forward or hold his hands with one of your arms across his back. Having everyone join hands can also help the child feel less frightened.

First-aid procedures

First aid is the immediate care of persons who are injured or ill. All staff must be trained in first-aid procedures and have access to a first-aid guidebook at all times.

Emergency situations are always upsetting. Being upset makes it difficult to think clearly. In these situations, it is very important to follow a system so you will be able to react quickly and correctly. First aid is a way to manage an illness or injury until further medical care can be obtained, if necessary. When giving first aid, there are two ways you can harm someone. The first way is by not treating an injury and the second is by further damaging the injury.

Remember these two very important rules of first aid:

- **Do no harm.**
- **Never move a hurt child except to save a life.**

When you provide first aid, it is absolutely critical that you remain calm and reassure the victim. A calm attitude will allow you to think clearly and act appropriately. At the time of an emergency injury or illness, ask other adults to remove the other children to an area away from the victim. This will clear the area so you can carry out the necessary first aid. It will also create a calmer atmosphere for the other children. Later, when the situation is taken care of, you and all others involved (including other children) will need the opportunity to work through your feelings about what happened.

Assess the injury

Follow these steps whenever you are faced with an emergency situation. If more than one person is injured, start with the one who appears to be in greatest danger.

1. **Find out what happened.** What caused the injury? How? Who is hurt? Is there still danger? Remember, never move a victim except to save a life. Am I calm and reassuring to the children? Who can help?

2. **Check for life-threatening problems.** Is the child conscious?

If the child is not conscious, is the child breathing (chest moving, air coming out of nose or mouth)? If not, lift only the jaw of child and give two quick breaths of mouth-to-mouth resuscitation. Is there a pulse in the neck? If not, start CPR.

If the child is conscious and old enough, ask questions such as, "What's your name?" to help determine the child's condition. Keep checking breathing and pulse as you proceed.

Wash any wounds to reduce chances of infection.

If there is a large amount of bleeding, it is most important to apply direct pressure on the wound to stop the bleeding. The wound should be washed to reduce the chance of infection only in cases where bleeding is insignificant or after the bleeding is stopped.

Providing first aid can present the risk of acquiring bloodborne infection. To reduce this risk, if contact with blood is anticipated, the first-aid responder should use disposable latex gloves. If gloves are unavailable, it is safest to maintain a barrier (e.g., gauze) between one's hands and the victim's blood.

3. **Call emergency medical services (EMS) if you have any doubt about the situation.** Ask another adult to call the emergency number first and then the person legally responsible for the child.

4. **Check for injuries.** Start at the head and work down unless the place of injury is obvious.

Eyes. Pull eyelids open and look at the pupils (dark circle in middle). Are they the same size? Are the pupils big or small? Are the child's eyes looking in the same direction?

Ears. Look for blood or fluid (don't be fooled by tears).

Scalp. Feel gently (without moving child's head) for bumps, dents, bleeding, or anything unusual.

Nose and mouth. Look for bleeding or tooth injury.

Neck. Recheck pulse and breathing. Feel for bleeding, swelling, or stiffness.

Chest. Feel gently for swelling, unusual position or motion of bones.

Back. Slide your hands under the child to check for bleeding or pain.

Abdomen. Check for bleeding, pain, or tight muscles.

Arms. Ask the child to move her or his hands, arms, and shoulders. If the child refuses to move any part, examine it very carefully without moving it. Start at the shoulder and feel carefully along both arms. Check for bleeding, swelling, pain, or any unusual shape or motion. Check pulse at the wrist (if it is not strong, check pulse at neck again). Feel hand bones. Check skin temperature.

Hips and legs. Ask the child to move as for the arms and check the feet, knees, ankles, legs, and hips. Are knees the same distance from the hips? Are feet warm or cold?

Keep the victim comfortable and warm with a clean blanket or clothing until help arrives. Provide detailed information to the emergency crew.

If you are handling the situation, administer the appropriate first aid.

5. **Regroup.** Check the condition of any other injured children. Talk with all present in calm, reassuring tones about how you are taking care of the injured child. Complete an incident report form

(Figure 8.5). Give one copy to the parents the day of the incident, put one copy in the child's file and one copy in the central injury log.

First-aid education

Staff

All staff should be trained in pediatric first aid including choking, seizures, and resuscitation. This training, done by qualified instructors, should be repeated at least every 3 years, or more often if possible, and whenever necessary to train new staff. The first-aid training should include a developmental approach to young children and injury prevention as well as how to handle emergencies appropriately from both a medical and psychological viewpoint. All staff must know your program's policies for emergencies in addition to basic first aid.

Children

Young children can begin to know how and from whom to get help. Teach children these basic, helpful concepts.

- Follow all safety rules.
- Tell an adult right away if something is wrong (someone is hurt or sick).
- Some things are dangerous (e.g., poisons, matches, tiny objects in the mouth).
- A person who is very hurt or sick may need to be alone with a helper.

Older preschool children also can be taught about basic care concepts such as cuts need to be cleaned with soap and water, direct pressure helps stop bleeding, burns should be treated with cold water. This information may help children to be more cooperative if they can understand why certain first-aid procedures are necessary.

Parents

Set up a program to help parents refresh their first-aid skills. You may consider inviting parents to your staff training or having a special meeting to review home first-aid procedures. You might want to put brief articles in your newsletter, if you have one. Keep parents informed when you hear about community education programs. First-aid resources are a great addition to a parent lending library, too.

CHOKING/CPR

For Infants Under One Year

Choking

Begin the following if the infant is choking and is unable to breathe. However, if the infant is coughing, crying, or speaking, DO NOT do any of the following, but call your doctor for further advice.

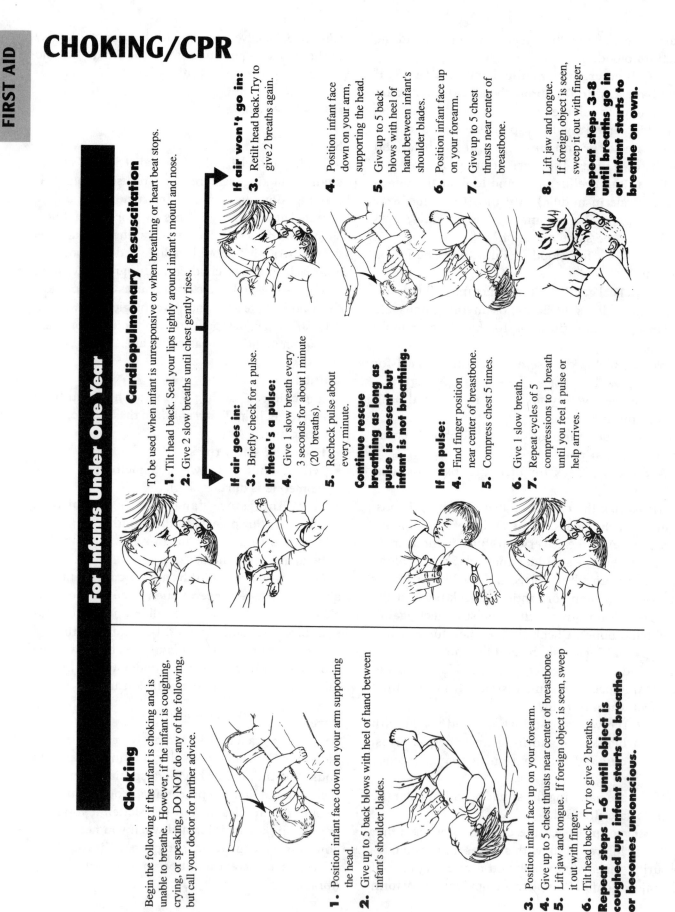

1. Position infant face down on your arm supporting the head.

2. Give up to 5 back blows with heel of hand between infant's shoulder blades.

3. Position infant face up on your forearm.

4. Give up to 5 chest thrusts near center of breastbone.

5. Lift jaw and tongue. If foreign object is seen, sweep it out with finger.

6. Tilt head back. Try to give 2 breaths.

Repeat steps 1-6 until object is coughed up, infant starts to breathe or becomes unconscious.

Cardiopulmonary Resuscitation

To be used when infant is unresponsive or when breathing or heart beat stops.

1. Tilt head back. Seal your lips tightly around infant's mouth and nose.

2. Give 2 slow breaths until chest gently rises.

If air goes in:

3. Briefly check for a pulse.

If there's a pulse:

4. Give 1 slow breath every 3 seconds for about 1 minute (20 breaths).

5. Recheck pulse about every minute.

Continue rescue breathing as long as pulse is present but infant is not breathing.

If no pulse:

4. Find finger position near center of breastbone.

5. Compress chest 5 times.

6. Give 1 slow breath.

7. Repeat cycles of 5 compressions to 1 breath until you feel a pulse or help arrives.

If air won't go in:

3. Retilt head back. Try to give 2 breaths again.

4. Position infant face down on your arm, supporting the head.

5. Give up to 5 back blows with heel of hand between infant's shoulder blades.

6. Position infant face up on your forearm.

7. Give up to 5 chest thrusts near center of breastbone.

8. Lift jaw and tongue. If foreign object is seen, sweep it out with finger.

Repeat steps 3-8 until breaths go in or infant starts to breathe on own.

CHOKING/CPR

Choking

Begin the following if the child is choking and is unable to breathe. However, if the child is coughing, crying, or speaking, DO NOT do any of the following, but call your doctor for further advice.

1. Place thumbside of fist against middle of abdomen just above the navel. Grasp fist with other hand.

2. Give up to 5 quick upward thrusts.

Repeat steps 1-2 until object is coughed up, or until child starts to breathe or becomes unconscious.

For Children Over One Year

Cardiopulmonary Resuscitation

To be used when child is unresponsive or when breathing or heart beat stops.

1. Tilt head back. Seal your lips tightly around child's mouth; pinch nose shut.

2. Give 2 slow breaths until chest gently rises.

If air goes in:

3. Briefly check for a pulse.

If there's a pulse:

4. Give 1 slow breath every 3 seconds for about 1 minute (20 breaths).

5. Recheck pulse about every minute.

Continue rescue breathing as long as pulse is present but child is not breathing.

If no pulse:

4. Find hand position near center of breastbone.

5. Position shoulders over hands.

6. Compress chest 5 times.

7. Give 1 slow breath.

8. Repeat cycles of 5 compressions to 1 breath until you feel a pulse or help arrives.

If air won't go in:

3. Retilt head back. Try to give 2 breaths again.

4. Place heel of 1 hand on child's abdomen above middle of navel and below rib cage.

5. Give up to 5 abdominal thrusts.

6. Lift jaw and tongue. If foreign object is seen, sweep it out with finger.

Repeat steps 3-6 until breaths go in or child starts to breathe on own.

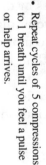

First aid for common situations

Call 911 or an emergency ambulance for any severely injured child.

BURNS AND SCALDS

Minor burns without blisters—Place burned extremity into cold water or cover burned part with a towel soaked in cold water until the pain stops (at least 15 minutes). Do not use ice.

Burns with blisters—Same as above. Do NOT break the blisters. Call your doctor for advice on how to cover the burn. ANY burn on the face, hands, feet, or genitals and any large burn should be seen by a doctor.

Large or deep burns—Call 911 or an emergency ambulance. Remove clothing. Do NOT apply medication. Keep child warm with a clean sheet and then a blanket until help arrives.

Chemical burns (see "Poisons—skin exposure"), **electrical burns**—Disconnect electrical power. Do NOT touch victim with bare hands. Pull victim away from power source with wood or a thick, dry cloth. ALL electrical burns need to be seen by a doctor.

CONVULSIONS (Seizures)

Protect the child from injury. Perform rescue breathing if child is blue or not breathing. If breathing, lay child on side. Put nothing in the mouth. Call 911 or an emergency ambulance.

EYE INJURIES

If anything is splashed in the eye, flush gently with water for at least 15 minutes. Call your poison center or doctor for further advice. Any injured or painful eye should be seen by a doctor. Do NOT touch or rub an injured eye. Do NOT apply medication. Do NOT remove objects stuck into the eye. Gently bandage the painful eye shut until you can get medical help.

FAINTING

Lay child on back with head to the side and legs raised. Do NOT give anything by mouth. Call your doctor. If child does not wake up right away, call 911 or an emergency ambulance.

FEVER

A child who feels hot to the touch, complains of being hot, or is sweating or chilling may have a fever. Take child's temperature. Give fever medication as recommended by your doctor to reduce fever. Do not sponge a child with ice or alcohol. If the child is hot from sun exposure or exercise, get child to cooler, shaded area to rest; give lots of liquids. Whatever you suspect the cause of fever may be, call your doctor. This is especially important for babies less than 3 months of age.

FRACTURES and SPRAINS

DO NOT MOVE A CHILD WHO MAY HAVE A NECK OR BACK INJURY because this may cause serious harm. If an injured part is painful, swollen, deformed, or if motion causes pain, suspect a fracture and splint it. Apply a cold compress and call your doctor or an ambulance.

HEAD INJURIES

DO NOT MOVE ANY CHILD WHO MAY HAVE A SERIOUS HEAD AND/OR NECK OR BACK INJURY because this may cause harm. Call 911 or an emergency ambulance for any of the following:
- Any loss of consciousness or drowsiness
- Persistent headache or vomiting
- Clumsiness or inability to move any body part
- Oozing blood or watery fluid from ears or nose
- Convulsions (seizures)
- Abnormal speech or behavior

For questions about less serious injuries, call your doctor.

NOSEBLEEDS

With child sitting, squeeze nostrils together between your thumb and index finger for 10 minutes. If bleeding persists, call your doctor.

POISONS

If a child is unconscious, becoming drowsy, having convulsions, or having trouble breathing call 911 or an emergency ambulance.

Swallowed poisons—Any non-food substance is a potential poison. Call your poison center immediately. Do not induce vomiting except on professional advice. Your poison center will give you further instructions.

Fumes, gases, or smoke—Get the victim into fresh air. Call 911 or fire department. If the child is not breathing, start CPR and continue until help arrives.

Skin exposure—If acids, lye, pesticides, chemicals, or any potentially poisonous substances come in contact with a child's skin, gently brush off dry material. Remove contaminated clothing. Wear rubber gloves if possible. Wash skin with large quantities of soap and water. Call your poison center for further advice.

SKIN WOUNDS

For all of these conditions, make sure the child is properly immunized for tetanus.

Bruises—Apply cold compresses for one-half hour. For extensive bruises, crushing injuries, or bicycle spoke injuries, call your doctor. For continued pain or swelling, call your doctor.

Cuts—Apply pressure with a clean cloth to stop the bleeding. If the cut is large and deep, call for help and maintain pressure until help arrives. For minor cuts, wash with soap and water and cover with dressing. If a cut may need stitches, seek medical care as soon as possible.

Scrapes—Wash scrape with soap and water. Cover with a nonstick dressing.

Splinters—Wash with soap and water. Do not soak splinter. Remove small splinters with tweezers. If not easily removed, call your doctor.

Puncture wounds—Do NOT remove large objects such as knives or sticks. Call your doctor. For minor puncture wounds, wash with soap and water and call your doctor. Your child may need a tetanus booster.

STINGS and BITES

Stinging insects—Remove the stinger with the scraping motion of a fingernail. Do NOT pull the stinger out. Put a cold compress on the bite to relieve pain. If hives, paleness, weakness, nausea, vomiting, tightness in the chest, breathing difficulty, or collapse occur, call 911 or an emergency ambulance. For spider bites, call your doctor or poison center.

Animal or human bites—Wash wound thoroughly with soap and water. Call your doctor.

Ticks—Place tweezers close to the head of the tick and pull tick away from point of attachment. Call your doctor if head remains attached or if child later develops symptoms such as headache, fever, or rash.

Snake bites—Call your poison center. Do not apply ice. Take the child to the emergency department. Splint injured arm or leg. Keep arm or leg elevated if possible.

TEETH

Baby (primary) teeth—If knocked out or broken, apply clean gauze to control bleeding and call a dentist.

Permanent teeth—If knocked out, find the tooth and rinse it gently without touching the root. Insert and gently hold the tooth in its socket or transport the tooth in cow's milk. Go directly to the dentist or an emergency department. Time is important.

If broken, save the pieces. Gently clean the injured area with warm water. Place a cold compress to reduce swelling. Go to the dentist immediately.

The first-aid information here should not be used as a substitute for the medical care and advice of your pediatrician. There may be variations in treatment that your pediatrician may recommend based on the individual facts and circumstances.

First-aid instructions from the *AAP First Aid Chart*, AAP Committee on Accident and Poison Prevention, revised April 1993.

Section D
Preventive health care

Major concepts

- Program staff are members of the preventive health team who aim to keep children well.

- Regularly scheduled health visits, including health screenings, are essential to maintain children's health.

- Health is assessed by the health team based on information from health histories, health observations, screening tests, and medical examinations.

- Adults must take care of their own health needs and concerns that may affect their job performance.

- Dental health is an important part of general preventive health care.

9

Preventive health care for children

Why preventive care is important

Health is defined by the World Health Organization as "... a state of complete physical, mental, and social **well-being** and not merely the absence of disease or infirmity." This total state of wellness is affected by the interrelationships between each area of a person's development. For example, when children are ill, tired, hungry, or poorly fed they cannot function well and may be cranky or inattentive. A child who has an undetected medical condition or who is neglected may become depressed or withdrawn. A child with a physical problem may develop emotional or learning problems; likewise, a child who has emotional upsets may develop physical symptoms as a result of eating and/or sleeping disturbances. Children's health is constantly changing, particularly during their early years.

Adults' health also affects their state of well-being. Adults, like children, require good preventive health care to keep well and function at their best.

Goals for preventive health care

Young children are at risk for developing a number of health problems such as hearing or vision difficulties, lead poisoning, developmental delays, and injuries. The goal of preventive care is to keep children well, rather than to treat them after they become sick. A comprehensive preventive health care plan has these goals:

- to detect medical conditions that may not be easily recognized that need medical attention (e.g., fluid in the ear, anemia, or "lazy eye"). Early identification and treatment of such problems may completely resolve them, while a delay in attention can result in more—or permanent—damage.
- to identify children who may be at high risk for

developing diseases due to hereditary factors, family health habits, or environmental factors
- to identify and follow signs in growth patterns, behavior, or development that could mean future health problems
- to evaluate the effectiveness of past or current treatments, such as tubes in ears, antibiotics, or patching an eye

The goals of routine checkups are

- to promote health through counseling, education, and guidance for anticipated problems
- to take specific preventive measures such as immunizations
- to identify potential health problems through screenings such as measurements of growth, vision, hearing, lead poisoning, and tuberculin testing
- to provide early detection and treatment of illnesses with symptoms (e.g., strep throat) to prevent complications
- to prevent disability from chronic diseases

It is crucial that children be seen regularly by health care providers to ensure that these goals are met.

The majority of pediatricians in the United States are members of the American Academy of Pediatrics (AAP). The AAP sets the minimum guidelines for routine health care for children. These are updated from time to time as new information about valuable preventive health measures becomes available. The guidelines in use at the time this manual was printed are shown in Figure 9.1. Members of the AAP receive updated versions of the guidelines when they are issued. Be sure a current version is being used by checking with an AAP member. Note that the guidelines are minimum requirements for healthy children who are

Figure 9.1. Recommendations for preventive pediatric health care

Committee on Practice and Ambulatory Medicine

Each child and family is unique; therefore, these **Recommendations for Preventive Pediatric Health Care** are designed for the care of children who are receiving competent parenting, have no manifestations of any important health problems, and are growing and developing in satisfactory fashion. **Additional visits may become necessary** if circumstances suggest variations from normal. These guidelines represent a consensus by the Committee on Practice and Ambulatory Medicine in consultation with the membership of the American Academy of Pediatrics through the Chapter Presidents. The Committee emphasizes the great importance of **continuity of care** in comprehensive health supervision and the need to avoid **fragmentation of care.**

A **prenatal visit** by first-time parents and/or those who are at high risk is recommended and should include anticipatory guidance and pertinent medical history.

	INFANCY							EARLY CHILDHOOD					LATE CHILDHOOD					ADOLESCENCE[2]			
AGE[3]	2–3 d[1]	By 1 mo	2 mo	4 mo	6 mo	9 mo	12 mo	15 mo	18 mo	24 mo	3 y	4 y	5 y	6 y	8 y	10 y	12 y	14 y	16 y	18 y	20y+
HISTORY Initial/Interval	●	●	●	●	●	●	●	●	●	●	●	●	●	●	●	●	●	●	●	●	●
MEASUREMENTS Height and Weight	●	●	●	●	●	●	●	●	●	●	●	●	●	●	●	●	●	●	●	●	●
Head Circumference	●	●	●	●	●	●	●	●	●	●											
Blood Pressure											●	●	●	●	●	●	●	●	●	●	●
SENSORY SCREENING Vision	S	S	S	S	S	S	S	S	S	S	S	O	O	O	O	S	O	O	S	O	O
Hearing	S	S	S	S	S	S	S	S	S	S	S	O	O	S[4]	S[4]	S[4]	O	S	S	O	S
DEVELOPMENTAL/ BEHAVIORAL ASSESSMENT[5]	●	●	●	●	●	●	●	●	●	●	●	●	●	●	●	●	●	●	●	●	●
PHYSICAL EXAMINATION[6]	●	●	●	●	●	●	●	●	●	●	●	●	●	●	●	●	●	●	●	●	●
PROCEDURES[7] Hereditary/Metabolic Screening[8]	●——→																				
Immunization[9]			●	●	●		●——→	●	●				●					●			
Tuberculin Test[10]						●	——→				●							●	——→		
Hematocrit or Hemoglobin[11]			←——			●	——→								●		——→				
Urinalysis[12]			←——			●	——→														
ANTICIPATORY GUIDANCE[13]	●	●	●	●	●	●	●	●	●	●	●	●	●	●	●	●	●	●	●	●	●
INITIAL DENTAL REFERRAL[14]											●										

1. For newborns discharged in 24 hours or less after delivery.
2. Adolescent-related issues (eg, psychosocial, emotional, substance usage, and reproductive health) may necessitate more frequent health supervision.
3. If a child comes under care for the first time at any point on the schedule, or if any items are not accomplished at the suggested age, the schedule should be brought up to date at the earliest possible time.
4. At these points, history may suffice: if problem suggested, a standard testing method should be employed.
5. By history and appropriate physical examination: if suspicious, by specific objective developmental testing.
6. At each visit, a complete physical examination is essential, with infant totally unclothed, older child undressed and suitably draped.
7. These may be modified, depending upon entry point into schedule and individual need.
8. Metabolic screening (eg, thyroid, PKU, galactosemia) should be done according to state law.
9. Schedule(s) per *Report of the Committee on Infectious Diseases,* 1991 Red Book, and current AAP Committee statements.

10. For high-risk groups, the Committee on Infectious Diseases recommends annual TB skin testing.
11. Present medical evidence suggests the need for reevaluation of the frequency and timing of hemoglobin or hematocrit tests. One determination is therefore suggested during each time period. Performance of additional tests is left to the individual practice experience.
12. Present medical evidence suggests the need for reevaluation of the frequency and timing of urinalyses. One determination is therefore suggested during each time period. Performance of additional tests is left to the individual practice experience.
13. Appropriate discussion and counseling should be an integral part of each visit for care.
14. Subsequent examinations as prescribed by dentist.

NB: **Special chemical, immunologic, and endocrine testing** is usually carried out upon specific indications. Testing other than newborn (eg, inborn errors of metabolism, sickle disease, lead) is discretionary with the physician.

Key: ● = to be performed S = subjective, by history O = objective, by a standard testing method

The recommendations in this publication do not indicate an exclusive course of treatment or serve as a standard of medical care. Variations, taking into account individual circumstances, may be appropriate.

AAP News, July 1991 RE9224

Recommendations are due to change in 1995. Check with the American Academy of Pediatrics for the most current information on preventive pediatric health care.

receiving competent parenting and who have no significant health problems. Some doctors and clinics do not follow the AAP guidelines. Some health programs do not pay for preventive health care that meets these guidelines. Despite these barriers, children should still receive the recommended services.

Ideally, all preventive care and illness care should be provided by a single source of medical care, the child's "medical home." Fragmentation of care by inappropriate use of emergency rooms for minor illnesses and seeking care from a variety of different providers without careful maintenance of a comprehensive medical record result in poor health care. However, when the child's regular source of care does not provide all the routine minimum services as outlined in Figure 9.1, every effort should be made to find community agencies to fill in the gaps (e.g., Society for Prevention of Blindness provides vision screening, lead detection programs do blood testing). Information obtained from special screening programs should always be

Each observer has a different perspective in obtaining health information about a child. To have a total picture of the child, all observations from the health team must be shared and seen as a whole.

forwarded (with parental consent) to the child's usual source of health care to be considered with the rest of the child's health data.

How health is assessed

A child's health should be assessed by individuals who have unique skills and experience with the child. This health team should be coordinated by the child's physician or another member of the health team as the child's special needs or family preference suggests. In many agencies the coordinator of services is called a "case manager." The child's health team consists of the child's parents, teachers, and others who regularly observe and interact with the child in addition to health professionals (see Figure 9.2). Each health team member has a special perspective to offer about growth, development, and overall health. This information should be shared with the health team coordinator or case manager so that a comprehensive picture of the child can be created. The clear designation of the health team coordinator or case manager is especially important for children with multiple health and developmental problems.

The assessment process is based on information from a variety of sources: health histories, observations by the health team, screening tests, and medical examinations. Health assessment and follow-up care are often separated into three categories: **screening, diagnosis,** and **treatment.**

- **Screening** is the use of quick, inexpensive, and simple procedures to identify children who may have a problem in a specific area. Health screening tests typically produce one of these three possible results:

Screening result	Action needed
• apparently healthy (negative)	• none
• possibly at risk	• repeat screening test
• at risk (positive)	• refer for further diagnosis and possible treatment

- **Diagnosis** is a more detailed evaluation to find out if there is, in fact, a health problem and, if so, what it is. When making a diagnosis, the health professional may use health histories,

Figure 9.2. Potential health team members

An **allergist** is a medical doctor with a special interest and training in diseases of the immune system including allergies (certified by the American Board of Allergy).

An **audiologist** is a specialist in hearing problems.

A **dentist** is a specialist who cares for and treats the teeth and gums.

A **neurologist** is a medical doctor with special interest and training in brain and nervous system disorders.

A **nutritionist** is a professional with interest and training (a master's degree) in nutrition, who evaluates a person's food habits and nutritional status. This specialist can provide advice about normal and therapeutic nutrition, feeding equipment, self-feeding techniques, and food service.

An **occupational therapist** evaluates and treats children who may have difficulty performing self-help, play, or other independent activities, particularly involving the use of hands.

An **ophthalmologist** is a medical doctor who evaluates, diagnoses, and treats disease, injuries, or birth defects that affect the eyes.

An **optician** advises in the selection of frames and fits the lenses prescribed by the **optometrist** or **ophthalmologist** to the frames. An optician also fits contact lenses.

An **optometrist** examines the eye and related structures to determine the presence of visual problems, eye disease, or other problems.

An **orthopedist** is a medical doctor who evaluates, diagnoses, and treats diseases and injuries to muscles, joints, and bones.

An **otologist** is a medical doctor who screens, diagnoses, and treats ear disorders.

An **otorhinolaryngologist** (ENT doctor) is a medical doctor who screens, diagnoses, and treats ear, nose, and throat disorders.

A **pediatrician** is a medical doctor who specializes in prevention and management of childhood diseases and problems, including developmental and behavioral concerns. (Certified by the American Board of Pediatrics or the Osteopathic Board of Pediatrics or English or Canadian equivalents.)

A **physical therapist** evaluates and plans physical therapy programs and equipment to promote self-sufficiency primarily related to gross-motor skills such as walking, sitting, and shifting position.

A **psychiatrist** is a medical doctor who screens, diagnoses, and treats psychological, emotional, behavioral, and developmental or organic problems. **Child psychiatrists** have additional training in diagnosing and treating these problems of children.

A **psychologist** screens, diagnoses, and treats people with social, emotional, psychological, behavioral, or developmental problems. **Child psychologists** specialize in diagnosing and treating children.

A **social worker** provides services for individuals and families experiencing a variety of emotional or social problems. These services may include individual, family, or group counseling; advocacy; referral; or consultation with programs, schools, clinics, or social agencies.

A **speech-language pathologist** screens, diagnoses, and treats children and adults with communication disorders. This person may also be called a **speech clinician** or **speech therapist**.

Adapted from *Mainstreaming Preschoolers Series* by U.S. Department of Health and Human Services, 1978. Washington, DC: U.S. Government Printing Office.

dietary information, laboratory test results, family/teacher observations, X-rays, or physical and psychological examinations.

- **Treatment** is designed to control, minimize, correct, or cure a disease or abnormality (e.g., eyeglasses, dental fillings, therapy). *Treatment is the key to an effective program.* Without it, screening and diagnosis are meaningless.

Health histories

Health histories provide important information about the child's prior health experiences and risks for future disease. The family health history may help predict what illnesses the child may inherit or develop. The physician will take a detailed health history including information about birth, illnesses, hospitalization, all treatments, immunization status, and current health concerns.

Programs for young children should also have a history form, but it needs to cover only major health problems and developmental concerns. This information can help explain a child's current behavior and past experience.

Parents know a great deal about their own child. However, unless there is a specific request for it, few parents will review their child's nutritional, immunization, health, and family history. Even the most alert parent may innocently overlook the health needs of a rapidly changing and growing child because of other urgent demands.

When your program requests a child's health history, you will help reinforce the parents' role in keeping important health information. You can assist parents in reviewing the child's health record for general health strengths and weaknesses. A developmental health history form is presented in Figure 9.3. Use it as a guide to develop one that meets your needs.

Observations

Physical health

Physical health observations include observable signs of health or illness (coughing, vomiting, swelling) and symptoms that are internal and must be described to be known to others (nausea, headache, stomachache).

Since young children often cannot describe how they feel, your objective observations usually provide the best clues. Precise physical observations are the most helpful. It is more useful to say, "Jeffrey has a frequent dry cough, flushed cheeks, and a runny nose with thick yellow mucus" than to say, "Jeffrey looks sick." Report your specific observations rather than drawing conclusions or making a diagnosis. For instance, say, "Jennifer has a sore throat and an oral temperature of 102°" rather than saying "Jennifer has strep throat." State measurable facts whenever possible. A form to record symptoms of minor illness helps focus attention on significant observations (see Figure 18.1 on page 262).

Use all your senses (smell, hearing, seeing, touching) when making health observations. Observe clues such as the texture of skin, breath odor, the appearance of a bruise, or the sound of a cough. Sometimes it is difficult to judge what is significant. Observe the group in general and compare individual children. For example, do most of the children need help zipping their coats? If so, the fact that Susan asks for help is not a concern. If a child differs significantly from others in the group, it is worth noting.

Each observer has a different perspective in obtaining health information. Parents compare a child to her or his typical appearance or behavior or to siblings or friends. Teachers may have a similar view but also observe children in a group setting with many children of the same age. The physician or health provider uses the knowledge and experience from medical practice. Each view is valuable but limited; to have a total picture of the child, all observations from the health team must be shared and seen as a whole.

Development

A child's physical health is only one aspect of her or his life. An equally important aspect is the development of language, gross- and fine-motor skills, social-emotional competence, and cognition (thinking). Problems in these areas often can be identified and worked out during the early years. Program staff are ideally suited to observe such problems and should develop capabilities in these areas.

1. **Developmental milestones.** Knowledge of general child development with in-depth informa-

Figure 9.3. Developmental health history

Child's name _____ Birth date _____ / _____ / _____
                          (Last)   (First)

Nickname _____

Physical health

What health problems has your child had in the past? _____

_____

What health problems does your child have now? _____

_____

Other than what you listed above—

Does your child have any allergies? If so, to what? _____

_____

_____

How severe? _____

Does your child take any medicine regularly? If so, what? _____

_____

Has your child ever been hospitalized? If so, when and why? _____

_____

Does your child have any recurring chronic illness or health problem (such as asthma or frequent earaches)?

_____

Does your child have a disability that has been diagnosed (such as cerebral palsy, seizure disorder, developmental delay)?

_____

Do you have any other concerns about your child's health? _____

_____

_____

Development (compared to other children this age)

Does your child have any problems with talking or making sounds? Please explain.

_____

_____

Figure 9.3 *continued*

Does your child have any problems with walking, running, or moving? Please explain. _____

_____

Does your child have any problems seeing? Please explain. _____

_____

Does your child have any problems hearing? Please explain. _____

_____

Does your child have any problems using her or his hands (such as with puzzles, drawing, small building pieces)? Please explain.

_____

_____

Daily living
What is your child's typical eating pattern? _____

_____

_____

Write **N/A** (nonapplicable) if your child is too young for the following questions to apply.

What foods does your child like? _____

Dislike? _____

How well does your child use table utensils (cup, fork, spoon)? _____

_____

How does your child indicate bathroom needs? Word(s) for *urination:* _____

Word(s) for *bowel movement:* _____

Special words for body parts: _____

What are your child's regular bladder and bowel patterns? Do you want us to follow a particular plan for toileting?

_____

_____

For toddlers, please describe use of diapers or toileting equipment (such as potty, toilet seat adapter).

_____

Figure 9.3 *continued*

What are your child's regular sleeping patterns?

Awakes at _____ Naps at _____ Goes to bed at _____

What help does your child need to get dressed? _____

_____

Social relationships/play

What ages are your child's most frequent playmates? _____

Is your child friendly? _____ Aggressive? _____ Shy? _____ Withdrawn? _____

Does your child play well alone? _____

What is your child's favorite toy? _____

Is your child frightened by (circle all that apply) Animals? Rough children? Loud noises? The dark? Storms? Anything else?

_____

Who does most of the disciplining? _____

What is the best way to discipline your child? _____

_____

With which adults does your child have frequent contact? _____

How do you comfort your child? _____

_____

Does your child use a special comforting item (such as a blanket, stuffed animal, doll)? _____

_____

Parent's signature _____

Date _____

tion about children at particular ages provides a general framework to identify children whose abilities fall outside the normal range. These milestones must be viewed flexibly because a child's development is greatly influenced by childrearing styles, culture and ethnic norms, and by the child's own temperament.

Figure 9.4 contains a useful guide to observe children from age 3 to 5 in group settings. This guide will help you identify signs of potential trouble in areas of development. Use it as a screening **aid**, not a developmental test or standard assessment tool because it is neither of these.

The NAEYC (1989) publication, *Developmental Screening: A Guide,* provides a review of several developmental screening instruments. These standardized tools are frequently used by health providers as a framework for reviewing the range of normal childhood behaviors and developmental skills for children.

2. **Observation and documentation.** Write down behaviors that might suggest problems in a child's development. (You can keep file cards in your pocket and note on them the day, time, activity, and behavior you have observed.) Ask other staff members to also observe and record the child's behaviors. Then look for patterns in the child's behavior. Is the behavior influenced by particular children or adults who are present or by times of the day or days of the week? You may also need to look for additional information in the child's environment. Perhaps there is a new baby in the family or an undiagnosed medical condition. Determine the appropriate next steps to take, and plan a meeting to discuss your concerns with the child's parent(s).

3. **Communication.** Develop your ability to communicate concerns about unusual or delayed development in a supportive, non-threatening manner. Parents are experts on their children and should be involved in discussions about developmental concerns early in the screening process. Their input can help you identify which behaviors are appropriate for the family and culture and which are not, and which behaviors or traits are of particular concern to the parents. Often they have questions similar to yours but may not have wanted to bother the staff or appear to be overly anxious. Dealing with these concerns in a respectful partnership can be a great help and support.

4. **Referral and consultation.** Seek information on community resources for referral and consultation. Many communities have a wide array of experts on every aspect of child development. Once a problem has been identified and confirmed by parents and other staff members, you should be familiar enough with your community to be able to make an appropriate referral to a competent and sympathetic diagnostician. A list of local services should be developed and kept at the center so that referrals can be made easily.

Major health screenings

Value of screening for the apparently well child

The AAP recommends a minimum number of screening tests for sound health care; Head Start requires its programs to perform a similar set. These tests try to identify conditions which, if undetected and untreated, may seriously handicap a child for life. These conditions are important to discover, occur quite often, and generally respond to early treatment. Early treatment is often more effective and less costly than later treatment and may also prevent the development of other problems.

For instance, children with undetected hearing loss risk developing language, learning, and behavior problems. Children with eyes that are not straight and children with a marked difference in visual acuity between eyes risk developing amblyopia (loss of vision in one eye due to lack of normal use). If decreased vision is not treated during the early years, treatment in the school-age years is slow and often unsuccessful.

Screening generally involves short and simple procedures because it is intended for large numbers of apparently well children. A good screening may identify a few children who turn out not to have a problem, but it should miss very few who do have the problem. Without screening, problems may go unnoticed or, if the signs or symptoms are recognized, their significance may not be understood.

Another reason for screening the apparently well child is that young children are in a period of rapid growth and development. There are milestones that the child can be expected to reach within a certain

Figure 9.4. Developmental red flags for children age 3 to 5

Teachers and parents of young children frequently wonder if particular behaviors are something they should worry about. There is no way to make these decisions simply or with total certainty. Observation and screening tools are always limited because they summarize enormous amounts of information. The Preschool Enrichment Team, Inc., has developed this material as a development observation tool for children age 3 to 5.

The most useful tool in observing young children is a **thorough knowledge of normal growth and development. There is no substitute.** The process of development varies with each individual child, but normal development follows a predictable sequence of stages. Interruptions in the **pattern** and **sequence of stages** should put an observer on the alert.

Small variations in the **timetable** of a child's development are of much less concern. Each age and stage of development is affected by the personality of each child and represents the skills the child has developed: motor, language, cognitive, personal-social. Children are continuously changing and emerging from younger stages into older stages in all four areas, thereby combining characteristics of different stages.

What are red flags?

Red flags are behaviors that should warn you to **stop, look,** and **think.** Having done so, you may decide there is nothing to worry about, or that a cluster of behaviors signals a possible problem. These guidelines will help you use red flags more effectively.

- Behavior descriptions are sometimes repeated under different areas of development. It is difficult to categorize children's behavior. Your job is to notice and describe what you see that concerns you. Do not try to decide into what category it fits.
- Look for **patterns** or **clusters** of red flags. One, or a few in isolation, may not be significant.

- Observe a child in a variety of situations to watch for the behaviors that concern you.
- Compare the child's behavior to the norm which should include children who are 6 months younger or 6 months older as well as the same age.
- Note how the child has grown during the past 3 to 6 months. Be concerned if you feel the child has not progressed.
- **Know the order and timetable of normal growth and development.** What may be a red flag at one age can be a perfectly normal behavior at another.
- Keep in mind that each child's development is affected by personality, temperament, family structure and dynamics, culture, experiences, physical characteristics, and the match of child and family to your program.
- Use a detailed skills list to develop a skills profile for the child.

Consultation and referral

None of us knows all there is to know about normal growth and development. Use all of your available resources to help you when you think a child may have a problem.

- Describe in detail what you see that concerns you. Do not try to conclude what it means or to label it. It is much more helpful to parents, consultants, and to the child to have descriptions, not conclusions.
- Talk with the child's parent(s) even if you're not sure that a problem exists.
- Wait and watch for a while **if** the problem seems mild and you have observed growth in the past 3 to 6 months. If no growth in the area of concern can be described, then it is time to ask for help.
- Know that if you recommend further evaluation of a problem and your concerns are confirmed, you have helped a child and family begin to solve a problem.
- Also, be glad if further evaluation does not indicate that there is a problem at this time.

Figure 9.4 *continued*
NOTE: *These categories are intended to guide your observation of children age 3 to 5 only.*

MAJOR DEVELOPMENTAL AREAS

Social-emotional development
including
- relationships
- separations
- involvement
- focusing
- affect
- self-image
- anxiety level
- impulse control
- transitions

Red flags
Be alert to a child who, compared with other children the same age or 6 months older or younger,
- does not seem to recognize self as a separate person, or does not refer to self as "I"
- has a great difficulty separating from parent
- is anxious, tense, restless, compulsive, cannot get dirty or messy, has many fears, engages in excessive self-stimulation
- seems preoccupied with own inner world. Conversations do not make sense.
- shows little or no impulse control, hits or bites as first response, cannot follow a classroom routine
- expresses emotions inappropriately (laughs when sad, denies feelings); facial expressions do not match emotions
- cannot focus on activities (short attention span, cannot complete anything, flits from toy to toy)
- relates only to adults. Cannot share adult attention, consistently sets up power struggle, or is physically abusive to adults
- consistently withdraws from people, prefers to be alone; no depth to relationships; does not seek or accept affection or touching
- treats people as objects, has no empathy for other children, cannot play on another child's terms
- is consistently aggressive, frequently hurts others deliberately; shows no remorse or is deceitful in hurting others

How to screen
1. Observe child.
- Note overall behavior. What does the child do all day? With whom? With what does the child play?
- Note when, where, how frequently, and with whom problem behaviors occur.
- Describe behavior through clear observations. Do not diagnose.

2. Note family history.
- Makeup of family. Who cares for child?
- Has there been a recent move, death, new sibling, or long or traumatic separations?
- What support does family have—extended family, friends?

3. Note developmental history and child's temperament since infancy.
- activity level
- regularity of child's routine—sleeping, eating
- distractibility
- exposure to drugs including alcohol and infections during pregnancy
- intensity of child's responses
- persistence/attention span
- positive or negative mood
- adaptability to changes in routine
- level of sensitivity to noise, light, touch

Community resources
- child's health care provider
- mental health center
- family service organization
- child guidance center
- school system's early childhood special needs coordinator
- birth-to-6 resource directory or regional offices, Department of Education
- early intervention programs
- integrated preschool programs and outreach and training teams
- regional offices of your department of public health
- libraries for additional reading

Figure 9.4 *continued*

Motor development—Fine motor, gross motor, perceptual

including

- quality of movement
- level of development
- sensory integration

Red flags

Pay extra attention to

- the child who is particularly uncoordinated and who
  - —has lots of accidents
  - —trips, bumps into things
  - —is awkward getting down/up, climbing, jumping, getting around toys and people
  - —stands out from the group in structured motor tasks—walking, climbing stairs, jumping, standing on one foot
  - —avoids the more physical games
- the child who relies heavily on watching own or other peoples' movements in order to do them and who
  - —may frequently misjudge distances
  - —may become particularly uncoordinated or off balance with eyes closed
- the child who, compared to peers, uses much more of her or his body to do the task than the task requires and who
  - —dives into the ball (as though to cover the fact that she or he cannot coordinate a response)
  - —uses tongue, feet, or other body parts excessively to help in coloring, cutting, tracing, or with other concentration
  - —produces extremely heavy coloring
  - —leans over the table when concentrating on a fine-motor project
  - —when doing "wheelbarrows," keeps pulling the knees and feet under the body or thrusts rump up in the air
- the child with extraneous and involuntary movements who
  - —while painting with one hand, holds the other hand in the air or waves
  - —does toe walking much of the time
  - —shows twirling or rocking movements
  - —shakes hands or taps fingers

- the child who involuntarily finds touching uncomfortable and who
  - —flinches or tenses when touched or hugged
  - —avoids activities that require touching or close contact
  - —may be uncomfortable lying down, particularly on the back
  - —reacts as if attacked when unexpectedly bumped
  - —blinks, protects self from a ball even when trying to catch it
- the child who compulsively craves being touched or hugged. Or, the older child who almost involuntarily has to feel things to understand them. These children may
  - —cling to, or lightly brush, the teacher a lot
  - —always sit close to or touch children in a circle
  - —be strongly attracted to sensory experiences such as blankets, soft toys, water, dirt, sand, paste, hands in food
- the child who has a reasonable amount of experience with fine-motor tools but whose skill does not improve proportionally, such as
  - —an older child who can still only snip with scissors or whose cutting is extremely choppy
  - —a child who uses extremely heavy crayon pressure
  - —an older child who still cannot color within the lines on a simple project
  - —an older child who frequently switches hands with crayon, scissors, paintbrush
  - —an experienced child who tries but still gets paste, paint, sand, water everywhere
  - —a child who is very awkward with, or chronically avoids, small manipulative materials
- the child who has exceptional difficulty with new but simple puzzles, coloring, structured art projects, and drawing a person, and who, for example, may
  - —take much longer to do the task, even when trying hard, and produce a final result that is still not as sophisticated compared to peers
  - —show a lot of trial-and-error behavior when trying to do a puzzle
  - —mix up top/bottom, left/right, front/back, on simple projects where a model is to be copied

Figure 9.4 *continued*

Motor development—Fine motor, gross motor, perceptual *continued*
—use blocks or small cubes to repeatedly build and crash tower structure and seem fascinated and genuinely delighted with the novelty of the crash (older child)
—still does a lot of scribbling (older child)

How to screen
1. Note level and quality of development as compared with other children in the group.

Community resources
- child's health care provider
- Registered Physical Therapist (RPT), Registered Occupational Therapist (OTR), preferably with pediatric experience
- school system's early childhood special needs coordinator
- rehabilitation center
- regional office of department of public health
- hospital/physical or occupational therapy department
- American Physical Therapy Association, local chapter
- American Occupational Therapy Association, local chapter

Speech and language development
including
- articulation (pronouncing sounds)
- dysfluency (excessive stuttering—occasional stuttering may occur in the early years and is normal)
- voice
- language (ability to use and understand words, grammar, etc.)

Red flags
- articulation. Watch for the child
  —whose speech is difficult to understand, compared with peers
  —who mispronounces sounds
  —whose mouth seems abnormal (excessive under- or overbite, swallowing difficulty, poorly lined-up teeth, drooling)
  —who has difficulty putting words and sounds in proper sequence
  —who cannot be encouraged to produce age-appropriate sound
  —who has a history of ear infections or middle ear disorders

  NOTE: Most children develop the following sounds correctly by the ages shown (i.e., don't worry about a 3-year-old who mispronounces *t*).
  2 years—all vowel sounds
  3 years—*p, b, m, w, h*
  4 years—*t, d, n, k, h, ng*
  5 years—*f, j, sh*
  6 years—*ch, v, r, l*
  7 years—*s, z,* voiceless and voiced *th*
- dysfluency (stuttering). Some dysfluency is normal in 3- to 4-year-olds. Note the child who, compared with others of the same age,
  —shows excessive
    repetitions of sounds, words (m-m-m, I-I-I-I)
    prolongations of sounds (mmmmmmmmmmmmmmm)
    hesitations or long blocks during speech, usually accompanied by tension or struggle behavior
    putting in extra words (um, uh, well)
  —shows two or more of these behaviors while speaking

hand clenching	breathing irregularity
eye blinking	tremors
swaying of body	pitch rise
pill rolling with fingers	frustration
no eye contact	avoidance of talking
body tension or struggle	

  —is labeled a stutterer by parents
  —is aware of her or his dysfluencies
- voice. Note the child whose
  —rate of speech is extremely fast or slow
  —voice is breathy or hoarse
  —voice is very loud or soft
  —voice is very high or low
  —voice sounds very nasal
- language (ability to use and understand words). Note the child who
  —does not appear to understand when others speak, even though hearing is normal
  —is unable to follow one- or two-step directions
  —communicates by pointing, gesturing

Figure 9.4 *continued*

Speech and language development *continued*
—makes no attempt to communicate with words
—has small vocabulary for age
—uses parrot-like speech (imitates what others say)
—has difficulty putting words together in a sentence
—uses words inaccurately
—demonstrates difficulty with three or more of these

making a word plural	using possessives
changing tenses of verb	naming common objects
using pronouns	telling functions of common
using negatives	objects
using prepositions	

NOTE: Two-year-olds use mostly nouns, few verbs. Three-year-olds use nouns, verbs, some adverbs, adjectives, prepositions. Four-year-olds use all parts of speech.

How to screen
1. Observe child. Note when, where, how frequently, and with whom problem occurs.
2. Check developmental history—both heredity and environment play an important part in speech development.
3. Look at motor development—it is closely associated with speech.
4. Look at social-emotional status—it can affect speech and language.
5. Write down or record speech samples.
6. Check hearing status.
7. Note number of speech sounds or uses of language.
8. Check language used by family.

Community resources
- child's health care provider
- school system's early childhood special needs coordinator
- communication disorders department at college or university
- speech clinic
- hospitals
- medical schools
- Head Start program

- speech/language program
- early intervention program
- American Speech-Language-Hearing Association
- also see Social-emotional development resources on page 107

Hearing
Even a mild or temporary hearing loss in a child may interfere with speech, language, or social and academic progress. If more than one of these red flag behaviors is observed, it is likely that a problem exists.

Red flags
- speech and language. Look for the child
  —whose speech is not easily understood by people outside the family
  —whose grammar is less accurate than other children of the same age
  —who does not use speech as much as other children of the same age
  —who has unusual voice (hoarseness, stuffy quality, lack of inflection, or voice that is usually too loud or soft)
- social behavior (at home and in school). Look for the child who
  —is shy or hesitant in answering questions or joining in conversation
  —misunderstands questions or directions; frequently says "huh?" or "what?" in response to questions
  —appears to ignore speech; hears "only what he wants to"
  —is unusually attentive to speaker's face or unusually inattentive to speaker, turns one ear to speaker
  —has difficulty with listening activities such as storytime and following directions
  —has short attention span
  —is distractible and restless; tends to shift quickly from one activity to another
  —is generally lethargic or disinterested in most day-to-day activities
  —is considered a behavior problem—too active or aggressive, or too quiet and withdrawn

Figure 9.4 *continued*

Hearing *continued*
- medical indications. Look for the child who
  —has frequent or constant upper respiratory tract infections, congestion that appears related to allergies, or a cold for several weeks or months
  —has frequent earaches, ear infections, throat infections, or middle ear problems
  —has had draining ears on one or more occasions
  —is mouth breather and snorer
  —is generally lethargic; has poor color

How to screen
1. Use pure tone audiometry tests for hearing, age 3 and older.
2. Use tympanometry for middle ear function, all ages.
3. Note history (behavioral and medical).

Community resources
- child's health care provider
- communication disorders or audiology department at college or university
- hearing or speech and hearing clinic
- school system
- audiologist
- ear, nose, throat specialist (otorhinolaryngologist)

Vision
including
- skills
- acuity (ability to see at a given distance)
- disease

Red flags
- eyes
  —are watery
  —have discharge
  —lack coordination in directing gaze of both eyes
  —are red
  —are sensitive to light
- eyelids
  —have crusts on lids or among lashes
  —are red
  —have recurring sties or swelling
- behavior and complaints
  —rubs eyes excessively
  —dizziness, headaches, nausea on close work
  —attempts to brush away blur
  —itchy, burning, scratchy eyes
  —contorts face or body when looking at distant objects, or thrusts head forward; squints or widens eyes
  —blinks eyes excessively; holds book too close or too far; inattentive during visual tasks
  —shuts or covers one eye; tilts head
  —eyes appear to cross or wander, especially when tired

How to screen
1. Note child's medical history. Has child had an eye exam? If not, recommend one.
2. Screen using a screening tool appropriate for young children such as the Snellen E chart or Broken Wheel cards.

Community resources
- for screening—contact service organizations such as women's club, Lions club
- to be trained to screen—contact Society for Prevention of Blindness or your department of public health. Your health consultant may be able to help.
- for eye examination—refer to an ophthalmologist or optometrist
- for Self-Instructional Preschool Vision Screening Package—contact Preschool Enrichment Team, Inc., 276 High Street, Holyoke, MA 01040

Adapted from material by Preschool Enrichment Team, Inc., 276 High Street, Holyoke, MA 01040.

range of time. Given the child's basic body structure, growth should follow a predictable pattern. The child should be able to accomplish certain tasks by a certain age. An abnormal screening test result is a clue that something is wrong, that a further look is needed. Abnormal screening results should be interpreted by the child's usual source of health care so appropriate further evaluation can be planned. Premature referral to a specialist in one area may neglect the possibility that the abnormality is part of a multisystem problem.

To be valuable, a screening program must include
- parent education about the screening
- parent involvement and consent
- use of a valid, reliable tool appropriate for the age
- practice by the screener
- screening and rescreening all children who may have a problem before making referrals
- written information provided to the parents when further examination is suggested
- parental choice of the health professional to follow up
- information received from the health professional about examination results

See page 98 for the recommended schedule of screening tests.

Vision screening

Developmental vision problems may be most effectively corrected during the preschool years. This is especially true in the areas of vision acuity (the ability of each eye to distinguish detail both near and far) and vision skills (the ability to use both eyes efficiently and effectively as a coordinated team).

All 3- and 4-year-old children should have a full eye examination that includes evaluation of general eye health, near and far vision acuity, and several types of vision skills. This type of screening can be performed in a pediatrician's or family practitioner's office or by a vision specialist. Some vision problems can interfere with a child's coordination and developmental skills. Every child should participate in a basic vision screening program. Many people believe that preschool children are too young to be tested. In fact, most **can** cooperate with a vision screening program. Two types

of effective and efficient vision screening can be done by program staff.

Informal screening is done by observing the child at play. The persistent symptoms listed in Figure 9.4 may indicate the need for a thorough eye exam.

Formal screening is done with an age-appropriate, standardized screening tool designed to identify some of the most common problems found in young children. Other problems may only be found through further testing.

The Snellen E (Tumbling E) and the Broken Wheel tests are recommended formal screening tools for 3- to 5-year-old children. See page 288 in Appendix 1 for ordering information. Various picture identification tests are generally considered less accurate. If you are interested in doing vision screening, it is important that you receive training; talk first with your health consultant.

Any screening program is valuable only if follow-up occurs. Parents should choose specialists who have training and experience with young children and who seem to enjoy working with this age child.

We know that visual development corresponds to other developmental patterns. We also know that young children are visually more skilled than previously understood. For screening purposes, 3-year-olds are expected to pass at 20/40; 4-, 5-, and 6-year-olds should pass at 20/30; and 7-year-olds at 20/20. These norms are for screening purposes only.

Do not assume that children will outgrow vision problems. Some problems get worse. Early detection permits early treatment that will correct the problem more completely and that is less expensive than later treatment.

Any child who cannot perform well on basic vision screening by age 4 should be referred to a vision specialist.

Hearing screening

A child who does not hear clearly will have trouble imitating sounds and developing language. Behavior can also be affected. Learning to read and to write will be difficult. Finally, permanent hearing loss may occur. Hearing problems may be hereditary or the result of certain illnesses during pregnancy or early childhood. Temporary or intermittent hearing loss may be caused by chronic ear infection, a heavy buildup of wax in the ear, or chronic fluid in the middle ear.

Hearing loss may be readily observed when the loss is fairly severe. There are signs that can alert adults to milder loss also. An infant who does not hear well will not startle at a sudden noise, will not search with the eyes for the source of a noise, will not respond to a musical toy or a parent's voice unless the parent is seen, and will be slow to imitate sounds and respond to simple commands or the sound of her or his name. Older children with hearing problems may have smaller vocabularies, use shorter sentences, have an unusual voice, and seem to understand less than other children the same age.

Hearing screening for infants can be easily performed around 6 months of age using a set of toys that make noise at specific frequency. The test always involves making the noise out of sight (about 3' away) from the child to see if the child turns to the direction from which the noise came. This is the Downs Hearing Screen (after Marion Downs who developed the procedure). Some health professionals use this test routinely. Others rely on reports about how the child responds to sound from parents.

The **pure tone audiometry** is the typical hearing test and checks a child's ability to hear quiet sounds at four different pitches or frequencies. It can be done on 3- and 4-year-olds with ease and can be used with some 2-year-olds. The test requires putting a toy in a box or raising the hand when a sound is heard through the earphones.

The following two tests may be appropriate primarily for selected high-risk children. **Tympanometry** measures the pressure required to move the eardrum (middle ear) and the way the eardrum moves. If fluid is present in the middle ear, it may cause negative pressure and decrease the eardrum's ability to move. Fluid in the middle ear can affect the child's ability to distinguish sounds clearly. This test can be done on children age 3 and older.

Acoustic reflex screening measures the control of a muscle in the middle ear in response to a loud sound. If the contraction (reflex) is absent, there may be fluid in the ear or incomplete healing from a recent infection. This test can be done on very young children.

Because children are more comfortable and secure in familiar surroundings with familiar adults, screening may be more successful if you bring the screeners to your program. Prepare the children for what to expect, and follow through on referrals. Be sure to notify the child's usual source of health care about any screening results to avoid duplication and to promote coordination of screening results with the rest of the child's health data.

Measuring height and weight

Height and weight should be measured regularly and recorded on a chart that permits comparison with normal growth patterns. These measurements are one of the best ways to detect physical growth patterns that may indicate a serious problem. Head circumference (measurement around the head) should also be measured for children from birth to 12 months of age.

Growth measurements will usually be done by the child's health care provider. Growth measurements should be graphed over time to show the pattern of the child's growth compared with other children the same age and the relationship of length/height and head circumference to weight. Figure 9.5 provides sample graphs of growth measurements patterns. Children whose length/height growth percentile differs by more than 1 percentile curve from their weight/growth percentile, or whose growth data are below the 5th percentile curve, need further evaluation. You should receive this information with the child's physical examination report. In some cases, you may also want to measure the children's height and weight as part of the health curriculum. These measurements integrate learning about mathematics, science, self, and health.

Anemia screening

Hematocrit or hemoglobin are commonly used to screen children for the presence of anemia once during each period of childhood (see Figure 9.1 on page 98). Anemia is the condition that results when the body does not have enough circulating red blood cells to carry oxygen from the lungs to the tissues and/or not enough iron to make hemoglobin (the chemical that carries oxygen to the red blood cells).

Figure 9.5. Physical growth NCHS percentiles* (girls: birth to 36 months)

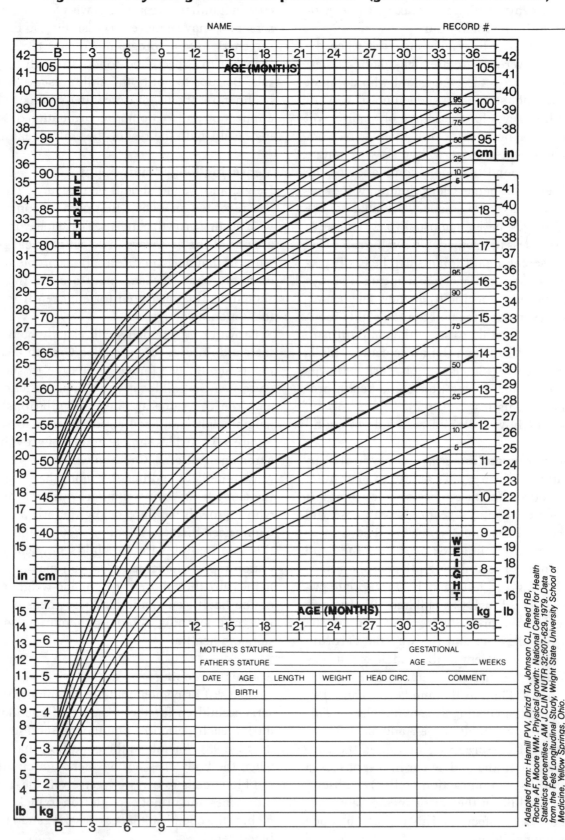

Used with permission of Ross Products Division, Abbott Laboratories, Columbus, OH 43216. From NCHS Growth Charts, © 1982 Ross Products Division, Abbott Laboratories.

Figure 9.5. Physical growth NCHS percentiles* (boys: birth to 36 months)

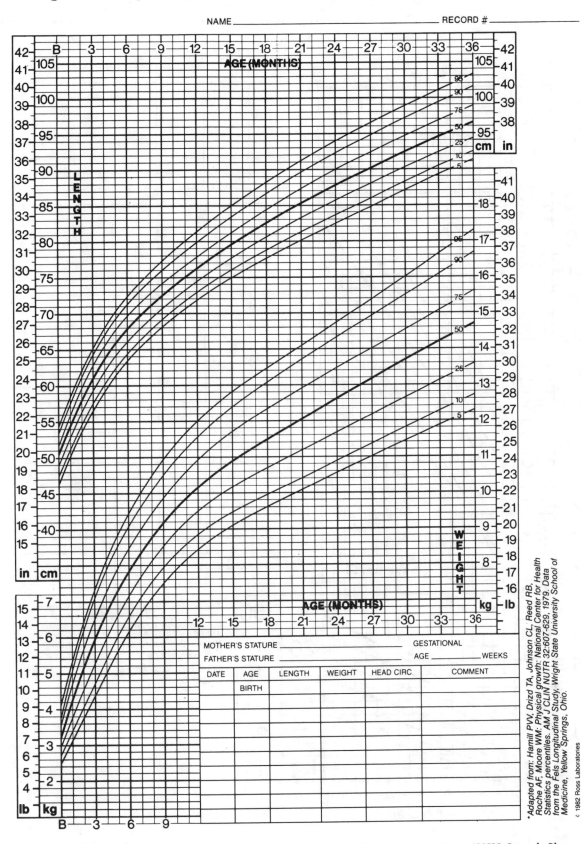

Used with permission of Ross Products Division, Abbott Laboratories, Columbus, OH 43216. From NCHS Growth Charts, © 1982 Ross Products Division, Abbott Laboratories.

Figure 9.5. Physical growth NCHS percentiles* (girls: 2 to 5 years)

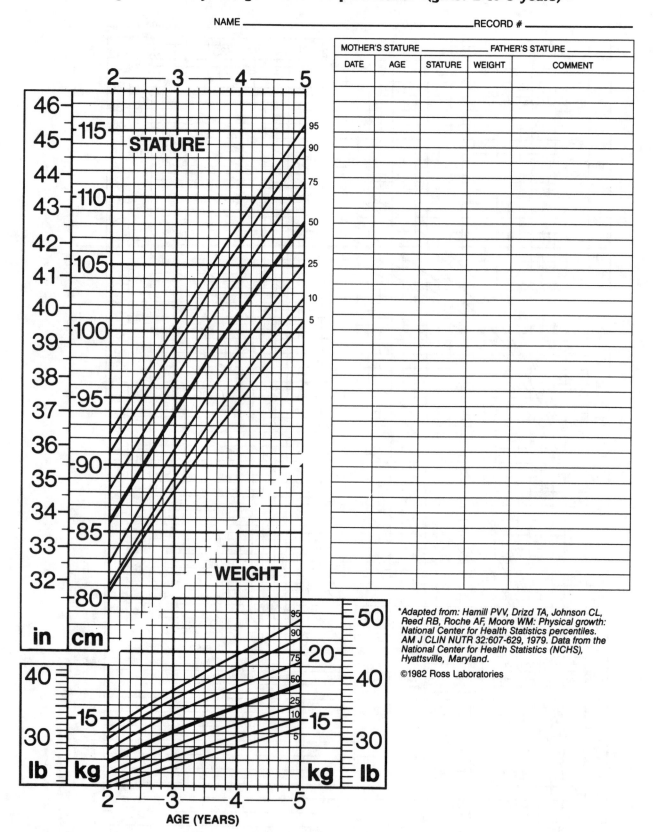

Figure 9.5. Physical growth NCHS percentiles* (boys: 2 to 5 years)

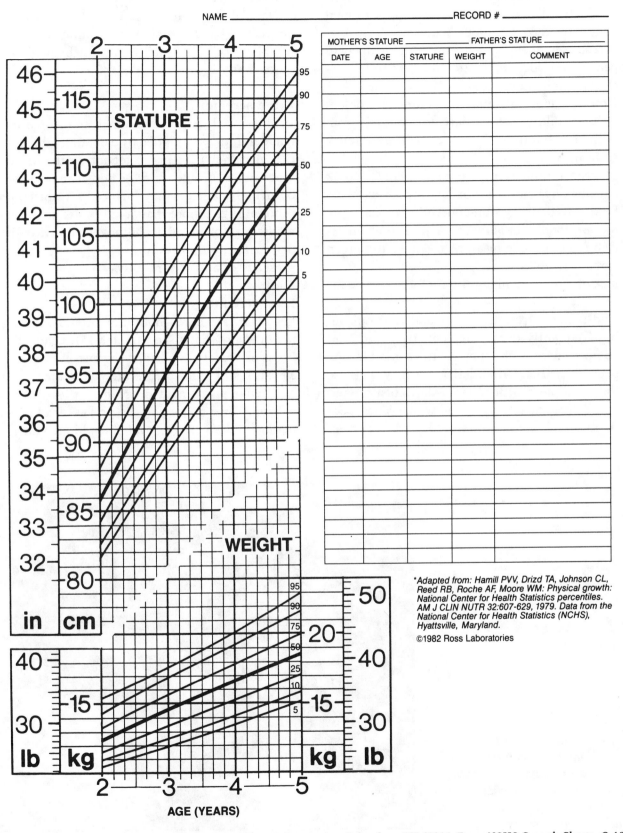

*Adapted from: Hamill PVV, Drizd TA, Johnson CL, Reed RB, Roche AF, Moore WM: Physical growth: National Center for Health Statistics percentiles. AM J CLIN NUTR 32:607-629, 1979. Data from the National Center for Health Statistics (NCHS), Hyattsville, Maryland.

©1982 Ross Laboratories

Iron is needed to form hemoglobin, the substance in blood that carries oxygen from the lungs to the body cells. Without enough iron, our blood cannot carry the oxygen our bodies need. Lack of iron results in anemia. An anemic child is likely to appear tired, pale, and inattentive, and to be susceptible to infection.

Iron deficiency anemia is a common problem for young children, particularly for children from low-income families. Causes of iron deficiency anemia include

- overconsumption of milk (more than 24 to 32 oz. per day) resulting in low intake of other foods, particularly iron-containing foods
- too few foods containing iron in the diet. (Iron-rich foods include meat, fish, beans, and green leafy vegetables.)
- lack of high-iron, high-nutrient foods served for snacks
- lead toxicity. Iron deficiency and lead poisoning frequently occur together. Iron and lead compete with each other for the same binding sites in the body. Iron deficiency may increase the absorption of lead from the intestine and make the toxic effects of lead worse. Therapeutic doses of iron are often required to correct

the iron deficiency when accompanied by lead poisoning.

Normal values for hematocrits in children are above 35% (of the total blood volume occupied by red blood cells); normal values for hemoglobin is more than 11 grams.

Urine screening

Urine is produced by the kidney and stored in the bladder until it is emptied by urinating. Abnormalities in kidney function, infection in the urine, or biochemical problems in the body can be detected by urinalysis. Normally, urine does not contain protein, sugar, more than a few white or red cells, nitrites, ketones, or urobilinogen. Pretreated paper strips are dipped into urine to determine the presence of any abnormality.

Lead screening

Lead is everywhere—both in nature and in manufactured products (see Chapter 15). Lead screening is extremely important because even very low elevations of lead, before any symptoms appear, can cause permanent problems in learning and behavior. Two major ways to prevent lead poisoning in children are removal of lead in the environ-

Each child's development is affected by personality, temperament, family structure and dynamics, culture, experiences, physical characteristics, and the match of child and family to your program.

ment and lead screening. The current tests for lead recommended by the AAP and CDC are a finger-stick or venous (usually taken from the vein at the inside of the elbow) blood test to most accurately detect elevated lead levels. Ideally, blood level screening should be a part of routine health care for children. Both the AAP and CDC recommend that risk for possible lead exposure be assessed at children's health visits between the ages of 6 months and 6 years. Health providers may use a set of questions with parents to help identify those at risk of high exposure to lead. Children at risk are those identified as living in or frequently visiting a house built before 1960 with peeling or chipping paint **or** undergoing recent or planned remodeling/renovation; having a sibling, housemate, or playmate being treated for lead poisoning; living with an adult whose job or hobby involves exposure to lead; or living in an area where lead poisoning is common. Such children should be screened more frequently than other children for blood lead levels. At least one screening test for lead is recommended for all children who are between 9 to 12 months of age, with a second test if possible again at 24 months of age. This screening recommendation is controversial and may be modified in areas where community-wide screening has found no lead problems.

Medical examinations

A medical examination is a comprehensive review by a physician or nurse practitioner of all the health information gathered from the health history, health observations, and screening tests. The examination includes an interview with the parent or guardian to get current health information and a record of immunizations, a complete physical examination, and laboratory and screening tests as necessary (e.g., blood or urine). A dentist or eye specialist may also be involved. Medical examinations should be done frequently during the first 3 years of life and yearly after age 3. The results of medical examinations should be reported in detail on the child's health assessment form (Figure 9.6). At a minimum, the form should include

- a description of any health condition that may affect the child's participation in child care
- a history of significant illness and/or hospitalizations
- the record of immunizations received with exact date of each
- reports of any screening or assessment
- any significant observations of the parents' or siblings' health
- notations about physical, mental, and social development

A complete and detailed health assessment form should give you an accurate picture of the child's unique development and health status. It should help you have realistic expectations and to plan appropriate activities. If the form is incomplete, the director or health consultant should help the parent contact the health provider for additional information. If any of the information is unclear, you should ask questions. Your program's health policies should require that these forms (based on an examination dated according to the AAP guidelines for routine health care) be on file prior to the child's first day of attendance. The forms should be updated each year for children older than 3 years of age and at least every 6 months for younger children. Health information should be considered confidential and should not be disclosed without written consent of the parent(s) or guardian.

Figure 9.6. Child health assessment

CHILD'S NAME _____   PARENT/GUARDIAN _____

DOB _____ HOME PHONE _____   ADDRESS _____

CHILD CARE FACILITY/SCHOOL _____   _____

CHILD CARE FACILITY/SCHOOL PHONE _____   WORK PHONE _____

I give my consent for my child's Physician and Child Care Provider to discuss my child's health concerns

_____
SIGNATURE   DATE

Note: A copy of the EPSDT exam report attached to a copy of the child's immunization record may be substituted for this form.

HEALTH HISTORY AND MEDICAL INFORMATION PERTINENT TO ROUTINE CHILD CARE AND EMERGENCIES:

DATE OF EXAM _____

ALLERGIES TO FOOD OR MEDICINE:

LENGTH/HEIGHT _____ IN/CM %ILE _____	WEIGHT _____ LB/KG %ILE _____	HEAD CIRCUMFERENCE _____ IN/CM %ILE _____	BLOOD PRESSURE _____/_____

PHYSICAL EXAMINATION	NORMAL	ABNORMAL/COMMENTS
HEAD/EARS/EYES/NOSE/THROAT		
TEETH		
CARDIORESPIRATORY		
ABDOMEN/GI		
GENITALIA/BREAST		
EXTREMITIES/JOINTS/BACK/CHEST		
SKIN/LYMPH NODES		
NEUROLOGIC/TONE		
DEVELOPMENTAL (E.G. DDST)		

VACCINE	BIRTH TO 1 MO	2 MO	4 MO	6 MO	12–15 MO	18 MO	4–6 YRS	11–12 YRS	14–16 YRS
HEP B	X								
HEP B		X		X					
DTP/Td		X	X	X	X		X	X	
POLIO		X	X	X			X		
HIB		X	X	X	X				
MMR					X		X		
VARICELLA					X				
OTHER									

X = 1 dose   *Note: Ages and number of boosters may vary when immunizations start at older ages.*

SCREENING TESTS	DATE	NORMAL	ABNORMAL/COMMENTS
LEAD			
ANEMIA (HGB/HCT)			
URINALYSIS (UA)			
TUBERCULOSIS (TB)			
HEARING			
VISION			

DATE OF LAST DENTIST'S EXAMINATION _____

Note: Age appropriate health services and immunizations must follow the schedule recommended by The American Academy of Pediatrics, 141 Northwest Point Blvd, Elk Grove Village, IL 60007

HEALTH PROBLEMS OR SPECIAL NEEDS   **RECOMMENDED TREATMENT/MEDICATIONS/SPECIAL CARE** *(Attach additional sheets if necessary)*

MEDICAL CARE PROVIDER   NEXT APPOINTMENT: MONTH _____ YEAR _____

ADDRESS   MD
                                                                                    DO
PHONE   DATE   SIGNATURE OF PHYSICIAN OR CRNP   CRNP

This form corresponds to the recommendations as of 5/95. Check with your Health Department for changes annually.

Reprinted from *Model Child Care Health Policies* with permission of the PA Chapter of the American Academy of Pediatrics.

10
Adult health

Staff are the key ingredient in a good program for young children. They are very concerned about the potential health hazards of their work. Hazards include an increased risk of getting illnesses; presence of toxic substances in art supplies, cleaning agents, and pesticides; back problems due to frequent heavy lifting and furniture and an environment designed for children; poor lighting; high noise levels; clutter; and stress.

Another major health hazard is caused by the tendency of staff to ignore their own health needs because they lack health benefits and time off and because they feel responsible for meeting children's needs first. Programs can alleviate some of these concerns by establishing an adult health plan; by creating a positive, healthful environment; by assisting adults to look after their own health needs; and by providing adequate benefits packages.

Ways to promote good health

Staff must care for themselves to be able to provide the best care for children. To help the staff in **your** program, take the time to look at your environment and program demands. How can you make yourselves more comfortable? What policies need to be revised to meet adult needs? Are you encouraging good health? Can sick adults stay home without guilt and loss of pay?

With staff and administration working together, it is possible to adjust a facility and program to the needs of the adults and the children. Here are examples of simple solutions to adult health problems:

- Require initial and ongoing health assessments to identify individual susceptibility to the known occupational risks of early childhood programs—infectious diseases, back injuries, rashes, stress, environmental exposures, etc.

- Negotiate benefits packages to meet staff needs, including paid leave (annual, sick, and/or personal), medical insurance, and other options.
- Provide a high counter with stools, or an adult-size table and chairs, for staff who do clerical, administrative, or curriculum planning work. Bring in adult-size folding chairs for staff meetings. Place a telephone book on a child-size chair to make it a much more comfortable seat.
- Set aside private adult space and provide adequate backup to ensure **genuine** breaks to alleviate stress.
- Train staff in proper techniques for lifting and bending to prevent leg and back strains (Figure 10.1).
- Provide gloves to use with cleaning agents to help prevent skin irritation.
- Establish preventive health policies that can reduce exposure to childhood illnesses, and practice preventive health procedures to help keep adults and children healthy.
- Include break and substitute plans in personnel policies.

Your adult health plan

Health examinations

The foundation for an adult health plan is the requirement that all adults (staff and volunteers) who work or wish to work in your program have periodic health exams. The results of such exams must be strictly confidential and can be given to the employer only with the staff member's permission. Your adult health plan must specify the following for each type of examination:
- content of the exam
- who can perform the exam

Figure 10.1. Suggestions on how to protect your back

Posture

Having a firm, flattened abdomen and holding your stomach in when you stand and sit provide needed support for the lower spine.

Sitting

When you sit, it's important to maintain a normal spine curve. A sitting position produces greater loads on the lower back than either standing or walking. Select a chair with a firm seat and adequate lower back support. Keeping your knees bent and resting your back against the chair will prevent back strain. Don't sit too long. Get up, stretch, and walk around occasionally.

Driving

When driving a car, move the seat forward to keep the knees higher than the hips. Often, a small pillow or towel rolled behind the lower back will provide extra support.

Standing

Standing can be hard on your back. Try not to work for long periods in a bent-over position. Muscles and good posture help to keep your spine in the balanced, neutral position. Abdominal muscles pull up in front and buttock muscles pull down in back to maintain the natural curve of the spine. This allows you to hold a balanced standing posture for long periods without tiring. Another technique is to stand with one foot elevated to a comfortable level. Switch feet every so often.

Sleeping

Sleeping rests the back. When you are lying down, your back doesn't have to support your body weight. It is important to use a firm mattress. Sleep on your side with knees bent or on your back with knees elevated.

Lifting techniques

Everyone has a lifting technique that seems most comfortable. But there are basic rules that apply to all. These rules will help control and prevent back pain.

- Step up close to your work area or to a load. Don't overreach to grasp or lift.
- Get a firm footing. Keep your feet parted; one alongside, one behind the object.
- Grip the object with the whole hand. Get a firm grip with the palms of your hands because the palms are stronger than the fingers alone.
- Draw the object close to you, with arms and elbows tucked into the sides of your body to keep your body weight centered.
- Bend knees, lift with your legs—let your powerful leg muscles do the work of lifting, not your weaker back muscles.
- Avoid lifting about the waist, but, if you must, reposition your grip to keep the weight centered. Arching your back during a lift makes nerve roots susceptible to pinching and can cause weak muscles to be strained.

Twisting during a lift is a common cause of back injury. If you have to turn with a load, change the position of your feet. By simply turning the forward foot out and pointing it in the direction you intend to move, the greatest danger of injury by twisting is avoided.

Proper maintenance and preventive care are the keys to a healthy back. Continue to learn how your back works and what you can do to keep it strong and flexible.

- how often it must occur
- special examinations for special roles, if any
- who receives the findings
- where the examinations can be performed
- who pays for the exam

For examinations to be effective, the health professional conducting the exam must know the nature and demands of the adult's job. For instance, a chronic lower back problem may not interfere with the job performance of a social worker but surely would affect the teacher of a toddler group.

Pre-employment exams. Ideally, the results of a health exam should be received before **a job offer is made final and before contact with the children begins.** It is hard to deal with health concerns after an individual has begun to develop relationships, and an exam that follows employment may reveal health problems to which other staff and the children have already been exposed. Information about health problems should be used to accommodate a qualified child care worker, not to discriminate against someone with a disability.

Pre-employment exams should be concerned with the prospective employee's

- physical and emotional fitness for the job
- freedom from contagious diseases including tuberculosis (TB) screening by the Mantoux method. (The Mantoux method is a test performed with a syringe and needle, *not* the multipuncture test.)
- immunization status and history of childhood infectious diseases including measles, mumps, rubella, diphtheria, tetanus, polio, and chicken pox
- assessment of need for immunizations against influenza, pneumococcus, and hepatitis B; and, if of childbearing age or planning pregnancy, from risk of exposure to chicken pox, cytomegalovirus (CMV), and parvovirus (Fifth Disease)
- condition(s) that might require emergency care
- limitation(s) in common situations such as difficulty being outdoors, skin conditions affected by frequent handwashing, allergy to art materials
- medication or special diet requirements that might affect job performance
- household members and their status regarding infectious diseases (for family child care or group home care)
- vision and hearing acuity

Pre-employment exams for bus drivers must include special tests, such as visual fields, color and depth perceptions, and an electrocardiogram (EKG).

Make sure that your pre-employment exams test for poorly controlled health conditions that might affect the safety of the children (a poorly controlled seizure disorder or obvious lack of stamina, for example). If these conditions are identified after a person has been hired, you may wish to make adjustments to allow the person to continue working by providing a change to part-time work, a change in role, or a temporary leave of absence.

Other periodic health exams. When you develop your adult health plan, specify which of these additional exams are required:

- periodic screening tests for TB by the Mantoux method every 2 years for all staff (or as recommended by local health department)
- prior to completion of a probationary period or if health concerns have been raised
- after a severe or prolonged illness, to help identify continued disabilities, necessary modifications, and expected transition time to resume a full work role
- upon return from a job-related injury, when a written release protects the program from liability for allowing the adult back on the job
- whenever a health condition seems to be affecting job performance, regardless of when the last assessment was done
- when a promotion or reassignment to another role could be affected by the adult's health status
- whenever there are liability issues such as adults with a history of back injuries, more than one heart attack, mental illness, or stress-related conditions
- after certain infectious diseases to ensure the adult is no longer contagious

For an example of a staff health appraisal form, see Figure 10.2 on page 124.

Infectious diseases

Infectious diseases are common in groups of young children, but most are not serious and would probably spread at a similar rate from children to adults

Figure 10.2. Child care staff health assessment

******** **Employer should complete this section.** ********

Name of person to be examined: _____

Employer for whom examination is being done: _____

Employer's Location: _____ Phone number: _____

Purpose of examination: ☐ pre-employment (with conditional offer of employment)　☐ annual re-examination

Type of activity on the job: ☐ lifting, carrying children　☐ close contact with children　☐ food preparation
☐ desk work　☐ driver of vehicles　☐ facility maintenance

******** **Part I and Part II below must be completed and signed by a licensed physician or CRNP.** ********
Based on a review of the medical record, health history, and examination, does this person
have any of the following conditions or problems that might affect job performance?

Date of exam: _____

Part I: Health Problems
(circle)

visual acuity less than 20/40 (combined, obtained with lenses if needed)? ....yes ....no

decreased hearing (less than 20 db at 500, 1000, 2000, 4000 Hz)?...yes ....no

respiratory problems (asthma, emphysema, airway allergies, current smoker, other)? ....yes ....no

heart, blood pressure, or other cardiovascular problems?..yes ....no

gastrointestinal problems (ulcer, colitis, special dietary requirements, obesity, other)?.................................yes ....no

endocrine problems (diabetes, thyroid, other)?...yes ....no

emotional disorders or addiction (depression, drug or alcohol dependency, other)?.....................................yes ....no

neurologic problems (epilepsy, Parkinsonism, other)?...yes ....no

musculoskeletal problems (low back pain, neck problems, arthritis, limitations on activity).......................yes ....no

skin problems (eczema, rashes, conditions incompatible with frequent hand washing, other)? ....yes ....no

immune system problems (from medication, illness, allergies and sensitivities to materials)?.......................yes ....no

need for more frequent health visits or sick days than the average person? ....yes ....no

other special medical problem or chronic disease that requires work restrictions or accommodation?.........yes ....no

Part II: Infectious Disease Status
Immunizations now due/overdue for:

　dT (every 10 years)...yes ....no

　MMR (2 doses for persons born after 1989; 1 dose for those born in or after 1957) ....yes ....no

　polio (OPV in childhood or IPV every 4 years) ....yes ....no

　hepatitis B (3 dose series)..yes ....no

　varicella (2 doses or had the disease)..yes ....no

　influenza...yes ....no

　pneumococcal vaccine...yes ....no

Female of childbearing age susceptible to CMV or parvovirus? ....yes ....no

Evaluation of tuberculosis status shows a risk for communicable TB? ....yes ....no

Mantoux test date_____　Result_____

(Tuberculosis status must be determined by performing the Mantoux test (intradermal, intermediate strength PPD injection with needle and syringe) for persons not previously tested positive for tuberculosis infection. For individuals over 55 years of age, and anyone with pulmonary symptoms, the Mantoux test should be performed twice if the first test is negative. The second test should be performed 1-3 weeks after the first test. Anyone with a previously positive Mantoux test who has symptoms suggestive of active TB should have a chest x-ray. All newly positive Mantoux tests should be followed by x-ray evaluation.)

Please attach additional sheets to explain all "yes" answers above. Include the plan for follow up.

MD
DO
CRNP

_____　_____　_____
(Date)　(Signature)　(Printed last name)　(Title)

Phone number of physician or CRNP: _____

I have read and understand the above information.

_____　_____
(Date)　(Patient's Signature)

This form corresponds to the recommendations as of 5/95. Check with your Health Department for changes annually.

Reprinted from *Model Child Care Health Policies* with permission of the PA Chapter of the American Academy of Pediatrics.

in a large family. However, because staff care for a number of young children, many of whom cannot control their body fluids and have not yet learned principles of hygiene, there is the potential for spread of infections to other employees, children, family members, and in the case of a pregnant employee or parent, to the fetus. Therefore, it is important that the employee be familiar with common infections and the measures to take to prevent them. **Details on these infections and ways to reduce their spread are contained in Chapter 17.**

Preventing infection. Two important barriers that help prevent the spread of infection are immunization and hygiene.

- Immunization—Safe, effective vaccines against many serious diseases including measles, mumps, rubella, diphtheria, tetanus, polio, and varicella (chicken pox) are available. Immunity against these diseases is strongly recommended for all staff (paid and volunteer); some states require staff to be immune. Vaccine for influenza virus (given yearly) may be advisable. Older adults may need pneumococcal vaccine. For employees whose job duties could reasonably be expected to expose them to contact with blood or other potentially infectious materials, the Occupational Safety and Health Administration (OSHA) regulations require that hepatitis B vaccine be offered by the employer.
- Handwashing—Careful handwashing after contact with potentially infectious body fluids along with proper handling of contaminated items is **the most effective measure to prevent most spread of infectious diseases. All blood and other body fluids from all children should be handled as potentially infectious.** (See Chapter 4, Figure 4.2.)

Special safeguards for pregnant women. Women of childbearing age should be aware that they can be exposed in child care to infectious diseases that can cause significant health problems for fetuses. These infections include rubella, measles, mumps, varicella (chicken pox), hepatitis B, cytomegalovirus, herpes, parvovirus, and HIV infection. Contact your health care provider for current information.

The first five diseases can be prevented by immunization. Routine immunization (or other proof of immunity) is strongly recommended for the first four diseases: measles, mumps, rubella, and chicken pox. Workers should be offered hepatitis B vaccine within 10 days of starting a job which could expose that employee to blood or body fluids that contain blood, i.e., giving first aid or cleaning up blood spills. Strict attention to handwashing and care with all children's blood and body fluids are the most effective safeguards for women susceptible to those infections for which there are no vaccines. Women who are or plan to become pregnant should discuss their susceptibility and occupational exposure with their obstetricians.

When not to come to work

It is expected that children will catch colds and flu. Adults working daily with young children are also likely to become ill. Yet, because of the difficulty of arranging for and keeping dependable substitutes, many programs have inadequate substitute policies. The result is that many keep staff working when they are ill, convincing themselves that they really are not that sick. **Upgrading substitute coverage is critical to a well-run program even though creating a reliable substitute policy is a difficult task.** The best illness guideline to follow is this:

Ask adults who cannot comfortably and capably perform their daily activities to remain at home. Personnel policies should be written to allow and encourage adults to stay at home when they feel too sick to work.

Staff will often come to work when they are sick because of fear of lost pay or feelings of guilt due to inadequate substitute coverage. All staff must make a choice that balances their personal concerns and those of the program. Clearly, adults with serious illness such as meningitis or chicken pox should not be at work in a program for young children. Adults with other contagious diseases (e.g., strep throat, lice, impetigo) may return after treatment is begun (see Chapter 17). Adults with diarrhea should not work until well or until a physician has determined the diarrhea is not infectious.

Substitutes and breaks

Follow these suggestions for substitute and break policies.

Substitutes

- Consider joining with other programs to hire a sub who rotates. This allows each program some guaranteed coverage and provides dependable employment for the sub. If nobody is absent on the scheduled day, the sub can supervise while regular staff attend parent conferences, planning sessions, or a similar type of meeting.
- Set a decent salary for substitutes.
- Regularly evaluate your substitute policy. Keep the sub list active; call subs periodically to make sure they are still available.
- Let parents know about the substitute procedure.

Breaks. Because of the cost of hiring additional staff, most programs must work with remaining personnel during staff breaks. When staff cover more than one group of children on the same day, they must pay extra attention to handwashing routines to avoid carrying germs from one group to another. Use these suggestions to cope with limited staff:

- Nonteaching staff can cover breaks on different days of the week.
- Assign parents, students, and community members as floaters. The key to making this plan work is regular scheduling and dependable volunteers! Be sure volunteers receive a thorough orientation to their duties and have the same monitoring skills and health as regular staff.
- In a well-staffed program, designate one member as a floater during break time for a week at a time. This person can become familiar with each of the classrooms and also gain perspective on the program.
- Overlap staff shifts. Perhaps afternoon shifts can begin during the last half hour of the morning shift. Although this model is more expensive, it covers breaks and also allows teachers time to communicate.
- Provide a quiet, separate, and relaxing space for staff. Even if space is limited, a comfortable chair placed in front of a window can serve as a place to relax. If at all possible, the budget should pay for refreshments for the staff.

11
Dental health

The type of hygiene and dental care children receive, along with diet and heredity, will determine their dental health throughout life. Your program can help prevent dental disease by serving well-balanced, nutritious food and by limiting sugared and sticky foods. You can also promote dental health by providing fluoride tablets or drops, with parental permission, if the local water supply is not adequately fluoridated; by teaching children and staff about good dental care by having them all brush their teeth during the day; and by looking for dental problems.

Healthy foods for teeth

High-sugar foods are clearly linked to tooth decay. Avoid or limit sweet drinks, candy, jelly, jam, cake, cookies, sugared gelatin, and sweetened, canned fruit. Low-sugar, fresh fruit and vegetables make a great snack or dessert alternative.

Here are some important facts about sugar and teeth.

- Natural sugars (such as maple syrup and honey) are just as harmful to teeth as refined sugar.
- Sticky sweets (such as caramel) are particularly harmful because they remain on the teeth longer than other sweets.
- Eating a sweet all at once is better than eating one for a long time (such as a lollipop) or often (such as popping mints or hard candies every 20 minutes).
- Sweet, sticky fruits, such as raisins and dates, should be eaten with a meal.
- Frequent snacking is not a good idea because the teeth are attacked by the decay process each time food is put in the mouth.
- Never put a baby to bed with a bottle of milk, formula, sweetened liquids, or fruit juices. The sugars in all of these liquids stay on the teeth for a long time and cause serious decay called nursing bottle mouth.
- **Never reward good behavior with candy or other sweets.**

Please refer to Chapter 12, Nutrition in programs for young children, for more information.

Fluoride

Fluoridation of public water supplies is the single most effective method to prevent tooth decay. When children have fluoride in their drinking water, or fluoride supplements from birth, their tooth decay can be reduced about 50%! Find out if your community fluoridates its water. If not, consider using fluoride drops or tablets (with parents' permission). After 2 years, 25 to 35% of the children's decay could be reduced. Contact your state or local health department to locate resources for a preschool fluoride program. Fluoride toothpaste is also helpful as long as the child does not swallow it. Because swallowing fluoride toothpaste could result in mottled teeth, use of toothpaste should be delayed until about age 3.

Brushing teeth

Very young children can learn good habits that will last into adulthood. Brushing teeth after lunch and/or snacks has the double benefit of cleaning teeth **and** teaching a good habit. This routine, if it is organized well, will probably not take more than 5 minutes a day. Here are some points to remember:

- Each child must have her or his own toothbrush, labeled by name, that must **never** be shared.
- Toothbrushes must be stored so they stay clean and open to the air. The bristles should not touch any surface. One method is to use a Styrofoam

egg carton. Clean the carton with alcohol, turn it upside down, and punch a hole in the bottom of each egg compartment. Store the brushes bristle-side up so they do not touch each other.

- Most dentists and hygienists recommend a small toothbrush with soft, rounded, nylon bristles; a straight handle; an even brushing surface; and a head small enough to reach every tooth. When the bristles become bent, the brush doesn't clean well and should be replaced. Brushes should be replaced about every 3 months.

- For children over 3 years of age, and younger children who can rinse their mouth well, use a small amount (about the size of a pea) of toothpaste with fluoride and encourage children to spit it out. Use this toothpaste only for children who will not swallow it because swallowed toothpaste can cause irregular doses of fluoride

and mottling of teeth. To discourage children from eating toothpaste, do not use a highly flavored one.

- Have an adult supervise toothbrushing.

- Teach children proper brushing technique. Use the circular motion which is easy and effective. Follow these guidelines for proper brushing:
  —Direct the bristles at a 45° angle where the teeth and gums meet.
  —Brush the outside and inside surfaces of the teeth. Place the bristles of the toothbrush where the teeth and gums come together. Move the brush in a short, circular motion, back and forth, brushing the gums and the teeth.
  —Scrub back and forth on the chewing surfaces.
  —Follow a systematic routine to help ensure that all areas get brushed each time. Begin with the top teeth in the back on the right side. Brush the outside surface. Follow the arch around to the left side. Follow this same pattern for the inside surfaces. Brush the chewing surfaces on both sides. Brush the bottom teeth following the same routine.
  —Brush the tongue.

Dental health education

Children and parents must understand the importance of good dental health. Children can be taught effectively through an integration of dental education activities with their regular activities. Parent programs can be publicized through articles in your newsletter, parent handouts, posters, or films. Brochures that describe particular problems, conditions, or resources are frequently available from state or local health departments. Also, some dentists or hygienists are willing to come to the classroom. A field trip to a dentist who enjoys working with young children can be a wonderful introduction to regular dental care.

Dental care

Encourage parents to follow healthy dental routines and to get regular dental care. Your program might provide the names of children's dentists (pedodontists) or family dentists who work regularly with young children. Some area resources may include dental health clinics, dental school

Teach children proper brushing technique. Both children and parents must understand the importance of good dental health.

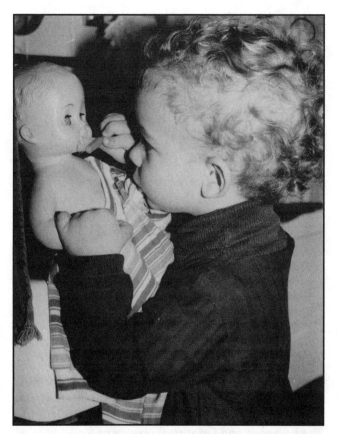

Try to make dental visits an important adventure. A good first trip will help mold children's feelings for many years.

clinics, community health centers, and, for emergencies, hospital emergency rooms.

A child's first visit to the dentist should be by 3 years of age, or when all 20 baby teeth are showing (see Figure 11.1). Since children usually need little treatment at this stage, the dentist can form a friendly and relaxed relationship with the child. The dentist can also look for early signs of future problems such as overcrowding or poor dental hygiene (cleanliness).

Try to make dental visits an important adventure. Tell children that the dentist is a friendly doctor who will help keep their teeth and mouth healthy. Talk about the visit in a positive, matter-of-fact way as you would any new experience. It is important to prevent fear. Avoid statements that suggest the visit may be unpleasant, such as, "It won't hurt." If you are fearful about dental visits, try not to let the children know. A good first trip will help mold children's feelings for many years.

Figure 11.1. Dental referral criteria

For most children younger than age 3, a visit to a dentist is purely an educational experience. However, there are cases when consultation with a dentist is recommended. Listed below are things to observe in young children. If you answer "no" to any of the questions, you should recommend that the child's parents consult a dentist.

Soft tissues (tongue, lips, cheeks, gums)
- Can the child stick the tongue tip completely out of the mouth?
- Can the child swallow with the teeth together (without the tongue pushing through)?
- Are the upper and lower lip the same size?
- Is there a clear distinction between lip and skin of face?
- Is the color inside the cheeks even throughout?
- Are all gum tissues the same color? Are gums free of pimples and/or swelling?

Hard tissues (teeth)

Number
- Does the child have at least 1 or 2 teeth by age 1? At least 12 by age 2?
- Are there the same number of teeth on either side of the middle of the jaw?
- Are teeth on either side the same shape?

Bite
- When the child closes the mouth, do the top teeth bite over the bottom teeth? Do the back teeth meet?
- Do all the teeth come in contact when the jaw is closed?
- Are the teeth spaced out, not crowded?

Color
- Are the teeth milky white? Are they all an even color?
- Do any stains and colors come off easily with a toothbrush?

Oral hygiene
- Are the teeth clean?
- Does the mouth have a clean, sweet odor?

You can help promote children's dental health by observing carefully. Suggest that the parent take the child to the dentist as soon as possible if any of these problems occurs.

- redness, swelling, or bleeding of the gums
- swelling of the face
- complaints of pain
- very dark or discolored teeth or holes in teeth
- complaints when the child eats hard, hot, cold, or sweet food
- broken teeth
- spaces from first teeth that fell out early
- constant bad breath

Special dental problems

Broken tooth
Contact the parent and request that the child be taken to the dentist immediately. If a broken tooth is not cared for, it can be lost.

Knocked out tooth
Contact the parent and dental provider immediately and **save the tooth!** Sometimes it can be replanted in the jaw. DO NOT clean the tooth. Simply put it in a wet cloth or a glass of water or milk. **Rush** the child and the tooth to the dentist (within 30 to 90 minutes if possible). The sooner the child sees the dentist, the better the chance of saving the tooth.

Toothache
Ask the parent to call the dentist at once. The dentist will find the cause of the toothache and will reduce the pain as quickly as possible. If emergency care is needed, there are temporary, emergency measures to use only when a child is in extreme pain. If a cavity can be seen in the tooth that aches, flush out any food particles with warm water. Oil of clove may be put directly into the aching tooth.

Acetaminophen can be swallowed for temporary relief of pain (use only with parental permission). Do not place acetaminophen directly onto the tooth. Arrange a dental appointment immediately.

Thumbsucking
Thumbsucking during the first several years should cause no concern. It gives the baby a feeling of pleasure and security. However, if the child continues thumbsucking beyond the age of 5, it can affect the position of the incoming permanent teeth and the shape of the jaws. The pressures of thumbsucking may push the teeth out and narrow the dental arches. Eventually orthodontic care may be needed. Work with the parents and their health care provider to help the child find a caring way to eliminate this habit.

Baby bottle tooth decay
Baby bottle tooth decay is a condition that can destroy the teeth. The teeth most likely to be damaged are the upper front teeth, but others may also be affected. Baby bottle tooth decay is caused by the frequent and lengthy exposure of a child's teeth to liquids containing sugars (milk, formula, fruit juice, and other sweetened liquids).

Using frequent bottles of these liquids as a pacifier is not a good idea. Allowing a child to fall asleep with a bottle during naps or at night can do serious harm to the child's teeth because the liquids pool around the teeth for long periods. If a child falls asleep with a bottle, remove it and use a wet washcloth, paper towel, or napkin to wipe the liquid from all tooth surfaces.

Bleeding around a tooth
Apply ice to the area as soon as possible and for as long as possible to minimize bleeding into the tooth and discoloration.

Section E
Nutrition

Major concepts

Guidelines for nutritious meals and snacks for children

- Provide a variety of foods each day. One food cannot supply all the nutrients a child needs.

- Establish regular times for meals and snacks.

- Offer portions appropriate to a child's age; discourage overeating.

- Offer nourishing snacks between meals to round out a well-balanced diet. Be aware that children often need more food than they are able to eat at a regular mealtime. Limit snacks that do not provide important nutrients.

- Encourage eating habits that are consistent with good dental health.

- Avoid serving foods with excess salt, fat, and sugar.

12
Nutrition in programs for young children

Good nutrition is an essential ingredient of quality child care. Tasty, colorful, nutritious foods and a pleasant, relaxed eating environment contribute to a child's sense of well-being. A child develops lifelong eating habits as a result of early eating experiences. As a child care provider, you need to know the nutritional requirements of children and how to provide a nutritious diet. Equally important is the atmosphere you create at meals and snacktime.

Feeding infants

During the first year of life, infants experience more changes in diet than at any other time in life. During this time, they grow rapidly and develop motor skills. They quickly progress from sucking liquids through a nipple to feeding themselves table foods (see Figure 12.1). Although feeding skills are developed in a systematic order, each child progresses through this sequence at her or his own pace. During this period, interaction with adults has a strong influence on the infant's development of self-feeding skills and acceptance of a variety of foods.

See Figure 12.2 for guidelines on feeding infants.

Breast milk is best

Breast milk is the recommended food for infants because it is uniquely suited to support their growth. Breast-fed infants should be given vitamin D and fluoride supplements. Bottle-fed infants should be given iron-fortified formula and possibly fluoride. Until about 4 to 6 months of age, infants are not physically ready to eat and digest any foods except breast milk or formula.

Your program can help promote breast-feeding and support nursing mothers by following some simple guidelines.

• Provide a quiet, private place with a comfort-

able chair where the mother can nurse before departure, on arrival, or during her work breaks.
• Try to establish a bottle-feeding schedule that ensures the baby is eager to nurse when the mother arrives (i.e., set the feeding time for at least 2½ hours before her arrival).
• Follow the guidelines for safe storage and handling of expressed breast milk (page 157).
• Be informed about the basics of breast-feeding and support the mother. With adequate rest, nutrition, and fluids, most mothers are able to maintain their breast milk supply when they bottle-feed part-time. A full supply of breast milk can be maintained, especially if the mother breast-feeds full-time while the baby is with her.

Introducing solid foods

Experts recommend starting solid food when infants are between 4 and 6 months old. Until this time, the infant's digestive tract is not able to completely break down the food; consequently, allergic reactions or sensitivities to solid food may be more likely. Also, the infant's neuromuscular skills needed for self-feeding and swallowing are not well developed. Therefore, it is best not to begin semi-solid foods (e.g., rice cereal) before 4 to 6 months. Cereals should not be mixed with milk or formula in the bottle unless a doctor recommends it. Between 6 and 8 months, add vegetables and fruits to the diet. At about 8 or 9 months, offer food in ¼" cubes or food with lumps (including table food the baby can easily chew, mash, or swallow whole). By the end of the first year, the baby should be eating most table foods.

Use the following guidelines to help you introduce solid foods:
• Allow time for the baby to get used to the feel and taste of solid foods.

Figure 12.1. Developmental sequence of feeding skills

Age (months)	Oral & neuromuscular development	Feeding skills implications	Special notes
Birth to 1	Rooting reflex	Turns mouth toward nipple or object that brushes cheek	Breast-fed babies need vitamin D and fluoride supplements. Formula-fed babies need no supplements except possibly fluoride.
2 to 4	Sucking reflex	Begins when lips are touched	
	Swallowing reflex	Initially involves only the back of the tongue. By 9 to 12 weeks, the front will begin to become involved.	
4 to 6	Extrusion reflex		Pushes out any food placed on front of tongue
	Sucking reflex becomes voluntary		
	Holds head erect		
	Mouth poises for nipple—anticipates food/bottle on sight		
	Extrusion reflex diminishes, giving way to chewing motion	Begin introduction of solid foods as infant's need for calories and certain nutrients increases that cannot be provided by breast milk or formula alone	Start with rice cereal. Prepare with 1 tablespoon formula or breast milk. Gradually increase consistency as baby gets used to it.
	Begins to reach mouth with hand		See Food component for infants (Figure 12.2)
	Grasps objects voluntarily		
		Uses tongue to move food in mouth Texture of food may be increased	
	Moves jaw and tongue laterally Sits with support		
6 to 8	Puts lips to rim of cup	Begin to offer beverages from a cup	Breast milk or formula is still the most important food in baby's diet
	Puts most objects into mouth	Encourage finger food	
	Grasps spoon, nipple, or cup rim	Holds own bottle well. Removes food quickly from spoon with lips.	

Figure 12.1 *continued*

Age (months)	Oral & neuromuscular development	Feeding skills implications	Special notes
6 to 8 *cont.*	Sits without support for brief periods Begins voluntary biting and early chewing	Increase texture to soft, mashed table foods	Offer strained, mashed, or bite-size pieces of cooked or soft, fresh or canned fruits and vegetables
8 to 10	Sits without support	Feeds self finger foods. Use soft table foods cut in small pieces.	Wheat products may be started. Begin meat and poultry (chopped or strained) and eggs.*
10 to 12	Chews up and down Closes lips around rim of cup Has neat pincer grasp Ceases drooling Tries to use spoon	Gradually increase texture; offer whole fruits and vegetables Drinks from cup or glass with help Offer finger foods in small pieces	May try small amounts of whole-grain cereals
12 to 18	Increased rotary motion of jaw Growth rate slows considerably Increases independence	Tries to use spoon. Give some thick foods that will stick to spoon. Can chew meats Appetite decreased, may refuse food. Provide small amounts. Uses spoon, may be upside down. Mostly feeds self Holds glass/cup with two hands to drink Discards bottle	Cheese or yogurt may replace some milk

*Note: Because egg whites may promote allergies, some recommend not introducing eggs before 11 months.

From *Guidelines for Feeding Infants and Young Children* by Nutrition Services of Vermont Department of Health, Burlington, VT, 1979; revised 1991, 1993. Adapted with permission.

Figure 12.2. Food components for infants

0-3 MONTHS	4-7 MONTHS	8-11 MONTHS
	MORNING	
4-6 fluid oz. breast milk or iron-fortified formula	4-8 fluid oz. breast milk or iron-fortified formula	6-8 fluid oz. breast milk, iron-fortified formula, or whole cow's milk
	0-3 tablespoons dry, iron-fortified infant cereal (optional before 6 months, but introduce by 6 months)	1-4 tablespoons fruit of appropriate consistency
		2-4 tablespoons dry, iron-fortified infant cereal
	MID-DAY	
4-6 fluid oz. breast milk or iron-fortified formula	4-8 fluid oz. breast milk or iron fortified formula	6-8 fluid oz. breast milk, iron-fortified formula, or whole cow's milk
	0-3 tablespoons dry, iron-fortified infant cereal (optional—see above)	1-4 tablespoon's fruit *and/or* vegetable of appropriate consistency
	0-3 tablespoons strained fruit and/or vegetable (optional, but if introduced, introduce as close to 6 months as possible)	2-4 tablespoons dry, iron-fortified infant cereal *and/or* 1-4 tablespoons fish, lean meat, poultry, or cooked dry beans or peas (all of appropriate consistency), *or* ½ to 1½ oz. cheese *or* 1-3 oz. cottage cheese *or* 1 egg yolk (introduce at 11 months of age)
	SUPPLEMENT SNACK	
4-6 fluid oz. breast milk or iron-fortified formula	4-6 fluid oz. breast milk or iron-fortified formula	2-4 fluid oz. breast milk, iron-fortified formula, or whole cow's milk, *or* 2 oz. full-strength fruit juice
		0-½ slice hard toast or 0-2 crackers or teething biscuits (optional) suitable for infants, made from whole-grain or enriched flour

Note—On the infant's arrival at the facility, the caregiver must ascertain what foods and/or formula the infant was fed at home in order to determine the infant's nutritional needs.

* Lean meat is beef, pork, or veal without visible fat. Luncheon meats and frankfurters are high in fat and are *not* considered lean meat.

Add finger foods at 8 to 10 months to encourage self-feeding. All foods should be easy for the baby to gum and small enough to swallow whole.

- Introduce a variety of foods to help build good food habits throughout life, but take care to **add only one new food at a time.** Wait 3 to 5 days to see if the new food is well tolerated.
- Start feeding solids with a small spoon. Let the baby suck the food off the tip of the spoon. Never put solids in a bottle—the baby may consume too many calories and delay learning to handle solid foods differently from sucked liquids.
- Add **finger foods** (such as meat and cheese tidbits, cooked or soft vegetable strips and fruit sections) at 8 to 10 months to encourage self-feeding. All foods should be easy for the baby to gum and small enough to swallow whole.
- Introduce **table foods** at about 9 months to supplement the protein provided by breast milk or formula. As table foods are introduced to the infant, it is important that an adult sit with the child.
  —Use cooked turkey, chicken, lean hamburger, or fish that has been strained, chopped, or cut into small pieces to make chewing easier.
  —Serve cooked, mashed dried beans or peas for

additional protein. Avoid spoonfuls of peanut butter (spread it on bread or crackers and serve with moist food and beverages), and avoid any nuts, carrots, hot dogs, whole grapes, raisins, popcorn, corn, and large chunks of any food due to the potential for choking.
  —Add wheat products only after 8 months because wheat is a common cause of allergies.
  —Serve no more than two to three eggs per week (soft-cooked or scrambled) after children are 11 months old. Before then, feeding eggs may promote development of egg allergies.
  —Offer a variety of **100% fruit juices** (dilute by mixing 1 part juice with 1 part water). Avoid juice drinks which are mostly water and sugar. Offer fluids from a cup at meals after 6 months.
  —Offer plain water, especially during hot weather. Children need to learn to drink unflavored beverages.

Beginning cow's milk

Provide breast milk or formula, which are particularly nutritious and more digestible, to infants until they reach at least 6 months of age. Cow's milk can be introduced between 6 and 12 months, but many pediatricians prefer to have infants stay on formula until 12 months of age because formula is a convenient source of protein. Keep the following in mind:

- Do not serve low-fat or skim milk until 2 years of age because these milk products have too few calories and too much protein for infants. Infants who are fed low-fat or skim milk may not consume enough calories. Whole milk contains the fat, cholesterol, and vitamin E babies need for brain and nerve development.

Ask parents to discuss their child's diet with their pediatrician, nurse, and/or nutritionist.

Avoiding baby bottle tooth decay

Do not allow infants or toddlers to go to bed with a bottle or to drink from a bottle lying down. Formula, milk, juice, and sweetened drinks contain sugars that can decay existing or erupting teeth, creating a condition known as nursing bottle mouth. This may lead to early loss of teeth particularly the front upper and lower teeth. As a result, the child may not be able to chew food properly and crowding may occur in the adult teeth. If an infant wishes to take a bottle to bed, fill it with plain water. Better yet, try to have the child drink the bottle before lying down. Children who drink their bottles lying down are prone to ear infections.

Weaning

Weaning is the process of replacing the bottle or breast with a cup. The "right time" to wean depends upon whatever works best for the mother and the baby.

- A cup can be introduced around 6 to 8 months of age. A cup without a spout top is recommended because this spout continues to promote sucking fluids.
- A toddler can be completely weaned from the bottle or breast sometime during the first half of the second year (12 to 18 months of age).
- Weaning can be accomplished by gradually offering more fluids in a cup at meals and between meals.
- Naptime and bedtime bottles and nursings should gradually be replaced by soothing and relaxing activity such as reading stories, rocking, or singing lullabies.

Feeding toddlers

A toddler's growth rate slows down during the period from 18 months to 3 years. As a result, a toddler eats less. Toddlers are demanding and energetic by nature. As they explore and gain control over themselves and their environment, they feel successful and become more independent. They begin to take more responsibility for what and how much they eat. For example, toddlers may go on food jags where they eat only a few foods.

You and the children's parents are responsible for **what** children are offered to eat, as well as **where, when,** and **how** food is offered. The toddler is responsible for **how much** food she or he eats. Your role is to help the child establish positive attitudes about eating and to ensure a nutritionally adequate diet. You can help toddlers become independent by encouraging them to select from a variety of acceptable foods. Observe how

energetic toddlers are, and how they grow, play, and eat. Be reassured that most toddlers are well nourished if a variety of nutritious foods are available.

How much is enough?

When too much food is put on a child's plate the child feels overwhelmed and may not even try to eat. A good rule to follow is to offer a child-size portion consisting of ¼ to 1/3 of a usual adult portion, or 1 tablespoon per year of age, whichever seems more appropriate. Give less than you think toddlers will eat and let them ask for seconds. Use the Food components for toddlers, preschoolers, and school-age children guide (Figure 12.3) to estimate appropriate portion sizes for toddlers. These are minimum amounts for a nutritionally adequate diet and are not intended to limit the amount toddlers are allowed to eat.

There will be daily variation in both types of foods and calories consumed by toddlers. Children 1 to 3 years of age consume approximately 1000 to 1300 calories per day (some days less, some days more). **On a weekly average, a toddler should be eating a nutritionally balanced diet.**

The eating environment

A pleasant, relaxed eating environment helps toddlers develop positive attitudes about food. Establish regular mealtimes and snacktimes. Make sure toddlers sit at a comfortable height in relation to the table surface with their feet touching the floor. Use plates and utensils appropriate to children's sizes and skills. Offer silverware, but don't insist toddlers use it. If you allow toddlers to touch, smell, and explore food, they are more likely to eat it. Toddlers can be finicky about the appearance of their food and often prefer to have food separated on their plate. Helping toddlers develop positive attitudes about eating is much more important than achieving fine-tuned table manners.

Encourage toddlers to try new foods, and occasionally praise them for eating well. Don't praise children for eating large quantities because this interferes with their self-regulation. Serve small portions, and encourage toddlers to try one bite. Prior to a meal, try to help toddlers relax and settle down. If children are tired or overstimulated from play, they may not feel like eating.

Figure 12.3. Food components for toddlers, preschoolers, and school-age children

Breakfast	1-2 years	3-5 years	6-12 years
Milk, fluid	½ cup	¾ cup	1 cup
Juice (full-strength) *or* fruit or vegetable	¼ cup	½ cup	½ cup
Bread *and/or* cereal (whole-grain or enriched)			
Bread	½ slice	½ slice	1 slice
Cereal			
Cold/dry *or*	¼ cup	⅓ cup	½ cup
Hot/cooked	¼ cup	¼ cup	½ cup

Lunch or Supper	1-2 years	3-5 years	6-12 years
Milk, fluid	½ cup	¾ cup	1 cup
Lean meat* *or* meat alternate			
Lean meat, fish, or poultry cooked			
(lean meat without bone)	1 ounce	1½ ounces	2 ounces
or Cheese	1 ounce	1½ ounces	2 ounces
or Egg	1	1	1
or Cooked dry beans or peas	¼ cup	⅜ cup	½ cup
or Peanut butter (smooth)	2 tablespoons	3 tablespoons	4 tablespoons
or Nuts and/or seeds**	½ ounce**	¾ ounce**	1 ounce**
Fruit and/or vegetable			
(two or more total)	¼ cup	½ cup	¾ cup
Bread or bread alternate			
(whole grain or enriched)	½ slice	½ slice	1 slice

Supplement (Snack)—Select two of the four components (midmorning or midafternoon supplement)

	1-2 years	3-5 years	6-12 years
Milk, fluid	½ cup	½ cup	1 cup
Lean meat* or meat alternate	½ ounce	½ ounce	1 ounce
(see above) *or* yogurt	¼ cup	¼ cup	½ cup
Juice (full-strength) *or* fruit *or* vegetable	¼ cup	½ cup	½ cup
Bread *and/or* cereal (whole-grain or enriched)			
Bread	½ slice	½ slice	1 slice
Cereal			
Cold/Dry or	¼ cup	⅓ cup	½ cup
Hot/cooked	¼ cup	¼ cup	½ cup

Note—On the child's arrival at the facility, the caregiver must ascertain what food was fed at home in order to determine the child's nutritional needs.

* Lean meat is beef, pork, or veal without visible fat. Luncheon meats and frankfurters are high in fat and are *not* considered lean meat.

** This portion can meet only one half of the total serving of the meat/meat alternate requirement for lunch or supper. Nuts or seeds must be combined with another meat/meat alternate to fulfill the requirement. For determining combinations, 1 ounce of nuts or seeds is equal to 1 ounce of cooked lean meat, poultry, or fish. CAUTION: Children under five are at the highest risk of choking. Any nuts and/or seeds must be served to them in a prepared food and be ground or finely chopped.

Copied with permission from *Caring for Our Children—National Health and Safety Performance Standards: Guidelines for Out-of-Home Child Care Programs.* American Public Health Association & American Academy of Pediatrics. Washington, DC, and Elk Grove Village, IL 1992, page 353.

Basic nutrition facts

Food groups and major nutrients

Foods can be divided into groups according to the major nutrients they contain. See Figures 12.2 and 12.3 for details about daily minimum servings of food components required by infants, toddlers, preschoolers, and school-age children.

Snacks

Snacks are an important part of a well-balanced diet. For preschoolers, snacks are especially important because their stomachs are small and they usually can't eat enough in three meals to meet energy needs or satisfy appetites. Within 3 hours after a meal, young children will usually be hungry. Foods eaten at snacktime can often provide nutrients missing from the rest of the day's food. The challenge is to help preschoolers eat nutritious snacks and to do so at appropriate times during the day. Good snacks are those that help provide children with essential nutrients they may be missing the rest of the day.

Serve snacks that are nutritious and contain some protein, some fat, and some carbohydrate to be satisfying and tasty. A list of nutritious snack ideas is provided in Figure 12.4. Snacktimes often offer good opportunities for children to try new foods. Avoid such commercial snack foods as chips, sweet cakes, candies, and fruit drinks. These all have limited nutritional value for the calories they contain.

Appetite

Preschool children are not growing as fast as they did in infancy so their appetites decrease. A small appetite may also result if a child is tired, excited, ill, or in strange surroundings. Because no one food contains all the nutrients our bodies need, serve a variety of foods such as fruits, vegetables, protein foods, and unsweetened cereals. Preschoolers generally enjoy eating the same foods as adults.

Preschoolers often have unstable eating habits. Children may be less hungry because they are in a slow growth stage or practicing newly discovered independence. Be aware of any change in a child's appetite that lasts longer than a few days, and talk to parents or caregivers to try to find the reason.

Figure 12.4. Ideas for nutritious snacks

Fruits and vegetables

- **Keep them fresh**—Apples, oranges, grapes, cherries, strawberries, blueberries, bananas, cantaloupe, watermelon, grapefruit, etc.
- **Apple sandwich**—Slice an apple, spread peanut butter on the slices, and make a sandwich. Or, add a slice of cheese between the slices.
- **Yogurt sundae**—Children can make their own . . . just supply bowls, plain yogurt, cut up fruit, and toppings of chopped nuts, sunflower seeds, wheat germ, or dry cereal.
- **Fruit kabobs**—Skewer fresh fruit and low-fat cheese cubes, pitted dates, or prunes on long straws or long toothpicks (for older children). Serve kabobs with a dip made with plain, low-fat yogurt sprinkled with cinnamon or a few drops of vanilla flavoring, or well-stirred, mixed fruit yogurt.
- **Fruit juice surprises**—Divide 1 cup of cut up fruit (apple, banana, orange, strawberries) into four glasses. Add 3 cups of unsweetened fruit juice and chill.
- **Veggie kabobs**—Skewer (see note above) cut up fresh vegetables such as cherry tomatoes, zucchini, carrots, cucumbers, green peppers, mushrooms, and low-fat cheese cubes. Serve with salad dressing or a dip made with mashed beans, yogurt, or cottage cheese and seasoned with herbs.
- **Toss a salad**—or invite children to a homemade salad bar. Set out dishes of cut up veggies for children to create their own salads.
- **Celery stuff-its**—Fill celery with part-skim ricotta cheese mixed with unsweetened crushed pineapple. Or, fill celery with peanut butter and add a few raisins (this is called "Ants on a Log").
- **Lettuce roll**—Spread tuna or chicken salad, peanut butter, or low-fat ricotta cheese on a lettuce leaf, roll it up, and eat.

Freezer delights

- **Frozen dixies**—Freeze one of the following in a paper cup with a Popsicle stick: applesauce, crushed pineapple, fruit yogurt (mixed well or made with fruit juices).
- **Frozen strawberry yogurt pops**—Blend 1 cup

Figure 12.4 *continued*

of frozen strawberries until smooth. Mix the strawberries with 1 cup of plain, low-fat yogurt and 3 to 5 tablespoons of honey. Pour into paper cups with a Popsicle stick in the center and freeze 1 to 2 hours until firm. Remove cup from frozen yogurt and serve. Makes seven pops.

- **Banana pops**—Mix 2 cups of low-fat, plain yogurt with 1 cup of mashed banana, 1 teaspoon of vanilla, and ½ cup of chopped walnuts (optional). Pour into six 4-oz. paper cups, insert Popsicle sticks in the center, and freeze until firm. Remove cup from frozen pop and serve.
- **Banana rockets**—Coat peeled, ripe bananas with orange juice or orange juice concentrate (to prevent discoloration), wrap in foil or plastic wrap, and freeze. Or, roll chilled, juice-coated bananas in chopped nuts or granola, press firmly to coat, and freeze until firm.

Homemade convenience snacks
- **Trail mix**—Combine dried fruits and dry cereal together, and divide into plastic bags or paper cups.
- **Cheese popcorn**—Make popcorn and sprinkle with grated Parmesan cheese. Add melted butter or margarine if desired.
- **Going crackers**—Crackers and cheese, crackers and peanut butter (with or without jelly), crackers and dip . . . just be sure to choose your crackers carefully. Crackers that are lower in fat or sodium include Melba toast, matzo, rice cakes, Wasa, Rye Krisp, bread sticks, unsalted saltines, zwieback, and graham crackers.
- **Yummo wrap-ups**—Have children make their own using flour tortillas spread with peanut butter, dried fruit, and raisins—ideal for hikes. Or, use part-skim ricotta cheese and cinnamon or jam.
- **Nachos**—Cut corn tortillas into six triangles and top with grated mozzarella cheese. Place in the oven (or toaster oven) at 350° to crisp the tortillas and melt cheese. Serve with salsa.
- **Natural soda pop**—Combine half a glass of fruit juice (orange, grape, apple, or pineapple) with half a glass of club soda or seltzer. Add ice and enjoy.

Blender snacks
- **Blender basics**—For a shake, blend 1 cup of plain yogurt, 1 cup of chopped fruit (strawberries, bananas, etc.), and ½ cup of fruit juice (orange, pineapple, or grape). The shakes will be thicker if made with frozen fruit.
- **Melon cooler**—In blender, mix 1½ cups of ice cubes, 1½ cups of cubed watermelon, honeydew, or cantaloupe, and ½ teaspoon of lemon juice until smooth. Serve immediately. Makes 2½ cups.
- **Ambrosia shake**—In blender, mix four sliced, ripe bananas, ½ cup of orange juice, ¼ teaspoon of vanilla, 4 cups of low-fat, skim, or reconstituted nonfat, dry milk. Makes six servings.
- **Fruit soup**—In blender, combine ¼ cup of orange juice, ½ of a small banana, ½ of an apple, 1 teaspoon of lemon juice, 2 tablespoons of plain, low-fat yogurt, ¼ cup of strawberries, a dash of cinnamon, and a dash of dried mint. Chill before serving. Makes three ½-cup servings.

Barbara Storper, M.S., R.D., Massachusetts Nutrition Resource Center, 150 Tremont Street, Boston, MA 02111. Reprinted with permission.

Variety is essential
Adults can help children develop good food habits and eat the essential nutrients by offering a wide variety of foods (both different foods and the same foods prepared in different ways, e.g., raw carrot sticks, cooked carrots, carrot salad). Gradually introduce a wide variety of foods to increase food acceptance. Pay attention to what foods children eat, and encourage them to eat foods from different food groups.

Food habits are learned
Food habits and the ability to eat wisely are **learned!** Children are great imitators and often mimic actions of people around them. New foods will be accepted more readily if you follow these guidelines:
- Introduce only one new food at a time.
- Serve the new food with familiar foods.

- Serve only small amounts of the new food.
- Introduce new foods only when children are hungry.
- Talk about the new food—taste, color, texture.
- Let children see you eating and enjoying the new food!
- Encourage children to taste the new food. If they reject it, accept the refusal and try again in a few weeks. As foods become more familiar, they are more readily accepted.
- Find out what is not liked about the rejected food. Often the food will be accepted if it is prepared in a different way.

Food as reward or punishment

Sometimes you may be tempted to use food as a reward, pacifier, or punishment. How many times have you said, "No dessert until you clean your plate," thereby implying dessert is a better part of the meal? Children do need positive encouragement, but using food as a reward places undue emphasis on certain foods. Praise, a smile, or a hug serve just as well. Avoid using food for reasons other than to satisfy hunger. Make desserts nutritious so that if only the dessert is eaten, the child will have good food.

Food safety

Follow these suggestions to avoid food-related problems:

- Be aware that foods that are round, hard, small, thick and sticky, smooth, or slippery are a choking hazard and should not be given to children under 4 years of age. Examples of such foods include nuts, hard candy, popcorn, whole grapes, raw peas, dried fruit, pretzels, marshmallows, spoonfuls of peanut butter, and chunks of meat larger than can be swallowed whole. If a child chokes while eating, these foods can easily be breathed into the lungs. (Hot dogs may be used only if sliced lengthwise and then cut into bite-size pieces.)
- Do not feed honey to infants younger than 1 year of age. Honey can cause botulism in infancy. Check food and formula labels to be sure that honey has not been used as a sweetener.
- Infant food should be cut into chunks smaller than a ¼". Toddler food should be cut into chunks smaller than a ½".

- Styrofoam cups and plates should not be used for children under 4 years old.
- Be sure that at least one staff member knows how to remove food caught in a child's throat using a modified Heimlich maneuver (see the first-aid section, page 90 and 91). It is common for children learning to eat finger foods to gag and cough. Immediate attention is required if the child chokes, i.e., turns blue or is not making voice sounds.
- Be sure all staff are aware of any children's food allergies. Be especially alert for foods that may cause allergic reactions that are served at birthday parties or other occasions when parents may not be aware of the problem. Staff must also be aware of emergency steps to be taken should the allergic child consume the problem food.
- Children are not allowed to eat while walking, running, playing, lying down, or riding in vehicles.

Activity and physical exercise

Activity has a lot to do with a child's appetite and nutritional status. Active children need more calories than inactive ones; this means that they have a better chance of getting all required nutrients. Adequate physical exercise year-round, preferably on a daily basis, is important to a child's development because it

- stimulates healthy appetites
- uses calories and maintains muscle tissue
- improves coordination
- encourages children to express themselves and develop social skills

Common nutritional concerns

Fats

There is a growing concern about the role of fat in heart disease and controversy about the kind of fat and amount of cholesterol permissible in children's diets. Polyunsaturated and saturated fats are important nutrients to include in the proper ratio. **Polyunsaturated fats** are the liquid vegetable oils that contain essential fatty acids that the body cannot manufacture. **Saturated fats** are the solid fats found in beef, pork, lamb, chicken, and dairy products and are the ones to be limited. Some fat from both sources is necessary to maintain the proper balance of fatty acids in the body. Foods such as hot dogs, luncheon meats, and potato chips are high in saturated fat and salt and should be limited in a child's diet.

Sugar

Many factors determine how foods affect your child's teeth. The more often your child snacks on foods containing sugars and starches, the greater the chance for tooth decay. You can easily avoid serving foods high in sugar to children. There is really no reason to sweeten food. Avoid honey, in any form, in the first year of life because it can cause botulism, a toxic condition for infants.

Honey, molasses, raw sugar, and refined sugar all contain the same number of calories. Never add sweetener to vegetables, fruits, fruit juice, or cereal. Avoid serving empty calorie foods such as candy; sweetened beverages; and refined, sweetened baked goods that provide mainly calories and low levels of essential nutrients.

Salt

High-salt diets may lead to the development of high blood pressure in people with a family background of hypertension (high blood pressure).

Salt intake can be reduced by not salting food at the table, decreasing the amount of salt used in cooking, and limiting salty foods (pickles, canned soups, chips, salty crackers, and salted nuts). Don't overlook the hidden sources of salt found in hot dogs, bacon, sausages, condiments, and canned and some frozen foods. Since preference for salty foods is learned, it can be changed.

Vegetarian diets

A well-planned vegetarian diet can provide all the nutrients a child needs for growth and activity. Vegetarian diets are often high in fiber and low in cholesterol and saturated fat, and they have many positive health benefits. However, because of this there is also the possibility that the child will not get enough calories. Vegetarian diets may include different food restrictions. Figure 12.5 describes vegetarian eating patterns.

Figure 12.5. Types of vegetarian diets

	FOODS CONSUMED				
Diet	**Beef and pork**	**Fish and poultry**	**Milk and milk products**	**Eggs**	**Vegetables, fruits, breads, cereals, and nuts**
Nonvegetarian	X	X	X	X	X
Semi-vegetarian		X	X	X	X
Lacto-ovo-vegetarian			X	X	X
Ovo-vegetarian				X	X
Lacto-vegetarian			X		X
Vegan (total vegetarian)					X

Adapted from Ivens & Weil (1984).

Vegetarian diets that include dairy products and eggs readily provide all the needed nutrients for young children. Vegan or total vegetarian diets that omit all animal protein can be nutritionally inadequate and may not provide enough protein, calcium, iron, zinc, vitamin D, and vitamin B^{12}. These very strict vegetarian diets may also be low in calories due to their high bulk and low fat content. In addition, problems of short stature, underweight, and rickets have occurred in children on very restrictive vegetarian diets.

Legumes, seeds, or nuts, when combined with grains, provide a good protein source. But to get enough protein, children on vegan or strict vegetarian diets need to eat more food than children who eat meat, fish, poultry, and cheese. The number of servings from each food group will be different for a child eating a vegetarian diet, particularly a vegan diet. Parents who wish to have their children follow a vegan diet should be referred to a dietician or nutritionist to ensure that intake of nutrients and calories is adequate for their child's growth.

Milk

If children drink too much milk, they may spoil their appetites for other foods and may develop iron deficiency anemia. Offer water if a child is thirsty.

If a child doesn't drink much milk, try not to make an issue of it because this is just a phase. Left alone, the child will probably go back to drinking milk. A preschool child needs approximately 16 to 24 ounces (2 to 3 cups) of milk daily. Other foods rich in calcium, such as hard cheese and yogurt, can be substituted for milk (see Figure 12.6).

Some children may have lactose intolerance, a lack of intestinal enzymes to digest the milk sugar/ lactose. (See page 146.)

Special nutritional problems

Early childhood programs must follow orders of parents or the physician in preparing and feeding a child's special diet. A nutritionist should be consulted for assistance in menu planning.

Obesity

Obesity is a complex problem with multiple causes including overeating, poor food choices, inactivity, social or emotional factors, and genetics. Helping

Figure 12.6. Dietary sources of calcium

Excellent

Yogurt, low-fat or whole milk, plain or fruit flavored
Skim milk
Low-fat milk (1 or 2%)
Buttermilk
Whole milk
Swiss cheese
Sardines, canned with bones

Good

Cheeses: cheddar, Muenster, mozzarella, blue
American or Swiss pasteurized process cheese food
Parmesan cheese, grated
Tofu*
Dry skim milk, instant
Mackerel, canned, solids and liquids
Salmon, pink, canned with bones
Collard greens, cooked

Fair

Blackstrap molasses
Vanilla, soft-serve, frozen dairy products
Figs, dried
Kale, cooked
Mustard greens, cooked
Ice cream, vanilla
Chickpeas, cooked
Broccoli, cooked
Cottage cheese, creamed

*Calcium content of tofu differs according to the processing method. Tofu contains calcium if it is processed with a calcium coagulant such as sulfate. Look on the nutrition label or in the ingredient list. Nigari is a popular tofu coagulant that does *not* contain calcium.

children learn healthy eating and exercise habits is the key to preventing obesity. Although you can't always predict whether an overweight child will become an overweight adult, many children who become obese will remain so throughout life. Obesity can significantly affect a child psychologically and emotionally and can result in low self-esteem.

Many young children learn eating and activity

patterns that can lead to obesity later in life. Using food as a reward or pacifier, force feeding, providing very large portions, and requiring clean plates may contribute to obesity. Physical activity is essential to maintain a normal weight. Surprisingly, it is often inactivity rather than calorie intake that results in obesity.

The goal of weight management for children is **to limit further weight gain.** Children will grow slimmer as they grow into their weight. Actual **weight loss is not generally recommended** as children need adequate nutrients and calories for growth. Low-fat, nutritious meals and snacks are essential to good weight management.

How to manage/prevent obesity in young children

- Encourage children to be physically active.
- Do not let the child eat while watching television, and limit television viewing to no more than 2 hours per day.
- Limit high-calorie foods (foods high in fat, sugar, or both).
- Limit excessive drinking of sweetened beverages such as fruit drinks, powdered or syrup-based drink mixes, and chocolate milk that can add many extra calories each day. A child's thirst can be satisfied with water after the proper amount of milk has been consumed.
- Use low-fat or skim milk with children older than 2 years old.
- Put food on small plates.
- Provide high-fiber, filling, crunchy foods.
- Limit eating to small meals at designated eating times (three meals plus two snacks, preplanned for portion control and nutrient balance).
- Provide lots of nonfood rewards. (Plan activities rather than special foods for birthday parties, holidays, and other celebrations.)
- Help children learn to deal with emotions or stress without turning to food.
- Remember that **your** food habits and attitudes will influence those of the children around you.

Iron deficiency

See page 113 and 118 for a description of anemia.

How to manage anemia

- Encourage the child to consume a varied, well-balanced diet that includes iron-rich foods.

- Provide increased amounts of iron-rich foods at meals and snacks. Good sources of iron include liver, dried beans and peas, lentils, beef, pork, lamb, whole wheat and enriched breads, and cereal products. Raisins and peanut butter also contain a small amount of iron. Iron from animal sources is absorbed better than iron from plant sources.
- Serve iron-rich foods with a source of vitamin C. Vitamin C increases the body's ability to use iron. The amount of iron absorbed from plant sources can be increased significantly when these foods are combined with a food high in vitamin C. For example, with chili serve spinach, broccoli, or tomato slices; with split pea soup serve half an orange, cantaloupe cubes, or strawberries. These fruits and vegetables provide fiber and vitamin C and make the iron in the bean dishes more available for use by the body.
- Limit milk to 24 ounces per day and assure adequate intake of other foods, particularly iron-containing foods.

Failure-to-Thrive

Some children do not grow properly. They are small or thin for their age; their height may be short for their age, or their weight may be low for their height. They may tire easily, be inattentive, disinterested in eating, and undernourished. This complex syndrome, known as Failure-to-Thrive (FTT), may be due to medical, nutritional, or psychosocial factors.

FTT can be a sign of child abuse or neglect. The child care provider should be especially alert to other possible signs of child abuse/neglect (see Chapter 14) that would require immediate reporting to child protective services.

How to manage FTT syndrome

- Refer the child immediately for a complete medical, nutritional, and social evaluation.
- Consult a nutritionist who can plan a nutritionally appropriate diet and support the family, child, and early childhood program during the critical period of weight gain.
- Be available to assist the family with carrying out the recommended treatment plan.
- Watch children who fail to thrive closely, even when the crisis is past.

Food allergies and intolerances

Infants and young children sometimes have food allergies or are intolerant of certain foods. An allergic reaction occurs when a child becomes sensitive to a particular food and the immune system produces increased amounts of antibodies. The allergic reaction can be avoided only by avoiding the food.

Foods that commonly cause allergic reactions are nuts, peanuts, eggs, cow's milk protein, wheat, fish, shellfish, citrus fruits, and berries.

A food intolerance means that the child has some metabolic factors (e.g., does not manufacture an enzyme or chemical needed to digest a certain food substance) that make it difficult or impossible to digest or use that food. Sometimes foods can be modified so that the child can tolerate them. Intolerance to the sugar in cow's milk (lactose) is a common problem in infants and children. Soy formulas are frequently used alternatives to cow's milk or regular formula for children with milk allergies or lactose intolerance.

When the allergic child eats a food to which she or he is sensitive, symptoms such as diarrhea, vomiting, abdominal pain, rash, irritability, breathing problems such as wheezing, and even death may occur. The relationship between allergies and hyperactivity is controversial. Hyperactivity is not caused by food allergies. If the child is hyperactive *and* has food allergies, the behavior may be worse when the symptoms of allergy are present. Thus, the hyperactive child will do better if allergies are controlled. Reactions to food allergies may be immediate or delayed; symptoms may be mild to severe, depending on the type and amount of food eaten and the age of the child.

How to manage food allergies and intolerances

- Consult a nutritionist concerning diet planning for the child.
- Eliminate or decrease the problem food(s) from the diet depending on the severity of the reaction.
- Read labels to identify hidden sources of the problem foods or substances.
- Work with parents to find acceptable substitutes for problem foods.
- Plan menus carefully to ensure adequate nutrition, particularly if a child has multiple food allergies or if the child is allergic to major food groups.
- Make sure the child gets critical nutrients from other sources: calcium and vitamin D if child is allergic or intolerant to milk; vitamin C if child is allergic to citrus fruits.

Milk allergies and lactose intolerance

Some children are allergic to the milk protein and are unable to tolerate any milk products including dry milk solids added to margarine, for example. This allergy is often outgrown between the ages of 2 to 5 years.

Other children are unable to digest the sugar in milk, called lactose, due to a low level of the enzyme lactase in the intestine. Lactose intolerance is more common in children from African-American and Asian backgrounds. Children with lactose intolerance may suffer from abdominal pain, bloating, gas, and diarrhea.

How to manage lactose intolerance. Tolerance of lactose varies. Many children can tolerate small amounts of lactose (e.g., 8 ounces of milk) if intake of these foods is spaced throughout the day. Encourage children to try cheese and other fermented dairy products, such as yogurt, that have a lower lactose content and are better tolerated. Lactose-free, soy-based formulas are available as substitutes for regular infant formula or cow's milk.

Encourage parents to try hydrolyzed milk (milk in which the lactose has been made more digestible by the enzyme lactase). You can buy hydrolyzed milk in many stores. Lactase is also available separately to be added to regular milk or chewed as a tablet for the same effect. See Figure 12.6 for alternative sources of calcium.

The diet of a child with a milk allergy or intolerance should be evaluated regularly. Because calcium requirements are met primarily through eating dairy products, these children may not get adequate calcium unless other adjustments are made in their diet. Fish, tofu, and dark, leafy vegetables are also good sources of calcium.

Hyperactivity

Additive-free diets for the treatment of hyperactivity have not been found to be of value. Diets that eliminate artificial food colorings and salicylates (aspirin-like compounds) are not harmful to children and may improve the nutritional value of the child's diet. However, they have not been shown to affect the hyperactivity itself. Any such diet, therefore, should be carefully planned along with appropriate medical and psychological treatment. A nutritionist should be consulted to ensure nutritional adequacy.

Feeding children who have special needs

Children with special needs have the same needs as all children for care and feeding. Often these basic needs are overlooked in the concern for the child's disability. **Nutritional problems** (such as poor food intake, inability to chew or swallow normally, inadequate weight gain, short stature, obesity, or iron deficiency anemia) and **behavioral problems** associated with eating frequently accompany the problems of children with special health care needs and therefore place them at nutritional risk. Infants or children with special needs may have feeding needs that require more patience, time, and understanding than usual. Special adaptive equipment may be necessary also.

Healthy foods and dietary supplements have an important role in helping the child with HIV/AIDS maintain weight, strength, and energy and may help fight infections. At times, the child may be able to follow a normal diet. During bouts with illness from fever, diarrhea, nausea, or weight loss, the child may require a special diet and food supplements. The child's health care provider and nutritionist can make recommendations.

Whatever the disease or disorder, the child's growth and development to her or his full potential must be promoted. Good nutrition always contributes to optimal growth and development and can decrease or prevent some debilitating effects.

Use the services of a nutritionist or dietician to ensure that families and staff have the knowledge, skills, and support to provide optimal nutritional care to a child with special needs. If necessary, involve occupational and physical therapists, social workers, or other health providers to help solve any complex problems.

Concentrate on creating a pleasant eating environment where all children can learn to eat in a manner appropriate to their developmental levels. It is essential to involve parents in meeting the special nutritional needs of the child with a disability because the major part of the child's food needs must be met at home.

Special nutritional concerns for children with disabilities

- **Obesity**—Obesity is a common nutritional problem with many special health care needs. Prevention is especially important since obesity is difficult to reverse once it is present. Treatment for obesity should include a calorie-controlled diet and physical activity. A nutritionist can help you plan a diet that is appropriate in calories and other nutrients. By reinforcing appropriate eating behavior through nonfood rewards, you can help the child learn to control the types and quantities of foods consumed. Increased physical activity can help use calories, improve muscle tone, and relieve tension. Parents, health care providers, and the child all need to be involved. See page 144 and 145 for further discussion of this topic.

- **Underweight**—Some children with chronic illness/special needs/developmental delays are underweight. Nutritionists can be helpful in determining the causes of underweight and in developing treatment plans. When conventional foods do not meet a child's nutritional needs, special dietary supplements may be used.

- **Behavioral problems**—Occasionally, children with disabilities develop behavior problems associated with eating. Discuss any problems with parents immediately and involve appropriate health care providers to develop a workable treatment plan.

- **Inborn errors of metabolism**—A child with phenylketonuria (PKU) or any other inborn error of metabolism needs to be on a carefully controlled diet in order to promote normal growth and development and ensure intake of adequate nutrients. For the most part, food for the child's meals and snacks should be provided by the family. Other children should not share their food.

- **Other metabolic problems**—Conditions such as diabetes require only minor changes in the menu. Ask the child's parents or a nutritionist to give you a meal plan to be used as a guide.

- **Developmental delays**—Some infants and toddlers may experience delay(s) in normal development that may affect advances in self-feeding. In some children, the amount or type of food eaten can lead to underweight or certain nutrient deficiencies. Check with the child's pediatrician and/or nutritionist to develop an appropriate diet and feeding plan to advance feeding within the child's abilities.

Nutrition education

Childhood is the best time to develop good food habits because early experiences with food have a strong impact on a child's future eating habits and health. Poor diet has been associated with the development of many of the chronic diseases in this country: heart disease, stroke, high blood pressure, some forms of cancer, diabetes, and tooth decay. Nutrition education can significantly enrich the lives of children and provide a means for learning about their life and culture. Children who understand themselves and their environment develop a positive self-image, an essential ingredient for effective learning of any kind. Nutrition education teaches young children how to be selective about food and combats misinformation from television advertising.

Dietary habits are established early in life. The habits children learn during their preschool years will significantly affect their future health.

Dietary guidelines for all ages

The U.S. Department of Agriculture and the Department of Health and Human Services have published dietary guidelines intended to promote the health of all Americans. A copy of "The Food Guide Pyramid: A Guide to Daily Food Choices" is available for $1.00 (check or money order) from Consumer Information Center, Department 159-Y, Pueblo, CO 81009. These guidelines form the basis of any nutrition education activities you conduct for children, staff, or parents. Guidelines include

- Eat a variety of foods.
- Eat lots of fresh fruits and vegetables.
- Maintain desirable weight.
- Avoid too much fat, saturated fat, and cholesterol.
  —Choose lean meat, fish, poultry, and dried beans and peas as protein sources.
  —Use skim or low-fat milk and milk products (preschool children and adults only).
  —Limit your intake of fat and oils, especially those high in saturated fat such as butter, cream, lard, hydrogenated fats (some margarines), shortenings, and foods containing palm or coconut oil.
  —Trim fat off meats.
  —Broil, bake, or boil, rather than fry.
  —Moderate your use of foods that contain fat, such as breaded and fried foods.
  —Read labels carefully to determine both the amount and type of fat present in foods. For

Childhood is the best time to develop good food habits because early experiences with food have a strong impact on a child's future eating habits and health.

example, choose margarines with liquid vegetable oils as the first ingredient.

- Eat foods with adequate starch and fiber.
  —Choose foods that are good sources of fiber and starch, such as whole grain breads and cereals, fruits and vegetables, and dried beans and peas.
  —Use starchy foods rather than foods that have large amounts of fats and sugars.
- Avoid too much sugar.
  —Use less of all sugars, including white sugar, brown sugar, raw sugar, honey, and syrups.
  —Read labels for clues of sugar content. If the word *sugar, sucrose, glucose, maltose, dextrose, lactose, fructose,* or *syrup* appears first, then there is a large amount of sugar.
  —Select fresh fruit or fruit packed in water, its own juice, or with light rather than heavy syrup.
  —For good dental health. limit how often you eat sugar and sugar-containing foods. Avoid eating sweets between meals.
- Avoid too much sodium (salt).
  —Cook without salt or with only small amounts of added salt.
  —Try flavoring foods with herbs, spices, and lemon juice.
  —Add little or no salt to food at the table.
  —Limit use of salty foods such as potato chips, pretzels, salted nuts and popcorn, condiments (soy sauce, steak sauce, garlic salt), pickled foods, cured meats, some cheeses, and some canned vegetables and soups.
  —Read food labels carefully to determine the amounts of sodium (salt).
  —Use lower sodium products, when available, to replace those you use that have a higher sodium content.

In addition to these guidelines, meet the special nutritional needs of infants and toddlers.

  —Encourage breast-feeding unless there are special problems.
  —Delay introduction of solids until babies are 4 to 6 months old.
  —Do not add salt, fats, or sugar to children's food.
  —Use adequate amounts of fat to assure adequate calories.

Nutrition education with children

Teaching children to eat wisely and moderately is an investment in the future. The foods children eat influence their growth, development, capacity to learn, and overall behavior. All children deserve an equal opportunity to learn about foods, to explore different foods, and to learn why eating a varied, nutritionally adequate diet is necessary to reach one's growth potential. Social, economic, cultural, and psychological factors play an important role in determining what and how much we eat. Successful nutrition education helps children develop flexible, enjoyable, healthy eating habits.

Figure 12.7 identifies ideas for nutrition education activities that will foster the development of positive eating practices and enhance a child's emotional and psychological growth. These learning experiences can be easily integrated into daily routines. For example, eating together at mealtime and snacktime or during special occasions is an opportunity for children to socialize. Visits to local farms and farmers' markets will put children in touch with local surroundings and create an awareness of how food is grown and sold in places other than a supermarket.

The cultural and ethnic customs of our society influence the food we eat. Cultural heritage often determines whether a particular food will be eaten, regardless of its nutritional value. A wide variety of cultures and food habits can make eating interesting and fun.

Involve parents

Your program can't be the **only** advocate of good nutrition; parent involvement is essential. The combination of foods eaten at home and at child care should provide all the necessary nutrients for a child. Parents and teachers need to educate themselves about the types and amounts of food necessary for good nutrition. Here are some suggestions to involve parents:

- Ask parents to assist in planning menus. If parents are interested, provide an educational meeting on the principles of good nutrition involved in menu planning for young children.
- Include articles in your newsletter about your nutrition education activities. Ask parents for ideas for future programs, and invite parents to

Figure 12.7. Ideas for nutrition education

Developmental areas	Knowledge/skills used	Activity
Good self-image	Develop skills to choose widely	Have children plan, prepare, and serve simple nutritional snacks. For example, have children prepare "Ants on a Log"—celery stuffed with peanut butter and topped with raisins.
Appreciation of health	Gain knowledge of how food promotes growth and development	Ask children to discuss what foods help their teeth grow and stay healthy.
Enjoyment of food through all the senses	Experience various foods through sight, sound, smell, feel, and taste	Have children try to identify different fruits such as a banana, orange, and apple using one sense (sound, smell, feel, taste) at a time and check their answers through sight.
Appreciation of ethnic background	Share cultural background	Choose the cultural heritage of one or more children as a theme for a day's meals and snacks. Discuss at mealtimes how factors such as climate help shape food habits.
Self-expression	Foster creativity	Have children try various whole grain breads by first baking the bread and then tasting it. Encourage children to shape the dough in different ways.

See Wanamaker, Hearn, & Richarz (1979) for many more ideas.

---

participate in classroom activities. Ask parents to contribute articles to the newsletter about nutrition activities with their children at home.

- Send menus home with children to show parents what meals and snacks are planned. Offer parents new ideas for providing nutritious foods at home. Ask parents to share creative meal and snack ideas with each other. Have a contest for the best idea.
- Invite parents to participate with their children at a potluck dinner with a special ethnic food unique to their culture.
- Talk with parents about any eating or nutritional problems you notice. Encourage good eating behaviors such as always sitting down for snacks and meals. Make appropriate referrals and provide regular progress reports.
- Sponsor educational programs for parents on nutrition and consumer issues. Help parents understand how they can encourage positive eating habits at home. Use the dietary guidelines (page 136 and 139) as a starting point.
- Remind parents about ways to involve their child with food in the home, such as
  —Allow your child to help prepare food.
  —Let the child share in cleanup activities.

—Encourage your child to talk with you about food.

- Make available a list of community food and nutrition services including school feeding programs, food stamps, WIC (Supplemental Food Program for Women, Infants and Children), and emergency feeding agencies.

Community nutrition resources

A resource list of community nutrition programs, local nutritionists with whom you can consult, and emergency food agencies will help you make appropriate referrals when necessary.

Child and Adult Care Food Program (CACFP)

The Child and Adult Care Food Program is a federally sponsored program that helps provide nutritious meals to children enrolled in child care centers or family child care programs throughout the country. It also introduces young children to many different types of foods and helps teach them good eating habits. It is funded by the U.S. Department of Agriculture and (in most states) is administered by the U.S. Department of Education as an adjunct to the School Lunch Program.

Who can participate? The program is limited to public and private nonprofit organizations providing licensed or approved nonresidential child care services. Private, for-profit programs may qualify if they receive compensation under Title XX of the Social Security Act for at least 25% of the children who are receiving nonresidential care.

Child care and after-school programs can operate in the program either independently or through a sponsoring organization that accepts final administrative and financial responsibility for the program. Home-based child care programs must participate under a sponsoring organization; they cannot enter the CACFP directly.

Children 12 and younger are eligible to participate in the program. For children of migrant workers, the age limit is 15 years. People with physical or mental disabilities are eligible, regardless of age, if they receive care at a center or home where the majority of enrollees are 18 or younger.

Eligibility requirements. All private institutions (except for-profit Title XX organizations) must have tax-exempt status under the Internal Revenue

Code of 1954, or must have applied to the Internal Revenue Service (IRS) for it at the time they apply for the Child and Adult Care Food Program. If an institution takes part in other federal programs for which it needs nonprofit status, it already meets this requirement. Home-based child care programs are not required to be tax exempt but their sponsoring organizations must have tax-exempt status if they are private. Local IRS offices can provide information on how to obtain tax-exempt status. **All institutions,** except sponsoring organizations, **must have child care licensing or approval.**

Meal service. All participating institutions must serve meals that meet the U.S. Department of Agriculture nutritional standards. Institutions may receive payment for up to three meals per child per day; one of these meals must be a snack.

Available assistance. Generally, payments to programs are limited to the number of meals served to enrolled children multiplied by the appropriate rates for reimbursement. The rate of payment varies according to the family size and income of children participating in the program. Increased payment is provided for low-income children. Some state administering agencies may base payment on the maximum rates or actual costs, whichever is less.

Meals served by home-based child care providers under the CACFP are paid for at different rates for each type of meal served that meets program requirements. The sponsoring organization must pass the full food-service payment to the home, unless the sponsoring organization provides part of the home's food service. Providers receive payment for meals served to their own children only when (1) their children meet the family size and income standards for free or reduced-price meals and are participating in the CACFP, and (2) other nonresident enrolled children are present and participating in the program. Separate administrative funds are provided to sponsoring organizations based on the number of homes they administer.

Civil rights. The CACFP is available to all eligible children regardless of race, color, national origin, sex, age, or disability. If you believe you have been treated unfairly in receiving food services for any of these reasons, write immediately to Administration Food and Nutrition Service, 3101 Park Center Drive, Alexandria, VA 22302.

Additional information. To obtain information about the CACFP in your area, write or call Director, Child Nutrition Division, Food and Nutrition Services, U.S. Department of Agriculture, 3101 Park Center Drive, Alexandria, VA 22302. 703-756-3590. You can also call your Department of Education, Bureau of School Nutrition Services.

Food Distribution Program
Through the Food Distribution Program, the USDA purchases surplus foods from U.S. markets and distributes them to state agencies for use by eligible local agencies. The foods go to schools and institutions participating in the child nutrition programs (school lunch, school breakfast, summer feeding, and after-school programs), to nutrition programs for the elderly, to low-income families on Indian reservations, and to hospitals and prisons.

Licensed child care programs are eligible to participate in the food distribution program. Programs already enrolled in the CACFP automatically receive an application for the Food Distribution Program. If their applications are approved, they can elect to receive commodities or cash.

Food Stamp Program
The Food Stamp Program helps low-income households purchase the foods they need for good health. Participating families get coupons, free of charge, that they exchange for food at authorized stores. People can apply for food stamps at their local food stamp office.

WIC
The Special Supplemental Food Program for Women, Infants and Children, commonly known as WIC, is a federally funded food and nutrition education program for pregnant, postpartum, and breast-feeding women; infants; and children younger than age 5 who are low income and at nutritional risk. WIC is operated by local health clinics and other authorized community agencies.

Nutritionists counsel WIC participants concerning specific dietary needs, eating patterns, and use of WIC foods (milk, cheese, eggs, 100% fruit juice, iron-fortified cereals, peanut butter, dried peas and beans, infant formula, and infant cereal). WIC's goal is to promote changes in eating, food preparation, and shopping habits that will positively affect health.

WIC programs provide supplemental foods in one of three ways: they obtain foods from local firms and distribute them directly; they arrange for home delivery; or they give mothers vouchers to exchange for specified items at authorized grocery stores. Contact your health agency.

Nutrition Education and Training Program (NET)
Federal Nutrition and Training Program funds are granted to states for the dissemination of nutrition information to children and for in-service training of teachers and food service personnel. The program is for all children in public and private schools and in residential and nonresidential child care.

Child care programs can apply to the state coordinator of NET for small grants to start nutrition education programs. Selected resources are available for loan through the Food and Nutrition Information Center, National Agricultural Library, 10301 Baltimore Blvd., Beltsville, MD 20705. 301-504-5719.

Expanded Food and Nutrition Education Program (EFNEP)
EFNEP serves limited-resource youth and families with young children. It is regarded by many as the nutrition education component of the Food Stamp Program. Home economists and nutrition specialists teach paraprofessionals who, in turn, teach participants about food purchasing and budgeting, storage, preparation, choosing healthy foods, meal planning, and sanitation. Contact your local county extension office, the state leader of home economics at your state land-grant university, or the Extension Service at the U.S. Department of Agriculture, Washington, DC 20250.

Running a food service
Operation of a food service program for young children involves menu planning, food purchase and preparation, food service, and a number of issues related to environmental health, sanitation, and infectious disease control. See Chapters 3, 4, and 17 for further information and guidelines.

Menu planning

Plan your menus around the nutritional and developmental needs of young children by using the meal pattern developed by the USDA Child and Adult Care Food Program as a minimum standard (see Figures 12.2 and 12.3). Figure 12.8 provides sample menus and shows how the meal pattern translates into meals and snacks. If you cannot represent all the food groups at one meal, serve the missing one at snacktime.

Prepare written menus that show a week at a time and post them for staff and parents. Vary menus by season and avoid recycling whole weeks of menus more than once a month. Provide nutritious snacks mid-morning or mid-afternoon for children who attend less than 4 hours. When children stay for 4 hours or longer, either the program or the parents must provide meals in addition to snacks. Use a menu-planning worksheet to ensure consistency in each day's menu (see Figure 12.9).

Provide children with nutritious foods they like and can eat easily. Fibrous foods are difficult for young children to eat. Preschoolers usually do not like food that is very hot or very cold. Cut foods into bite-size pieces. Serve a variety of finger foods or foods that can be easily picked up. In cooking, try to preserve natural colors and textures so food looks appealing.

Consider setting up a menu planning committee to involve interested people in developing your menu. This committee might consist of a program director, a teacher or teacher's assistant, a cook, a parent(s), and a nutritionist. If you use cyclical menus, you may only have to meet once a month or every 6 weeks.

Here are some other factors to consider as you plan menus:

- Inventory—Keep an inventory of the foods on hand to help you determine future menus and how much of a particular food you need to order during a menu cycle.
- Budget—Recognize that the budget is an important factor in planning a menu. If your program is not being reimbursed by the Child and Adult Care Food Program for meals served, your food costs will be a large part of your budget. Consider shopping at food cooperatives or food banks.
- Equipment—Consider the availability and capacity of equipment when planning menus. Ask the following questions: Is the oven large enough to accommodate the amount of food to be baked? Is there room in the refrigerator to store foods?
- Storage space—Check the availability of storage space before you plan the menu. Is there enough dry storage space for the number of cases of dry goods you'll need to order?
- Cultural diversity—Serve foods that represent different cultural food patterns and are familiar to children as a natural way to establish rapport with the children and their families. This practice will also educate children about various cultures and their food preferences.
- Season—Some foods, particularly fruits and vegetables, are more available during various times of the year. Plan your menus to include the fruits and vegetables that are in season. They are more economical and taste better.

Guidelines for food preparation and service

These procedures for food preparation and service can be used by cooks and others involved with food service.

Food purchasing

- Be sure that suppliers of food and beverages meet local, state, and federal codes.
- Be sure that the meats and poultry you purchase have been inspected and passed for wholesomeness by federal or state inspectors.
- Use only pasteurized milk and milk products. If you use dry milk, prepare it in a clean container and refrigerate or use it immediately.
- Do not use home-canned foods or food from dented, rusted, or bulging cans or cans without labels.

Food storage

- Store all perishable foods at temperatures that will prevent spoilage (refrigerator temperature, 45° F. or lower; freezer temperature, 0° F. or lower).
- Place thermometers in the warmest part of the refrigerator and freezer (near the door) and check them daily.
- Set up refrigerators so that there is enough shelf space to allow for air circulation around shelves and refrigerator walls. This will help maintain proper food temperatures.

Figure 12.8. Menu planning and sample menus

NAME OF FACILITY _____

Menus are planned that are appealing, nutritious and culturally sensitive. Menus will promote use of food as a learning opportunity. New and familiar foods are combined in each month's cycle of menus. Menus are posted in _____
_____weekly.
site in facility

Parents are encouraged to submit recipes to _____for consideration.
title of staff

Menus are recycled every_____weeks to provide variety and avoid repetitions in food service. To promote variety, meals will have a combination of cooked and raw foods. Menus will include foods attractive to children with contrasting colors, and foods served in forms young children can manage easily. Menus are prepared by _____
title of staff
using guidelines from *A Planning Guide for Food Service in Child Care Centers*, U.S. Department of Agriculture, Food and Nutrition Service; The National Health and Safety Performance Standards; and the expertise of a local nutrition specialist.

Pattern	1st Day	2nd Day	3rd Day	4th Day	5th Day
Breakfast					
Juice or fruit or vegetable	Orange Juice ½ cup	½ Banana sliced	Apricot halves ½ cup	Fruit cup ½ cup	Grapefruit sections ½ cup
Cereal, bread, or bread alternate	Biscuit 1	Cornflakes ⅓ cup	Blueberry Muffin ½ to 1 muffin	Toast ½ to 1 slice	Rolled oats ¼ cup
Milk	Milk ¾ cup	Milk ¾ cup	Milk ¾ cup	Milk ¾ cup	Milk ¾ cup
Other Foods	Baked, scrambled eggs 2 tbs.			Hard-cooked egg ½ egg	
Morning Snack (select two of these four components)					
Milk	Milk ½ cup		Milk ½ cup		
Meat or meat alternate		Cheese wedge ½ oz.			Peanut butter
Fruit, vegetable, or juice		Fruit or vegetable juice ½ cup		Orange juice ½ cup	Grape juice ½ cup
Bread or bread alternate (including cereal)	Toast ½ slice sprinkled with cinnamon		Dry Cereal ⅓ cup	Toasted raisin bread ½ slice	Enriched soda crackers 2

Figure 12.8 *continued*

Pattern	1st Day	2nd Day	3rd Day	4th Day	5th Day
Lunch or Supper					
Meat or meat alternate	Meat loaf 1 slice (1½ oz. meat)	Baked chicken (1½ oz. meat)	Chicken vegetable soup ½ cup (1 oz. meat, ¼ cup vegetable)	Spaghetti and meat sauce ½ cup (1½ oz. meat)	Fish sticks (1½ oz. fish)
Vegetables and fruits (two or more)	Green beans ¼ cup Pineapple cubes ¼ cup	Mashed potatoes ¼ cup Peas ¼ cup Carrot stick	Green pepper stick Sliced peaches ¼ cup	Peas ¼ cup Green salad ¼ cup	Green beans ¼ cup Fresh pear half ¼ cup
Bread or bread alternate	Bread ½ slice	Roll small	Peanut butter and jelly sandwich ¼ (1 tbs. peanut butter)	French bread ½ slice	Corn bread 1 square
Milk	Milk ¾ cup	Milk ¾ cup	Milk ¾ cup	Milk ¾ cup	Milk ¾ cup
Afternoon Snack (select two of these four components)					
Milk		Milk ½ cup		Milk ½ cup	
Meat or meat alternate					Cottage cheese dip ½ cup with zucchini sticks
Fruit, vegetable, or juice	Mixed fruit juice ½ cup		Apple juice ½ cup	Turnip stick	
Bread or bread alternate (including cereal)		Oatmeal cookie 1	Soft pretzel 1	Peanut butter cookie	Melba toast 3

Figure 12.9. Menu planning worksheet

USDA Child Nutrition Program meal and snack pattern	Monday	Tuesday	Wednesday	Thursday	Friday
Breakfast Juice, fruit, or vegetable Cereal, bread, or bread alternate Milk Other foods					
Morning snack (select two of these four components) Milk Meat or meat alternate Fruit, vegetable, or juice Bread or bread alternate (including cereal)					
Lunch or supper Meat or meat alternate Vegetables and fruits (two or more) Bread or bread alternate Milk					
Afternoon snack (select two of these four components) Milk Meat or meat alternate Fruit, vegetable, or juice Bread or bread alternate (including cereal)					

- Always examine food when it arrives to make sure it is not spoiled, dirty, or infested with insects.
- Store unrefrigerated foods in clean, rodent- and insect-proof, covered metal, glass, or hard plastic containers. (Large shortening cans available from bakeries are ideal for storing flour and other commodities.)
- Store containers of food above the floor (about 6") on racks or other clean slotted surfaces that permit air circulation.
- Keep storerooms dry and free from leaky plumbing or drainage problems. Repair all holes and cracks in storerooms to prevent insect and rodent infestation.
- Keep storerooms cool (about 60° F.) to increase the food's shelf life.
- Store all food items separately from nonfood items.
- Use an inventory system: **The first food stored is the first food used.** This will ensure that stored food is rotated. Inspect food daily for spoilage.

Preparing and handling infant formula and foods sent from home. **Always** wash hands and utensils before handling breast milk, infant formulas, and foods. Be sure to follow directions on the packages regarding shelf life and preparation. If breast milk or formula is to be warmed, bottles should be placed in a pan of hot (not boiling) water for 5 minutes; shaken well; and, the milk temperature should be tested before feeding. Special care should be taken in cleaning and/or disinfecting bottles and nipples.

- Breast milk—Any breast milk sent from home should be in the infant's bottle with the child's name and the date. Breast milk should be refrigerated for a maximum of 48 hours. Breast milk may be frozen. The container in which the milk is collected and frozen, as well as the type of storage used (i.e., freezer unit of the refrigerator, self-contained freezer, or standing deep freeze) appear to affect the length of time breast milk may be safely stored. Frozen breast milk should be thawed under running cold water or in the refrigerator. Do not refreeze previously frozen breast milk.
- Concentrated infant formula—This should be sent from the child's home in its original, factory-sealed container and reconstituted according to package directions. Refrigerate until immediately prior to use. Never reuse a bottle of milk that has been warmed and/or used to feed an infant.

- Ready-to-feed infant formula—This can be served as is, unless parents provide instructions for a special formula preparation. Accept only factory-sealed containers.
- Powdered formula—Reconstitute as directed on the container.
- Junior foods—Serve commercially prepared junior foods from a **serving dish,** not the food jar. Cover, date, and refrigerate open jars of junior foods and use the contents within 48 hours.

Food preparation and handling

- Wash all raw fruits and vegetables before use. Wash tops of cans before opening.
- Thaw frozen foods in the refrigerator or put quick-thaw foods in plastic bags under cold running water for immediate preparation. DO NOT thaw frozen foods by allowing them to stand at room temperature.
- Use a thermometer to check internal temperatures of the following foods to be sure they have been cooked evenly:
  —Poultry—heat to a minimum temperature of 165° F.
  —Stuffing—heat to a minimum temperature of 165° F. in a **separate** pan. (**Do not** cook stuffing inside poultry.)
  —Pork and pork products—heat to a minimum of 160° F.
- Prepare these potentially hazardous foods as quickly as possible from chilled products, serve immediately, and refrigerate leftovers immediately.
  —meat salads, poultry salads, egg salads, seafood salads, and potato salads
  —cream-filled pastries
  —other prepared foods containing milk, meat, poultry, fish, and/or eggs
- Prevent the growth of bacteria by maintaining all potentially hazardous foods at temperatures lower than 45° F. or higher than 140° F. during transportation and while holding until service. Bacteria multiply most rapidly between 45° and 140° F.
- Cover or completely wrap foods during transportation.
- Never reuse a spoon that has been used even once for tasting.
- Make sure each serving bowl has a spoon or other utensil for serving food.

- Reserve food for second serving times at safe temperatures in the kitchen.
- Leftover food from serving bowls on the table must be thrown away with these possible exceptions
  —raw fruit and vegetables that can be thoroughly washed
  —packaged foods that do not spoil
- Place foods to be stored for reuse in shallow pans and refrigerate or freeze immediately to rapidly bring temperature to 45° F. or lower.
- Leftovers or prepared casseroles held in the refrigerator must be discarded after 2 days.
- Leftover foods should not be sent home with children or adults because of the hazards of bacterial growth during transport.
- Keep lunches brought from home in the refrigerator until lunch time.

Storage of nonfood supplies

- Store all cleaning supplies (including cleaning agents) and other poisonous materials in **locked** compartments or in compartments well above the reach of children and separate from food, dishes, and utensils.
- Store poisonous and toxic materials, other than those needed for kitchen sanitation, in **locked** compartments **outside** the kitchen area.
- Store insect and rodent poisons in **locked** compartments in an area apart from cleaning materials to avoid contamination or mistaken usage.
- Bait put into food storage areas should be boxed and separated to prevent a possible contamination of food supplies.
- Clearly label all containers of poisonous material as poison and include information on appropriate antidotes.

Cleaning and care of equipment

- Cracked or chipped dishes or utensils may harbor bacteria. Throw them away. Avoid utensils with chipped or painted handles.
- Wash dishes using an approved method (see Chapter 4, page 34).
- Wash equipment frequently.
  —Clean range tops during food preparation as needed and on a daily basis.
  —Clean ovens and overhead hoods at least weekly.
  —Wash the inside and outside of refrigerators weekly with the bleach solution; defrost when ice is a ¼" thick.

—Wash tables with the bleach solution before and after each meal.
- Set up a cleaning schedule to prevent contamination of food as follows:
  —Wet mop **floors** daily; scrub as needed.
  —Wash and disinfect **food preparation surfaces** between preparation of different food items (e.g., meat and salad) and between different meats (e.g., pork and chicken).
  —Wash and disinfect **cutting boards** after cutting any single meat, fish, or poultry item. (Use only hard, nontoxic, nonwood boards that are free of cracks, crevices, and open seams.)
  —Wash and disinfect **can openers** daily.
  —Clean and disinfect **utensils** between use on different food items.
- Special notes
  —**Air dry all food contact surfaces** after cleaning and disinfecting. Do not use wiping cloths.
  —Make sure no food contact surfaces are made of cadmium, lead, zinc, granite enamelware, or other toxic materials.
  —Do not use cyanide to polish or clean silver.
  —Be sure that there are sufficient garbage cans to hold all garbage. These cans should have tight-fitting lids and be leakproof. Line garbage cans with plastic liners; empty and clean the cans frequently. Keep the garbage area clean at all times.

Insect and rodent control

- For flying insects, use only approved pyrethrin-based insecticides or a flyswatter in the food preparation areas. Use products in accordance with directions and cautions appearing on their labels. Do not allow insecticides to come in contact with raw or cooked food, utensils, or equipment used in food preparation and serving or with any other food contact surface. Do not use insect strips that hang from the ceiling.
- Insecticides for crawling insects should be applied only by certified insect control personnel. A staff member should monitor where the insecticides are applied to be certain that food preparation surfaces or child contact areas are not contaminated.
- Be sure all doors and windows have screens in good condition. Keep screens closed at all times. Close all openings to the outside to prevent rodents and insects from entering.

Section F
Special health issues

Major concepts

- All children are children first. The child's special needs do not define the whole.

- Children with special health conditions do best when their needs are met by health and mental health professionals and specialists, program staff, and parents working together as a team.

- Most children with mild and moderate special health care needs can be served in group programs when proper prior planning has been done by the team.

- Staff, along with other members of the team including parents, need to observe these children carefully for signs and symptoms of special health care needs.

- A wide variety of community resources at the state, regional, and local levels are available to assist programs and families.

- Some conditions, such as lead poisoning and abuse and neglect, are preventable. Other conditions, such as chronic health problems or physical disabilities, may not be preventable. All these special health issues require appropriate intervention, regular monitoring, and daily care.

- Whenever possible, children with special health care needs should *not* be excluded from activities. Rather, give these children extra help, change your expectations, or modify the materials or activity.

- Your program must make "reasonable accommodation" to serve any child and must *not* discriminate on the basis of disability or special health care needs.

13
Children with special needs

Children with a wide range of problems or disabilities—those with speech and language problems, problems getting along with other children, chronic illnesses, family difficulties, abusive or neglectful parents, or developmental delays or physical impairments—can benefit from being in group situations with children who do not have special needs. The lives of other children and staff can also be greatly enriched by including children with special needs in mainstreamed early childhood programs.

Some children with special needs will require extensive individual program planning and extra services. Others will need staff to help them in minor ways or for limited times. Whatever the special need, staff must be attentive to reactions of the child, family, other children and families in the program, and other staff members; and they must

be flexible in planning. Each program needs to be realistic about what it can do to safely and appropriately meet the special needs of a child.

You should be aware that you cannot deny care to a child simply because the child has a disability. The Americans with Disabilities Act (ADA), which went into effect in 1992, states that people with disabilities are entitled to equal rights in employment; state and local public services; and public accommodations such as preschools, child care centers, and family child care homes. Each child's needs must be **evaluated on an individual basis** to determine whether a program can **reasonably accommodate** the child's needs. (See Figure 13.1 for information to assist you in understanding the provisions of the Americans with Disabilities Act and a flowchart to guide your thinking in determining whether or not

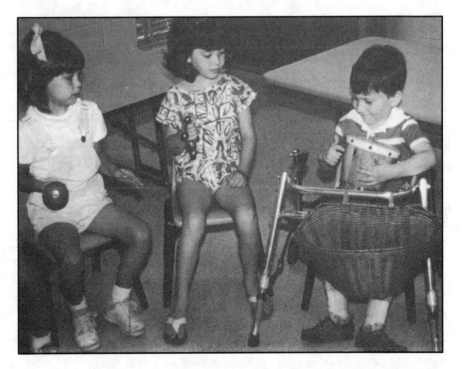

Children with special needs who are given the opportunity to play and learn with other children in the classroom learn more about themselves and how to cope with the give-and-take of everyday life.

Figure 13.1. The ADA: "A New Way of Thinking" Title III: Public Accommodations

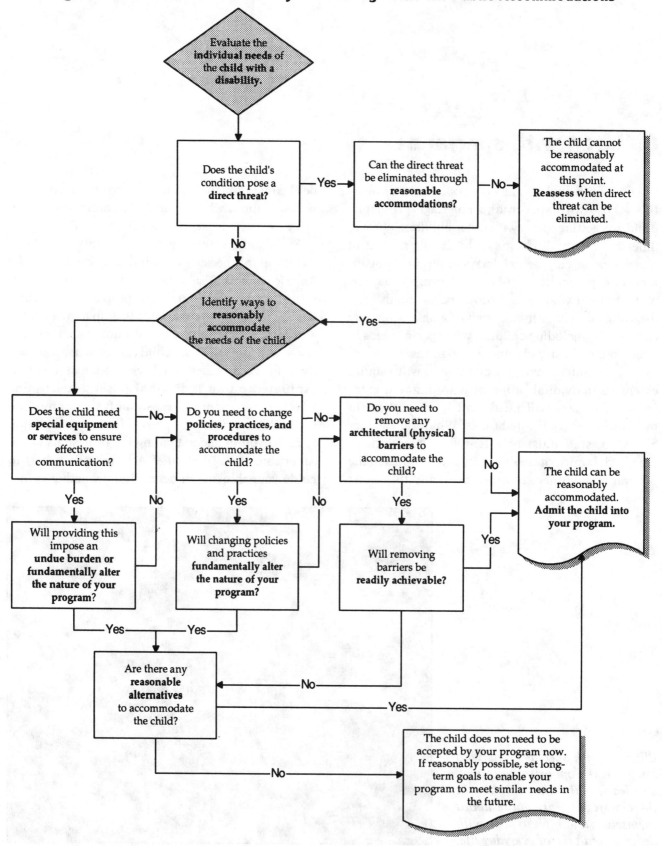

Figure 13.1 *continued*

ADA GOAL:

> To *reasonably accommodate* individuals with disabilities in order to *integrate* them into the program to the extent feasible, given *each individual*'s limitations.

ADA PRINCIPLES:

- INDIVIDUALITY
    the limitations and needs of *each* individual;

- REASONABLENESS
    of the accommodation to the *program* and to the *individual;*

- INTEGRATION
    of the individual *with others* in the program.

TYPES OF ACCOMMODATIONS:

- AUXILIARY AIDS AND SERVICES
    special equipment and services to ensure effective communication;

- CHANGES IN POLICIES, PRACTICES AND PROCEDURES;

- REMOVAL OF BARRIERS
    architectural, arrangement of furniture and equipment, vehicular.

REASONS TO DENY CARE:

- ACCOMMODATION IS UNREASONABLE, and there are no reasonable alternatives.

    □ For **auxiliary aids and services**, if accommodations pose an *UNDUE BURDEN* (will result in a significant difficulty or expense to the program);

    □ For **auxiliary aids and services**, or **changes in policies, practices or procedures**, if accommodations *FUNDAMENTALLY ALTER* the nature of the program;

    □ For **removal of barriers**, if accommodations are *NOT READILY ACHIEVABLE* (cannot be done without much difficulty or expense to the program).

- DIRECT THREAT

    The individual's condition will pose or does pose a significant threat to the health or safety of other children or staff in the program, and there are no reasonable means of removing the threat.

your program can reasonably accommodate the needs of a particular child.

Several other chapters in this manual may also provide helpful information. For example, Chapter 6 presents safety issues to consider with a particular special needs child in mind. Chapter 8 offers emergency-related advice that may have special importance for a program including children with special needs. Chapter 14 presents information on abused or neglected children, and Chapter 16 describes chronic health conditions you may encounter.

Inclusion

Inclusion, as a value, supports the right of all children, regardless of their diverse abilities, to participate actively in natural settings with their communities. A natural setting is one in which the child would spend time had she or he not had a disability. Such settings include but are not limited to home and family, play groups, child care, nursery schools, Head Start programs, kindergartens, and neighborhood school classrooms. Support for inclusion extends to full and successful access to health, social service, education, and other supports and services that promote full participation in community life for young children and their families (The Division for Early Childhood 1993).

Benefits of inclusion

Research on children has shown repeatedly that the early years of life are critical for learning and growth. It is during this time that children's cognitive, speech and language, physical, social, and emotional development can be most influenced. If their special needs are recognized and met during these years, children with disabilities will have a much better chance of becoming competent and independent adults. Children with special needs who are given the opportunity to play and learn with other children in the classroom learn more about themselves and how to cope with the give-and-take of everyday life. This is one of the first steps they can make toward developing independence. When children with special needs participate in regular early childhood settings that provide for their special needs and have teachers who know how to adapt teaching techniques and activities, they will have a head start toward achieving their fullest potential.

Inclusion helps children

When children with special needs participate in an early childhood program as welcome members of the class, they learn self-reliance and master new skills. When they work and play with other chil-

Inclusion allows all children the opportunity to make friends with many different individuals.

dren, children with special needs are encouraged to strive for greater achievements. Working toward greater achievements helps them develop a healthy and positive self-concept.

Inclusion can be an especially valuable method for discovering undiagnosed problems. Some disabilities don't become evident until after children enter elementary school, and by then much important learning time has been lost. Teachers and caregivers of young children have the opportunity to observe and compare many children of the same age, making it easier to spot problems. See Chapter 9 for additional information on developmental milestones.

Inclusion can help nondisabled children, too. They can learn to accept and be comfortable with individual differences. Some studies show that children's attitudes toward children with special needs become more positive when they have the opportunity to play together regularly. They learn that children with special needs share with them the ability to do some things better than others. Inclusion allows all children the opportunity to make friends with many different individuals.

Each child is an individual with different needs and abilities.

Inclusion helps parents
Inclusion can also be helpful for the parents of children with special needs. These parents may feel less isolated, when you, the other members of the staff, and specialists share the responsibility for teaching their child. They can learn new ways to help their own child. As they watch their child progress and interact with other children, parents can begin to think about their child more realistically. They will see that some of the behaviors that concern them are probably typical of all young children, not just children with special needs.

Inclusion helps teachers
Inclusion can also have advantages for you. You will have the chance to make a significant impact on a child with special needs. The techniques you develop for working with a child with special needs will enhance your ability to meet the range of individual needs of all children in your program. In fact, many of the most effective teaching techniques were first developed for children with disabilities. Finally, working with children with spe-

cial needs is a chance to broaden both your teaching and personal experience.

How is inclusion carried out?
Inclusion can be carried out in a variety of ways. Your decisions about the best ways to include a particular child with special needs will depend upon the child's strengths and needs. Each child is an individual with different needs and abilities. This is just as true for a child with special needs who displays a broad range of behavior and abilities. Your decisions will also be influenced by the parents, staff, and resources and services within your community. The most integrated setting appropriate to meeting the special needs of a child should be *individually* determined for a *particular* child at a *particular* time and reassessed *regularly*.

Inclusion involves the efforts of many people working as a team. This team includes teachers, the child's parents, other specialists providing consultant services on a full- or part-time basis, agencies serving children with special needs, and the public schools. The identification of team members and development and coordination of their efforts is both a challenge and a critical requirement for meeting the needs of a child with special needs.

Staff's feelings and attitudes toward children with special needs

Each staff member will probably bring different attitudes and experience different feelings, both positive and negative, when including a child with special needs in the program. Different needs may evoke different emotions and responses. You may feel sympathy, pity, repulsion, caring, anger, fear, and/or acceptance. Each of these feelings may affect how you respond to a child with a special need.

Feeling sorry for the child may lead to an overly protective attitude; you may try to shelter the child from experiences that are part of daily life. Pity may prevent you from seeing the child's strengths and expecting the most from the child. Your anger may flare up when you realize the extra responsibility or work required as you deal with a child with special needs. You may experience fear and insecurity if you do not have adequate information about the condition or feel that you are not capable of meeting the child's needs. Your feelings

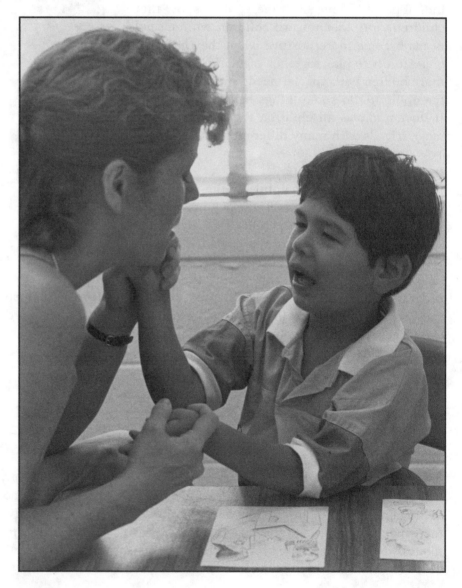

Children must be provided with positive role models so that they learn to interact with others in a kind, accepting way. When they are given an opportunity to watch adults relating comfortably to children with special needs, children take the first step toward learning peer acceptance.

of acceptance and caring may happen immediately or may develop as you get to know the child and view her or him as an individual.

Regardless of your feelings, it is best to first admit and acknowledge them to yourself. Then, share these feelings with other staff who are supportive and who may help you deal with your feelings in a healthy way. Most of you did not choose special education as a career and may feel unprepared to work with various special needs. Often teachers have found that working on a daily basis with children who have special needs has helped to ease their anxiety and fear. These teachers have taken steps to learn about the specific special need and have learned to see the children as children first. They have learned to place emphasis on the whole child rather than on the child's limitations. Learning to see beyond a particular special need is a skill you can develop.

Resources and support

You are not expected to be an expert in special education; however, there are many ways you can prepare yourself to work with a child with special needs. You can read about a particular disability; you may find that the child's parents have a wealth of information to share. You can visit other classrooms where children with similar special needs are being taught.

Specialists, particularly those who have worked with or evaluated the child, may have valuable suggestions and resources to share. Seek permission from the parent to contact the child's health care provider and others who are working with the child so child care goals, activities, and evaluations for the child can be coordinated among all the members of the child's team. Training sessions, conferences, or workshops can provide excellent background material. National associations and professional organizations may be able to send you specific information on a disability and may serve as an important resource for parents. A list of national associations is provided in Figure 13.2.

Your local hospital, college, clinic, or other community agencies may be able to provide you with information and assistance. Your state or local school system may be responsible for providing services to preschool children with special needs under Public Law 94-142, the Education of the Handicapped Act as amended by Public Law 99-457. The law also established the Early Intervention Program for Infants and Toddlers with Disabilities (known as the Part H program) directed to the needs of children from birth to their third birthday. Amended again in 1990, the name was changed to the Individuals with Disabilities Education Act, or IDEA (P.L.101-476). Your school system's special education director or Child Find Coordinator can provide information specific to the services available in your community.

Modifying your program

When children with special needs are enrolled, modifications or adaptations in the policies, equipment, practices, or routine may be needed to facilitate these children's active participation in your program. The primary goal of inclusion is to enable all children to participate actively in the activities of the program and to allow them to operate as independently as possible. For this reason, a program that enrolls children with special needs should meet these objectives:

- adapt the program to ensure successful participation
- develop all children's feelings of competence
- promote peer acceptance
- avoid overprotection
- strengthen the teamwork between parents, teachers, and other specialists

Adapt the program

The selection and adaptation of materials and activities for children with special needs requires problem solving and a little creativity. Special materials may be required and may need to be purchased. Examples of such materials are

- eating utensils with special grips or edges
- puzzles with large pieces and/or knobs for children with fine-motor problems
- books with large pictures for children with visual impairments
- a magnifying glass
- art materials that are hypoallergenic
- low-sugar foods for parties and snacks

Figure 13.2. National resources for children with special needs

Alexander Graham Bell Association for the Deaf, 3417 Volta Place, N.W., Washington, DC 20007. 202-337-5220.

Disseminates information on deafness.

American Academy of Pediatrics, 141 Northwest Point Boulevard, P.O. Box 927, Elk Grove Village, IL 60009-0927. 708-228-5005 or 800-433-9016.

The AAP is heavily involved in public education, teaching parents and children about the importance of medical care, both preventive and therapeutic, as well as providing pamphlets and information for parents on a variety of children's common health problems.

American Diabetes Association, National Service Center, 1660 Duke Street, Alexandria, VA 22314. 703-549-1500.

Affiliates throughout the states offer camps, classes, self-help groups, and support for children, adults, and family members. Its publications include the magazine *Forecast.*

American Heart Association, 7272 Greenville Avenue, Dallas, TX 75231. 214-373-6300.

The association offers educational materials on a variety of disorders such as stroke, heart disease, and smoking, as well as preventive measures such as nutrition and exercise.

American Lung Association, 1740 Broadway, New York, NY 10019. 212-315-8700.

Contact your local branch for general information pamphlets.

American Speech-Language-Hearing Association, 10801 Rockville Pike, Rockville, MD 20852. 301-897-5700 or 800-638-8255 (Voice/TDD).

Education and professional organization for speech, language, and audiology. Free public information is available upon request.

The Arc, 500 East Border Street, Suite 300, Arlington, TX 76010. 800-433-5255, TDD 817-277-0553.

Serves professionals and parents and addresses issues of persons with developmental disabilities of all age levels. Disseminates information on developmental disabilities, parent needs, and many other topics. A catalog and brochure are free upon request.

Autism Society of America, 7910 Woodmont Avenue, Suite 650, Bethesda, MD 20814. 301-657-0881.

Provides information about autism and the various options, approaches, and systems available to parents, family members, and professionals who work with children with autism. List of publications and local chapters available upon request.

Child Care Law Center, 22 Second Street, 5th Floor, San Francisco, CA 94105. 415-495-5498.

A nonprofit legal services organization dedicated to improving and expanding available child care services. A network of volunteer attorneys offers training and educational seminars for both lawyers and laypersons; provides technical assistance on legislative analysis; offers advocacy support for improved child care policies on local, state, and federal levels; and develops and distributes publications to meet the needs of both providers and lawyers. Publication order form available upon request.

Clearinghouse on Disability Information, U.S. Department of Education, 330 C Street, S.W., Washington, DC 20202-2524. 202-205-8241.

Responds to inquiries on a wide range of topics, especially on federal funding for programs serving the disabled, federal legislation, and programs benefitting people with disabilities. *The Pocket Guide to Federal Help for the Disabled Person* is free upon request.

Figure 13.2 *continued*

Council for Exceptional Children, 1920 Association Drive, Reston, VA 22901. 703-620-3660 (Voice/TDD).

Provides information on children with special needs. Children with special needs include those who have disabilities, developmental delays, are gifted/talented, and are at risk of future developmental problems.

The Division for Early Childhood of the Council for Exceptional Children, 2500 Baldwick Road, Suite 15, Pittsburgh, PA 15205. 412-937-5430.

DEC is an organization designed for individuals who work with or on behalf of children with special needs, birth through age 8, and their families. DEC promotes parent-professional collaboration in early childhood intervention services and advocates for policy planning and best practice in prevention and intervention that supports young children with special needs and their families in integrated settings. A list of publications and position papers is available upon request.

Epilepsy Foundation of America, 4351 Garden City Drive, Landover, MD 20785. 301-459-3700 or 800-332-1000.

Provides free information on epilepsy and education materials dealing with seizure disorders, provides referral services, monitors related legislative activity, and is a strong advocate to help obtain needed services and rights for persons with epilepsy and their families. Many affiliates have job placement programs and support groups.

Head Start, P.O. Box 1182, Washington, DC 20013. 202-205-8572.

Head Start programs include services for children with disabilities who meet income-level requirements. To locate a Head Start program in your area, check the telephone directory or contact the local board of education.

Learning Disabilities Association of America, 4156 Library Road, Pittsburgh, PA 15234. 412-341-1515.

Provides information on advocacy, publications, and new developments related to children with learning disabilities.

March of Dimes Birth Defects Foundation, 1275 Mamaroneck Avenue, White Plains, NY 10605. 914-428-7100.

Catalogs are available for the listing of programs and services.

National Association for the Visually Handicapped, 22 West 21st Street, 6th Floor, New York, NY 10010. 212-889-3141.

Provides free learning materials for parents to help their children, including large-print books and a monthly newsletter, and to keep families informed on the new techniques used with people with visual impairments.

National Audiovisual Center, National Archives Fulfillment Center, 8700 Edgeworth Drive, Capitol Heights, MD 20743-3701. 301-763-1896.

Catalogs are available for audiovisual materials by subject area, i.e., special education.

National Down Syndrome Congress, 1605 Chantilly Drive, Suite 250, Atlanta, GA 30324. 800-232-6372.

Provides information packets to child care providers and parents on the disorder. Acts as a referral service to provide contact with local parent/support groups. Services include personal responses to questions, an annual conference, *Down Syndrome News* magazine, and information packets.

National Easter Seal Society, 70 East Lake Street, Chicago, IL 60601. 312-726-6200 or 800-221-6827.

Provides rehabilitation services to people with physical disabilities and provides contact with your local Easter Seal Society.

Figure 13.2 *continued*

National Hemophilia Foundation, SOHO Building, 110 Greene Street, Room 303, New York, NY 10012. 212-219-8180.

Provides a number of free pamphlets and literature on hemophilia and debilitating conditions that can result from it; provides referral services.

National Information Center for Children and Youth with Disabilities (NICHY), 1255 23rd Street, N.W., Washington, DC 20037. 202-884-8200.

Free information service to ensure that all children and youth with disabilities have a better opportunity to reach their fullest potential. Services include personal response to questions, referral to other organizations, information packets, publications, and technical assistance to parents and/or professional groups.

National Information Center for the Educational Media (NICEM), Access Innovations, Inc., P.O. Box 40130, Albuquerque, NM 87196. 505-265-3591.

Maintains and indexes nonbook materials in all subject areas.

National Information Clearinghouse for Infants with Disabilities and Life-Threatening Conditions, Center for Developmental Disabilities, University of South Carolina, Benson Building, 1st Floor, Columbia, SC 29208. 800-922-9234 (Voice/TDD).

Provides information and individualized referrals about community resources and services that meet the needs of infants with disabilities and life-threatening conditions.

National Mental Health Association, 1021 Prince Street, Alexandria, VA 22314. 703-684-7722.

Provides referral services for the general public. Makes available a large collection of free literature. For further information, call the number here or refer to your local Yellow Pages listings for "Mental Health."

National Organization for Fetal Alcohol Syndrome, 1815 H Street, N.W., Suite 710, Washington, DC 20006. 202-785-4585.

Disseminates information and material on fetal alcohol syndrome.

National Pediatric HIV Resource Center, 15 South 9th Street, Newark, NJ 07107. 201-268-8251 or 800-362-0071.

Office of Special Education Programs, U.S. Department of Education, 400 Maryland Avenue, S.W., Room 3086, Switzer Building, Washington, DC 20202-3511. 202-205-5507.

Administers Public Law 94-142, the Education for All Handicapped Children Act, that guarantees appropriate free public education for children with handicapping conditions.

Orton Dyslexia Society, Chester Building, Suite 382, 8600 LaSalle Road, Baltimore, MD 21286. 800-222-3123.

Provides general information packet and catalog of article reprints on dyslexia.

Sickle Cell Disease Foundation of Greater New York, 127 West 127th Street, Room 421, New York, NY 10027. 212-865-1500.

The foundation is a support base for locating local chapters who provide services and information to educate the public about the disease.

United Cerebral Palsy Association, Inc., 1522 K Street, N.W., Suite 1112, Washington, DC 20005. 800-872-5827 (Voice/TDD).

Provides general information and materials specific to cerebral palsy.

Staff can also adapt materials already available. For example, they can

- apply masking tape to brush handles and crayons so children can get a firmer grip
- slit a rubber ball and slide the paint brush or crayon through it so the children can grab it better
- cut out fabric to paste on a storybook to make it more tactile
- lower an easel
- use more visuals to accompany classroom discussions for children with hearing problems or more listening activities for children with visual difficulties
- use a wedge, standing table, bolster, or other special equipment
- eliminate pets or plants in the room if a child's asthma or allergies are aggravated by them

Adaptations to the environment may depend on the type and severity of a child's problem. For example, if a classroom is to accommodate a child in a wheelchair, the staff can do the following:

- measure traffic lanes between areas to ensure that the child can maneuver from one area to another
- check the height of tables to ensure that the arms of the wheelchair fit under them, or find an alternate seating arrangement
- add blocks under a table to slightly increase the height
- explore the use of a scooter board instead of a wheelchair, if appropriate, for mobility around the classroom
- confirm ready access to and from the building
- add ramps instead of, or in addition to, steps
- position a water tray or a table so the child can reach it

Developing feelings of competency

All children need to feel a sense of competence. For some children, learning and relating take more time and effort. To ensure successful experiences for all children, staff can

- observe children closely to see what interests them
- talk with children about themselves, their families, pets, experiences
- break tasks into a sequence

- allow sufficient time to use new skills before moving on to something new
- offer a variety of materials and activities suited to different levels of ability
- provide an emotionally safe classroom by respecting all children
- focus on the **process** of learning rather than the end result
- accept different answers from different children
- set clear and realistic goals for each child

Promote peer acceptance

Children must be provided with positive role models so that they learn to interact with others in a kind, accepting way. When they are given an opportunity to watch you and other adults relating comfortably to children with special needs, they take the first step toward learning peer acceptance. Children should be given factual information about disabilities to dispel misunderstandings and diminish fear. Staff can encourage the acceptance of a child with special needs in the following ways:

- Always answer children's questions accurately, using language that is easily understood.
- Reassure children that disabilities are not catching (contagious).
- Provide simulation activities so that children can have some idea what it is like to have a special need. For example, whisper or put cotton in ears so that children know what a hearing loss is like. Lead children on a blindfold walk so that they can experience the loss of vision.
- Plan activities that allow the other children to see the child with a special need in a successful role.
- Have materials routinely available that depict all types of people. For example, include books about children with special needs in the reading corner, and include dolls or puppets with disabilities (commercially available from Mattel).
- Invite adults with disabilities into the classroom and have them participate.
- Focus on the similarities as well as the differences among people.
- Use a model showing competence and adaptation rather than a deficit model emphasizing weakness.

Avoid overprotection

Overprotection limits a child's opportunities to grow to full potential. Pity and fear may limit a teacher's ability to allow a child with a special need to take risks, to respond to limits, to engage in conflict, and to experience **real** success and failure. Staff can avoid overprotection by remembering the following concepts:

- Limits need to be set for all children (a child with a special need must also wait for a turn on the slide).
- It is important to provide many options and activities in the classroom so that children do not become overly dependent on adult direction.
- All children should be encouraged to try new activities they wouldn't naturally choose.
- Your attitude and feelings will be conveyed to the children, who see you as an important role model. If you avoid overprotection, the children will follow.

Strengthen teamwork

Including a child with special needs makes the necessity for teamwork even greater. To ensure that the special needs of a child and family are met, parents, teachers, and administrators must communicate closely and regularly. Collaboration on the following tasks is especially important:

- identify the special needs of a child
- plan and implement a program responsive to the child's needs
- note any changes in the child's condition
- talk or meet with other specialists who provide therapeutic services
- share information, observations, concerns, and the progress of the child
- obtain special materials, information, and resources to help work with the child

When team members focus on providing a child and family with a supportive, caring environment, the personal feelings of role possessiveness, inferiority, or superiority can often be eliminated. Focusing helps a team see each member's contribution as essential to achieving the goals for the child.

Types of disabilities

The Individuals with Disabilities Act (P.L. 101-476) defines the following types of disabilities. You may want to check with your local school system for the definitions applicable to services to children with special needs in your own community.

Autism—A developmental disability significantly affecting verbal and nonverbal communication and social interaction, generally evident before age 3.

Deafness—A hearing impairment that is so severe that a child is impaired in processing linguistic information through hearing, with or without amplification.

Deaf-blindness—Simultaneous hearing and visual impairments, the combination of which causes severe communication and other developmental and educational problems.

Hearing impairment—An impairment in hearing, whether permanent or fluctuating, which adversely affects a child's educational performance.

Mental retardation—Significantly subaverage general intellectual functioning existing concurrently with deficits in adaptive behavior.

Multiple disabilities—Simultaneous impairments (such as mental retardation/blindness, mental retardation/orthopedic impairment, etc.), the combination of which causes severe educational problems.

Orthopedic impairment

A severe orthopedic impairment that adversely affects a child's educational performance. The term includes impairments caused by a congenital anomaly (e.g., clubfoot, absence of some limb, etc.), impairments caused by disease (e.g., poliomyelitis, bone tuberculosis, etc.), and impairments from other causes (e.g., cerebral palsy, amputations, and fractures or burns) that cause contractures.

Other health impairment—Having limited strength, vitality, or alertness, due to chronic or acute health problems such as a heart condition, tuberculosis, rheumatic fever, nephritis, asthma, sickle-cell anemia, hemophilia, epilepsy, lead poisoning, leukemia, or diabetes. According to the clarification statement of the Office of Special Education and Rehabilitative Services, eligible children with Attention Deficit Disorder (ADD) may also be classified under "other health impairment."

Serious emotional disturbance—A condition exhibiting one or more of the following characteristics over a long period and to a marked degree that adversely affects educational performance: (a) an inability to learn which cannot be explained by intellectual, sensory, or health factors; (b) an inability to build or maintain satisfactory interpersonal relationships with peers and teachers; (c) inappropriate types of behavior or feelings under normal circumstances; (d) a general pervasive mood of unhappiness or depression; or (e) a tendency to develop physical symptoms or fears associated with personal or school problems. The term includes children who have schizophrenia. The term does not include children who are socially maladjusted unless it is determined that they have a serious emotional disturbance.

Specific learning disability—A disorder in one or more of the basic psychological processes involved in understanding or in using language, spoken or written, which may manifest itself in an imperfect ability to listen, think, speak, read, write, spell, or to do mathematical calculations. The term includes such conditions as perceptual disabilities, brain injury, minimal brain dysfunction, dyslexia, and developmental aphasia. The term does not include children who have learning problems that are primarily the result of visual, hearing, or motor disabilities; of mental retardation; of emotional disturbance; or of environmental, cultural, or economic disadvantage.

Speech or language impairment—A communication disorder such as stuttering, impaired articulation, a language impairment, or a voice impairment.

Traumatic brain injury—An acquired injury to the brain caused by an external physical force resulting in total or partial functional disability or psychosocial impairment or both. The term does not include brain injuries that are congenital or degenerative or brain injuries induced by birth trauma.

Visual impairment including blindness—A visual impairment that, even with correction, adversely affects a child's educational performance. The term includes both children with partial sight and those with blindness.

Adapted from *Disabilities Which Qualify Children and Youth for Special Education Services Under the Individuals With Disabilities Education Act (IDEA)*. Fact Sheet of the National Information Center for Children and Youth with Disabilities (NICHY). 1994.

Within each type of disability there may be a wide range of functioning. It is important, therefore, to understand both the characteristics of a disability as well as the particular special needs of individual children. These terms should never be used to simply label children. They should be used to assist you in identifying resources, services, support systems, and appropriate training.

14
Child abuse and neglect

Many factors contribute to the maltreatment of children, making the identification, treatment, and prevention of child abuse and neglect complex. There are several types of child abuse and neglect and each leaves a permanent mark on the victim.

No standard definition is used by all professionals who deal with child abuse and neglect. Every state has one or more legal definitions that are used

All communities—urban, suburban, and rural—experience child abuse that occurs regardless of ethnicity, race, religion, or income level.

to establish official reporting procedures. Various agencies also develop their own definitions for reporting and accepting cases of abuse and neglect. However, most definitions have common elements. The National Committee for Prevention of Child Abuse (NCPCA) defines child abuse as a **"nonaccidental injury or pattern of injuries to a child for which there is no 'reasonable' explanation."** Child abuse includes

- nonaccidental injury
- neglect
- sexual molestation
- emotional abuse

It is impossible to identify how many children are abused each year because the definitions of abuse and neglect, as well as reporting practices, vary from state to state. It is estimated, however, that at least 1,000,000 children are abused each year and that between 2,000 and 5,000 die each year as a direct result of child abuse. All communities—urban, suburban, and rural—experience child abuse that occurs regardless of ethnicity, race, religion, or income level.

Identification of abused and neglected children

Educators are required to report all suspected cases of abuse and neglect. As an educator, you may feel that you lack the information required for accurate identification of those cases and be concerned about how such reporting will affect your relationship with the family and other staff. In fact, many parents are grateful when support and assistance are offered to them. The following indicators are provided to help you identify suspected cases of abuse and neglect in children. Many of these indicators are signals that the child is

possibly being abused; however, some could also be caused by other physical, environmental, or emotional problems. Failure to thrive, or poor growth, can be a sign of any type of abuse or neglect.

Physical abuse

A physically abused child is one who has received injuries from shaking, beating, striking, burning, or other similar acts. You should *suspect* **physical abuse** has occurred when any of these conditions exists.

- repeated or unexplained injuries (burns, fractures, bruises, bites, eye or head injuries, bilateral clustered injuries) beyond the usual bumps and bruises of active children

The following are often seen in cases of abuse or neglect. They should be considered in light of explanations provided, medical history (especially if inconsistent), and the developmental abilities of the child to engage in the activities said to cause the injury.

Bruises and welts

- bruises on any infant, especially bruises on the face
- bruises on the backside of a child's body
- bruises in unusual patterns that might be made by an instrument (e.g., belt buckle or strap) or human bite marks
- clustered bruises that might indicate repeated contact with a hand or object
- bruises in various stages of healing

Burns

- immersion burns indicating dunking in a hot liquid ("sock" or "glove" burns on the arms or legs or "doughnut" shaped burns of the buttocks or genitalia)
- cigarette burns
- rope burns
- dry burns indicating that a child has been forced to sit upon a hot surface or has had a hot instrument applied to the skin

Cuts, tears, or scrapes

- cuts of the lip, eye, or any portion of an infant's face
- any cut or scrape on external genitalia

Head injuries

- absence of hair or bleeding beneath the scalp due to hair pulling
- black eyes
- bruised, bloody, swollen eyes
- swollen mouth or jaw
- loosened or missing teeth

Children who are physically abused may appear to have "minor" physical injuries; however medical examination may indicate evidence of serious injuries, including retinal (eye) hemorrhages (shaken-baby syndrome), multiple healing fractures, and sexually transmitted diseases.

Other conditions that may indicate physical abuse include

- frequent complaints of pain
- wearing clothing to hide injuries, wearing clothing inappropriate for weather conditions
- reports of harsh treatment
- frequent lateness or absenteeism; parents arrive too early or leave child after closing
- unusual fear of adults, especially parents
- malnourished or dehydrated appearance
- avoidance of logical explanations for injuries
- withdrawn, anxious, or uncommunicative behavior; outspoken or disruptive behavior, especially if this is a change from the child's usual behavior
- lack of seeking and/or giving affection
- evidence that the child was given inappropriate food, beverage, or drugs

Emotional abuse

An emotionally or psychologically abused child is one who has been verbally abused by her or his parent(s) or who has had excessive or inappropriate demands placed on her or his emotional, social, or physiological capabilities. A parent may emotionally abuse a child by rejecting, ignoring, terrorizing, isolating, or corrupting a child. You should *suspect* **emotional abuse** has occurred when any of these indicators are present:

- is generally unhappy and seldom smiles or laughs
- is aggressive and disruptive or unusually shy and withdrawn
- reacts without emotion to unpleasant statements and actions

- displays behaviors that are unusually adult or childlike
- exhibits delayed growth and/or delayed emotional and intellectual development
- has low self-esteem
- receives belittling or degrading comments from her or his parents
- fears adults

Note, however, that some indicators may be present due to a developmental or behavioral disorder.

Sexual abuse

A sexually abused child is one who has been exploited for any sexual gratification such as rape, incest, fondling of the genitals, exhibitionism, and/or voyeurism. You should *suspect* **sexual abuse** has occurred when a child exhibits any of these indicators.

Physical indicators

- difficulty in walking or sitting
- torn, stained, or bloody underclothing
- complaints of pain, itching, or swelling in genital area
- pain when urinating
- bruises or bleeding in external genitalia, vaginal or anal areas, mouth, or throat
- vaginal discharge
- venereal disease or vaginal infections

Behavioral indicators

- unwilling to have clothes changed or to be assisted with toileting
- holds self, wants to be changed although not wet
- unwilling to participate in physical activities
- extreme changes in behavior such as loss of appetite)
- withdrawn or infantile behaviors; may go back to earlier behaviors (bed-wetting, thumb sucking)
- extremely aggressive or disruptive behavior
- unusual interest in or knowledge of sexual matters (normally, 3-year-olds may masturbate frequently and show great interest in body parts, especially the genitalia); expressing affection in ways inappropriate for a child of that age
- poor peer relationships
- fear of a person or a strong dislike of being left somewhere or with someone
- child reports sexual assault

Physical and emotional neglect

A child who is a victim of physical or emotional neglect is one who has not received sufficient physical, emotional, intellectual, or social support from her or his caretaker(s). The level of neglect may range from beginning stages to truly gross proportions. You should *suspect* **physical neglect** when a child

- lacks supervision
  —very young children left unattended
  —children left in the care of other children too young to protect them
  —children inadequately supervised for long periods or when engaged in dangerous activities
- lacks adequate clothing and good hygiene
  —children dressed inadequately for the weather
  —persistent skin disorders resulting from improper hygiene
  —children chronically dirty and unbathed
- lacks medical or dental care
  —children whose needs for medical or dental care or medication and health aids are not met
- lacks adequate education
  —children who are chronically absent
- lacks adequate nutrition
  —children lacking sufficient quantity or quality of food
  —children consistently complaining of hunger or rummaging for food
  —children suffering severe developmental lags
- lacks adequate shelter
  —structurally unsafe housing or exposed wiring
  —inadequate heating
  —unsanitary housing conditions

In identifying neglect, be sensitive to

- different cultural expectations and values
- different childrearing practices

Neglect is not necessarily related to poverty; it reflects a breakdown in household management, as well as a breakdown of concern for and caretaking of the child.

Characteristics of families at risk for child abuse

All adults have the capacity to strike out in anger, fear, pain, or frustration, and this capability makes it possible for all of us to be potential child abusers. Yet most people have the ability to control these violent impulses. Abuse occurs as a symptom of excess stress and unhealthy adaptations to mental health problems. Child abuse can happen when adults

• are isolated, without support
• have unmet needs for nurturance and dependence
• feel that their failures outnumber their successes
• were abused themselves and lack nurturing childrearing experiences
• are under stress
• keep their frustrations inside until they finally boil over or cannot control their emotions
• are under the influence of alcohol or other drugs that reduce their ability to control impulses

Many of the causes of child abuse can also be traced to societal or personal problems such as marital difficulties, economic problems, unemployment, the loss of a supportive, community feeling in our neighborhoods, and the acceptance of violence as a way of dealing with problems.

How early childhood educators can help abused children and stressed families

Early childhood programs are the only places where young children are seen on a daily basis for an extended time by professionals trained to observe their appearance, behavior, and development. You may be the first person to suspect (and to report) abuse and neglect. When you suspect that something is amiss, you should try to gather some more data to substantiate your suspicions.

Children who are abused or neglected will not be able to learn or participate to their maximum potential. These children may carry emotional scars for life. Depending on the kind and/or severity of abuse and neglect, long term physical effects can include motor impairment, loss of hearing or vision, mental retardation, and/or learning and emotional problems. Thus it is essential that you take action to interrupt the cycle of abuse and neglect by helping children and parents receive needed treatment. Your trusting relationship with children is a major factor in helping children and families cope with and resolve such difficult situations.

Legal and ethical issues

All states have mandatory reporting laws for child abuse. Most states require (and no state forbids) the reporting of suspected child abuse and neglect by educators. Many states provide penalties for those who are mandated to report suspected child abuse but who fail to do so. On the other hand, **every** state provides immunity from civil or criminal liability. (See NAEYC's Code of Ethical Conduct and Statement of Commitment 1992.)

Problems you may encounter

You may have mixed feelings about reporting suspected abuse. You may not want to become involved or you may feel that parents have the right to discipline their child in their own way. You may also be reluctant to face the fact that someone you know may be a possible abuser. This is a natural feeling but must be overcome. Once you are aware that your involvement is required and that child abuse and neglect differ from acceptable childrearing practices, much of this reluctance should disappear.

At times it will be difficult to decide whether or not to tell a parent beforehand that you are going to make a report. Of course, if you feel that a child is in imminent danger and you believe the parent may disappear with the child, call the appropriate agency immediately and do not tell the parent. Most frequently, however, you will be faced with a situation where you know and care about the parent, and the child is not in imminent danger. You may worry that telling the parent will evoke hostility and anger, that may spur the parent to remove the child from your program. However, if you fail to inform parents they may feel betrayed or deceived. As a general rule, it is probably better to inform the parent of your decision to make a report. You might start by explaining that, as an educator, you are **required** to report all instances of known or suspected child abuse. Although they may be very angry, they will see that you had no choice in the matter.

You may also have had previous experiences with reporting suspected child abuse and neglect and may be reluctant to become involved again. Perhaps you felt that a social worker discouraged you from reporting, or was unresponsive, or that a case was not adequately handled. Perhaps you have heard of cases where nothing was done and that abuse continued or escalated. These concerns are often valid. But a previous bad experience does not mean that next time things will not be handled better. You must file a report regardless of previous experiences. The law requires it, with no exemptions. Abused and neglected children cannot be protected unless they are first identified and reported.

You may worry about endangering your relationship with the child's parents by reporting your suspicion. Although the identity of the reporter of child abuse is supposed to remain anonymous, parents will suspect who reported them by the nature of the information contained on the report. Many abusive parents are grateful for the identification—a guilty secret for them. This is especially true if supportive services result from making the report. Each case requires individual handling, but in general, it is best to advise the parent that a child abuse/neglect report is being filed **as required by law,** that the person filing the report is seeking help for the family. Even if the parent adamantly denies any abuse or neglect, filing of **suspected** abuse or neglect is required so concerns about the problem can be aired and put to rest.

You should get a copy of your state's child abuse reporting statute. This can be obtained from a local department of social services, law enforcement agency, district attorney's office, or the Department of Health and Human Services regional office of child development. Check how the report will be handled once filed so you can explain the procedure to parents when you inform them about your responsibility to report their child. Every program has a responsibility to inform staff of appropriate federal, state, local, and program regulations regarding child abuse and neglect.

Your program should have a written policy on child abuse and neglect. At minimum this policy should include

- requirements for reporting suspected child abuse and neglect
- a code of conduct for staff relating to their behavior with children
- procedures for investigating staff or job applicants for child abuse and neglect
- decision-making guidelines for hiring staff previously accused, indicted, and/or found guilty of child abuse and neglect

Reporting procedures

What and when to report
You must consult your state statutes to determine just what is considered child abuse and neglect. **No state requires that the reporter have proof that abuse or neglect has occurred before reporting.** The law may specify reporting of suspected incidents or include the phrase *reason to believe.* **Incidents must be reported as soon as they are noticed** because waiting for proof may involve grave risk to the child.

Where to report
Each state specifies one or more agencies to receive reports of suspected child abuse and neglect. Usually this agency is the department of social services, human resources, or public welfare. **It is important to know who receives reports of suspected child abuse and neglect in your jurisdiction.** Some states maintain a 24-hour hot line just for reports of suspected child abuse or neglect.

How to report
Some states vary with regard to the form and contents of reports of suspected child abuse and neglect. All states require that an oral or written report (or both) be made to the specified agency. Usually the information included in the report should contain

- the name, age, and address of the child
- the name(s) and address(es) of the parent(s)
- the name and location of the reporter (sometimes not required, but extremely helpful)

Preventing abuse and neglect in programs for young children

Discipline
Your program should have a philosophy and policy that provide guidelines for disciplining children. **Corporal punishment should not be used,** and children should not be punished in any way that interferes with their daily functions of living such as eating, sleeping, and toileting. Expectations should be developmentally appropriate for children, and limits should be realistic. Children should be taught positive and appropriate words,

actions, and ways of relating to other children and adults. Adults should model positive patterns of interaction and communication with all children and families.

If you know or suspect that a staff member has abused or neglected a child you should contact the appropriate agency immediately.

Injury

If a child arrives with an injury requiring immediate medical attention, you should take the child to a doctor or to an emergency room for treatment. If you notice bruises, cuts, burns, or other injuries on a child, you should ask the parent how the injury occurred, what treatment has been provided, and what care or precautions must be taken.

As a routine practice, you should keep careful records for every child, noting all injuries received while in your program and any other injuries that come to your attention. In your record, include a description of the injury, date, time, and how it was received, if known; any statements by parent or child; and treatment given. Always notify parents immediately if any injury or illness occurs. See Chapter 8 for further information.

Sudden Infant Death Syndrome

One of the most difficult situations to deal with is the death of a child, and one of the most frightening types of death is that of a sleeping, apparently healthy infant who dies for no apparent reason. Sudden Infant Death Syndrome (SIDS), also known as crib death, is a well-recognized event in the health care field and is the major cause of death in infants after the first month of life (up to 2 deaths per 1,000 live births). We do not yet fully understand the causes of Sudden Infant Death Syndrome, but we do know that it is not caused by suffocation, aspiration, or regurgitation; and that the infant does not struggle or make any noises to alert a caretaker.

The American Academy of Pediatrics recommends placing healthy infants on their sides or backs when put down for sleep. This practice has reduced the risk of SIDS. It is not recommended for premature infants with breathing difficulties or infants with stomach problems.

Studies by the Consumer Product Safety Com-

mission have associated the unsafe use of soft bedding as a contributor to infant deaths. Parents and caregivers are advised to put babies to sleep on a firm, flat sleeping surface and never on top of soft, fluffy products such as pillows, comforters, or sheepskins.

Because of the obvious trauma that an unexpected death of a healthy baby can cause, however, child care providers have been accused of abuse or neglect in such circumstances. In the very unlikely event that an apparent SIDS death occurs in your program, you should be aware that an autopsy can verify that there was no identifiable cause of death (disease, suffocation). If the need arises, contact your state public health department and state chapter of the national SIDS support program for help for the family, the staff, and other families in the program who will understandably be very upset by knowing about a SIDS case in a family in the program.

Accusations of abuse in the program

If a complaint of child abuse is filed against your program or staff, it will be investigated. Your program should have a policy specifying the internal steps that will be followed during the investigation. It is possible that a teacher may be removed from the classroom and given a job that doesn't require interaction with children. Staff may be suspended or given leave with or without pay during the investigative period. Parents of other children in the program may be contacted. Staff members' past employment records may be checked. Do not panic, but it may be wise to contact an attorney.

Screening potential staff

During the hiring process, you should find out if the applicant has been convicted of any violent and/or sex-related crimes or of driving under the influence of alcohol or drugs. Ways you can learn about an individual include

- an interview with the candidate
- a reference check
- observation of the candidate in the job for which she or he is applying, if possible
- a search for information from those who know the candidate, including past co-workers and parents

- a check of public records related to child abuse and neglect convictions

A probationary (trial) period for new employees is strongly recommended. During this time, you will have the chance to monitor new staff members by observing and discussing their performance. Parents may be encouraged to drop in and visit the new employees as well. Each new employee must receive a copy of your program's written policies on staff conduct and on reporting procedures for suspected child abuse.

The most important step program directors can take to guard against child abuse and neglect is to ensure that there is adequate daily supervision of all staff and that children cannot be taken to any area of the child care program where they cannot be easily viewed by other adults. The physical layout of the center should reduce the likelihood of isolation or privacy of individual caregivers with children, especially where children may be undressed or have their private parts exposed.

Working with families and children

As a sensitive, perceptive teacher or director, you may note the early warning signs of a potentially abusive or neglectful situation. This is, of course, the best time to act. You should become aware of, and let parents know about, community agencies that provide needed support services such as respite care, counseling, temporary shelter, drug treatment, and food stamps. Share your knowledge of child development and childrearing techniques with parents. Let them know if you recognize signs of stress in their children. Share your concerns with parents and help them share their concerns with you.

Your early attention and intervention could save a child from harm and maintain a family's integrity. Make it a part of your job to get to know parents so you can build a trusting, sharing relationship with them.

Another part of prevention is educating young children about their right to say *no*. Particularly in the area of child sexual abuse, children can learn to try to stop the abuse and how to tell a trusted adult about the experience. The concept about teaching children about "good touches" and "bad touches" is controversial. Care must be taken not to teach children that genital touching or fondling is "bad" since such touching is a normal and "good" part of mature sexual practice, and masturbation is commonplace among preschoolers. Children can be taught that doctors must check "private parts," but that otherwise, private parts should not be shown to anyone without checking with a parent. There are many excellent materials for young children on this topic. Figure 14.1 presents a guide for evaluating these materials.

Figure 14.1. Considerations when examining materials on child sexual abuse/ personal safety for young children

Content

_____ Does the material teach assertiveness, build self-esteem, and help children develop problem-solving skills?

_____ Is it appropriate for the age group recommended? Is it easy to understand?

_____ Does it portray a range of touches that are good, as well as touches that are bad, without implying that genital touching itself is bad?

_____ Does it describe verbal as well as physical abuse?

_____ Does it encourage children to trust their own feelings and instincts?

_____ Does it teach children whom to tell if there is abuse? Does it identify the range of people who make up a child's support system? Will the child understand that there are others to tell if one person doesn't believe her or him?

_____ Do the pictures, examples, and/or music avoid frightening a child?

_____ Is the material free from bias? Does it include a variety of male and female, racial and ethnic, urban and rural situations? Does it avoid stereotypes?

_____ Is the material sensitive to the needs of children with disabilities?

_____ Does the material teach caution with strangers without making children fearful of helpful strangers, such as police officers? Are children made aware that most adults are trustworthy?

_____ Does it discuss family abuse in an appropriate way?

_____ Is the material compatible with classroom/ school philosophy?

Curriculum package

_____ Is there a teacher's guide? Does it recognize that a teacher may be uncomfortable teaching about child sexual abuse and may not be well informed on the subject?

_____ Does the curriculum provide supplemental materials for parents and teachers and explain how the materials are to be used?

_____ Are the curriculum and guide complete? Is everything contained in the package or does it specify all the materials you need? Can you get the materials?

_____ What is the cost of the curriculum and other materials? Is the package cost-effective?

_____ Is it flexible? Does it allow the teacher to combine activities or to choose from a variety of activities?

_____ Does it help the teacher to deal with disclosure once a child has confided?

_____ Are any audiovisuals short enough to keep a child's attention?

_____ Does it suggest ways to involve parents?

_____ Is the material pretested? What are the expected outcomes of using the curriculum? Are the stated purpose and outcome compatible?

Adapted from the Head Start, Region III, Task Force on Child Abuse and Neglect.

Figure 14.2. National resources for information on child abuse and neglect

These organizations provide information, resource lists, and/or training on various aspects of child abuse and neglect. You should also check with your local public health and mental health agencies for state and local resources.

Center on Children & the Law, c/o American Bar Association, 1800 M Street, N.W., Suite 200 South, Washington, DC 20036. 202-331-2250.

Child Welfare League of America, 440 First Street, N.E., Suite 310, Washington, DC 20001. 202-638-2952.

Children's Defense Fund, 25 E Street, N.W., Washington, DC 20001. 202-628-8787.

Clearinghouse on Child Abuse and Neglect Information, P.O. Box 1182, Washington, DC 20013. 800-394-3366.

National Abandoned Infants Assistance Resource Center, Family Welfare Research Group, School of Social Welfare, University of California at Berkeley, 1950 Addison Street, Suite 104, Berkeley, CA 94704-1182. 510-643-8390.

National Child Abuse Hotline (a referral service). 800-422-4453.

National Committee for Prevention of Child Abuse, 332 S. Michigan Avenue, Suite 1600, Chicago, IL 60604. 312-663-3520.

Parents Anonymous, 520 South LaFayette Park Place, Suite 316, Los Angeles, CA 90057. 800-421-0353.

15
Lead poisoning

Lead poisoning is the damage caused by too much lead in the body. Even small amounts of lead can interfere with a child's learning and behavior. Large amounts may cause serious damage to the brain, kidneys, nervous system, and red blood cells. Young children are at greatest risk for lead poisoning because of their natural curiosity and hand-to-mouth activity. They are exposed to many sources of lead in their normal environment and absorb a high proportion of the lead to which they are exposed, especially if their diets lack adequate iron or calcium.

Knowledge of lead poisoning should be an essential aspect of training for all early childhood educators. Educate parents about the dangers of lead poisoning and encourage them to have their children screened even if the state does not require it. Each child's medical history should contain lead screening results.

Sources of lead

Most lead poisoning happens when lead paint chips or leaded dust is swallowed. While most paints sold since the mid-1970s have not contained lead, many older homes and public buildings still have layers of lead-based paint. Children become lead poisoned from eating, chewing, or sucking on lead-painted surfaces or items coated with lead dust. Typical sources include railings, window wells and sills, doorsills, toys, furniture, and jewelry. Children are easily lead poisoned if they are around old buildings that are being renovated or redecorated. Children touching things with sticky fingers are likely to pick up the contaminated dust or material.

Soil is often overlooked as a source of lead. Soil can be contaminated by paint that has weathered or been scraped or sanded off buildings. Lead can also accumulate in soil from the residue of auto exhaust from gasoline containing lead. Children playing outdoors who get dirt on their hands and then put their hands in their mouths can become lead poisoned. Lead is most highly concentrated in house dust and in soil within 3' of a building or in areas close to busy streets, parking lots, and driveways.

Dust and fumes created by renovation and sandblasting are also important lead sources. Adults working in lead-related jobs or crafts can also contribute to a child's exposure by bringing home lead dust on their clothes, hands, and hair. Another source of lead is lead solder used with water pipes in new construction, or in older plumbing, lead pipes.

Lead screening

Most children who are lead poisoned show no symptoms. Early symptoms such as headache and stomachache, tiredness, fussiness, and poor appetite are vague and can be easily mistaken for a viral infection, teething, or stress. A blood test is the best way to find out if a child is lead poisoned.

Risk for possible lead exposure should be assessed at children's health visits between the ages of 6 months and 6 years. The current tests to screen for lead recommended by the AAP and CDC are a finger-stick or venous (usually taken from the vein at the inside of the elbow) blood test. If an elevated blood-lead level is found, children will be referred to their health care providers for follow-up.

Treatment and follow-up

If an initial lead screening test by finger-stick sample is elevated, the child must have a venous lead test since finger-stick blood screening tests can be contaminated by lead on the hands of the child or the person drawing the blood. A venous blood test is the only way to verify an accurate lead level.

The child's health care provider will decide on treatment based on the venous lead test. For low levels of lead poisoning, the medical treatment may be limited to removing the source of lead and testing the child's blood frequently to ensure that she or he is no longer being exposed. Sometimes iron is prescribed because the lead present in the blood interferes with the body's ability to manufacture healthy red blood cells.

Children with higher levels of lead poisoning may be treated with a chelating agent. Chelation removes lead from the body and causes it to be passed through the kidneys. This treatment, consisting of either daily injection or oral drug therapy, is usually managed in a hospital or clinic setting. Children who have very high lead levels may require more than one course of treatment.

Following the diagnosis and treatment of lead poisoning, children must continue to have frequent blood-lead tests to determine if additional treatment is necessary or to detect evidence of re-exposure. Lead-poisoned children should have careful developmental testing to identify learning or behavioral problems. Although the medical treatment for lead poisoning cannot reverse brain damage, an enriched environment may help children overcome or compensate for their disabilities.

Serious poisoning can occur in any household. Children in the same household of a child with an elevated blood-lead level should also be tested if exposure is believed to have occurred in the household. If other locations such as playgrounds, schools, child care centers, or family child care homes are identified as being a source of lead exposure, children in those environments should also be tested frequently. A cleanup of environmental lead by qualified personnel should be undertaken to remove the lead from these settings.

Environmental management

When a child is identified as lead poisoned, her or his dwelling should be inspected by a state or local health inspector. All deteriorating paint and all accessible, chewable lead paint must be removed from interior surfaces, common areas, and exterior surfaces. Each case must be followed until the deleading is completed and the child's lead level is normal.

Deleading is very hazardous. Specific safety precautions must be taken to prevent poisoning workers as well as the occupants. Steps must also be taken to prevent contaminating other parts of the building, children's play areas, and soil. No children or pregnant women should be present during deleading, renovation, or sandblasting. Check with your department of public health for specific information. Be sure your child care program facility is lead-free.

Measures to protect children

Early childhood programs and parents must work to protect children by taking the following steps:

- Comply fully and promptly with all applicable state and local regulations regarding lead testing and removal.
- Assure that all children have been properly lead screened/tested.
- Have soil tested. Contact your nearest agricultural extension service for information.
- Cover areas of peeling paint with fresh paint, heavy wallpaper, or plasterboard. Do not remove the paint or do the repairs yourself since lead dust can be toxic.
- Never let a child dig in contaminated soil.
- Have a professional who is certified to remove lead hazards remove or cover contaminated soil (pave; sod; or add mulch, gravel, or new topsoil).
- Plant bushes close to buildings to discourage play there.
- Plan gardens and play areas away from painted structures and busy roads.
- Install a fence or bushes as a barrier between busy streets and play areas and gardens.
- Have the drinking water tested for lead. Do not use the hot water from the faucet for drinking or cooking. Open the cold water faucet and let the water flow until it is as cold as it will get before using it for drinking or cooking.
- Do not store or serve food or beverages in leaded crystal pitchers or lead-glazed dishware. Some imported ceramic ware has a lead glaze.
- Wash all fruit and vegetables before eating them.
- Never heat food in the can or store food in an open can.
- Provide a diet rich in iron and calcium, low in fats.

- Never use home remedies that contain lead (e.g., greta, azarcon).
- If a parent is exposed to lead in the workplace, work clothes should be left at work or laundered immediately at home. The parent should shower or bathe before contact with the children.

Use the same measures recommended to control the spread of germs to help prevent lead dust buildup on hands and surfaces.

- Clean your own and children's hands frequently, especially before preparing food or eating, after touching pets or shoes, gardening, playing in soil, or crawling.
- Wet-mop floors, window wells, and sills frequently with weak detergent solution.
- Provide clean teething toys to discourage chewing on railings, painted items, or paper products.
- Teach children to throw away any food that falls on the floor.
- Keep indoor toys inside and outdoor toys outside.
- Encourage everyone to wipe off dusty shoes on a mat outside the door of the facility.

For additional information, contact National Lead Information Center Hotline 1-800-LEAD-FYI.

16
Chronic health conditions

Almost every early childhood program includes several children with chronic health problems or medical conditions. For example, more than 1 of every 10 preschool children has some type of allergy. Other less common conditions are asthma, heart problems, and epilepsy.

Children with chronic health conditions already in programs generally have mild forms of the problems and, most of the time, are able to participate in the normal routines. Even children with more severe forms of these conditions, or with less common chronic illnesses, can be involved in programs with sound planning.

General information about each chronic condition can usually be obtained by contacting a voluntary agency associated with the disease (see Figure 13.2). It is important that you get detailed information from parents about their children's health problems. When doing this, you need to ask specific questions. The child's health record should include an additional section that describe's the child's chronic illness (see Special care plan, Figure 16.1).

Allergy

What is it?
An allergic reaction is a special type of inflammatory (reddening and/or swelling) response in various parts of the body to a substance in the environment that most people tolerate without any problem. Hay fever, asthma, eczema, hives, and sinusitis are common allergic reactions.

How do people get allergies?
It is thought that the tendency to develop allergies largely is inherited from a parent or parents, although the parent may have had allergies only as a child or may have had one type of allergy while the child has another. Allergies develop when a person is repeatedly exposed to a substance and the body's immune system, normally protective against foreign substances, overreacts to the substance, causing symptoms.

What triggers an allergic reaction?
The foreign substances that cause an allergic person's body to react are called allergens. These allergens may be swallowed, inhaled, or touched. Common allergens include
- indoor and outdoor dust
- pollen from trees and weeds
- mold from plants, dead grass, and leaves
- animal fur and feathers
- insect venom (bee or other insect stings)
- foods such as eggs, nuts, chocolate, shellfish, cow's milk, and wheat

What are the symptoms of an allergic attack?
Allergic children do not have symptoms all the time. Rather, they have a **tendency** to react under certain conditions. For example, a child with an allergy to chocolate may be in perfectly good health unless she eats chocolate, in which case she may develop hives or abdominal pains.

Symptoms of an allergic reaction depend on which part of the body is especially sensitive to the allergen.

Allergens that are **inhaled** can cause
- asthma attacks
- sneezing, runny nose
- itchy eyes, dark circles under the eyes
- coughing

Allergens that are **ingested** (eaten) can cause
- swollen mouth

Figure 16.1. Special care plan

Facility name _____

Facility address _____

Child's name _____

Date of birth _____ Times and days in child care _____

1. Describe the child's special need during group care _____

_____

2. Child's present functional level and skills _____

3. What emergency or unusual episode might arise while the child is in care? How should the situation be

handled? _____

_____

4. Accommodation which the facility must provide for this child _____

_____

   (a) Are there particular instructions for sleeping, toileting, diapering, or feeding? _____

   _____

   (b) Are special emergency and/or medical procedures required? If so, what procedures are required?

   _____

   _____

   (c) What special training, if any, must staff have to provide that care? _____

   _____

   (d) Are special materials/equipment needed? _____

   _____

5. Other specialists working with the child (e.g., occupational therapist, physical therapist) _____

_____

Primary case manager _____ Telephone _____
                         (usually the doctor in charge)

Address _____

On-site child care facility case manager _____ Telephone _____

Reprinted from *Model Child Care Health Policies* with permission of the PA Chapter of the American Academy of Pediatrics.

- itchy throat
- nausea/vomiting, diarrhea
- hives/skin rash
  Allergens that are **touched** can cause
- itchy/blotchy skin
- skin rash/hives

In extremely rare instances, a child will develop an overall allergic response that causes the voice box to swell and makes breathing difficult. This reaction should be treated **immediately** by a physician since it can be fatal. Some people have this kind of reaction to bee stings and need to have available a bee sting kit that contains an injection to treat the reaction. This type of reaction is called anaphylaxis.

What is the treatment for allergies?

The most effective approach to treat allergies for most children with mild problems is to figure out what specific allergens cause the reaction and then avoid exposing the children to them. Some allergens are treated by medications, either taken regularly (everyday or during certain seasons) or when the child is having allergic symptoms. Desensitization (allergy shots) may be used with some children who have severe allergies and/or asthma.

What should staff do during an allergy attack?

Use common sense. If staff can identify the allergen, either **remove the child from the allergic environment or take the irritant out of the child's space.** If the allergen cannot be easily identified, and the child's symptoms do not decrease, the staff member should **try to keep the child calm, quiet, and comfortable while she or he contacts the parent or physician.** Severe reactions must be treated immediately according to the procedures the parents have specified.

Parents should be required to leave detailed instructions on what to do if any reaction occurs.

How should programs integrate children with allergies?

Most children with allergies require no special planning at all; common sense is the key to handling these children successfully. For example, if a child develops uncomfortable itchy eyes one spring day on the playground, she or

Keeping pets such as rabbits, guinea pigs, or other furry animals in group programs can cause problems for children with allergies.

he should be brought inside. Or, a child with a food allergy should not be given that food, and all the parents in the group with the allergic child could be asked not to bring birthday treats containing the food.

Some of the main problems for allergic children in group programs are

- keeping pets such as rabbits, guinea pigs, and other furry animals
- damp/moldy basements or bathrooms
- field trips to farms or zoos, hikes in the woods, or playing in leaf piles

Modifications in your program or physical space may be required to avoid allergic reactions.

Asthma

What is it?

Asthma is a respiratory problem in which breathing is difficult and often accompanied by a wheezing or whistling sound. Wheezing is caused by this combination of events in the lungs: the muscles surrounding the air tubes in the lungs tighten, the tissues lining the air tubes swell, and an extra amount of mucus is produced. The airways are narrowed because of these events, the child feels as if she or he needs to push to get air out, and air passing through makes a wheezing sound. Most children with asthma have attacks only occasionally. At other times, they are fine.

How do people get asthma?

Asthma can be caused by allergic and nonallergic triggers. Children with allergic asthma probably inherited the tendency from one or both parents. It is not yet clearly understood how children develop nonallergic asthma.

What triggers an asthma attack?

Because children's lungs are especially sensitive if they have asthma, a variety of factors can trigger an attack including

- allergens, such as dust, pollen, molds, feathers
- weather conditions, such as cold air, weather changes, windy or rainy days
- smoke, both cigarette and other types
- odors, such as paint fumes, aerosol sprays, cleaning materials, chemicals, perfumes
- infections, especially viral respiratory tract infections
- exercise, especially strenuous exercise in cold or damp weather
- sleeping with head not raised, especially when the child has a cold
- emotional upset

What are the symptoms of an asthma attack?

During an attack, a child has discomfort or tightness in the chest and has difficulty breathing. This is usually accompanied by the wheezing sound, especially when breathing out (exhaling). Sometimes coughing and spitting up mucus are part of the episode. Asthma attacks can frighten children, or they may appear tired and listless. In infants and toddlers wheezing is often not apparent. More common symptoms include a persistent rattling cough, rapid breathing, and retractions around the ribs when breathing.

What is the treatment for asthma?

Depending on the frequency of attacks and severity of the asthma, a range of treatments is available. Often, asthma attacks are mild and will calm down with rest or treatment within a short time. Keeping the child away from the irritants that are known to cause wheezing is the first step. Some children take regular medications to relax airways, making it easier to breathe; prevent exercise-induced asthma; decrease swelling; and relieve nasal/sinus congestion, itching eyes, sneezing.

Special equipment called nebulizers convert the medicine into a fine mist that can be inhaled. Some children with asthma use nebulizers on a regular basis or to treat an attack. Other children need asthma medications only during particular seasons or when they have colds.

What should staff do during an asthma attack?

You should have detailed instructions about what to do during an asthma attack, including a description of which symptoms are particularly worrisome. **An asthma record for each child must be attached to the child's general medical form** (see Figure 16.2). General guidelines include the following:

- Remove the child from the allergen if it is known.
- Try to keep the child calm and relaxed.
- Keep the child sitting upright.
- Encourage the child to drink fluids (but nothing ice cold).
- Administer medications as indicated by parents and doctors.
- Contact the parents/doctor immediately if the child does not improve with medication or the child displays signs of severe respiratory distress (e.g., breathing that is so rapid and labored that the child cannot play, talk, cry, or drink).

How should a program plan to accommodate children with asthma?

Most children with asthma can participate in the usual early childhood program's activities. Adults in contact with these children should know emergency procedures and what allergens to avoid in the classroom environment and in foods served. If a child tends to get asthma during exercise, staff should keep

Figure 16.2. Asthma record

Child's name _____

Parents' names and telephone numbers

_____ (work) _____ (home) _____

_____ (work) _____ (home) _____

Physician's name and telephone number

_____

1. Describe the child's asthma symptoms, including when they generally occur. What triggers an attack?

2. How are mild episodes (attacks) treated?

3. How are serious episodes treated?

4. Is this child on daily medication? _____
If so, give details here

Figure 16.2 *continued*

5. Are there any side effects of the medication—physical and/or behavioral?
If so, please explain.

6. Does strenuous activity seem to trigger episodes? _____
If so, under which conditions should this child not participate in sports?

7. Do weather conditions affect the asthma? _____
If so, how?

8. Does the child understand asthma? _____
If yes, does the child participate in the management of this condition? _____

Additional comments

Date _____

close watch during strenuous activity. If an asthma attack begins, the child should be kept quiet and encouraged to relax; after the attack, the child may be able to continue playing. Be sure to let parents know of the attack at the end of the day so that they can monitor the child's condition.

Parents of children with asthma know their children's limitations and should be consulted frequently so your program does not unnecessarily limit the child's activity.

Heart problems

What are they?
The heart is a muscle that pumps blood through the body. It is divided into four hollow parts called chambers. The blood goes from the heart to the lungs to pick up oxygen. The blood then returns to the heart so it can pump the blood out to the body. As the oxygen is used up, the blood returns to the heart and the process begins again.

Heart problems occur when one or more of these are not working properly:
- the pumping chambers
- the valves that separate the pumping chambers and keep the blood flowing in the proper direction
- the blood vessels leading to or from the heart

How do children develop heart problems?
Most heart problems in children are congenital (present at birth). These congenital defects begin in the early part of pregnancy when the heart is forming. Heart disease may also occur in children who have had rheumatic fever, an unusual complication of strep throat. They are left with scarred valves that do not properly control the flow of blood between pumping chambers.

What is the treatment for children with heart problems?
Many congenital heart defects are mild and do not require therapy. The most severe congenital heart defects and some heart disease from rheumatic fever can be corrected or vastly improved with surgery. Other heart defects can be treated with drugs or mechanical aids such as pacemakers.

Often children who have had rheumatic fever will take daily antibiotics to prevent them from catching another strep throat that could possibly cause further damage to their heart valves.

What are the symptoms of heart disease?
Congenital heart problems can be identified in infants who have a bluish color, difficulty breathing, or abnormal growth and weight gain. These

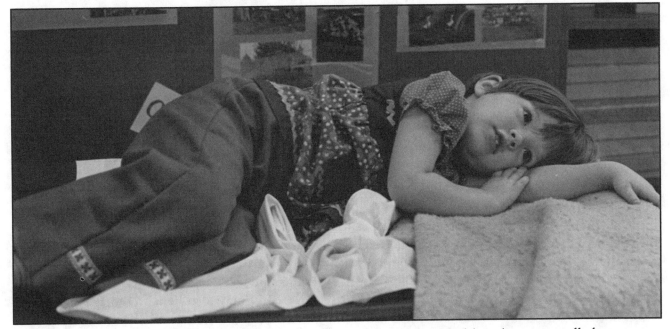

Know what behaviors a child is likely to have during and after a crisis and how long it usually lasts.

children, as well as those with rheumatic heart disease, may tire easily and feel weak. In most cases, heart problems are already known to parents before a child is enrolled. However, in case they are not, it is important to alert parents to any such symptoms as they may indicate heart disease.

How can programs accommodate children with heart problems?

Children with heart problems not fully corrected by surgery or children recovering from surgery may require modifications in the daily program because their stamina and endurance may not match that of other children. These modifications include

- shorter active play periods
- additional rest periods, longer naps
- more frequent smaller meals
- administration of regular medications

It is important to obtain detailed information from parents and doctors describing the types and amounts of activities in which these children can participate. Activity restrictions are unusual because children will generally pace themselves. If you are uncertain if a child should take part in a particular event (e.g., dance or movement), get advice from the doctor and/or parent. Make sure to explain to the other children the reasons for the child's limited activity and provide opportunities to excel in nonphysical areas. **Do not restrict the child beyond what is requested by doctors or parents.**

It is important that children with a history of rheumatic fever not contract strep throat. **If there are cases of strep throat in your program and you have a child who has had rheumatic fever, inform her or his parents immediately.**

Epilepsy/seizure disorder

What is it?

The brain serves as a master control center for almost all functions of the body including movement, thinking, feeling, and talking. It sends electrical charges along nerves to body parts and also receives and interprets these electrical signals.

Epilepsy is a disorder of the brain in which the brain sometimes becomes overloaded with electrical charges and produces a set of uncontrollable movements called seizures or convulsions. The loss of control is temporary, and the brain usually functions normally between seizures. Epilepsy is fairly rare compared to allergies; it is estimated that between 1 and 2% of all children have some form of seizure disorder. Among preschoolers, it is thought to be less than 1 child per 100.

The two most common types of seizures are *grand mal*, currently known as *generalized tonic-clonic seizures*, and *petit mal*, currently known as *absence seizures*.

- **Grand mal** seizures are the most dramatic seizures and affect the whole body. Grand mal seizures usually last only a few minutes. During this time the person becomes unconscious and may shake violently; drool at the mouth; and/or bite lips, cheeks, or tongue. The individual may also have no control over bladder and bowel movements. A deep sleep may follow the seizure. In some cases, the seizure is preceded by a special feeling that differs from person to person. This warning sign is called an aura and enables the person to get ready by lying on the floor to prevent a fall.
- **Petit mal** (absence) seizures are very short and usually frequent. The child may seem to stare blankly, blink, or experience slight twitching and then return to an activity. Though this behavior is often mistaken for daydreaming, a child experiencing an absence seizure cannot be roused out of the seizure as one can do with a daydreaming child. Petit mal seizures are most common in young children. Children with petit mal often have hundreds of brief (absence) seizures each day.

How do children get epilepsy?

There are many different known causes of seizures in children, including

- high, rapidly rising fever
- infection, such as viral encephalitis
- metabolic or body chemistry imbalance
- head injury/trauma (complication at birth or afterward)
- poisoning, such as lead poisoning

Heredity may also be a factor. For many children with epilepsy, however, there is no known explanation for the brain's malfunctioning.

What triggers an epileptic seizure?

Some children's seizures have known triggers including fatigue, blinking lights, scary amusement rides such as roller coasters, certain sounds or odors, or rapidly rising fever. For other children there are no known triggers.

What is the treatment for epilepsy?

At present, there is no cure for epilepsy. However, almost half of all people with epilepsy have their seizures completely controlled by medications and other treatments. An additional 30% of people with epilepsy have their seizures substantially, although not totally, controlled.

Most children with epilepsy (other than fever-related seizures) will be taking daily medication. Information on the medication, possible side effects, and seizure triggers should be obtained from parents and physicians.

What should staff do during a grand mal seizure?

Although a grand mal seizure appears frightening, it is not dangerous to the child if it does not last beyond 15 minutes and generally will pass without complications. These steps should be taken by staff members during a grand mal seizure.

- Remain calm.
- Remember that there is no way to stop a seizure once it has begun, except by methods available to a physician.
- If the child is on the floor, leave her or him there; if the child is elsewhere, place her or him, on either side, on the floor.
- Clear the area of hard, hot, sharp, or pointed objects.
- Place a soft pillow or clothing under the child's head.
- Loosen tight clothing.
- Turn the head to the side so the child can breathe and saliva cannot collect in the throat.
- Do not place any sticks or other objects in the mouth during a seizure!
- Do not try to interfere with or stop the seizure movements (except to prevent serious injury from knocking against something).
- Record the time of onset of the seizure and follow how long the seizure lasts. If you do not follow the time on the clock, the seizure usually seems longer than it actually is.
- Stay with the child until the seizure ends (usually 2 to 3 minutes) and help her or him to a comfortable place to rest for a while. Help to clean up and change clothes if the child was incontinent of urine and/or stool during the seizure.
- Have a treatment plan prepared for seizures that last more than 15 minutes (status epilepticus). Emergency contacts and transportation to a hospital should be arranged immediately.
- Reorient the child to activities.

It is critical that the child not be made to feel awkward after a seizure. The teacher should discuss seizures with the child's group in advance so the other children will be prepared.

What should a program do to integrate a child with epilepsy?

Most children with epilepsy take medication to control their condition and therefore no special planning is needed for them. It is important, however, to train staff in emergency procedures and get complete medical information from parents and physicians. In the case of children who have occasional seizures, the staff should know which activities might be dangerous and should prepare the other children to be helpful if they see a grand mal seizure.

As with other conditions, the child with epilepsy should not be restricted from participating in the full program unless specific limitations are imposed by parents or physicians.

What are febrile seizures?

Febrile seizures are seizures in children younger than 4 years that usually occur as the child's temperature is rising. They last less than 15 minutes and cause no permanent harm. Once a child has been evaluated and found to have febrile seizures, no treatment is needed other than cooling off the child during illness with fever.

Sickle-cell anemia

What is it?

Anemia is a general term for a blood disorder caused by too few red blood cells or too little hemoglobin—the pigment that gives the red blood cells their color. These red blood cells are important to the breathing process and they feed the body's other cells; therefore, people with anemia often seem to be tired or to lack energy.

With sickle-cell anemia, the normal round red cells take on a sickle shape under conditions of decreased oxygen. They have difficulty moving through the smaller blood vessels and become damaged or destroyed. Sickle-cell anemia is most commonly found in Black children and young adults.

How do people get sickle-cell anemia?

Sickle-cell anemia is a disease that children inherit from their parents. Parents may be unknowing carriers and pass the defective gene on to their children. Both parents must pass on a defective gene to produce a child with sickle-cell anemia, but either parent can pass on a defective gene to produce a child who carries the sickle-cell *trait*.

What happens during a sickle-cell crisis?

Sickle-cell anemia affects children differently. A small percentage are able to participate in all activities, but a far greater number have intermittent periods of fatigue and pain. When a large number of sickled cells stick together in a blood vessel, the blockage is called a crisis. It usually causes extreme pain in the place where it occurs. Common locations are the hands, feet, legs, and abdomen.

What triggers a sickle-cell crisis?

A sickle-cell crisis can be set off by an infection, fatigue, unusual stress, overexertion, or dehydration. At times, a crisis occurs without any identifiable trigger.

What is the treatment for sickle-cell anemia?

Sickle-cell anemia is not curable, although it can sometimes be controlled by medication. Its complications can often be treated. Children with sickle-cell anemia should avoid overexertion and infections. Many children with sickle-cell anemia take daily antibiotics to prevent infections. Some children with sickle-cell anemia require hospitalization to deal with painful crises and infections.

How should a program prepare to integrate a child with sickle-cell disease?

Because a child with sickle-cell disease is particularly vulnerable to infection, the decision to place such a child in a group setting is a delicate one that should be reached jointly by parents, physicians, and staff. A child with a mild case may be able to participate fully and should be encouraged to do so. You should have detailed information on the child's ability to engage in physical activities, beginning symptoms of illness or infection, and procedures to handle a sickle-cell crisis should it occur. Discuss the child's illness with other children in the group in a sensitive way.

Detailed emergency procedures must be available as well as several possible contact persons who know about the condition.

Diabetes

What is it?

Diabetes is a condition in which the pancreas, a gland located behind the stomach, does not produce enough of a natural chemical called insulin. Insulin is a very important substance that helps the body store and use (metabolize) sugar (glucose). All cells in the body need glucose to work properly since it is their main fuel or food for energy. Without insulin, these cells cannot use the glucose already in the blood and do not get enough nourishment.

There are two forms of diabetes:

- insulin-dependent diabetes (also called Type I or juvenile-onset diabetes)
- non-insulin-dependent diabetes (also called Type II or maturity-onset diabetes)

Almost all children have the insulin-dependent form, which means they must add insulin to their bodies daily through injections, usually two each day. In addition to the insulin, each child needs to follow a special diet. Insulin and diet must be balanced with exercise. Food makes the glucose (blood-sugar) level rise; exercise and insulin make it fall.

Problems can result from an imbalance among these factors. The most common reaction, when the blood-sugar level is too low, is called an insulin reaction or hypoglycemia. Much rarer is a blood-sugar level that is too high; this results from not enough insulin to allow sugar to be used. Acids and fruity-smelling ketones build up. The person starts to breathe differently and can become unconscious if the situation is not corrected. This condition is called ketoacidosis and can lead to a diabetic coma. This comes when a child is ill over the course of a few days.

How do children get diabetes?

The causes of diabetes are not yet fully known. However, it is generally thought that a child inherits the tendency to develop diabetes. Many diabetic children have a family history of the disease. A viral illness triggers a reaction where the body makes antibodies against the pancreas cells that produce insulin; the cells become permanently damaged and can no longer produce enough insulin.

What is the treatment for diabetes?

Most insulin-dependent diabetic children must have injections twice daily. They must stay on a diet that is specifically planned for their normal activity level and temperament. Exercise is necessary to control diabetes. Finally, using a simple procedure several times each day, the blood or urine should be tested to determine their blood-sugar level. Although diabetes is not curable, in most cases it can be controlled so that children may lead full lives.

What triggers an insulin reaction?

An insulin reaction occurs when the glucose level is too low, either because of too much exercise or too little food. An insulin reaction is usually sudden.

What are the symptoms of an insulin reaction?

There are warning signs that an insulin reaction is going to occur. Often a child will feel these symptoms coming on and alert a staff member.

- staggering/poor coordination
- irritability/unusual behavior
- pale color/sweating
- confusion/disorientation
- excessive hunger
- trembling/crying
- headache and dizziness
- abdominal pain or nausea

- blurred vision
- drowsiness/fatigue

If an insulin reaction is not treated immediately, unconsciousness and convulsions may occur.

What should a staff member do during an insulin reaction?

- Follow the procedures, approved in advance, by the parents and physicians.
- Provide sugar immediately in the form of orange juice, other sugar-containing juice, or granulated sugar.
- Reassure the child.
- Call parents or physician if there is no improvement within 10 to 15 minutes.
- When the child is feeling better, provide a small snack.
- Invite the child to resume activities.

How should a program prepare for a child with diabetes?

- Collect basic information about the child's diabetes prior to enrollment using the special care plan (Figure 16.1). Note additional information on emergencies that may occur as well. Make sure you get information on signs and symptoms the child usually exhibits before an insulin reaction, when insulin reaction is most likely to occur, and the most effective treatment and amount.
- Acquaint all staff with the signs of an *insulin reaction* and how to treat it. Post general procedures in each classroom.
- Make sure every staff member has quick access to sugar or the sugar-containing foods suggested by the child's physician.
- Prepare meals in accordance with the child's special requirements. Work out meal plans with the parents and/or consulting dietician.
- Give meals and snacks on time.
- Have the child eat an extra bit of food before strenuous exercise, if prescribed.
- Assist in monitoring the child's blood-sugar level if requested. Review this or any other special requirement with the parent and physician.
- Explain insulin reactions to the other children so they can inform an adult if a reaction occurs.

Children with diabetes should not be unduly restricted from involvement in all activities.

Review of emergency planning considerations

These summary points, adapted from *Mainstreaming Preschoolers* (Healy, McAvearey, Von Huppel, & Jones 1978) apply to all programs serving children with chronic health conditions.

- Prepare for emergency situations by talking to parents or the child's doctor.
- Be aware of what may cause a crisis and how often it may occur.
- Be aware of how the child may behave before a crisis.
- Know what behaviors the child is likely to have during and after a crisis and how long it usually lasts.

- Ask the parent/doctor to describe, demonstrate, or train you in what you are to do during and following the crisis. Can you do it alone or should you get help?
- Prepare a list of typical classroom activities. Ask the child's doctor to check off activities that must be avoided and to describe modifications so the child can participate.
- Prepare other children for possible health crises by giving them a simple explanation when discussing other emergencies. Assure children that the staff will be able to handle all such situations.

Section G
Managing illnesses

Major concepts

- Your program must establish detailed policies about preventing and handling illness, including policies about attendance by sick children and staff.

- You can help to prevent the spread of disease by following appropriate precautions.

- Always consider all body fluids from children, adults, and animals to be POSSIBLY INFECTIOUS. These include stool, urine, blood, and fluids from the eyes, nose, throat, and skin. It is essential that you handle fluids carefully and clean up after them, even when this process is complicated.

- Despite your best efforts, children and adults will get sick. It is an expected part of life.

- Become familiar with signs and symptoms of illness. Encourage the parents of sick children to consult their health care provider for diagnosis, guidance, and care.

- Recognize that many illnesses DO NOT require exclusion. Most mildly ill children can safely attend if they feel well enough to come.

- Discuss options available for sick child care with parents at the time of enrollment. Be sure parents understand your policies about illness.

- Take active steps to educate staff, parents, and children about infectious illnesses, techniques to prevent their spread, and proper care of ill children.

The March 1997 reprinting of *Healthy Young Children* includes the American Academy of Pediatrics' "Recommended Childhood Immunization Schedule—United States, January–December 1997" (see Figure 17.1 on page 204). There were no revisions within the text of the manual.

17
Infectious diseases

Infectious diseases are illnesses caused by infection with specific germs—viruses, bacteria, fungi, or parasites. *Contagious* or *communicable* diseases are infectious diseases that can spread from one person to another.

Contagious diseases are one of the major problems that programs for young children must face. They cause discomfort, suffering, and absences for both children and staff. Occasionally, outbreaks of serious diseases may occur. If precautions are not taken, these serious diseases can spread quickly. The germs that cause infections and contagious diseases are spread in four main ways:

- through the intestinal tract (via the stool)
- through the respiratory tract (via fluids from the eyes, nose, mouth, and lungs)
- through direct contact or touching
- through blood contact

This chapter will give you information about some of the contagious diseases that occur in early childhood programs. It will also discuss some common infectious diseases that are not contagious.

The five commandments of infectious disease control

1. Prevent illness from spreading
The viruses and bacteria that cause infectious illnesses thrive in warm, wet, and stuffy environments. Conversely, these infectious agents have difficulty growing in clean, dry environments where there is lots of fresh air. To prevent the spread of illness, take these steps.

- Require correct handwashing procedures for adults and children (see Figure 4.1).
- Air out the rooms daily, and take the children outside often.

- Allow sufficient space between cots, cribs, and other furniture.
- Clean and disinfect areas for diapering, toileting, and eating, as well as toys and furniture.
- Reduce germs by cleaning the environment with soap and water and then disinfecting with the bleach solution (see Figure 3.1 on page 18).
- Remember that an ounce of prevention is worth a ton of cure.

Refer to Chapters 3 and 4 for detailed information on these topics.

Infectious illnesses are often spread by people who do not look or feel sick. Body fluids from these people get into the air, food, or onto surfaces where they are breathed, eaten, or touched by others. To control the spread of illness

- teach children and staff how to catch a sneeze/cough correctly and how to dispose of tissues. Sneeze and cough away from other people and toward the floor. If you sneeze or cough into your hands or into a tissue, you will have to wash your hands!
- use running water, liquid soap, and individual paper towels for handwashing
- do not allow sharing of personal items

2. Require certain immunizations
All children in your program must be immunized against the diseases of diphtheria, tetanus, pertussis, poliomyelitis, measles, mumps, rubella, Haemophilus influenzae (Hib), and varicella (chicken pox) (see Figure 17.1 on page 204) at appropriate ages unless they are exempted by your state laws for religious or medical reasons. **You must exclude children who are not properly immunized.**

Figure 17.1 shows childhood immunization schedules typically recommended by state public

Figure 17.1. Recommended childhood immunization schedule—United States, January–December 1997

Vaccines[1] are listed under the routinely recommended ages. Bars indicate range of acceptable ages for vaccination. Shaded bars indicate *catch-up vaccination*: at 11–12 years of age, hepatitis B vaccine should be administered to children not previously vaccinated, and Varicella vaccine should be administered to children not previously vaccinated who lack a reliable history of chicken pox.

Age ▶ Vaccine ▼	Birth	1 month	2 months	4 months	6 months	12 months	15 months	18 months	4–6 years	11–12 years	14–16 years
Hepatitis B[2,3]	Hep B-1		Hep B-2		Hep B-3					Hep B[3]	
Diphtheria, Tetanus, Pertussis[4]			DTaP or DTP	DTaP or DTP	DTaP or DTP		DTaP or DTP[4]		DTaP or DTP	Td	Td
H. influenzae type b[5]			Hib	Hib	Hib[5]	Hib[5]					
Polio[6]			Polio[6]	Polio	Polio[6]		Polio[6]		Polio		
Measles, Mumps, Rubella[7]						MMR			MMR[7] or MMR[7]	MMR[7]	
Varicella[8]							Var			Var[8]	

Approved by the Advisory Committee on Immunization Practices (ACIP), the American Academy of Pediatrics (AAP), and the American Academy of Family Physicians (AAFP).

[1] This schedule indicates the recommended age for routine administration of currently licensed childhood vaccines. Some combination vaccines are available and may be used whenever administration of all components of the vaccine is indicated. Providers should consult the manufacturers' package inserts for detailed recommendations.

[2] **Infants born to HBsAg-negative mothers** should receive a 2.5 μg of Merck vaccine (Recombivax HB) or 10 μg of SmithKline Beecham (SB) vaccine (Engerix-B). The 2nd dose should be administered ≥ 1 month after the 1st dose. **Infants born to HBsAg-positive mothers** should receive 0.5 mL hepatitis B immune globulin (HBIG) within 12 hours of birth, and either 5 μg of Merck vaccine (Recombivax HB) or 10 μg of SB vaccine (Engerix-B) at a separate site. The 2nd dose is recommended at 1–2 months of age and the 3rd dose at 6 months of age. **Infants born to mothers whose HBsAg status is unknown** should receive either 5 μg of Merck vaccine (Recombivax HB) or 10 μg of SB vaccine (Engerix-B) within 12 hours of birth. The 2nd dose of vaccine is recommended at 1 month of age and the 3rd dose at 6 months of age. Blood should be drawn at the time of delivery to determine the mother's HBsAg status; if it is positive, the infant should receive HBIG as soon as possible (no later than 1 week of age). The dosage and timing of subsequent vaccine doses should be based upon the mother's HBsAg status.

[3] Children and adolescents who have not been vaccinated against hepatitis B in infancy may begin the series during any childhood visit. Those who have not previously received 3 doses of hepatitis B vaccine should initiate or complete the series during the 11–12 year-old visit. The 2nd dose should be administered at least 1 month after the 1st dose, and the 3rd dose should be administered at least 4 months after the 1st dose and at least 2 months after the 2nd dose.

[4] DTaP (diphtheria and tetanus toxoids and acellular pertussis vaccine) is the preferred vaccine for all doses in the vaccination series, including completion of the series in children who have received ≥ 1 dose of whole-cell DTP vaccine. Whole-cell

DTP is an acceptable alternative to DTaP. The 4th dose of DTaP may be administered as early as 12 months of age, provided 6 months have elapsed since the 3rd dose, and if the child is considered unlikely to return at 15–18 months of age. Td (tetanus and diphtheria toxoids, absorbed, for adult use) is recommended at 11–12 years of age if at least 5 years have elapsed since the last dose of DTP, DTaP, or DT. Subsequent routine Td boosters are recommended every 10 years.

[5] Three *H. influenzae* type b (Hib) conjugate vaccines are licensed for infant use. If PRP-OMP (PedvaxHIB [Merck]) is administered at 2 and 4 months of age, a dose at 6 months is not required. After completing the primary series, any Hib conjugate vaccine may be used as a booster.

[6] Two poliovirus vaccines are currently licensed in the United States: inactivated poliovirus vaccine (IPV) and oral poliovirus vaccine (OPV). The following schedules are all acceptable by the ACIP, the AAP, and the AAFP, and parents and providers may choose among them:

1. IPV at 2 and 4 months; OPV at 12–18 months and 4–6 years
2. IPV at 2, 4, 12–18 months, and 4–6 years
3. OPV at 2, 4, 6–18 months, and 4–6 years

The ACIP routinely recommends schedule 1. IPV is the only poliovirus vaccine recommended for immunocompromised persons and their household contacts.

[7] The 2nd dose of MMR is routinely recommended at 4–6 years of age or at 11–12 years of age, but may be administered during any visit, provided at least 1 month has elapsed since receipt of the 1st dose and that both doses are administered at or after 12 months of age.

[8] Susceptible children may receive Varicella vaccine (Var) at any visit after the first birthday, and those who lack a reliable history of chicken pox should be immunized during the 11–12 year-old visit. Children ≥ 13 years of age should receive 2 doses, at least 1 month apart.

health departments. Ideally, these schedules would not be interrupted, and most children would complete their basic series of immunizations before the age of 18 months. In reality, however, appointments are missed and immunization schedules are disrupted. **Partial immunizations do not provide complete protection against disease.** For this reason, children with delayed or disrupted schedules must receive makeup immunizations according to the schedule for children who are not immunized in the first year of life.

To determine if a child is eligible to enter your program

- ask the parents to obtain a completed Certificate of Immunization (or a Child health assessment, Figure 9.6) from their health care provider
- determine the child's age
- compare the immunization record with the recommended schedule in Figure 17.1 to see if all immunizations are up-to-date
- if you have questions, call your health consultant

The AAP recommends that if a child is not up-to-date on the immunizations, she or he may be admitted on the condition that the child has a clinic appointment for the necessary immunizations within 1 month and continues with follow-up as needed. Refer the family to local physicians or the health department where they can obtain the necessary immunizations.

Additional information on vaccine-preventable diseases is provided later in this chapter.

3. Report some illnesses

Every state has laws that require early childhood programs to report the occurrence of certain infectious diseases to the state department of public health. Because reportable diseases vary from state to state, you need to contact your local board of health for the current list. **Be sure to include this list and a reporting procedure in your health policy.** The purpose of reporting certain diseases is to enable your board of health and/or state department of public health to conduct investigations and take appropriate measures to prevent further spread of contagious diseases.

For some diseases, an individual occurrence must be reported (e.g., hepatitis and meningitis). Other diseases must be reported when an *outbreak* (involving more children or staff) occurs. Generally, an *epidemic* (a large number of cases in a short period) should be reported, even if the disease is not listed (e.g., flu, mononucleosis, conjunctivitis, or pneumonia).

Special reporting requirements usually exist for illnesses caused by consumption of contaminated food. If a number of your staff and children experience stomach cramps, vomiting, diarrhea, and/or dizziness, suspect food contamination and report the situation to your local board of health.

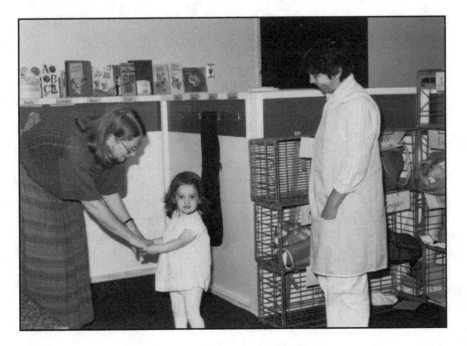

Many illnesses do not require exclusion from group programs. Most mildly ill children can safely attend if they feel well enough to participate.

Finally, there are a number of diseases, such as Acquired Immune Deficiency Syndrome (AIDS) and sexually transmitted diseases (STDs), that must be reported directly to your state public health department. Physicians, health care providers, and laboratories who diagnose these diseases are generally the mandated reporters.

4. Exclude some children
Contrary to popular belief and practice, only a *few* illnesses require exclusion of sick children to ensure protection of other children and staff. Figure 17.2 lists exclusion guidelines.

With most other illnesses, children have either **already exposed** others before becoming obviously ill (e.g., colds) or **are not contagious at some point after beginning treatment** (e.g., strep throat, conjunctivitis, impetigo, tuberculosis, ringworm, parasites, head lice, and scabies). The waiting periods after the onset of treatment vary with the disease (see specific disease descriptions later in this chapter).

Children who are carriers of viral illnesses such as cytomegalovirus (CMV), hepatitis B, or HIV infection **can and should be admitted.**

When your program allows mildly ill children to attend, consider these steps to better meet their needs.

- Maintain a small room or area where they can spend a quiet day.
- If the child's illness might worsen with outdoor play, assign one staff person to remain with this child when others go outside.

Refer to Chapters 18 and 19 for additional information.

5. Be prepared!
Don't wait until an epidemic hits! Do some advance planning and take these steps:

- Insist that staff learn and follow handwashing, cleaning, and ventilation guidelines.
- Choose a health consultant who knows about infectious disease in early childhood settings.
- Have the telephone numbers of your local board of health and the state department of public health posted and readily available.
- Make sure children's immunizations are up-to-date before you admit them. Update immuniza-

tion status records for all children immediately after each immunization.

- Staff should also be up-to-date on their immunizations in order to protect themselves and the children.
- Make sure parents recognize their responsibilities for taking their sick child to the health care provider and for reporting a contagious illness to you. Do not expect parents will read all the material you give them. Review health procedures orally at enrollment and send a letter annually to all parents. Describe each of your health policies and ask them to
    —call or write when their child is ill and tell you the problem
    —call or write if a health care provider makes a specific diagnosis (such as strep throat)
    —tell you **immediately** if Hib or meningococcal disease is diagnosed
    —keep their child home if she or he has an excludable illness
    —call and discuss with you whether or not their child should attend when she or he has mild diarrhea or an infectious disease and if it has been treated
    —inform you of any changes in emergency numbers where they can be reached each day
- **Be watchful!** Learn to look for signs of infectious disease. Call or send a note home if you suspect a problem.
- Inform staff and parents of contagious diseases that occur in your program.

DISEASES SPREAD THROUGH THE INTESTINAL TRACT

Infectious diarrheal diseases, pinworms, hepatitis A
These diseases are caused by germs (viruses, bacteria, or parasites) that multiply in the intestines and are passed out of the body in the stool. Anyone can catch these diseases, and they can be caught repeatedly (except for hepatitis A). Programs that care for children in diapers are especially at risk because staff and children may get stool on their hands frequently. When stool containing these germs gets on hands or objects, it can inadvertently be swallowed. Swallowing as few

Figure 17.2. Criteria for excluding an ill or infected child from an early childhood program

Exclude children and adults with these illnesses or symptoms—

Temperature, oral temperature 101° or greater, rectal temperature 102° or greater, axillary (armpit) temperature 100° or greater, accompanied by behavior changes or other signs or symptoms of illness, until medical evaluation indicates inclusion in the facility

Signs of possible severe illness, including unusual lethargy, irritability, persistent crying, difficult breathing, uncontrolled coughing

Uncontrolled diarrhea, defined as an increased number of stools compared with the child's normal pattern, with increased stool water and/or decreased form that is not contained by the diaper or toilet use

Vomiting two or more times in the previous 24 hours unless the vomiting is determined to be due to a noncommunicable condition and the child is not in danger of dehydration

Mouth sores with drooling unless the child's physician or local health department authority states the child is non-infectious

Rash with fever or behavior change until a physician has determined the illness not to be a communicable disease

Purulent conjunctivitis, defined as pink or red conjunctiva with white or yellow eye discharge, often with matted eyelids after sleep, and including a child with eye pain or redness of the eyelids or skin surrounding the eye, until 24 hours after treatment has begun

Infestation (e.g., scabies, head lice), until 24 hours after treatment was begun

Tuberculosis, until the child's physician or local health department authority states the child is non-infectious

Impetigo, until 24 hours after treatment was begun

Streptococcal pharyngitis, until 24 hours after treatment has been initiated, and until the child has been afebrile for 24 hours

Varicella (chicken pox), until 6 days after onset of rash or until all lesions have dried and crusted

Shingles, only if the sores cannot be covered by clothing or a dressing, until the sores have crusted

Pertussis, which is laboratory confirmed, or suspected based on symptoms of the illness, or suspected because of cough onset within 14 days after having face-to-face contact with a laboratory-confirmed case of pertussis in a household or classroom, until 5 days of appropriate chemoprophylaxis (currently, erythromycin) has been completed

Mumps, until 9 days after onset of parotid gland swelling

Hepatitis A virus infection, until 1 week after onset of illness or until after immune serum globulin has been given to appropriate children and staff in the program, as directed by the responsible health department

Measles, until 6 days after rash appears

Rubella, until 6 days after rash appears

Source: American Academy of Pediatrics, & American Public Health Association. (1992). *Caring for our children—National health and safety performance standards: Guidelines for out-of-home child care programs.*

as 10 Shigella or Giardia germs can cause an intestinal tract illness. Salmonella and Campylobacter germs must be swallowed in larger quantities to cause illness. Children or staff with disease-causing germs in their stool may not act or feel sick or have diarrhea. Laboratory tests are the only way to tell if a particular stool has these germs in it. These tests are sometimes done as part of an effort to control an outbreak of disease.

If cases of infectious diarrhea, pinworms, or hepatitis A occur, notify parents, staff, and your health consultant. Also, report specified infectious diarrhea and hepatitis A to your local board of health (refer to local reporting requirements).

How to stop spread of intestinal tract diseases

Because children and staff who have intestinal tract diseases don't always feel sick or have diarrhea, the best method for preventing spread of these diseases is to have a constant prevention program in place. Take these **special precautions:**

- **Insist on frequent, thorough handwashing for both staff and children** (see Figure 4.1).
- **Insist on general cleanliness.** (See Chapters 3 and 5 for detailed information on cleaning, disinfecting, and diapering.)
- **Separate children into three groups whenever possible:** infants, diapered children, and toilet-trained children. Try to have a staff member work with only one group to avoid carrying germs from group to group. (Note: Because this type of grouping may not meet administrative or child development needs, directors will have to consider a variety of factors when grouping children and assigning staff. If mixing staff and child groups must occur, minimize the number of people involved and emphasize careful handwashing for all concerned.)

Infectious diarrheal diseases—Giardia, Shigella, Salmonella, and Campylobacter

People have diarrhea when they have **more stools than normal** for them and the stools are **loose, watery, and unformed.** (Exception: Breast-fed babies may have stools that are normally unformed.)

Infectious diarrhea is caused by viruses, parasites, or bacteria and can spread quickly from person to person. **Non-infectious** diarrhea can be caused by food allergies, food intolerances (e.g., milk/lactose intolerance), toxins (e.g., certain types of food poisoning), chronic diseases (e.g., cystic fibrosis), or antibiotics (e.g., ampicillin) and does not spread from person to person.

This section gives detailed information on infectious diarrhea caused by Giardia, Shigella, Salmonella, and Campylobacter. Other infectious diarrheal agents including parasites (e.g., cryptosporidium, amoeba), other bacteria (e.g., Yersinia), and other viruses (e.g., rotavirus) are not discussed in detail, but the general stop-spread instructions in this section apply to all of these diseases.

Exclusion guidelines

- When children or staff have uncontrolled diarrhea **and** fever, or diarrhea that cannot be contained by diapers or routine toileting procedures, or vomiting (or have severe or bloody diarrhea) . . . **exclude** until fever and diarrhea are gone and treated if necessary.
- When children or staff have mild diarrhea but are not sick . . . **take special precautions or exclude.** (Also make sure they receive appropriate management with fluids and diet.)
- When children or staff are found to have infectious diarrheal germs in their stool (positive stool cultures) but have no diarrhea or illness symptoms . . . **take special precautions** but do not exclude them. (Also make sure they receive appropriate management.)
- When staff who normally prepare food or feed children have positive stool cultures . . . **do not allow them to prepare food or feed children** until they have documentation of appropriate treatment followed by two negative stool cultures taken 48 hours apart. (Cultures should not be taken until 48 hours after medication is completed if antibiotics are used.)

Special precautions

- **strictly enforce all** handwashing, diapering, toileting, and cleaning procedures; **and**
- set up a separate room or area where added staff attention is provided

Return guidelines. Excluded children and staff may come back after treatment and when severe diarrhea is gone. **Continue to take special precautions** until all those with **positive** stool cultures have had **two negative** stool cultures after treatment.

How to stop spread of infectious diarrheal diseases

- Follow handwashing and cleanliness procedures.
- Keep track of the number of cases of diarrhea and take these steps:
  - —If **one** person has diarrhea, use **special precautions** or **exclude** her or him based on exclusion guidelines.
  - —If **two** or **three** people have diarrhea, use **special precautions** or **exclude** them. Ask parents to have stool samples cultured and/or examined for ova (eggs) and parasites by health care providers. Inform staff and parents (see Figure 17.3). Talk to your health consultant.
  - —If **more than three** people have diarrhea, do all of the above **AND** call your local board of health for help. Use your state's definition of an outbreak and follow those procedures.

Giardia lamblia

What is it? Giardia lamblia is an intestinal parasite in the small bowel that may cause chronic diarrhea, stomach cramping, bloating, pale and foul-smelling stools, weight loss, and fatigue. Although most children who have Giardia do not have these symptoms, they are still passing Giardia cysts in their stools and are infectious if untreated.

Who gets it and how? Giardia is very common—between 3 and 20% of all people have it. It spreads quickly in programs for young children, especially when children in diapers are present. The microscopic Giardia cysts are spread by contact with stool, by drinking untreated water, and sometimes by drinking water in areas where the water supplies are contaminated. Environmental sanitation is **very** important in reducing spread.

How is it diagnosed? Stool must be examined under a microscope to identify Giardia cysts. Because Giardia is present in stools only off and on, several examinations must be made.

How is it treated? Persons with Giardia who are ill and/or have diarrhea should receive medication. Persons who do not have symptoms should

not be treated routinely. Although there is no consensus regarding treatment for asymptomatic Giardia infection, consideration should be given for treatment of asymptomatic infection based on the potential for transmission or re-infection.

When should people with Giardia be excluded and allowed to return? See infectious diarrhea exclusion and return guidelines.

Where to report it? Notify parents and staff if a child or staff member is diagnosed with Giardia (see Figure 17.3). Also notify your health consultant and your local board of health. Make family and household members in contact with a person with Giardia diarrhea aware of their possible exposure to this parasite, especially if they are involved in food handling or preparation. If they develop diarrhea, they should immediately see their health care provider and get a stool test.

Shigella

What is it? Shigella is a family of bacteria that causes symptoms ranging from mild diarrhea to diarrhea with blood and mucus. In severe cases, it can cause dehydration, fever, severe cramps, vomiting, headache, and even convulsions (in young children).

Illness generally begins 1 to 4 days after swallowing the bacteria. Although symptoms usually disappear without treatment after 4 to 7 days, bacteria may still be passed out in the stool for several more weeks.

Who gets it and how? Shigella is most common in children younger than 5 and can be a significant problem in groups. It is spread when diarrheal stools get on hands or objects and then onto other children's hands and mouths. It can also be spread through stool-contaminated food, drink, or water. As few as 10 swallowed bacteria can cause a Shigella infection. Environmental cleaning and sanitation is **very** important in reducing spread.

How is it diagnosed? A test called a stool culture must be performed. Up to 72 hours may be required to grow the bacteria from a stool sample. If Shigella infection is found in a child or staff member, the stools of all other children and staff should be cultured.

How is it treated? Children and adults who have Shigella in their stool should receive antibiotic

Figure 17.3. Letter to parents about diarrheal diseases

Dear parent or guardian:

_____ A child in our program has a diarrheal disease.

_____ Your child may have a diarrheal disease.

Please take the following precautions:

1. Watch your child and members of your family to see if they develop diarrhea, stomach cramps, gas, and/or nausea.

2. If your child develops severe diarrhea, diarrhea with fever or vomiting, or diarrhea with blood or mucus, **do not send your child to the program.**

3. If your child develops mild diarrhea, **please call us** to discuss whether attendance is recommended.

4. In either case, we may ask your health care provider to do the tests for bacteria and parasites in the stool. We may ask you to get tests for your child and for other family members who develop diarrhea.

5. Be sure to remind your health provider that your child is in a child care program so your child's management and the needs of the other children can be considered. **If your child's test is positive,** keep your child home until any serious diarrhea or illness is over **and** our program's health consultant decides whether any special precautions are needed for your child to return.

6. Keep us informed about how your child is doing and about any test results or treatment.

Information about diarrheal diseases

What are they? Diarrheal diseases are caused by germs (bacteria, parasites, or viruses) that multiply in the intestines and are passed out of the body in the stool. Anyone can get diarrheal diseases and they can be caught repeatedly. People with these germs in their stool may not actually have diarrhea or feel sick. Laboratory tests are the only way to tell if a particular stool contains germs.

Five diarrheal diseases commonly found in early childhood programs are listed here, along with the symptoms they typically cause.

The disease which may be causing illness at our center has been circled. If no disease has been circled, the specific cause of the diarrheal disease is not yet known.

How do you catch diarrheal diseases? When people do not wash their hands well after going to the bathroom, changing diapers, or helping a child go to the bathroom, microscopic diarrheal germs stay on their hands and the children's hands. The germs can then spread to food or drink or to objects and, eventually, to other people's hands and mouths. The germs are then swallowed by the other people, multiply in their intestines, and cause an infection.

Obviously diarrheal diseases can spread easily among young children who normally get their hands into everything and may not wash their hands well.

Figure 17.3 *continued*

Name	Caused by	Symptoms
Rotavirus	A virus	Most cases of winter diarrhea in children younger than 2 years, usually preceded or accompanied by vomiting and low-grade fever. May also have runny nose and cough.
Giardia lamblia	A microscopic parasite	Mild to severe diarrhea, bad-smelling diarrhea, gas, stomach cramps, nausea, lack of appetite, and/or possible weight loss
Shigella	Microscopic bacteria	Mild to very severe diarrhea, fever, stomach pain, and/or diarrhea with blood or mucus
Salmonella	Microscopic bacteria	Mild to severe diarrhea, fever, and/or painful stomach cramps
Campylobacter	Microscopic bacteria	Mild to severe or bloody diarrhea, fever, stomach cramps, and/or vomiting

How do you know if you have a diarrheal disease? Some of these diseases can be diagnosed by examining the stool under a microscope, some by growing the germs in the laboratory, others by special chemical tests. Since the germs are usually passed in the stools off and on, stool samples taken on several days may need to be examined.

How can you stop the spread of diarrheal diseases in your household?
- **Be sure everyone thoroughly washes their hands after using the bathroom or helping a baby or child with diapers or toileting and before preparing or eating food.** Babies and children need to have their hands washed, too, at these times. Ask us if you are unsure of the steps required for proper handwashing.
- If someone in your family develops diarrhea, ask your health care provider to consider doing a test for germs in the stool. **This is critical for family or household members who handle or prepare food as a job and can stop spread within families.**
- Medication may be recommended for children and adults who have diarrheal diseases. Your health care provider will decide about treatment for your child and/or other family members.

medication that shortens both the duration of the illness and length of time that bacteria are passed with the stools.

When should people with Shigella be excluded and allowed to return? See infectious diarrhea exclusion and return guidelines. Infected children or adults should be excluded until after treatment and cessation of diarrhea.

Where to report it? Notify parents and staff if a child or staff member is diagnosed with Shigella (see Figure 17.3). Also notify your health consultant and your local board of health. Family and household members in contact with a person with Shigella diarrhea should be made aware of their possible exposure to the bacteria, especially if they are involved in food handling or preparation. If they develop diarrhea, they should immediately see their health care provider and get a stool culture and antibiotic treatment if necessary.

Salmonella

What is it? Salmonella is a family of bacteria that causes diarrhea accompanied by stomach cramps, pain, and fever. These symptoms usually develop in less than 24 hours after bacteria are swallowed, but may not develop until 72 hours and may disappear untreated in 2 to 5 days. Bacteria may be present in the stool for several weeks after the diarrhea is gone. Very rarely, Salmonella causes a bloodstream infection or infects a part of the body (such as a joint). People who do not have diarrhea but are passing Salmonella bacteria in their stools are called carriers.

Who gets it and how? Children younger than 5 and adults older than 70 get it most often. Salmonella can cause severe infections in these people as well as those with underlying diseases, such as sickle-cell anemia or cancer. In group programs for children, Salmonella is usually spread from stool to mouth. Children pass it easily when stool goes from one child's hand to an object or directly to another child's hands.

Salmonella can also be spread by contaminated food or drink and is frequently found on eggshells and in uncooked meat or poultry. Therefore, thoroughly cook all foods, especially eggs, poultry products, and beef, and refrigerate any leftovers. Do not use unpasteurized (raw) milk or raw eggs because they are frequently contaminated with Salmonella bacteria.

Pet turtles can be carriers of Salmonella.

How is it diagnosed? A stool culture must be performed. Up to 72 hours may be required to grow bacteria from a stool sample.

How is it treated? Medication is not usually given for Salmonella. In fact, medication can actually lengthen the time the germ is found in the stool. People who do need treatment in order to prevent severe complications include infants under 3 months of age, people with sickle-cell disease or suppression of the immune system, and the elderly.

When should people with Salmonella be excluded and allowed to return? The American Academy of Pediatrics "Red Book" (1994) recommends that when Salmonella is identified in a child or staff person, that person should be excluded until three consecutive stool cultures are negative and symptoms are gone; other children and staff with symptoms should have stool cultures and follow-up as needed. Persons without symptoms do **not** need to be cultured. If there is an outbreak, the decision to exclude or separate children should be made in consultation with public health officials.

Where to report it? Notify parents and staff if a child or staff member is diagnosed with Salmonella (see Figure 17.3). Notify your health consultant and your local board of health. Make family and household members in contact with a person with Salmonella diarrhea aware of their possible exposure to the bacteria, especially if the people are involved in food handling or preparation. If they develop diarrhea, they should immediately see their health care provider and get a stool culture.

Campylobacter

What is it? Campylobacter is a family of bacteria that can cause diarrhea with fever, stomach cramps, and vomiting in adults and children. The diarrhea may be severe and bloody. Campylobacter infections occur 1 to 7 days after the bacteria are swallowed. Usually symptoms disappear without treatment in 1 to 7 days, but there may still be bacteria in the stools for several weeks if treatment is not received.

Who gets it and how? Campylobacter are spread stool to mouth.

The bacteria can also be spread through food (especially poorly cooked poultry products), unpasteurized milk, and contaminated water. When puppies and kittens have this germ in their stools, they may infect people.

How is it diagnosed? A stool culture must be performed. Up to 72 hours may be required to grow bacteria from a stool sample.

How is it treated? Adults and children with Campylobacter in their stools should receive medication. This will reduce the chance of spread to others. Treatment with erythromycin usually gets rid of the bacteria in stool within 2 or 3 days.

When should people with Campylobacter be excluded and allowed to return? See infectious diarrhea exclusion and return guidelines. Infants and children in diapers should not return after having diarrhea until they have received at least 2 days of erythromycin treatment and the diarrhea has subsided.

Where to report it? You must report cases of Campylobacter to parents and staff (see Figure 17.3). Also notify your health consultant and your local board of health. Family and household members in contact with a person with Campylobacter diarrhea should be made aware of their possible exposure to the bacteria, especially if the people are involved in food handling or preparation. If they develop diarrhea, they should immediately see their health care provider and get a stool culture.

Pinworms

What are they? Pinworms are tiny worms that infect people (but not animals) and live in the lower intestine. The female worms (resembling short, white threads less than a ½" long) come out through the anus at night and lay their microscopic eggs around the opening. In some people, this causes intense itching of the anus and sometimes the vagina/vulva; in others, nothing. Pinworms do not cause teeth grinding or bed-wetting and are not dangerous, just irritating.

Who gets them and how? It is estimated that 5 to 15% of people in the United States have pinworms (the rate is higher in other countries). Children frequently have pinworms, and members of an infected child's household can be infected and reinfect a treated child. When children or adults scratch their itchy bottoms, the microscopic eggs can come off onto the fingers or under the fingernails. These people may put their fingers into someone's mouth or food, and eggs may be swallowed that will hatch into worms in the intestines. People can also keep reinfecting themselves by swallowing eggs that are on their own hands. Pinworms can also be indirectly spread through contact with clothing or bedding that has been contaminated with eggs.

How are they diagnosed? The worms crawl out at night to lay their eggs while the child lies still and sleeps. The easiest way to find them is to inspect a 1" circular area around the child's anus about 1 hour after the child has gone to sleep. By spreading the buttocks and looking with a flashlight, a parent can see the worms crawling toward the opening of the anus. A health care provider can make the diagnosis by asking the parent to apply the sticky side of transparent tape around the anal area so any eggs on the skin will stick to it. This is best done first thing in the morning before bathing. The tape is then placed sticky side down on a slide and examined under a microscope to see if there are any eggs.

How are they treated? Several medicines are available for treatment of this infection. Often the health care provider will treat the whole family if one person in the home is infected and may repeat treatment 2 weeks later.

Should people with pinworms be excluded? No. Children and adults do **not** need to be excluded.

Where to report it? Notify parents and staff so they may watch for symptoms in themselves and/or their children (see Figure 17.4).

Special stop-spread information

In addition to following handwashing and cleanliness procedures, staff should be sure each child has her or his own crib or mat with its own sheets. Each child's clothing should be stored separately in plastic bags and sent home for laundering.

Hepatitis A

What is it? Hepatitis A is an infection of the liver caused by the hepatitis A virus. Although the virus causes a total body illness, it is spread through the intestines and stools. The illness often occurs from 2 to 8 weeks (typically 4 weeks) after the virus is

Figure 17.4. Letter to parents about pinworms

Dear parent or guardian:

_____ A child in our program has pinworms.

_____ Your child may have pinworms.

Please take these precautions:

1. Check your child for pinworms, using the information given below.

2. If you think your child may have pinworms, call your health care provider for instructions.

3. If your child does have pinworms, please tell us.

4. **Remember to wash your hands and your child's hands carefully after going to the bathroom and BEFORE eating or preparing food.** This will help prevent spread of pinworms to family members.

Information about pinworms

What are they? Pinworms are small, white, threadlike worms that live in the large intestine and only infect people. The female worms crawl out through the anus at night and lay eggs on the skin around the opening. This can cause intense itching in this area. It does **not** cause teeth grinding or bed-wetting. It is not a dangerous disease, just a very irritating one.

Who gets them and how? It is estimated that 5 to 15% of the people in the United States have pinworms. Children frequently have pinworms, and members of an infected child's family can be infected and then reinfect a treated child. When children scratch their bottoms, the microscopic eggs can come off onto their fingers or under their fingernails. If they put their fingers into someone's mouth or food, the eggs may be swallowed and then hatch into worms in their intestines. Pinworms can also be spread through contact with clothing or bedding that has been contaminated with eggs.

What do you do about pinworms? Your health care provider will ask you to place sticky tape on your child's bottom first thing in the morning and will then look at the tape under the microscope. If there are pinworm eggs on the tape, she or he will give your child a medication to cure the infection. Your whole family may be treated, too, because other people in households are often infected as well but are not aware of it.

swallowed. Adults who have hepatitis A often suffer from tiredness, loss of appetite, nausea, fever, and jaundice (yellowing of the skin and whites of the eyes as well as dark brown urine and pale stools). These symptoms usually last from 1 to 2 weeks, although some adults may be sick for several months. Most young children who catch the virus have only a mild flu-like illness without jaundice, or no symptoms at all.

Who gets it and how? Anyone can get this infection that spreads quickly in groups of children who do not yet use the toilet and who cannot wash their own hands well. Because most young children with hepatitis A do not become ill, often the first sign of the infection is a jaundiced parent or staff member. Hepatitis A virus is passed out of the body in the stool and is spread by the stool to mouth method. Contact with stool-contaminated food, drink, or environmental surfaces can also spread the infection. The virus is **not found** in urine, saliva, or other body fluids and is **found only briefly** in the blood. A person is most contagious during the 2 weeks before the illness begins, when there are the most virus particles in the stool. Usually, within a week after the illness starts, the virus disappears from the stool.

How is it diagnosed? Hepatitis A is diagnosed by a blood test that indicates if a person currently has the infection, regardless of the presence of symptoms. Another blood test can detect whether the person has ever had the infection.

How is it treated? There is no treatment that **cures** hepatitis A. However, because the incubation period is so long, the illness can usually be prevented by giving persons exposed to hepatitis A a protective shot of immune globulin as soon as possible and at most within 2 weeks of their exposure to the virus.

When should people with hepatitis A be excluded and allowed to return? Exclude these people:
• those who are jaundiced
• those exposed to hepatitis A virus in the past 2 weeks, unless they receive immune globulin. If they do not receive immune globulin, exclude them for 6 weeks after the last case occurs.

People who are sick with hepatitis A can return to the program 1 week after the illness started AND when their fever is gone.

Where to report it? Notify parents and staff (see Figure 17.5). Also notify your health consultant and your local board of health.

Special stop-spread information
• Since the hepatitis A virus can survive on objects and environmental surfaces, it is important to clean *and* disinfect all surfaces. Strictly enforce handwashing practices and procedures for cleaning and disinfecting surfaces.
• Make sure all parents and staff notify the program if any person in their household is diagnosed with hepatitis A.
• If a household member comes down with hepatitis A, the child or staff member living there should get a blood test to see if she or he has the illness as well. If the test is negative, she or he should receive a shot of immune globulin. If the test is positive for hepatitis A, exclude as described above.
• You may have an **outbreak** if, in the course of 1 month,
  —one child in the program **OR** one staff person develops hepatitis A (diagnosed by blood test) or
  —people with hepatitis A are found in two or more households with children in group programs or staff.
• At this point, call your local board of health. They will help you investigate the possible outbreak and will also request that exposed children and adults be given the immune globulin shot by their own health care providers.
• When a case of hepatitis A occurs in a program that has children in diapers, **all** children and staff should get the immune globulin shot. If there are no children in diapers, only staff in direct contact with the infected child and children in the infected person's class need to get the shot.
• Additionally, any children who could have potentially shared eating or drinking utensils should be given immune globulin.
• If an outbreak of hepatitis A occurs in a program, all children enrolled or staff hired during

Figure 17.5. Letter to parents about hepatitis A

Dear parent or guardian:

A child or staff member in our program has been diagnosed with a viral infection called hepatitis A, and your child may have been exposed.

Information about hepatitis A

What is it? Hepatitis A is an infection of the liver caused by a virus. It can cause tiredness, fever, lack of appetite, nausea, and jaundice (yellowing of the skin and whites of the eyes, with darkening of the urine). The illness usually lasts 1 to 2 weeks. Young children do not usually show any symptoms even though they carry the infection and can spread it to other children and adults.

How do you get it? The virus lives in the intestines and is passed out of the body in the stool. The virus is microscopic, so you cannot see it. If people do not wash their hands well after toileting a child or themselves, or do not wash the child's hands, the virus can be spread to other people, food, drink, or other things. The germs can then be swallowed by another person, multiply in the intestines, and cause illness 2 to 8 weeks later. If a person has swallowed some germs, the illness may be prevented by a shot of immune globulin.

How is it diagnosed? Hepatitis A is diagnosed by a blood test.

What should you do about hepatitis A?

1. Be sure all members of your household thoroughly wash their hands **after** going to the toilet, helping a child go to the toilet, or changing a diaper. They must wash the children's hands, too. **These are the most important things to do!** Hands should also be washed before touching food, eating, or feeding.

2. If anyone in your household develops signs of hepatitis A, ask your health care provider to do a blood test. Tell us if it is positive.

3. Do any of the checked items:

_____ Ask your health care provider to give your child a shot of immune globulin. The immune globulin may be available free of charge to your physician from your state or local health department.

_____ Ask your health care provider to give immune globulin shots to the other people in your household.

the 6 weeks following the last case of hepatitis A should receive immune globulin before coming to the program to prevent further spread of the disease.

- If you have not recognized an outbreak for 3 or more weeks from the onset of the first case or if illness has occurred in three or more families, the disease is likely to have spread widely. Immune globulin should be considered for all the program staff and children and for all the household contacts of all enrolled children who are 3 years old or younger.

Hand, foot, and mouth syndrome (coxsackievirus)

What is it? Hand, foot, and mouth syndrome is a mild disease caused by coxsackievirus. Symptoms may include fever; sore throat; stomach pain and diarrhea; and a rash of tiny blisters on the palms of the hands, soles of the feet, and in the mouth. It is most common in the summer and fall.

Who gets it? Adults and children can get it but it is most common among young children.

How do they get it? Coxsackievirus is spread by stool to mouth. Stool gets on hands or objects and then onto other people's hands and mouths. The virus may also be spread by direct contact with discharge from the nose and throat. People usually get sick 3 to 6 days after being exposed to the virus.

How is it treated? There is no specific treatment available.

How is it diagnosed? Diagnosis is usually based on clinical symptoms described above.

Should people be excluded? No. If they are well enough to attend, there is no need to exclude. Because the virus is contagious before symptoms begin, other children and staff have already been exposed.

Where to report it? Notify parents, staff, and—if required—the local board of health.

Stop spread guidelines for coxsackievirus

Follow strict handwashing and personal hygiene procedures. Always wash hands, especially after using the bathroom or diapering or assisting a child in the bathroom and before eating or handling food.

DISEASES SPREAD THROUGH THE RESPIRATORY TRACT

Respiratory tract diseases are all spread through microscopic, infectious droplets of the nose, eye, or throat, most of which are shared via hand contact with infected fluids and then contact with surfaces that uninfected people touch to pick up the germs or breathe them in through airborne spread. Respiratory tract diseases may be mild (viral colds and strep throat) or life threatening (bacterial meningitis). Some of these diseases are more common in children (Hib—Haemophilus influenzae type b), whereas others like the viral cold affect all ages fairly equally.

When an infected person talks, coughs, sneezes, or blows the nose, infectious droplets get on objects such as hands, toys, or food and can be touched, mouthed, or eaten by others. When the germs in these infected droplets come in contact with the nose, eyes, or mouth of an uninfected person, they can multiply in the nose and throat and cause infection. Young children often fail to wash their hands after touching their noses or eyes and are in constant physical/oral contact with objects around them. Adults and children often put their hands around their eyes, mouth, and nose. As a result, respiratory tract diseases spread easily in a group setting.

Stop-spread methods for respiratory tract diseases

Handwashing and cleanliness are essential to stop the spread of all respiratory tract diseases.

- Ensure that staff and children thoroughly wash their hands after wiping or blowing noses; after contact with any nose, throat, or eye secretions; and before preparing or eating food.
- Do not allow food to be shared.
- Wash and disinfect any mouthed toys and frequently used surfaces (such as tables) according to the recommended schedule on page 30.
- Wash eating utensils carefully in hot, soapy water; then disinfect and air dry. Use a dishwasher whenever possible.
- Use disposable cups whenever possible; when reusable cups must be used, wash them in a sanitizing solution and allow them to air dry after each use. Label each child's cup.

Figure 17.6. Letter to parents about hand, foot, and mouth syndrome (coxsackievirus)

Dear parent or guardian:

_____ A child in our program has hand, foot, and mouth syndrome.

_____ Your child may have hand, foot, and mouth syndrome.

Information about hand, foot, and mouth syndrome

What is it? Hand, foot, and mouth syndrome is a mild disease caused by coxsackievirus. Symptoms may include fever; sore throat; stomach pain and diarrhea; and a rash of tiny blisters on the palms of the hands, soles of the feet, and in the mouth. It is most common in the summer and fall.

Who gets it? Adults and children can get it but it is most common among young children.

How do they get it? Coxsackievirus is spread by stool to mouth. Stool gets on hands or objects and then onto other people's hands and mouths. The virus may also be spread by direct contact with discharge from the nose and throat. People usually get sick 3 to 6 days after being exposed to the virus.

How is it treated? There is no specific treatment available.

How is it diagnosed? Diagnosis is usually based on clinical symptoms described above.

Should people be excluded? No. If they are well enough to attend, there is no need to exclude. Because the virus is contagious before symptoms begin, other children and staff have already been exposed.

What should you do? Follow strict handwashing and personal hygiene procedures. Always wash hands, especially after using the bathroom or diapering or assisting a child in the bathroom and before eating or handling food. Please notify us if your child develops this illness.

- Air out the rooms daily, even in winter.
- Have children play outdoors as often as possible. When indoors, open windows several times a day to maximize ventilation.
- Teach children and staff to cough or sneeze toward the floor or to one side away from people. If they sneeze or cough into a hand or tissue, they must properly dispose of the tissue and wash their hands.
- Wipe runny noses and eyes promptly, and wash hands afterward.
- Use disposable towels and tissues.
- Dispose of towels or tissues contaminated with nose, throat, or eye fluids in a step can with a plastic liner. Keep cans away from food and classroom materials.

COMMON RESPIRATORY TRACT ILLNESSES—RESPIRATORY VIRAL ILLNESSES

Colds, influenza

What are they? **Colds** are mild infections of the nose and throat that are caused by many different viruses. The most common of these is a rhinovirus (nose virus). Cold symptoms include stuffy or runny nose, sore throat, coughing or sneezing, watery eyes, fluid in the ears, fever, and general fatigue. **Influenza** is also caused by viruses (Influenza A or B) and has symptoms of high fever, chills, congestion, coughing, headache, and muscle aches. Most people who get influenza feel too ill to attend a group program.

Who gets them and how? Young children usually catch many colds each year and will catch even more if they have young siblings or attend a group program. **The virus concentration in respiratory secretions is usually highest 2 to 3 days before a person develops symptoms of illness.** Viruses continue to be present in respiratory secretions for 2 to 3 days after symptoms begin. As a result, infected children and staff have already spread viruses before they begin to feel ill. In fact, children and adults often have mild colds that may go undetected but still cause them to be contagious. Green nasal mucus (usually found toward the *end* of the cold) is not more contagious than the clear mucus (usually found at the beginning of the illness).

How are they diagnosed? These viral illnesses are usually diagnosed by their symptoms. The viruses can be grown in special cultures in laboratories, but this process is time consuming, expensive, and usually unnecessary.

How are they treated? No medicines or treatments can *cure* these viral illnesses. Health care providers usually suggest rest and plenty of fluids. Sometimes a viral infection can be complicated by secondary **bacterial** infection (e.g., ear or sinus infection, pneumonia). A person with high fever, persistent cough, or earache should be evaluated by a health care provider to see if there is a bacterial infection that requires antibiotic treatment. Aspirin (or products containing salicylate) should **NOT** be used for fever control if influenza or chicken pox is suspected because of the rare association between Reye's syndrome (vomiting, liver problems, and/or coma) and influenza and chicken pox.

When should people with viral illnesses be excluded? There is no need to exclude these children and staff, as long as they feel well enough to attend.

Yearly influenza vaccines are very important to prevent influenza and its complications among staff and children who have respiratory problems (e.g., asthma), heart defects, or immune deficiency (e.g., HIV/AIDS, cancer chemotherapy).

Roseola (Sixth disease)

What is it? Roseola is another viral infection that starts with a high fever (103° F. or above) and lasts 3 to 4 days. Soon after the fever ends, the infected person develops a lace-like rash over the whole body, but begins to feel well again.

Who gets it and how? Most cases of roseola occur in children ages 6 to 24 months. Infection is rare before 3 months or after 4 years of age. Roseola does not seem to spread easily although occasional outbreaks have been reported. Roseola is caused by a virus but it is not known how it spreads. The greatest numbers of cases tend to occur in spring to summer. It is not known how long an infected person is communicable. The estimated incubation period is 5 to 15 days from exposure.

How is it diagnosed? There is no diagnostic test available. Diagnosis is made on the basis of clinical symptoms.

How is it treated? There is no specific treatment for roseola other than supportive care to make the child more comfortable.

Should a child be excluded? No. They may attend when they feel well enough.

Stop-spread methods for common respiratory tract illnesses

Follow the stop-spread methods for respiratory tract diseases.

COMMON RESPIRATORY TRACT ILLNESSES— GROUP A STREPTOCOCCAL INFECTIONS

Strep throat, scarlet fever, impetigo

What are they? A variety of infections, including strep throat, scarlet fever, and impetigo, are caused by Group A Streptococci bacteria (see page 233 for a discussion of impetigo).

Strep throat infections are categorized by a very red, painful throat often accompanied by fever, tender and swollen lymph nodes (called glands by many people), headache, and stomachache. Sometimes a strep throat will be accompanied by coughing or less often a runny nose. The vast majority of sore throats in children and adults are caused by cold viruses, **not** strep bacteria.

Scarlet fever is a type of Streptococcal infection characterized by a skin rash. The rash usually consists of fine, red bumps that feel sandpapery and usually appear on the neck, chest, groin, and/or inner surface of the knees, thighs, and elbows. It may last only a few hours. Other scarlet fever symptoms include flushed cheeks, paleness around the mouth, and a red tongue that resembles the surface of a strawberry. Scarlet fever is no more serious than strep throat.

Rheumatic fever (abnormalities of the heart valves and inflammation of the joints) can develop 5 to 6 weeks after the occurrence of any type of strep infection that goes untreated. In rare instances, **kidney disease** can also follow an untreated strep infection. Therefore, it is very important that all cases of suspected strep infections be referred to health care providers for diagnosis and treatment if needed.

Who gets them and how? Strep throats occur most frequently in children older than 3 (and in adults), during the colder months, and in crowded situations. New information suggests that spread may occur among younger children in child care as in older children in schools. If one person in a family gets strep throat, other family members may also get it. The Group A Streptococci are transmitted from one person to another through microscopic respiratory secretions. The incubation period lasts 2 to 5 days. People with strep throat are generally not infectious, however, until their symptoms appear. They continue to be infectious until they have received treatment for a day or so.

How are strep infections diagnosed? Throat cultures are used to diagnose strep infections. Rapid tests are now commercially available. Although the specificity of these tests is generally high, sensitivity may vary. Therefore, negative rapid tests should be followed by a culture, if indicated.

How are they treated? Strep infections are usually treated with an oral antibiotic for 10 days, starting either at the onset of symptoms or after throat culture results are received. A single, long-lasting injection may also be used to treat strep.

When should people be excluded and allowed to return?
- People who are only mildly ill can continue to attend while awaiting the results of a strep culture, **IF** the doctor has not begun antibiotic treatment. (If the culture proves to be positive, send them home.)
- People who have a positive strep culture should stay home until after they have had **at least** 24 hours of antibiotic medicine and the fever is gone. Make sure that every dose of the antibiotic is taken for the next 10 days.

Where to report strep infections? Notify all parents if a child has a strep infection (see Figure 17.7).

Special stop-spread information for strep infections
- Follow the stop-spread methods for respiratory tract diseases.
- If there is a case of strep in the program, send children or staff with sore throats to their health care providers for throat cultures.
- Be alert to an outbreak. If there are any cases associated with rheumatic fever or kidney disease, talk to your health consultant about having all children and staff cultured.

Figure 17.7. Letter to parents about strep throat

Dear parent or guardian:

_____ A child in our program has strep throat.

_____ Your child may have strep throat.

Please take these precautions:

1. Watch your child for signs of a sore throat and other signs of strep (headache, fever, stomachache, swollen and tender neck glands).

2. If your child develops a sore throat and any of these other signs, please see your health care provider, tell her or him that another child in the program has strep, and ask to have your child tested for strep throat. If strep is found, your child should receive treatment.

Information about strep throat

What is strep throat? **Strep throat** is a sore throat caused by **streptococcus bacteria** that are passed around through nose and mouth droplets. It is very common in children. Most sore throats, however, are caused by **viruses** and are not treated with antibiotics.

Why is it important that your child receive treatment? **There are three main reasons:**

1. **Treatment reduces spread.** If not treated or not treated long enough, your child may continue to spread the infection to other members of your family or to other children.

2. **Treatment with antibiotics can usually prevent rheumatic fever.** Rarely, some children with strep throat later develop rheumatic fever—abnormalities of the heart valves and inflammation of the joints.

3. **Treatment will also prevent other rare, but possibly dangerous, complications.**

When can your child come back to the program? Your child can return after taking medicine for **at least 24 hours and the fever is gone.**

What should you do to prevent the spread of strep throat?

1. Thoroughly wash your hands and your child's hands after wiping noses and before eating or preparing food.

2. Wash dishes carefully in hot, soapy water or a dishwasher.

3. Do not allow children to share cups, spoons, or toys that are put into the mouth.

4. Do not allow sharing of food.

COMMON RESPIRATORY TRACT ILLNESSES

Chicken pox and shingles

What are they? **Chicken pox** is a very contagious disease caused by the varicella-zoster virus. It usually begins with a mild fever, symptoms of a cold, and an itchy rash. The rash appears with small, red bumps on the stomach or back and spreads to the face and limbs. These bumps rapidly become blistered and oozy, then crust over. People may have only a few bumps or may be totally covered.

Once a person has been infected with the varicella-zoster virus and gets chicken pox, the virus remains (without symptoms) in the body's nerve cells. In some people the virus becomes active again at a later time and is called shingles or zoster. With shingles a red, painful, itchy, blistery rash appears, usually in a line along one side of the body. There is no fever. The virus shed in the blisters of the rash can cause chicken pox in a person who has not had it, if that person has direct contact with the infected shingles blisters.

Who gets them and how? Anyone who is exposed to the varicella-zoster virus and has not had chicken pox or chicken pox vaccine will usually get it. If you had chicken pox once, you usually cannot get it again. Chicken pox is most common in school-age children whereas shingles is most common in adults. Chicken pox is generally not considered to be a serious disease in otherwise healthy children. However, teenagers, adults, and other people with weakened immune systems (e.g., individuals with HIV/AIDS or on cancer chemotherapy) can experience a more severe disease from this virus.

Pregnant women who are susceptible to chicken pox should be referred to their physician **IMMEDIATELY** after exposure. Women who get chicken pox when pregnant may not only have serious disease, but their babies may also have serious complications, including fetal abnormalities (e.g., of the limb, eyes, nervous system) or newborn chicken pox which can be fatal.

People with chicken pox are contagious from 1 to 2 days **before** the rash appears until 5 days after the rash begins. The disease is spread by close contact (sharing breathing space or direct touch-ing) with infected secretions from the nose, throat, or rash. It takes about 10 to 21 days from the time of exposure until a person develops the symptoms of chicken pox. Usually it is 14 to 16 days.

How is it diagnosed? Chicken pox and shingles are usually diagnosed by the typical appearance of the rash.

How is it treated? People at risk for serious complications of chicken pox (i.e., susceptible pregnant women, people with immune problems, adults with chronic lung or skin diseases) can be given VZIG (varicella zoster immune globulin) to prevent serious problems. For VZIG to work, it must be given within 4 days of exposure. Also, a specific antiviral medication can be given to people at risk to reduce the number of chicken pox spots and shorten the duration of the illness by about a day. This medicine must be given as soon as chicken pox is diagnosed and is not routinely recommended.

The symptoms may be treated, however, with anti-itching medicine and lotions, medicine for fever control, fluids, and rest. Aspirin (or products containing salicylate) should **NOT** be used for fever control because rarely Reye's syndrome (vomiting, liver problems, and/or coma) can result. Scratching should be avoided because it can increase scarring. A varicella vaccine has been recently licensed and is universally recommended as a single dose at 12 to 18 months of age. For further information, contact your health care provider.

When should people with chicken pox and shingles be excluded and allowed to return? Most child care programs have a policy that children and staff with chicken pox should be excluded. Children may return on the sixth day after the rash first appears (or when all blisters are crusted over and dry). In mild cases with only a few blisters, children may return sooner.

Children and staff with shingles shed the virus that causes chicken pox and could cause an outbreak of chicken pox. Therefore, unless the shingles rash can be completely covered, it is advisable that people with shingles stay home until the rash is crusted over and dry. The person with shingles must be very careful about personal hygiene.

Where to report it? Notify parents and staff about the occurrences of chicken pox (see Figure 17.8). Where required, chicken pox should be re-

Figure 17.8. Letter to parents about chicken pox

Dear parent or guardian:

_____ A child or staff member in our program has chicken pox.

_____ Your child may have chicken pox.

Information about chicken pox

What is it? Chicken pox is a very contagious infection caused by a virus. It usually begins with a mild fever and an itchy rash. The rash starts as small, red bumps that become blistery and oozy and then crust over.

How is it spread? It is spread through exposure to infected fluids from the nose, throat, or skin rash of someone with chicken pox. This can occur either by sharing that person's breathing space or by directly touching the infected fluids from the skin. Chicken pox is contagious from 1 to 2 days before the rash starts until 5 days after the rash began. After exposure, it takes 10 days to 3 weeks before the rash appears. Usually it appears in 14 to 16 days.

How is it treated? Chicken pox is generally not a serious disease and there is no specific treatment for it. The symptoms can be treated with plenty of fluids, rest, anti-itching medicines and lotions, and medicine for fever control.

ASPIRIN-(SALICYLATE) CONTAINING PRODUCTS SHOULD NOT BE USED FOR FEVER CONTROL IN CHILDREN WITH CHICKEN POX. There is a possible association between the use of aspirin and a rare but very serious disease called Reye's syndrome (vomiting associated with liver problems and coma).

What should you do about chicken pox?

1. Be sure your child has received chicken pox vaccine at or after 12 months of age, if your child has not already had the disease.

2. Watch your child for the next 10 days to 3 weeks to see if the chicken pox rash develops.

3. Do not send your child to our program with a suspicious rash. Ask your health care provider to diagnose the illness and to give you anti-itching medicine or lotions for your child if the itching is disturbing the child.

4. If your child develops chicken pox, you can return her or him to the program on the sixth day after the rash began or when all the blisters are dried up and crusted over.

5. Be aware that if one of your children develops chicken pox, other people in the family who have not had it will probably get it, too, because chicken pox is **very** easily spread.

6. If you are pregnant and think you have never had chicken pox, or if you have a weakened immune system, talk to your doctor **IMMEDIATELY.** Your doctor can check whether you are susceptible to chicken pox with a blood test. Women who get chicken pox when they are pregnant are more likely than other adults to develop serious complications. Babies born to mothers with chicken pox can develop high fevers and other serious problems. People at risk can be given VZIG (varicella zoster immune globulin) to prevent serious complications. For VZIG to work, it must be given less than 96 hours (4 days) after exposure to chicken pox.

Note: Since the 1995 publication of the Recommended U.S. Childhood Immunizaation Schedule, a varicella vaccine has been licensed and universally recommended as a singe dose at 12 to 18 months of age. The vaccine is also recommended for any child who has not yet had a documented case of varicella (chicken pox) or received the vaccine by 11 to 12 years of age. Contact your health care provider for more information.

ported to the state or local board of health. You do not need to report cases of shingles.

Special stop-spread information for chicken pox and shingles

The best way to prevent spread of these very contagious diseases is to be sure all children over 12 months of age and all adults who have not had chicken pox disease receive the vaccine. Keep infected people away from the program. The severity of the infection tends to increase with increasing age.

- Check the immunization and health records for every child and adult in the program for evidence of immunity to chicken pox (vaccine or disease).
- Develop a system for immediate notification if a child or staff member develops chicken pox or shingles.
- Keep a person with chicken pox (or shingles with a rash that cannot be completely covered) at home until the rash is **completely** dry and crusted.
- Watch closely for early symptoms in others for 3 weeks following the most recent case. If a child or staff member develops a suspicious rash, the person's health care provider should be contacted to discuss what to do.
- All child care providers should review their medical history and consult with their physician if they have never had chicken pox and may be susceptible.

Fifth disease (Erythema Infectosum)

What is it? Fifth disease (also known as "Erythema Infectosum") is a mild rash illness that usually affects children. It is called fifth disease because it was the fifth of six similar rash-causing illnesses to be described. Fifth disease is caused by a virus called parvovirus B19 that lives in the nose and throat and can be spread from person to person. Clusters or outbreaks of illness among children in school and early childhood programs are not unusual.

The first stage of illness consists of headache, bodyache, sore throat, low-grade fever, and chills. These symptoms last about 2 to 3 days and are followed by a second stage, lasting about a week, during which the person has no symptoms at all. In children, the third stage involves a bright red rash on the cheeks which gives a "slapped cheek"

appearance. This may be followed by a "lacy" rash on the trunk, arms, and legs. The rash begins 17 to 18 days after exposure. The rash may appear on and off for several weeks with changes in temperature, sunlight, and emotional stress. Adults may not develop the third-stage rash but may experience joint pain, particularly in the hands and feet. The disease is usually mild and both children and adults recover without problems. However, in rare situations some people, especially those with blood disorders such as sickle-cell anemia, may develop more severe symptoms.

Who gets it and how? Children and adults can get parvovirus B19. The virus can be spread by the respiratory route in close contacts such as in households, schools, and early childhood settings. When an infected person coughs, sneezes, or speaks, the virus is sprayed into the air. These contaminated droplets can then be inhaled or touched by another person. Women who develop fifth disease during pregnancy may pass the infection to their unborn fetuses. In rare situations, miscarriages and stillbirths have been associated with fifth disease during pregnancy.

Outbreaks often begin in late winter or early spring and may continue until June. In outbreak situations, 10 to 60% of the children may develop fifth disease. Many people have already caught this disease before adulthood. It is estimated that about half of the adults in the United States have been infected with parvovirus B19 and are now immune. This level of protection may be higher among early childhood program staff.

How is it diagnosed? The diagnosis in children is based on the clinical symptoms of the facial rash. There is a particular laboratory test that can detect newly formed antibodies to the parvovirus B19. This test may be used for pregnant women, persons with blood disorders, and people with deficient immune systems who may be at higher risk for complications from fifth disease.

How is it treated? There is no specific treatment for fifth disease. Health care providers may suggest treatment to relieve some symptoms.

Should children and adults be excluded? Children or staff with fifth disease should **not** be excluded. By the time they are diagnosed with the rash, they are no longer contagious.

Figure 17.9. Letter to parents about fifth disease

Dear parent or guardian:

_____ A child in our program has fifth disease

_____ Your child may have fifth disease

Information about fifth disease

What is it? Fifth disease is a mild rash illness that usually affects children. Fifth disease is caused by a virus called parvovirus B19 that lives in the nose and throat and can be spread from person to person.

The first stage of illness consists of headache, bodyache, sore throat, low-grade fever, and chills. These symptoms last about 2 to 3 days and are followed by a second stage, lasting about a week, during which the person has no symptoms at all. In children, the third stage involves a bright red rash on the cheeks which gives a "slapped cheek" appearance. This may be followed by a "lacy" rash on the trunk, arms, and legs. The rash begins 17 to 18 days after exposure. The rash may appear on and off for several weeks with changes in temperature, sunlight, and emotional stress. Adults may not develop the third-stage rash but may experience joint pain, particularly in the hands and feet. The disease is usually mild and both children and adults recover without problems. However, in rare situations some people, especially those with blood disorders such as sickle-cell anemia, may develop more severe symptoms.

Who gets it and how? Children and adults can get parvovirus B19. When an infected person coughs, sneezes, or speaks, the virus is sprayed into the air. These contaminated droplets can then be inhaled or touched by another person. Women who develop fifth disease during pregnancy may pass the infection to their unborn fetuses. In rare situations, miscarriages and stillbirths have been associated with fifth disease during pregnancy.

How is it diagnosed? The diagnosis in children is based on the clinical symptoms of the facial rash. There is a particular laboratory test that can detect newly formed antibodies to the parvovirus B19. This test may be used for pregnant women, persons with blood disorders, and people with deficient immune systems who may be at higher risk for complications from fifth disease.

How is it treated? There is no specific treatment for fifth disease. Health care providers may suggest treatment to relieve some symptoms. There is no vaccine to prevent fifth disease.

Must your child stay home? Children or staff with fifth disease do **not** have to stay home. By the time they are diagnosed with the rash, they are no longer contagious.

What should you do?
1. Watch for the symptoms of fifth disease and tell us if your child has fifth disease.
2. If you are pregnant, tell your health care provider about your possible exposure.
3. Always be careful about handwashing, especially after touching discharge from the nose and throat and before eating or handling food.

Where to report it? Notify parents, staff, and—if required—your local board of health.

Is fifth disease a problem for pregnant women? Miscarriages and stillbirths have been reported rarely in women who developed fifth disease during pregnancy. Birth defects have not been reported associated with this disease. Recent evidence suggests that the risk of an adverse effect during pregnancy is extremely low. However, women who develop fifth disease during pregnancy should be followed closely by their obstetrician.

How can I avoid getting fifth disease? Careful handwashing (especially after handling discharge from the nose and throat and before eating or handling food) is the best protection against spread of fifth disease. Currently, there is no vaccine against fifth disease.

The decision to try to decrease any person's risk of infection by not attending a child care environment where there is an outbreak should be made by the person after discussion with family members, health care providers, public health officials, and employers. A policy to routinely exclude members of high risk groups is not recommended.

SERIOUS RESPIRATORY TRACT ILLNESSES

Meningococcal illnesses

What are they? Bacteria called Neisseria meningitidis cause meningococcal illnesses that are serious and sometimes fatal. The most common of these illnesses is **meningitis,** an inflammation of the coverings of the brain. People with this type of meningitis **must** be hospitalized immediately and receive intravenous antibiotics. The disease usually starts suddenly with fever, chills, lethargy, and a rash of fine red freckles or purple splotches. Young children with meningitis show symptoms of unusual irritability, poor feeding, vomiting, fever, and excessive, high-pitched crying. Older children and adults may experience severe headache, neck pain, and stiffness.

Who gets them and how? Although older children and adults can get meningococcal illnesses, they occur most frequently in children younger than 5 years of age (and especially in babies 6 to 12 months of age). The bacteria are passed between people who are in close contact through coughing, sneezing, nasal discharge, saliva, and touching of infected secretions. These bacteria cannot live on environmental surfaces. People called carriers have these bacteria in their noses, throats, or mouths but do not have symptoms of the illness. Both sick people and carriers pass these germs to others. Usually illness occurs 1 to 4 days after a person has been exposed, although incubation can take up to 10 days. If one infection occurs at your center, there are more than the usual number of carriers and the risk of disease spread increases greatly.

How are they diagnosed? These infections are diagnosed by rapid tests and/or cultures of the spinal fluid or cultures of the blood. It may take up to 72 hours to grow and identify the bacteria.

How are these infections treated? People sick with these infections require hospitalization for special care and a closely supervised program of antibiotics. Sick people *and* those in contact with them should also take an oral medicine called rifampin to lower the risk of the spread of the disease to others. Antibiotic treatment of all children and adult contacts should begin as soon as possible, preferably within 24 hours of diagnosis of the first case. (NOTE: Pregnant women and people with liver disease should not take rifampin.)

When should people with meningococcal diseases be excluded and allowed to return? People with meningococcal disease are too ill to attend. They may return when they are well (after hospital treatment) and after they have taken rifampin for 2 days. Exclude all people who have been in close contact with a person who has meningococcal disease until their treatment with rifampin is started. If rifampin is not taken, contacts should be excluded for 1 week after onset of the last case. Children enrolled within 1 week of onset of last case should also take rifampin.

Where to report them? Notify all parents and staff **immediately** (see Figure 17.10). Parents of any child enrolled within 1 month of the last case should receive written information about meningococcal diseases so that they can take appropriate precautions. Also notify your health consultant and your local board of health.

Special stop-spread information
The best way to prevent spread of this very conta-

Figure 17.10. Letter to parents about meningococcal illnesses

Dear parent or guardian:

A child or staff member in our program has a serious infectious illness caused by bacteria named Neisseria meningitidis. The bacteria can spread between persons who share breathing space or are in close physical contact. There is a medicine called rifampin that can be taken to reduce the risk of infection in people in close contact with the ill person.

_____ Your child has been in close contact (same classroom or shared activities) with this child or staff member.

_____ Your child has not been in close contact with the ill person.

Please take these steps:

1. **Call your health care provider.** Tell her or him that your child is in a group program where another child or staff member has come down with a meningococcal illness. Indicate whether or not your child has been in close contact with the ill person.

2. **If your child has had close contact, our health consultant recommends that your child take a medication called rifampin (unless there is some reason why your child cannot take this drug). Rifampin can help eliminate the germ from someone else who has been exposed. We will help your child receive rifampin if it is recommended by our health consultant. Be sure to let your child's doctor know whether or not your child received rifampin.**

3. If your child has had close contact, do not return her or him to the program until the rifampin treatment has been started.

4. **Watch your child for signs of illness or a fever for the next 3 weeks. If your child becomes ill, take her or him to a doctor immediately whether or not rifampin was given.** The medicine is not always 100% effective. Neisseria meningitidis usually causes meningitis, an infection of the coverings of the brain, that is often fatal if not treated with antibiotics. Symptoms of meningitis include headache, stiff neck, fever, and chills.

5. Remember that our program will be very watchful during the next 3 weeks. We will notify you if anyone else becomes ill.

gious disease is to warn everyone that a case has occurred so that rifampin medication can begin.

- Develop a system for immediate notification if a child or staff member comes down with a meningococcal illness.
- Ask all staff and parents to contact their health care providers immediately.
- Notify your local board of health.
- Require that all close contacts of the ill person including people in the household and in the classroom take rifampin for 2 days. Classmates and staff in the ill person's class need to take the medicine as soon as possible. Children and staff in separate classes may not need rifampin. Speak with your health consultant and/or local board of health if you have questions about who is a close contact. Usually, the best way to assure that everyone who needs it gets rifampin is to have a doctor (e.g., health department consultant) prescribe the medication to be given to all the contacts in the child care program. Compliance is not usually achieved by asking each person to get a prescription from her or his own doctor.
- Make parents and staff aware the rifampin does NOT give absolute protection against disease. **Therefore, any child or adult who develops symptoms such as fever or headache requires prompt evaluation by a health care provider.**
- Monitor the situation closely for 2 to 3 weeks. Make sure all ill children are seen by their doctors and that you are notified if another person develops meningococcal disease.

Haemophilus influenzae type b illness (Hib disease)

What is it? Haemophilus influenzae type B (Hib) is bacteria that causes serious, sometimes fatal illnesses, most often in young children. Some of the diseases the bacteria can cause are

- epiglottitis—infection of the upper throat and entrance to the windpipe
- cellulitis—infection of the deep skin, especially of the face and neck
- meningitis—infection/inflammation of the coverings of the brain
- arthritis—infection and swelling of the joints
- pneumonia—infection of the lung
- bloodstream infections

Who gets them and how? These illnesses occur primarily in children younger than 5 years of age, most of them in children younger than 2. Epiglottitis is an uncommon problem found most often in children 2 to 4 years old, while the other diseases are most common in children younger than 2 years. Children in group settings may be at greater risk of catching these illnesses. Older children and adults rarely develop these illnesses. In recent years, widespread immunization of children against Hib has dramatically reduced the amount of Hib disease in the United States.

As with meningococcal illnesses, Hib disease requires relatively close contact in order to spread between people. Spread is more likely among children younger than 4, with the highest risk in children younger than 2. In programs where there are young children and everyone is in close contact, there may be an increased risk of a second infection following a first case.

The bacteria are passed from person to person, by direct contact or by breathing infected droplets of nose or throat fluids scattered in the air. The bacteria cannot live on environmental surfaces. Some people can carry the bacteria in their nose or throat for a period of time without becoming ill themselves. Both sick people and carriers may spread the bacteria to others who may then become ill.

How is it diagnosed? These illnesses are diagnosed by rapid tests and/or cultures of the spinal fluid or cultures of the blood. It may take up to 72 hours to grow and identify the bacteria.

How is it treated? People sick with these infections generally require hospitalization. Both sick individuals and other people sharing the household should take rifampin to reduce the risk of spreading Hib disease. Rifampin is an antibiotic that is used as a preventive treatment.

The AAP recommendations, detailed in the *Report of the Committee on Infectious Diseases* (1991), can be summarized as follows:

(a) Careful observation of child care Hib disease contacts is essential. Children who develop illnesses with fever shall receive prompt medical evaluation.

(b) When there is exposure to a child with Hib infection in a group of children less than 2 years of age, and the group members are in close contact for 25 or more hours a week (thus like household contact), rifampin treatment should be given to children and staff.

(c) Rifampin treatment is not required in child care programs where a single case has occurred and all contacts are older than 2 years.

(d) Rifampin treatment is indicated for children and staff in all child care programs regardless of the ages of the children when two or more cases of serious Hib disease have occurred among children within a 60-day period. If indicated, children enrolled within 1 week of the last case need rifampin.

(e) When rifampin treatment is used, all children enrolled, regardless of Hib immunization status, and staff should receive rifampin treatment. In multi-classroom settings, only classroom contacts need rifampin.

(f) Because therapy for systemic Hib disease does not prevent people from carrying Hib bacteria in their nose or throats, a child treated for Hib disease shall be given rifampin treatment before returning to the child care program, if rifampin has been used in her or his child care contacts.

(g) Representatives of the local health department should supervise antibiotic treatment when child care exposure to Hib has occurred and treatment is indicated.

A recently licensed vaccine for prevention of Hib infections is recommended for all children from 2 months to 5 years old, particularly those in group programs. This vaccine should be given during regular health care visits and requires 2 weeks to take full effect. It is not effective in preventing Hib in someone who has already been exposed or in preventing the immediate spread of Hib. Children may be at slightly increased risk of coming down with Hib disease during the week following the shot.

When should people with Hib disease be excluded and allowed to return? Exclude children and staff who are ill with Hib disease while they are ill and until they have initiated their treatment with rifampin. Exclude children who do not receive the rifampin as required by your policy on **preventive rifampin use for 1 week after onset of last case.**

Where to report Hib disease? Notify all parents and staff immediately (see Figure 17.11). Parents of any child enrolled within 1 month of the last case should receive written information about Hib

disease so that they can take appropriate precautions. Also notify your health consultant and your local board of health.

Special stop-spread information
- Develop a policy regarding preventive rifampin use.
- Develop a system for immediate notification if a child or staff member develops a Hib illness.
- Ask all staff and parents/guardians to contact their health care provider immediately.
- Notify your local board of health.
- Make parents and staff aware that rifampin does not provide 100% protection against disease. Therefore, any child or adult who becomes ill should be seen promptly by a health care provider.
- Make sure all ill children are seen by their doctors and that you are notified if another person develops Hib infection.
- Encourage parents to see that all attending children between 2 months and 5 years of age receive the Hib vaccine, and suggest it to parents for all children as they turn 2 months old. Many states now require Hib vaccine for children attending early childhood programs.

Tuberculosis (TB)

What is it? **Tuberculosis (TB)** is caused by bacteria called Mycobacterium tuberculosis that usually causes an infection of the lungs. Transmission of the disease occurs when an infected adult coughs TB bacteria into the air and another person who shares close breathing space inhales them. Except under unusual circumstances, TB is not highly contagious and generally requires prolonged or intense exposure to cause infection. Most persons who inhale TB bacteria are protected from infection by their immune systems that wall up the bacteria in tiny, hard capsules (tubercules). Bacteria in tubercules do not usually cause illness.

People who have been infected with the TB germ who do not have the disease can be identified by a positive Mantoux tuberculin skin test. People with positive skin tests are not contagious and do not feel ill. However, if their defense systems become weakened due to other health problems, the walled up germs could begin to multiply, break out of the capsules, and cause disease. Most cases of TB in

Figure 17.11. Letter to parents about Hib disease

Dear parent or guardian:

A child in our program has a serious infectious illness caused by bacteria named Haemophilus influenzae type b. (A short way of writing the name is *Hib.*) Hib can spread between people who are in close physical contact and share breathing space. Hib is not at all related to the regular flu.

_____ Your child has been in close contact (same classroom or shared activities) with this child or staff member.

_____ Your child has not been in close contact with the ill person.

Hib can cause very serious illnesses such as meningitis (infection of the coverings of the brain), pneumonia, arthritis, epiglottitis (infection of the upper throat), blood infections, and skin infections. All of these illnesses require hospital treatment and intravenous antibiotics. Because the bacteria can spread from child to child and because they can cause serious illness, we want to make you aware of the fact that your child may have been exposed.

[Insert a statement of your local health department's recommendations and policy regarding the use of rifampin to reduce the risk of spread.]

Please take these steps:

1. **Call your health care provider.** Tell her or him that your child is in a program where another child has come down with an illness caused by Haemophilus influenzae type b (Hib). Indicate whether or not your child has been in close contact with the ill person. Describe our program's policy on Hib and rifampin.

2. **Watch your child for signs of illness or a fever. If your child becomes ill, take her or him to your health care provider.** Watch your child especially carefully in the next week, and continue watching for a month.

3. Remember that our program will also be very watchful over the next month. We will notify you if another child comes down with this illness.

the United States are caused by such reactivation of old TB infection. A special anti-TB medicine can be taken to prevent an infected person from "breaking down" with TB. This medicine is usually taken by infants and children for 9 months and by adults for 6 to 12 months.

People who have active TB disease have symptoms of coughing, infected sputum, fever, weight loss, and abnormal chest X rays. More rarely, TB germs can cause disease in other body organs. Persons with TB disease in areas other than the lung are usually not contagious to others because the TB germ must be in the air and inhaled in order to cause infection in another person.

Who gets it and how? Anyone who shares breathing space with an adult with active TB lung **disease,** usually over a long period of time, can develop TB **infection.** Only a few of those infected, however, will develop TB **disease.** Infants, young children, pregnant women, and people with problems of the immune system (e.g., HIV/AIDS, diabetes, lymphoma, kidney failure, and malnutrition) are more likely to develop serious TB disease if infected.

When people with active lung disease cough, sneeze, or spit they spread bacteria into the air in microscopic droplets from the nose, mouth, and lung. These germs can be breathed by someone who shares close breathing space with an infected person over a prolonged period of time. TB is not spread by brief contact in large, spacious areas or by handling a diseased person's bedsheets, books, furniture, or eating utensils.

The TB germ is spread only from a person with active TB disease, usually in the lungs, to another person. Not all cases of TB disease are equally contagious. Advanced TB of the lung with extensive lung damage (as shown on a chest X ray) is more often accompanied by a wet cough and is thus much more contagious than lung disease with few X ray findings and little cough. Infants and children with TB disease are usually not contagious. This is because the TB germs are scattered in the lungs and children are less likely to cough up and spit out phlegm from their lungs.

How is it diagnosed? Infection with the TB germ is diagnosed by a tuberculin skin test (a Mantoux test). A test is called *positive* when there is a significant amount of swelling at the skin test site 48 to 72 hours after the test is placed. After a person first breathes TB bacteria, it may take 2 to 3 months for the skin test to become positive. A positive skin test indicates exposure to the TB germ at some time in the past, causing the body to develop a response of the defense system to contain the germ.

A positive test does not indicate if a person has had TB disease. Further evaluation by chest X ray and medical examination is used to determine if infection has been contained by the person's defensive system or has progressed to active disease. If a person has a positive Mantoux skin test AND symptoms (such as cough and fever), additional studies such as TB sputum cultures may also be done. The TB germ grows very slowly, and it can take up to 3 months before a culture shows growth of the germ.

How is it treated? TB is readily treated with several medications taken for 9 months. These medications usually make the person noncontagious within a few weeks. All household contacts of people with active TB should be tested. If they are less than 6 years of age or have a depressed immune system, then they should be treated with preventive medication. TB infection without disease (that is, a positive skin test only) can be prevented from progressing to disease by taking a single medication daily for a year.

When should people with TB be excluded and allowed to return? Anyone who has been diagnosed with active TB disease must be excluded from attending or working in programs for young children. Children and staff with TB disease may return after they have begun treatment and their health care provider states that they are not contagious. Adults usually become noncontagious within 2 to 4 weeks on medication. Children are rarely contagious since they usually do not have pus pockets in their lungs and cough up the germs as adults do with TB.

Where to report it? You must report **TB disease** to your local board of health. (TB **infection**—positive skin test without symptoms and with a normal chest X ray does not need to be reported.) Notify all staff, parents, and your health care consultant if a case of active TB disease occurs in your program. Your local board of health can help you to notify parents and can conduct an evaluation of exposed people, including free TB skin testing.

Special stop-spread information

- **ALL** adult staff (paid and volunteer) should receive a Mantoux test **before** they start to work. A Mantoux skin test is done by injecting a small amount of TB test solution under the skin with a syringe. If the test is positive and an X ray is recommended, it should be done before the person comes to work also. Any adult with TB lung disease, particularly if associated with extensive lung damage on chest X ray and wet cough, can present a significant risk to children and other adults. People with positive skin tests should receive an appropriate evaluation and medical clearance from their health care provider before beginning work. Staff should be retested for TB at least every 2 years or more frequently if recommended by the local health department.

- You may wish to require a TB skin test for newly entering children as part of their entrance physical examination. If you are located in an area where the rate of TB disease is higher than average, children should be retested for TB yearly. Your local board of health can give you information about the TB rate in your area.

- Ask your local board of health to conduct an evaluation of exposed people if a child or staff member is diagnosed with active TB. This evaluation should include TB skin testing of program children and staff and medical evaluation of anyone with a positive skin test. (The skin test needs to be repeated 2 to 3 months later because it may take several months to turn positive after the person is first exposed to the TB germ.)

DISEASES SPREAD THROUGH DIRECT CONTACT

Superficial infections and skin infections—Impetigo, ringworm, conjunctivitis, scabies, and pediculosis

These diseases are caused by superficial bacterial or viral infections or parasitic infestations. They are common and are not serious. They are spread by direct contact with infected secretions, infected skin areas, or infested articles. Because young children are constantly touching their surroundings and the people around them, these infections are easily spread among children and their teachers.

The direct contact method of disease spread is illustrated in these examples:

- A child has oozy sores on his arm. While playing with another child, he rubs his arm against hers. Some ooze gets on her arm and then into a cut or scratch on her skin.

- A child with head lice takes off his hat that has a louse on it. A second child puts on the hat and the louse climbs onto his head.

- A child has runny eyes. She rubs them with her hand, then puts her hand on a toy. Another child touches the toy, gets eye discharge on his hand, rubs his eyes, and puts eye discharge from the first child into his own eyes.

How to stop spread of superficial/skin infections

1. Follow these handwashing and cleanliness guidelines:

- Make sure staff and children thoroughly wash their hands after contact with any possible infectious secretions.
- Use **free-flowing water** for handwashing.
- Use liquid soap dispensers whenever possible.
- Always use disposable tissues or towels for wiping and washing.
- Never use the same tissue or towel for more than one child.
- Dispose of used tissues and paper towels in a lined, covered step can that is kept away from food and materials.
- Wash and disinfect toys at least daily. Wash or vacuum frequently used surfaces (wash tables, counters; vacuum furniture, floors) daily.

2. Make sure that each child has her or his own crib or mat and does not switch. Sheets and mats should be kept clean and stored so that the sleeping surfaces do not touch each other.

3. Do not allow children to share personal items such as combs, brushes, blankets, pillows, hats, or clothing.

4. Store each child's dirty clothing separately in plastic bags and send it home for laundering.

5. Wash and cover sores, cuts, and scrapes promptly and wipe eyes dry.

6. Report rashes, sores, running eyes, and severe itching to the parents so they can contact their health care provider.

Impetigo

What is it? Impetigo is a very common skin infection caused by Streptococcal (strep) or Staphylococcal (staph) bacteria. It may start as oozing at an injured spot on the skin (such as an insect bite, cut, or burn) and can easily be spread by the person's hands to other areas of the skin. Children often have impetigo on their faces. The rash looks oozy, red, and round; may have a flat, honey-colored crust; and may be itchy. In impetigo caused by either strep or staph bacteria, sometimes there are blisters that break easily leaving raw, red, oozy skin exposed. In impetigo caused by strep bacteria, kidney disease can develop under very rare circumstances. Impetigo is most commonly seen during warm, summer months.

Who gets it and how? Ordinarily the skin protects the body from bacteria. When the skin is broken (cut, scraped, bitten, scratched), bacteria can get under the surface, multiply, and cause an infection. Children often have multiple cuts and scrapes on their bodies that make them more vulnerable to impetigo than adults. Most children have impetigo at least a few times during their growing-up years. Impetigo bacteria are found all over infected skin, on the crusts, and in the ooze. They can be spread to another person who directly touches the skin or a surface contaminated by the ooze or crusts. Bacteria that get under the top protective skin layer of the second person multiply and cause infection.

How is it diagnosed? Impetigo can be diagnosed by the way it looks. Bacterial cultures are not usually needed. Strep and staph impetigo may look the same, although staph tends to cause blisters more often.

How is it treated? Usually some combination of a special soap, an antibiotic ointment, and sometimes an oral antibiotic is given.

When should people with impetigo be excluded and allowed to return? Children and staff do not need to be sent home in the middle of the day if a suspected impetigo rash is noticed. Wash a child's rash area with soap and water and cover it. **Wash your hands and the child's afterward.** Notify the parents when they come to pick up the child and tell them to check with the child's health care provider. Children and staff can come back after us-

ing medicine for 24 hours. The sores should be kept lightly covered until they have dried up.

Where to report it? Notify parents and staff (see Figure 17.12).

Special stop-spread instructions for impetigo

- When children hurt themselves and cause a break in the skin, wash the area thoroughly with soap and water and dry carefully.
- If you think a child may have impetigo, wash the rash with soap and water and cover it loosely with gauze, a bandage, or clothing. Be sure those who touch the rash wash their hands well. Dispose of any soiled tissues or bandages carefully, keep any dirty clothing in a plastic bag, and ask the parents to have the child seen by their health care provider.

Ringworm (tinea)

What is it? Ringworm (tinea) is a mild infection of the skin or nails caused by several different fungi. Ringworm infections are not serious and are easily treated. On the skin, ringworm appears as a flat, growing, ring-shaped rash. The edges of the circle are usually reddish and may be raised, scaly, and itchy; the center of the circle is often clear. Another type of ringworm fungus can cause the skin to become lighter in flat patches, especially on the trunk and face. On the scalp, infection begins as a small bump and spreads outward, leaving scaly patches of temporary hair loss. Scales, cracks, and blisters may be seen on the skin between the toes. A chronic infection of the nails can cause thickening, discoloration, and brittleness.

Who gets it and how? Ringworm is spread when infected skin touches healthy skin or when infected broken nails or skin flakes fall onto the floor, get onto hair scissors or clothes, and are touched later by other people. Dogs and cats can also spread ringworm.

How is it diagnosed? These infections can often be diagnosed by their typical appearance. Sometimes a special lamp is used to examine for ringworm. Occasionally, scrapings of suspicious skin may be examined under a microscope or cultured to see if a ringworm fungus is present.

How is it treated? An antifungal ointment is usu-

Figure 17.12. Letter to parents about impetigo

Dear parent or guardian:

_____ A child in our program has impetigo.

_____ Your child may have impetigo.

Please take these precautions:

1. Check your child's skin for an impetigo rash.

2. Take your child to your health care provider if you suspect your child has an impetigo rash so that medicine may be prescribed.

3. Tell us if your child is treated for impetigo.

4. If your child has impetigo, return her or him to the program after 24 hours of treatment has been given.

Information about impetigo

What is it? Impetigo is a skin infection common in young children. It is seen mostly on the face and around the mouth, but can occur any place on the skin. In impetigo infections, the skin becomes red and may ooze. There may be small bumps clustered together or larger red areas. These areas may have honey-colored crusts or blisters. Impetigo spreads quickly and is often itchy. Children may scratch the crusts off and cause a little bleeding.

What causes it? Impetigo is caused by common skin germs (such as strep and staph). These germs usually cause infection only when the skin gets injured (scraped, cut, or scratched). Impetigo can spread easily among young children who touch everything.

How is impetigo diagnosed and treated? Your health care provider can tell you if your child has impetigo. Usually it is treated with some combination of a special soap, an antibiotic ointment, and sometimes an oral antibiotic.

What should you do about impetigo? The most important thing is to keep the impetigo rash clean and dry. You may want to cover it lightly so the ooze and crusts cannot be spread to other people. People who touch the rash should wash their hands very well.

ally applied to the skin for several weeks. Antifungal medicine may be taken by mouth, particularly if the diagnosis is ringworm of the scalp or nails.

When should people with ringworm be excluded and allowed to return? There is no need to exclude children or staff with these common, mild infections once treatment has been started. Refer people with a suspicious rash to their health care providers for appropriate diagnosis and treatment, and allow them to return as soon as treatment has begun.

Where to report it? Notify parents and staff if more than one person in the program develops ringworm (see Figure 17.13).

Special stop-spread information for ringworm

Keep the environment as clean, dry, and cool as possible because ringworm fungi grow easily on moist, warm surfaces.

Conjunctivitis (pinkeye)

What is it? Conjunctivitis (pinkeye) is an infection of the eyes most often caused by a virus but also caused by bacteria. With this infection, the white parts of the eyes become pink and the eyes produce lots of tears and discharge. Sometimes the discharge is clear; when there is yellowish or greenish pus the infection is more likely to be caused by bacteria. In the morning, the discharge may make the eyelids stick together. (Some children and adults have allergies that can cause everything listed here except pus.) Conjunctivitis is a mild illness. Viral conjunctivitis will go away by itself in 1 to 3 weeks.

Who gets it and how? Children have conjunctivitis most often and spread it to people taking care of them or to other children when some pinkeye pus gets into an uninfected person's eyes. Children often pass the infection by rubbing their eyes, getting discharge on their hands, and touching someone or something. Conjunctivitis can also be spread when staff wash, dry, or wipe a child's face and then use the same washcloth, towel, paper towel, or tissue on another child's face. Staff could also get eye discharge on their hands when wiping a child's eyes and then pass it along as outlined above.

How is it diagnosed and treated? Symptoms of conjunctivitis are obvious; however, it is often difficult to tell if the cause is bacterial or viral. Occasionally the doctor will examine the discharge under a microscope or culture it. Often an antibiotic eye medicine will be given because treatment of bacterial conjunctivitis shortens the length of symptoms and decreases infectiousness. There is no treatment for viral conjunctivitis that will go away by itself but may last a week or more. It is recommended that children who have conjunctivitis be treated by rinsing out the eye and by sometimes using an antibiotic eye medicine to prevent spread of the infection.

When should people with conjunctivitis be excluded and allowed to return? Children with conjunctivitis do not need to be sent home in the middle of the day. Let parents know that the symptoms were noticed. Children with infectious conjunctivitis with white or yellow eye discharge can return after they have used antibiotic treatment for 24 hours. The parent should notify the program if the health care provider decides not to prescribe a medicine. Children with a clear watery eye discharge, no pain, no fever or eyelid redness do not generally require exclusion.

Where to report it? Notify parents and staff (see Figure 17.14).

Special stop-spread information for conjunctivitis

- Keep children's eyes wiped free of discharge, and always wash your hands after wiping a child's eyes.
- Teach children to wash their hands after wiping their eyes.
- Be sure articles that may touch children's eyes (such as prisms, toy binoculars, and toy cameras) are washed well with soap and water at least once daily.

Scabies

What is it? Scabies, a common skin infection, is caused by a microscopic parasite called a mite that infects only people. The female mite burrows under the skin to lay her eggs that hatch and start the infestation cycle again. An infected person usually has only 10 to 12 mites.

Symptoms of scabies do not appear until 2 to 6

Figure 17.13. Letter to parents about ringworm

Dear parent or guardian:

_____ A child in our program has ringworm.

_____ Your child may have ringworm.

Please take these precautions:

1. Check your child for ringworm, using the information given below.

2. Take your child to your health care provider if you think she or he has ringworm.

3. Tell us if your child has ringworm.

Information about ringworm

What is it? Ringworm is a rash caused by a fungus. On the body you may see red rings that are slightly raised, itchy, and scaly. On the scalp you may see circles of hair loss. On the feet you may see cracking and peeling between the toes. Another kind of ringworm causes whitish patches on the face or body. All of these forms of ringworm spread easily. Dogs and cats can also spread ringworm. Ringworm is not dangerous and can be treated easily.

How do people catch ringworm? Ringworm is spread by touching the rash on another person or touching the scales or broken hairs that have fallen off the rash.

How is ringworm diagnosed? Your health care provider can usually identify ringworm by looking at the rash. Sometimes other tests are needed.

When can your child come back? There is no need to exclude children or staff with these common, mild infections once treatment has been started.

Figure 17.14. Letter to parents about conjunctivitis

Dear parent or guardian:

_____ A child in our program has conjunctivitis (also called pinkeye).

_____ Your child may have conjunctivitis.

Please take these precautions:

1. Watch your child and members of your family for signs of pinkeye.

2. See your health care provider if your child develops pinkeye. Your child may need to be given an eye medication.

3. Do not send your child to the program until **the day after** you start giving the medicine. If your health care provider decides not to prescribe an eye medicine, ask for a note to send in with your child.

4. Tell us if your child is being treated for pinkeye.

Information about conjunctivitis

What is it? Pinkeye is an infection of the eyes. It is most often caused by a virus but can also be caused by bacteria. The white parts of the eyes become pink or red; the eyes may hurt, feel itchy or scratchy; and the eyes may produce lots of tears and discharge. In the mornings, the discharge (pus) may make the eyelids stick together. (Some children and adults have allergies that can cause everything listed here **except pus.**) Conjunctivitis is a mild illness and is NOT dangerous. Doctors usually prescribe an antibiotic eye medication just in case it is due to bacteria.

How do you catch conjunctivitis? The pus is infectious. If children rub their eyes, they get it on their hands. They can then touch someone's eyes or hands or touch an object (toy or table). If other children get discharge on their hands and then touch their own eyes, they can catch it. It can spread easily among young children who touch their eyes and everything else and who do not know how (or forget) to wash their hands.

What should you do if your child has conjunctivitis?
1. Keep your child's eyes wiped free of discharge. Use paper tissues and throw them away promptly.

2. **Always thoroughly wash your hands after wiping your child's eyes.**

3. Teach your children to wash their hands after wiping their eyes.

4. Ask your health care provider if your child needs to receive eye medication.

5. Be sure to wash carefully anything that touches your child's eyes (such as washcloths, towels, toy binoculars, and toy cameras).

weeks after initial exposure. On re-exposure, symptoms can start within days. Scabies symptoms include an intensely itchy rash (with red bumps and burrows—short, wavy, dirty-looking lines in the skin). An infected person's scratch marks may cover up the typical appearance of the rash. The rash usually appears on the sides of the fingers and finger webs, wrists, elbows, underarms, and belt lines. In infants, the head, neck, palms, soles, and buttocks may also be involved.

Who gets it and how? Anyone who has contact with the mite can become infested with scabies by skin-to-skin contact or by skin contact with clothes or bedding, for example. The mites can survive only 3 days off the body and cannot jump or fly. They require direct contact with skin to be spread.

How is it diagnosed? Scabies can be diagnosed by the typical appearance of the rash and accompanying symptoms and by examining skin scrapings under a microscope to see the mite or its eggs.

How is it treated? Scabies can be treated with one of several prescription mite-killing creams or lotions. These are applied once to the skin and then washed off after a specified period of time. Medicine to relieve the itching is often necessary. Even after effective therapy, itching can persist for as long as 4 weeks. Some doctors may treat all household members (even those without symptoms) once, due to the high likelihood of spread within a household.

When should people with scabies be excluded and allowed to return? Children or staff do not need to be sent home in the middle of the day if a rash that appears to be scabies is noticed. Ask parents to take infested children to their health care provider for treatment. An infested person can return the day after treatment is started.

Where to report it? Notify parents and staff (see Figure 17.15).

Special stop-spread information for scabies

- Wash and dry on the **HOT** cycle all washable items that came into contact with the child's skin during the 72 hours prior to treatment. Use a **HOT** dryer for 20 minutes.
- Store difficult-to-wash items (such as stuffed toys and pillows) in tightly closed plastic bags for 4 days before using again.

- Thoroughly vacuum any carpet or upholstered furniture.
- Talk with your health consultant if you think you have a major problem with scabies because it may be necessary to treat all children and adults in the group once.
- Do not use pesticide sprays because they can be harmful to people and animals.

Pediculosis (head lice)

What are they? Head lice are tiny insects that live only on people's scalps and hair. They hatch from small eggs, called nits, that are firmly attached to the individual hairs near the scalp and cannot be easily moved up or down the hair (as can specks of dandruff). Nits may be found throughout the hair but are most often located at the back of the scalp, behind the ears, and at the top of the head. The eggs hatch in about 10 days, with new lice reaching adulthood in about 2 weeks. The female louse is about the size of a sesame seed, can live for 20 to 30 days, and can lay about six eggs a day. The lice live by biting and sucking blood from the scalp. Lice can survive up to 8 hours between feedings and can do so off the body.

The major symptom of head lice is itching caused by the bite of the louse. Persistent scratching of the head and back of the neck should be viewed with suspicion. Often red bite marks and scratch marks can be seen on the scalp and neck, and a secondary bacterial infection can occur causing oozing or crusting. Swollen neck glands can also occur.

Who gets them and how? Head lice are not a sign of unclean people or homes. They can occur at any age and afflict either sex. Anyone who has close contact with an infested person or shares personal items can become infested. Lice are spread **only** by crawling from person to person directly or onto shared personal items, such as combs, brushes, head coverings, clothing, bedding, and towels.

How are they diagnosed? Diagnosis is usually made by finding nits—tiny, pearl gray, oval specks attached to the hair near the scalp. Use a magnifying glass and natural light when you search for them on the hair at the back of the neck, behind the ears, and at the top of the head.

Figure 17.15. Letter to parents about scabies

Dear parent or guardian:

_____ A child in our program has scabies.

_____ Your child may have scabies.

Please take these precautions:

1. During the next 6 weeks, watch for signs of an itchy rash that usually appears in lines.

2. If a rash develops, see your health care provider.

3. Tell us if your child has scabies.

Information about scabies

What is it? Scabies is a common skin rash caused by microscopic animals called mites that are found only on people. The mite digs under the skin and lays eggs that hatch. The new mites dig more paths and lay more eggs. The rash appears as red bumps and short, wavy lines in the skin (where the mites have dug). It is especially common between fingers and toes and at the wrists and ankles, but can occur anywhere. The rash is intensely itchy. Scabies is not dangerous, but it is very annoying. Anyone can get scabies from another person who has it or from clothes or bedding used by a person with scabies. The mites cannot jump or fly, but they can crawl. They can live for 3 days off the body.

What to do if your child has scabies
1. See your health care provider to get medicine to treat the scabies.

2. Wash all items such as clothes, hats, sheets, pillowcases, blankets, and towels, that your child has used, in **HOT WATER.** Dry these items on the hottest setting on the dryer.

3. Put things that you do not want to wash (pillows, blankets, toys, stuffed animals) away in tightly closed plastic bags for 4 days.

4. Thoroughly vacuum all carpets and upholstered furniture. Do not use pesticide sprays—they can be harmful to people and animals.

When can your child come back? Return your child to the program 24 hours after treatment was given. Sometimes your doctor may want to treat the whole family because scabies can spread so easily.

How are they treated? Treatment consists of getting rid of the lice from both the infested person and the surroundings and personal items. All household members and people with close physical contact should be examined for lice and treated if infested. Some health care providers may simultaneously treat all members of a household once.

To treat an infested person:

- Refer all persons who are infested with lice to their health care provider who will determine which medicine to use.
- Use these products very carefully. Always consult a physician before treating infants, pregnant or nursing women, or people with extensive cuts or scratches on the head or neck.
- After shampooing the hair with medicine, remove all the nits or eggs. This is a difficult and time-consuming process because the nits have such a firm grip on the hair. A solution of vinegar and water may help loosen the nits so you can remove them more easily with a special, fine-toothed, nit-removal comb.
- Check for nits daily for the next 10 days. If new nits or newly hatched lice appear, the treatment may need to be repeated. **Treatment should be repeated in 10 days to kill newly hatched lice** unless an ovicidal preparation is used.

To treat personal items and surroundings:

- Machine wash all washable and possibly infested items in **HOT** water. Dry them in a **HOT** dryer.
- Put difficult-to-wash items (stuffed toys, pillows) in a hot dryer for 20 minutes or dry-clean them.
- Seal items that cannot be washed or dried in a plastic bag for 30 days (the life cycle of a louse).
- Boil combs and brushes for 10 minutes or soak them for 1 hour in the bleach solution.
- Thoroughly vacuum rugs, upholstered furniture, and mattresses.
- Do not use insecticide sprays because they can be harmful to people and animals.

When should people with pediculosis be excluded and allowed to return? A child found to have an active case of head lice should be kept separate from other children. Notify the parent that the child may not return until treated. Other close contacts should be checked to determine if there are other cases. If your program is having a prob-lem with head lice, you should conduct morning head checks before the children mingle together. There is some disagreement among authorities about whether to require complete nit removal after treatment before allowing a child to return. Removal of nits is difficult, and the majority of nits will be killed by treatment. However, reinfestation is possible if some nits survive and hatch into adult lice. If the nits are not removed, you will not be able to tell whether reinfestation has occurred or there are only old nits. Program staff and the health consultant should decide on the best policy for both you and the parents. Regardless of the policy, to ensure successful treatment the children need to be checked for new nits for 10 to 14 days after therapy.

Where to report them? Notify parents and staff if a case of head lice occurs (see Figure 17.16).

Special stop-spread instructions for pediculosis

- Learn to recognize nits, and regularly check children's hair when there is a known case of head lice. Because almost all programs will have outbreaks of head lice periodically, and because the hysteria produced by head lice is far greater than their threat to health, this is a prime area for preventive, anticipatory parent information. A well-organized and prompt response to the first few cases can prevent a widespread problem.
- If a case is identified, your program should follow treatment procedures outlined above.

OTHER INFECTIOUS DISEASES

Cytomegalovirus (CMV), herpes simplex virus (HSV), sexually transmitted diseases (STDs)

These infections caused by direct contact (CMV by contact with saliva and urine; HSV and STDs most commonly through skin/mucous membrane contact) are more serious than the skin infections previously described. People with these infections may experience no symptoms, mild illness (such as cold sores), or a total body illness. Some infections (such as syphilis) are treatable, but others (such as cytomegalovirus) are not. Anyone can get these infections and can carry the germs in their

Figure 17.16. Letter to parents about head lice

Dear parent or guardian:

_____ A child in our program has head lice.

_____ Your child has head lice.

Please do not be alarmed, as this is a common occurrence in group programs. Head lice are not a sign of unclean people or homes.

Please take these precautions:

1. Check your child's hair for eggs (also called nits).

2. If you suspect your child has head lice, ask your health care provider to diagnose the problem and recommend appropriate treatment.

3. Tell us if your child is diagnosed as having head lice.

4. If head lice are diagnosed, do not return your child to the program until she or he has been treated.

Information about head lice

What are they? Head lice are tiny insects that live only on people's scalp and hair. They hatch from small eggs (nits) that are firmly attached to the individual hairs near the scalp and cannot be easily moved up or down the hair (as can specks of dandruff). They look like grains of sand. Nits may be found throughout the hair but are most often located at the back of the scalp, behind the ears, and at the top of the head. The eggs hatch in about 10 days, with new lice reaching adulthood in about 2 weeks. The female louse is about the size of a sesame seed, can live for 20 to 30 days, and can lay about six eggs a day. The lice live by biting and sucking blood from the scalp. Lice can survive up to 8 hours between feedings and can do so off the body.

How should you check for head lice? Usually, you probably will not see the lice, only the eggs. These are tiny, pearl gray, oval specks attached to the hair near the scalp. Look carefully, using a magnifying glass and natural light. Search for nits at the back of the neck, behind the ears, and at the top of the head.

How does a person get head lice? Anyone who has close contact with an infested person or shares personal items can become infested. Lice are spread **only** by crawling from person to person directly or onto shared personal items such as combs, brushes, head coverings, clothing, bedding, or towels.

What should you do about head lice?
1. If your child does have head lice, your health care provider may want to treat everyone in your family. Everyone should be checked, and anyone with nits should definitely be treated.

Figure 17.16 *continued*

2. To get rid of head lice

- **Use a special medicated shampoo or cream rinse that your health care provider prescribes or recommends. Use any of these products very carefully, and consult a physician before treating infants, pregnant or nursing women, or people with extensive cuts or scratches on the head or neck.**

- **Remove all nits** after shampooing the hair with medicine. This is a difficult and time-consuming process because the nits have such a firm grip on the hair. Using a solution of vinegar and water may help loosen nits so you can remove them with a special, fine-toothed, nit-removal comb.

- **Check for nits daily for the next 10 to 14 days.** Then repeat treatment to kill any newly hatched lice.

- **Clean personal items and surroundings:**

  —Machine wash all washable and possibly infested items in **HOT** water. Dry them in a **HOT** dryer.

  —Put difficult-to-wash items (stuffed toys or pillows) in a **HOT** dryer for 20 minutes or dry-clean them.

  —Seal items that cannot be washed or dried in a plastic bag for 30 days (the life cycle of a louse).

  —Boil combs and brushes for 10 minutes or soak them for 1 hour in a bleach solution of 1 tablespoon of bleach mixed with 1 quart of water.

  —Thoroughly vacuum rugs, upholstered furniture, and mattresses.

  —Do not use insecticide sprays because they can be harmful to people and animals.

When can your child return? Your child may come back as soon as the shampoo has been used, you have removed as many nits as possible from your child's hair, and you have cleaned or stored personal items. Remember that you must keep checking your child's hair for new nits for at least 2 weeks.

body secretions for months or years even though these carriers may not experience symptoms. The germs that cause these infections are spread when the secretions they are in (such as saliva) penetrate the skin or mucous membrane of another person. This process can occur when germs get on skin that is broken, cut, or scraped, or on mucosal surfaces such as the inside linings of the mouth, eyes, nose, rectum, or sex organs. These infections may also be transmitted from an infected mother to her newborn infant.

How to stop spread of these infectious diseases. You should assume that every body secretion is potentially contagious and should take these preventive actions:

- Insist that staff and children wash their hands well after any contact with blood, saliva, urine, stool, skin sores, or genital secretions.
- Make sure that staff and children place disposable items that are contaminated with body secretions (diapers, tissues, bandages, paper towels) in a covered step can that is lined with a disposable plastic bag and that is kept away from food and other materials.
- Store clothing and other personal items that become contaminated with body secretions separately in plastic bags, and send them home for laundering.
- Wash and disinfect surfaces and toys that become contaminated with body secretions or blood. Clean or dispose of cleaning items (mops, rags, and towels) properly.
- Do not permit aggressive behavior (biting, scratching).
- Do not allow sharing of personal items that may have been contaminated with blood or other body fluids (toothbrushes, washcloths, teething rings).

Cytomegalovirus infection

What is it? Cytomegalovirus is a very common infection found especially in young children. In most cases, CMV causes no symptoms. Occasionally, children or adults with CMV will experience mononucleosis-like symptoms (fever, swollen glands, fatigue). Persons infected with CMV often have the virus in their bodies for as long as several years. During this time, they continue to shed viruses into such body fluids as saliva, urine, genital fluids, and (rarely) blood. Once people are infected with CMV they develop substances called antibodies that prevent them from getting new CMV infections.

CMV concerns early childhood programs primarily because it can cause problems for pregnant women. If a pregnant woman **who has never had CMV** becomes infected, especially during the first trimester, the fetus may also become infected. If this happens, in rare cases the fetus may suffer mental retardation, hearing loss, or other sensory problems. The mother may not realize she is sick or may have only a mild, flu-like illness. Women who **have had CMV in the past** can also transmit the infection to their fetus, but it is far less likely to adversely affect the baby.

Who gets it and how? CMV is shed in highest rates by children from the ages of 1 to 3 years. The virus can also spread to people who have regular, close physical contact with children's secretions. At any given time, 20 to 80% or more of the children in a group may have CMV but show no signs of illness. Spread of the virus requires direct contact with infected fluids (saliva and urine) that are then transferred to a mucous surface (inside the mouth, genital tract, or lining of the eye) or into a person's bloodstream (through a break in the skin, needle stick, or blood transfusion). Spread between children can possibly occur by sharing mouthed objects or toys that have infected saliva on them. The virus can survive several hours on surfaces outside the body.

How is it diagnosed? Most people with CMV are not diagnosed because they show no symptoms. Diagnosis of the CMV virus can be made from cultures of infected fluids or by blood tests for the CMV antibodies.

How is it treated? Immune deficient people with severe effects of CMV may be given antiviral and immune globulin treatment to lessen the severity of the disease, but these treatments are not routine.

When should people with CMV be excluded? Children who are known to have CMV do not need to be excluded because the program probably has other children who have CMV.

Where to report it? There is no need to report CMV

infection, as it is common and frequently occurs unrecognized and undiagnosed in the community.

Special stop-spread information for CMV

- **Make sure that adults** (especially pregnant women or women trying to become pregnant) **always wash their hands after contact with children's urine, saliva, or blood.** Women who work in child care programs who might become pregnant should be referred to their personal physician or health department for counseling regarding the risk in your setting. This counseling may include testing for immunity against CMV infection.
- Do not share food or drinks.
- Do not share eating utensils or drinking glasses without washing and disinfecting them thoroughly.
- Do not kiss children on the mouth.

Herpes simplex viral infections

What are they? Oral herpes infection is extremely common. The first infection usually occurs in childhood, is mild, and often unnoticed. It may come in the form of **gingivostomatitis**—fever accompanied by widespread painful ulcerations (sores) in the mouth. HSV usually recurs as cold sores—single or multiple blisters around the lip. Rarely, HSV can be spread by direct touching to cause infection on a finger (**herpetic whitlow**—painful recurrent blisters of a finger) or eye (**herpetic keratitis**—recurrent ulcerations of the cornea).

Genital herpes infection occurs primarily in adults and is sexually transmitted. The first infection is frequently unnoticed and without symptoms. However, it can also cause painful genital blisters and ulcers accompanied by fever and can last 2 weeks. Recurrence is common and usually comes in the form of localized, less painful ulcers that go away in days and are not accompanied by fever. Recurrence may also be asymptomatic.

Herpes of the newborn most often occurs when a newborn infant passes through an infected birth canal. The resulting illnesses range in severity from skin blisters to total body disease with death or severe brain damage. An infant who survives may have recurrent skin blisters due to HSV.

Herpes infections in children are usually manifested as oral herpes which, while uncomfortable, are rarely serious. People who have severe eczema or immune system problems may have more severe infections with herpes.

Who gets them and how? Oral herpes infections are most common in young children; genital herpes infection (due to its sexual transmission) is more common in adults. Genital herpes may be seen in children in unusual circumstances or as a result of sexual abuse. HSV is shed into the secretions of the blisters and ulcers. Spread of HSV requires direct contact of virus-containing secretions with a mucous membrane (inside the mouth, lining of the eyes, rectum, or genitals) or with broken skin (such as a cut).

Because herpes viruses can survive as long as 4 hours on surfaces, mouthed objects contaminated by virus-containing saliva can transmit infections of the mouth. It would be unlikely for HSV from a child's mouth, skin, or genital lesion to cause genital herpes in another person, as transmission would require direct contact with the other person's genital area.

How are they diagnosed? Diagnosis is usually made based on the distinctive appearance of the blisters or sores. A doctor may also examine material under a microscope or do a special viral culture.

How are they treated? Antiviral therapy for HSV infections is available. Generally speaking, this therapy is used only for serious HSV infections (such as in the newborn, for people with immune problems, for infections of the brain or eye, or for certain cases of genital herpes).

When should people with HSV infections be excluded and allowed to return?

- Exclude children or staff with open, oozing skin sores that cannot be covered. Exclude all cases of herpetic whitlow if the sores are not crusted. **Do not exclude** children or staff with mouth sores or skin blisters that can be covered or with genital herpes. If the program has a large number of infants with oral lesions, consider excluding children who are drooling or have biting behaviors.
- Allow returns as follows:
  —Children with drooling or biting behavior can return when blisters are crusted over.

Figure 17.17. Symptoms/diagnosis/treatment of major sexually transmitted diseases

Gonorrhea

Cause
Bacteria (Neisseria gonorrhoeae)

Symptoms
Vaginal/rectal pus discharge or redness
Pain or pus during urination
Sore throat
Pus and eye discharge in newborn younger than
    1 week old*

Diagnosis
Culture of appropriate area

Treatment
Antibiotics

Chlamydia

Cause
Bacteria-like germ (Chlamydia trachomatis)

Symptoms
Vaginal/rectal pus discharge or redness
Pain or pus during urination
Pus and eye discharge in newborn younger than
    1 month*
Certain pneumonia syndromes in infants
    younger than 3 months*

Diagnosis
Culture or rapid test of scraping of infected area

Treatment
Antibiotics

Syphilis

Cause
Spirochete bacteria (Treponema pallidum)

Symptoms
Painless, hard ulcer, usually on genitals, with
    swollen groin glands
Body rash (symmetrical, brownish) with flu
    symptoms
Shallow ulcerations on mucosal surfaces
    (mouth)
Moist, gray genital warts
Syndrome of congenital syphilis*

Diagnosis
Blood test

Treatment
Antibiotics

Herpes simplex (genital herpes infection)

Cause
Virus

Symptoms
Recurrent, painful, tiny blisters or ulcers,
    usually on genitals
Swollen groin lymph nodes
Severe generalized disease of skin, brain, liver*

Diagnosis
Viral culture or scraping of infected area viewed
    under a microscope

Treatment
First (primary) infection: an antiviral ointment
    or oral medicine may be given
Recurrent infection: usually no treatment,
    occasionally oral antiviral medicine

*Mother-to-newborn transmission

—Children or staff with **skin blisters** that cannot be covered can return when the blisters are crusted over.

—Children or staff with **herpetic whitlow** can return when blisters are completely crusted over.

Where to report them? There is no need to report HSV infections unless they occur in newborn babies.

Special stop-spread information for HSV infections

- Do not kiss children on the mouth.
- Do not share eating utensils or drinking glasses without washing and disinfecting them thoroughly.
- Cover herpes lesions with a bandage.
- Make sure that staff who may touch blisters on children wear gloves during diapering or changing of a dressing.

Sexually transmitted diseases

What are they? Sexually transmitted diseases (including gonorrhea, syphilis, chlamydia, genital herpes simplex, hepatitis B, and HIV/AIDS) are infections caused by bacteria, viruses, or parasites that are transmitted by intimate sexual contact with infected secretions. CMV, hepatitis B, and HIV/AIDS, three viral infections discussed elsewhere in this chapter, can also be transmitted sexually because the viruses are present in genital secretions.

Who gets them and how? These diseases are primarily seen in sexually active adolescents and adults and are transmitted through intimate sexual contact. They are NOT spread through the air, by contact with objects such as toilet seats, or by casual contact. They are spread when infectious secretions come in direct contact with a mucosal surface (such as genitals). Some infections can be passed from mother to newborn during pregnancy or as the infant passes through an infected birth canal. These include gonococcal or chlamydial eye infections (ophthalmia neonatorum), herpes simplex of the newborn, congenital syphilis, CMV, hepatitis B, and HIV/AIDS.

Except in cases of newborn infants infected during pregnancy or the birth process, the presence of one of these infections in a child should raise the possibility of sexual abuse. (Refer to Chapter 14 for information about sexual abuse indicators and reporting requirements.) In children, CMV, hepatitis B, and oral herpes infections are almost always transmitted by other mechanisms and should **NOT** be considered possible indicators of sexual abuse.

How are they diagnosed? Sexually transmitted diseases can be diagnosed by a variety of tests. Figure 17.17 reviews the symptoms, diagnosis, and treatment of major sexually transmitted diseases.

When should people with sexually transmitted diseases be excluded? Do not exclude children who have sexually transmitted diseases. Make sure, however, that these children receive treatments specific to their infections and that appropriate reporting for investigations of possible sexual abuse is carried out.

Do not exclude staff members who have sexually transmitted diseases. Ask these adults to get appropriate treatment and counseling.

Where to report them? The following sexually transmitted diseases must usually be reported by the diagnosing health care provider directly to your state department of public health:

- gonorrhea
- syphilis
- chlamydial genital infection
- pelvic inflammatory disease
- granuloma inguinale
- lymphogranuloma venereum
- chancroid
- ophthalmia neonatorum
- neonatal herpes
- hepatitis B
- HIV/AIDS

If you suspect that occurrence of any of these diseases in a child was caused by sexual abuse, you must report these cases to the local child protective services or other identified agency responsible for investigating child sexual abuse.

Special stop-spread information for sexually transmitted diseases

- Watch for signs of sexual abuse (i.e., genital and anal tears, sores, discharge) when changing or toileting children.
- Insist that staff and children wash hands after any contact with genital areas.

INFECTIOUS DISEASES SPREAD THROUGH BLOOD

Hepatitis B and HIV/AIDS infection

Hepatitis B and HIV/AIDS are two serious viral infections that can be spread by contact with infected blood. The viruses that cause these illnesses can be spread when blood containing the virus enters the bloodstream of another person. Spread can occur when infected blood comes in contact with a broken surface of a mucous membrane (such as the inside lining of the mouth, eyes, nose, rectum, or sex organs). This can also happen when the skin is accidentally or intentionally punctured by a contaminated needle. An infected mother can also give these viruses to her newborn infant during the pregnancy, childbirth, or by breast-feeding. Once these viruses enter a person's body, they may stay for months or years. An infected person may appear to be healthy but can spread the viruses.

How to stop spread of infectious diseases spread through blood contact

Even though these diseases spread through blood contact are more difficult to catch or spread to another person than other diseases described in this chapter, you should **treat all blood and body fluids as if they were contagious.** Wear disposable latex or vinyl gloves whenever contact with blood may occur—during first aid and for clean-up. Make sure that you clean up all blood spills promptly with soap and water and then disinfect **all** blood-contaminated surfaces with the bleach solution (Figure 3.1) or other approved sanitizing solution (check the label for this use). Wash hands and exposed skin well with soap and water.

Hepatitis B

What is it? Hepatitis B is a viral infection of the liver. Symptoms of infection include fever, loss of appetite, nausea, jaundice (yellowing of the skin and whites of the eyes), and occasionally pain of the joints and a skin rash. Illness can range from infection without symptoms to the very rare event of rapid liver failure and death. As with hepatitis A infection, young children are less likely to be jaundiced or show symptoms of illness. Unlike hepatitis A infection, hepatitis B can cause long-term (chronic) infection with persistent shedding of the virus into body fluids and blood in some of those infected. People who have the virus in their blood for 6 months or more are called chronic carriers. These people can develop liver disease, cirrhosis with liver failure, and liver cancer, years after infection. An infected mother can transmit the infection to her newborn infant. Although these infants often show no obvious symptoms of hepatitis B, many can become chronic carriers if they are not treated.

Who gets it and how? Hepatitis B is spread when blood or body fluids containing the virus get onto skin or inside the mouth, eyes, rectum, or genital tract. Hepatitis B infections are more difficult to spread than hepatitis A infections (that are spread via infected stool). Hepatitis B infections occur most frequently in people who have contact with other people's blood (such as laboratory technicians or health care providers who may accidentally puncture their skin with blood-contaminated needles or intravenous drug abusers who may share needles). People who have hepatitis B can spread the infection to their sexual contacts via infected genital tract fluids. Transmission of infection in households occurs only rarely, in situations where there is sharing of personal items that may be contaminated with infected blood or saliva. Hepatitis B can also possibly spread, rarely, by bites that break the skin. In 30 to 40% of cases of acute hepatitis B, the risk factor is unknown.

How is it diagnosed? Hepatitis B infection is diagnosed by a blood test.

How is it prevented and treated? A vaccine for the prevention of hepatitis B is highly effective and considered very safe. This vaccine is recommended for all children and for people likely to be exposed to hepatitis B infection. The goal of the immunization program is to eventually achieve universal immunization of all people. If a person who has not had hepatitis B vaccine is exposed to hepatitis B through contact with infected blood, an injection of a special immune globulin should be given as soon as possible to prevent infection. Immunization should follow the immune globulin injection.

There is no cure, currently, for hepatitis B infection, although some immune treatments can reduce disease progression in some cases. Prevention is important to prevent the long-term, continuing infection that is associated with death from liver disease usually in adulthood.

Who should receive hepatitis B vaccine? The American Academy of Pediatrics, the Centers for Disease Control and Prevention, and the U.S. Public Health Services Advisory Committee on Immunization Practices have recommended that all children be given hepatitis B vaccine. For employees whose job duties could reasonably be expected to expose them to contact with blood or other potentially infectious materials (i.e., giving first aid or cleaning up blood spills), the Occupational Safety and Health Administration (OSHA) regulations require that hepatitis B vaccine be offered by the employer. For further details on these regulations, contact the regional office of OSHA listed under the Department of Labor in your telephone directory.

When should people with hepatitis B be excluded and allowed to return? A staff person ill with hepatitis B should stay home until she or he feels well and fever and jaundice are gone. A staff person with chronic hepatitis B infection who has open, oozing sores that cannot be covered should not attend until the skin sores are healed.

If hepatitis B were to spread in a child care setting it would most likely occur through direct blood contact via bites, scratches, or cuts that break the skin and allow the blood of an infected person to spread into the bloodstream of a noninfected person. Based on all research at this time, the **risk of disease spread in child care is considered very low and does not justify routine screening of children prior to enrollment.** Admission of a known hepatitis B carrier with specific risk factors such as biting, frequent scratching, generalized open skin rashes or sores, or bleeding problems should be assessed on a case-by-case basis by the child's physician, early childhood program, and responsible public health authorities. Hepatitis B carriers without behavior or medical risk factors should be admitted to child care without restrictions.

Where to report it? Notify parents and staff about **acute hepatitis B infections** and report these cases to your health consultant and local board of health. The center director and primary caregivers should be informed about a known hepatitis B carrier child. **If your program has one or more staff or children who are known carriers of hepatitis B,** caregivers and parents should be reminded about the advisability of getting the hepatitis B vaccine. Your health consultant, local board of health, and state department of public health can help you obtain information about prevention of hepatitis B and the availability of vaccine.

It is vital that you respect the confidentiality of the medical records of the hepatitis B carrier(s) and not stigmatize the individual carrier(s). Do not release the names of specific children to other parents, and in the affected classroom(s) use all precautions or procedures for ALL children and staff.

Special stop-spread instructions for hepatitis B

- Make sure that all staff and children follow the general procedures for thorough handwashing and cleanliness.
- **Always treat blood as a potentially dangerous fluid** and follow the stop-spread disinfecting guidelines at the beginning of this section.
- Do not allow sharing of personal items that may become contaminated with blood or body fluids, such as toothbrushes, food, or any object that may be mouthed.
- Place disposable items contaminated with blood in plastic bags in covered containers.
- Store clothing or other personal items stained with blood separately in a plastic bag to be sent home with the child for appropriate cleaning. Ask parents to wash and then **bleach** these articles.
- Clean surfaces or toys contaminated with blood or body fluids with soap and water and then disinfect with the bleach solution (Figure 3.1) as soon as possible after they are contaminated.
- Discourage aggressive behavior (biting, scratching). Supervise closely to avoid these behaviors.
- Use disposable gloves when you clean up blood spills. Wash your hands well afterward with soap and water.
- If a person has a significant exposure to blood (i.e., contact of non-intact skin or mucous membrane of mouth or eyes with any person's blood), then the bloodborne pathogens exposure protocol should be followed. According to OSHA regulations, this involves immediately washing the site well, documenting and reporting the expo-

sure to the supervisor, and having a medical evaluation within 24 hours to determine the need for preventive treatment and follow-up including laboratory tests, immune globulin, and hepatitis B vaccine.

- If you enroll children who are known chronic carriers of hepatitis B, strongly consider a vaccination program for non-immune employees and children, and discuss this action with your health consultant.

HIV/AIDS infection

HIV (human immunodeficiency virus) is a viral infection that can lead to AIDS (acquired immunodeficiency syndrome), a combination of illnesses that can be severe and life threatening. A person infected with HIV can remain healthy for many years; she or he may also alternate between sick and relatively healthy periods. Over time the virus can damage the person's immune system and other organs. Children with HIV/AIDS may experience symptoms such as delays in growth and development and repeated infections such as thrush, diaper rash, ear infections, and pneumonia. Many of the conditions that people with HIV/AIDS experience can be successfully treated with antibiotics and other medications. Currently there is no cure for HIV/AIDS and the illness tends to be progressive and fatal. However, new and effective treatments are being developed, and it has been shown that early diagnosis, treatment, and close medical follow-up has significantly improved the health and survival of children with HIV/AIDS.

Because new information about HIV/AIDS is constantly being generated, it is important for you not only to read what is in this manual but also to keep up with new developments. You should contact the AIDS coordinator at your state and local departments of public health for current information and guidance. Also, be aware of HIV/AIDS-related changes to laws or regulations that affect the operation of your program. If a child with known HIV/AIDS applies to your program, ask your state and/or public health department and the child's physician to help you decide if the child should attend and what procedures you should follow. For the most part, children with HIV/AIDS, particularly those who are asymptomatic, will be unlikely to need any special accommodations to be integrated into your program.

How is the disease detected? The presence of HIV infection is determined by a blood test. If a person develops symptoms of AIDS, a blood test for the presence of HIV helps confirm the diagnosis. However, many people may be infected with HIV and, during the latent period, not be aware of their HIV infection, though they are capable of transmitting the disease (see below). Therefore, there are people (including young children) who have HIV infection but are not aware of it.

Another complication in detecting HIV infection in infants is that the blood test detects antibodies to the virus and not the virus itself. Young infants receive antibodies from their mothers that stay in their bodies for as long as 15 months. Thus, infants may test positive for the HIV antibodies that came from their HIV-infected mothers, but they may not have the infection themselves. Only about 20 to 30% of infants born to mothers with HIV infection will actually turn out to be infected, though all test positive in the first few months. It may be difficult to accurately detect HIV infection by the HIV antibody test in an infant up to the age of 15 months. New blood tests, however, can detect the presence of the actual virus and provide early diagnosis of HIV infection within the first month of life.

How is the HIV infection transmitted? In this country the overwhelming majority of young children acquire HIV infection from their mothers during pregnancy or delivery. If the infant or young child develops HIV infection, the mother has HIV infection also. However, the mother's infection may also be latent, and she may be unaware that she is infected. Or, she may have AIDS. The only way that HIV infection is known to spread from one person to another is (1) through sexual intercourse, (2) from a mother to her infant during pregnancy, delivery, or breast-feeding, and (3) from the blood of an infected person entering the body of an uninfected person. This latter method of transmission most frequently occurs in IV drug users who *inject* drugs using needles contaminated with blood from other IV drug users. The other common method of transmission *was* by blood transfusion, donated by infected persons and received by uninfected persons. However, in this country all donated blood has been tested for HIV infection since 1985, and this mode of transmission is now rare. **HIV is spread only by blood or sexual fluids. HIV is not transmitted through urine, stool (diarrhea), vomitus, saliva (mouthing of toys and other objects), mucus, sweat, or any other body fluid that does not contain blood. HIV is *not* spread by casual contact.**

What are recommendations for attendance of children with HIV/AIDS?

- All children with HIV/AIDS should be admitted to the program as long as their own health and development status allows them to benefit from the program.
- Remember, no child in the program, regardless of known HIV infection, should be attending the program with bloody diarrhea or open, oozing mouth or skin sores that cannot be covered or successfully treated with medication.
- All programs should use appropriate precautions in the handling of all blood spills since the presence of infection that can be transmitted by blood will not always be known.
- Since HIV status is confidential information, and since transmission is possible only through blood which all programs must handle appropriately, there is *no* requirement that program staff or families of other children in the program be informed of the HIV status of a child. However, program directors and health care personnel should be informed of *any* child who is immunodeficient so that the presence of a contagious disease in the program can be communicated immediately to that child's family and doctor. This does not mean that HIV status must be disclosed. There are other causes for immune deficiencies, such as being treated for cancer and other immune diseases unrelated to HIV.

Can an adult who is HIV positive or who has HIV/AIDS work in early childhood settings? Since HIV infection is **not** spread by casual contact, there is no reason to exclude the person with HIV/AIDS while she or he feels well enough to work. As with any adult in child care, an adult with HIV/AIDS should not work if there are open, oozing sores which cannot be covered, until they are healed. Other restrictions are not needed. Adults with HIV/AIDS may be immunocompromised (their immune system is not working well to protect them from illnesses) and may be more likely to get infections. To protect their own health, they should consult their physicians regarding their occupational risk.

How can you protect against the spread of HIV infection? Transmission of HIV infection in the child care setting is only possible through blood from an infected child entering the body of an uninfected person. This is theoretically (and practically) possible only if the infected child or adult bleeds and others in the child care setting are exposed to infected blood through contact of the infected blood with a mucous membrane or opening in their skin. Therefore, as with hepatitis B, **always treat blood as a potentially dangerous fluid.**

- Children and adults with open skin lesions should keep these lesions covered.
- If contact with blood, bloody body fluids (e.g., bloody diarrhea), oozing skin lesions, or mucous membranes is anticipated, disposable latex (or reusable rubber for those allergic to latex) gloves should be used. Hands should be washed immediately after gloves are removed. If reusable rubber gloves are used, they must be washed and disinfected using the same procedures as for other contaminated surfaces and hung to dry.
- If gloves are unavailable, it is safest to maintain a barrier (e.g., gauze) between one's hands and the blood. Then wash hands and other exposed skin well afterward.
- It is theoretically possible that a bite by an uninfected child, into an infected child, if the bite draws blood, could result in transmission if blood from the infected child contacts an opening in the mucous membranes of the uninfected child. However, this has never been shown to happen in a child care setting. Because of this potential concern, and the much more likely danger of *other* infections resulting from bites, all biting should be taken seriously. Such behavior should be controlled by close supervision and by providing children with more acceptable alternatives to express aggressive impulses.

Other recommendations for programs enrolling children with HIV/AIDS

- Protect all children and staff by strictly following special procedures for cleaning and handling blood and body fluids.
- Protect children with HIV/AIDS from infections by communicable diseases (e.g., chicken pox or measles) by immediately notifying the parent and excluding them if there is an outbreak (until they are properly treated with hyper immune gamma globulin and/or until the outbreak no longer presents a threat).
- Protect the right to privacy of these children by maintaining confidential records and by giving medical information only to people with an absolute need to know and *only* with the consent of the child's parents/legal guardian.
- Provide in-service education for all staff in early childhood programs to ensure accurate information about HIV/AIDS.
- Help children with HIV/AIDS to lead as normal a life as possible.

VACCINE-PREVENTABLE DISEASES

Measles, mumps, rubella, polio, pertussis, diphtheria, and tetanus

Prior to the implementation of immunization programs, these seven diseases were a major cause of widespread illness, often with permanent medical complications and even death. The diseases were a problem especially for children, although adults were also affected. (Haemophilus influenzae type b infections, hepatitis B, and varicella [chicken pox] are now also preventable through vaccines. These diseases and the vaccines are discussed in detail in previous sections.)

Some people believe that these diseases are no longer a problem in the United States or that children can't get them anymore. **However, cases of these diseases do occur still, particularly in nonimmunized or inadequately immunized children and adults.** Incidence of many of these diseases is on the rise. Children and staff in group programs are especially at risk because the children may be too young to be fully immunized and because the close contact that occurs in the group allows easy spread of

any disease. In addition, programs that have a relatively young staff (born after the late 1950s) are at particular risk because this age group is too young to have gotten natural immunity from exposure.

How to stop spread of vaccine-preventable diseases

- Make sure that all children are immunized as completely as possible for their age (see Figure 17.1).
- Make sure that all adults working in your program (including volunteers) have immunity to diphtheria, tetanus, measles, mumps, rubella, polio, and varicella (chicken pox). Remember that all adults need boosters for diphtheria and tetanus every 10 years. (Adult vaccination against pertussis is not recommended.) Acceptable evidence of immunity in adults can be provided in several ways, that vary by the age of the adult and the specific disease, as listed here.

Diphtheria/tetanus—evidence of immunity
—documentation of completion of a primary series (three doses) within the past 10 years, or
—documentation of a primary series in childhood and regular boosters every 10 years since

Measles—evidence of immunity
—born before 1957, or
—documentation of vaccination with live measles vaccine on or after the first birthday, or
—laboratory evidence of immunity
(Vaccination for measles is recommended for adults older than 20 years who are not sure they are immune.)

Mumps—evidence of immunity
—born before 1957, or
—documentation of vaccination with live mumps vaccine on or after the first birthday, or
—laboratory evidence of immunity
(Vaccination for mumps is recommended for adults older than 20 years who are not sure they are immune.)

Rubella—evidence of immunity
—documentation of vaccination with rubella vaccine on or after the first birthday, or
—laboratory evidence of immunity

(A history of rubella, or even documentation of physician-diagnosed rubella, without laboratory confirmation, is not acceptable. Vaccination during pregnancy is generally not advised. Vaccination should be given after delivery.)

Polio—evidence of immunity
—documentation of vaccination with a primary series (three or more doses) of polio vaccine

- Notify your local board of health if a documented case of measles, mumps, rubella, polio, diphtheria, tetanus, or pertussis occurs in your program. They will assist you in starting any necessary identification and vaccination of susceptible children and adults. They will also instruct you on procedures for closely watching for any additional cases and for notifying other parents.

Measles

What is it? Measles is one of the most communicable viral illnesses and is the most serious of the common childhood diseases. Usually it causes a brownish-red, blotchy rash, that begins on the face and spreads down the body for 3 days, accompanied by high fever, cough, runny nose, and watery eyes. The illness lasts 1 to 2 weeks and can be complicated by ear infections, pneumonia, and encephalitis (inflammation of the brain). It can also cause miscarriages or premature delivery in pregnant women.

Who gets it and how? All people are at risk, but those most at risk for measles are generally
- children younger than 15 months old (who are too young to have been immunized) and preschoolers
- those refusing vaccination
- adolescents and young adults who may have received an earlier ineffective measles vaccine prior to 1968 or who graduated from school prior to the mandatory measles vaccination law. (Adults born prior to 1957 are generally considered immune.)

Measles is spread by large infected droplets or direct contact with the nasal or throat secretions of infected persons. It can also be spread by inhaling air that has tiny infectious droplets from sneezes or coughs. It is one of the most readily transmissible communicable diseases. The communicable period is greatest **prior to** and **just after** rash onset.

The incidence of measles is rising, and therefore immunization schedules have been changed to include two doses.

When should people with measles be excluded and allowed to return? Exclude anyone with measles until at least 4 days after the appearance of the rash. Exclude all children and adults who are not immune for 14 days after exposure to the last case during its infectious period or after the date of rash onset in the last case.

How to stop spread of measles
Measles is one of the few diseases we *can* prevent through prompt immunization after exposure. If a case is reported or suspected, all susceptible staff and children older than 12 months, who are without contradiction to vaccine, should be immunized WITHIN 72 HOURS OF EXPOSURE. Immunization within this period often prevents disease. Immune globulin, if given within 6 days of exposure, may decrease the severity of illness and should be offered to all those younger than 12 months, pregnant women, persons who are immunocompromised (have weak immune systems), and those with other contraindications to the vaccine. Those who receive immune globulin can still become infectious and should be excluded for 14 days after their exposure.

Where to report it? Notify parents and staff as well as your local board of health and your health consultant.

Mumps

What is it? The incidence of mumps is rising. Mumps is a viral infection that causes fever, headache, and swelling and tenderness of the salivary glands, particularly the gland at the angle of the jaw. This causes the cheeks to swell. Possible complications include meningitis (inflammation of the coverings of the brain and spinal cord), encephalitis (inflammation of the brain), deafness, and in adolescent or adult males, inflammation of the testicles. The virus may produce a miscarriage if a woman becomes infected during the first trimester of pregnancy.

Who gets it and how? Most adults born before 1957 have been infected naturally and are probably immune. Mumps may occur in nonimmunized children or adolescents and young adults who graduated from school prior to laws requiring mumps immunization. The mumps virus is found most often in saliva. It is transmitted by direct contact or by droplet spread of the virus in the air through sneezes or coughs. The virus may also be found in urine. Mumps is most infectious 48 hours **prior** to the onset of symptoms and may be communicable as long as 7 days prior to swelling.

When should people with mumps be excluded and allowed to return? Exclude anyone with mumps until 9 days after the onset of swelling or until the swelling has subsided (whichever is sooner). All persons who are susceptible should be immunized and then excluded until 21 days after the last case.

Where to report it? Notify parents and staff as well as your local board of health and health consultant.

Rubella (German measles)

What is it? Rubella (German measles) is a mild viral illness that causes a slight fever and (in about 50% of infections) a flat, red rash that begins on the face. The rash spreads to the rest of the body over the next 24 hours. The illness causes swelling of the neck glands—particularly those at the back of the neck. Adult women with rubella may experience swelling or aching of the joints that lasts about a week. Rarely, encephalitis (brain inflammation) or a temporary bleeding disorder (purpura) may occur, usually in adults.

The most serious problem with rubella is that if a pregnant woman becomes infected, her developing infant can also become infected. Stillbirth, miscarriage, or serious birth defects (e.g., heart defects, deafness, blindness, and mental retardation) can occur in the infant.

Who gets it and how? Rubella is most often seen in nonimmunized children and in a susceptible group of adolescents and young adults who gradu-

ated prior to school rubella vaccination laws. The virus is spread by large droplets in the air (through sneezes or coughs) or by direct contact with infected nasal or saliva secretions. Direct contact with blood, urine, and stool during the infectious period can also spread infection.

When should people with rubella be excluded and allowed to return? Exclude anyone with rubella until 7 days after the onset of the rash. All persons who are susceptible should be immunized and excluded until 21 days after exposure to the infectious case or after the date of rash onset in the last case has been reported.

Where to report it? Notify parents and staff as well as your local board of health and your health consultant.

Polio

What is it? Polio is caused by a virus and causes an illness that ranges in severity from a mild, unnoticed feverish illness to meningitis (inflammation of the coverings of the brain and spinal cord) to paralysis and even death.

Who gets it and how? Polio cases occur mainly among nonimmunized young children or members of groups that refuse immunization. The virus is spread by consuming food or water contaminated by the virus and direct contact with infected stool and throat secretions (phlegm, mucus). People are most infectious during the first few days before and after the onset of symptoms. However, the virus can be shed in the stool for up to 8 weeks.

When should people with polio be excluded and allowed to return? People with polio are infectious for up to 6 weeks. Due to the seriousness of this disease, it is unlikely they will return before then.

Where to report it? Notify parents and staff as well as your local board of health and your health consultant.

Diphtheria

What is it and how is it treated? Diphtheria is a very serious bacterial infection of the nose and throat. It causes a sore throat, swollen tonsils with a grayish covering, and swollen neck glands. It can lead to severe throat swelling that can block breathing. The bacteria also produce a toxin (a type of poisonous substance) that can cause severe and permanent damage to the nervous system and heart. Diphtheria is treated primarily with an antitoxin, along with antibiotics. Antibiotics are also given to others who were closely exposed to a person with diphtheria and to carriers of diphtheria bacteria. Close contacts who are unimmunized or have not received a diphtheria vaccine within the past 5 years should also be given the diphtheria vaccine.

Who gets it and how? Diphtheria occurs primarily among nonimmunized or inadequately immunized people. People need booster doses of diphtheria toxoid every 10 years after finishing the childhood primary immunization series, to maintain protection. The bacteria are spread by direct contact with discharge from the nose, throat, eyes, or skin sores of infected people. Articles or food contaminated with discharge can also spread infection.

When should people with diphtheria be excluded and allowed to return? Exclude all diphtheria patients and carriers of diphtheria bacteria. They should receive appropriate treatment and not return until two cultures from nose, throat, or skin sores are negative for the bacteria. These cultures should be taken at least 24 hours apart after treatment is completed.

Where to report it? Notify parents and staff as well as your local board of health and your health consultant.

Tetanus

What is it? The tetanus bacteria (that live in soil) can enter the body through a cut or wound and produce a poisonous substance that causes the muscles to go into spasms. Paralysis and even death can result. Tetanus has also been called *lockjaw.*

Who gets it and how? Tetanus occurs almost exclusively in nonimmunized or inadequately immunized people. People need booster doses of tetanus toxoid every 10 years after finishing the childhood primary immunization, to maintain protection. Unlike the other vaccine-preventable diseases, tetanus is NOT spread from person to person. It occurs when the bacteria in soil or dust are introduced into the body through a wound.

When should people with tetanus be excluded and allowed to return? Tetanus patients may attend when they feel well enough to return.

Where to report it? Notify your local board of health and health consultant.

Special stop-spread information for tetanus
Make sure that you clean all cuts, scrapes, and puncture wounds well with soap and water.

Pertussis (whooping cough)

What is it? Pertussis (whooping cough) is a very contagious bacterial infection of the respiratory tract. The disease begins with cold symptoms and within 1 to 2 weeks develops into repeated attacks of severe coughing that can last 1 to 2 months. The whoop sound (that gets its name from the sound a child makes when trying to draw a breath after a coughing spell) may not occur, especially in young infants or adults. During the severe coughing stage, seizures or even death can occur, particularly in a young infant, due to a lack of oxygen. Antibiotic treatment will reduce the infectiousness of an ill person but may not improve symptoms once a person has developed a severe cough. However, antibiotics are crucial in making people not infectious and preventing illness in contacts.

Who gets it and how? Cases generally occur in nonimmunized or inadequately immunized children. About half of all cases occur in children younger than 1 year old, and 70% of all cases occur in children younger than 5 years old. Many cases occur in adolescents and adults because protection from the vaccine lasts only 5 to 10 years after the last dose given at age 7. These adults, who may have very mild symptoms, can spread the infection into a susceptible group of young children. Therefore, immunization of young children is important because the most serious effects of the disease are most common among young children. The bacteria are spread by direct contact with discharge from the nose or throat of an infected person or by breathing infected droplets in the air where an infected person coughs. The period of greatest risk of spread is the early stage when it appears to be a cold.

When should people with pertussis be excluded and allowed to return? Exposed children should be observed carefully for respiratory symptoms for

14 days after contact ended. Be especially watchful of any child who is incompletely immunized. Exclude a person with pertussis until 3 weeks after the onset of cough or 5 days after starting appropriate antibiotic therapy. People with direct contact with a case of pertussis should receive antibiotic treatment to prevent the development or spread of the disease. Antibiotics can prevent illness and spread from occurring. Those refusing antibiotics should be excluded until 21 days after contact or after the last case has been reported.

Where to report it? Notify parents and staff as well as your local board of health and your health consultant.

NONCONTAGIOUS INFECTIOUS DISEASES

Otitis media, monilial infections, and tick-borne diseases

Some infectious diseases caused by bacteria, viruses, fungi, or parasites are not easily spread from person to person. Two of these noncontagious infections—otitis media (middle ear infection) and Candida (yeast infection)—occur frequently in young children. Tick-borne infections can also occur in young children.

Otitis media (middle ear infection)

What is it? Otitis media is an infection of the part of the ear behind the eardrum. There is a small passageway (the eustachian tube) from inside the throat to this middle ear. Bacteria and/or viruses can travel from the throat area through the eustachian tube to the middle ear and cause an infection. When infection occurs, pus develops, pushes on the eardrum, and causes pain and often fever. Sometimes the pressure is so great that the eardrum bursts, and the pus drains out into the ear canal. Although this can frighten a parent, the child feels better, and the hole in the eardrum will heal over.

Untreated ear infections can spread to the mastoid bone just behind the middle ear and cause mastoiditis. Before antibiotics were available for treatment, mastoiditis was a serious problem. Today, the biggest problem from otitis media is the potential for hearing loss. Fluid may remain in an ear for as long as 6 months after an infection is gone. This is called serous otitis media.

Who gets it and how? Middle ear infections are common in children between the age of 1 month and 6 years and most common before age 3. Some children develop ear infections a few days after a cold starts. Some children have one infection after another, whereas others never have any. The tendency to have infections runs in families. The bacteria and viruses that cause otitis media start out in the throat. About half of the cases of otitis are bacterial and about half are viral. It is impossible to tell which germ is causing the infection without inserting a sterile needle through the eardrum, pulling out some of the pus or fluid, and culturing it. This is somewhat difficult and done only for special reasons. In general, all middle ear infections are treated with antibiotics as if they were bacterial.

When should people with ear infections be excluded and allowed to return? Because ear infections themselves are not contagious, there is no reason to exclude a child with one.

Special care notes for children who have frequent ear infections

- Never use cotton swabs and never put anything smaller than your finger into a child's ear. Do not allow the child to do so, either.
- Do not feed or bottle-feed infants lying on their backs—it is easier for the food or milk (with mouth germs) to run down into the eustachian tube into the middle ear in that position.
- Be especially alert for any sign of hearing or speech problems. Refer the child to the family's health care provider or other community resources (see Chapter 9).

Special care notes for children who have ear tubes

- An ear tube creates a hole in the eardrum so fluid and pus may drain out and fluid will not build up. It usually stays in for 3 to 6 months.
- Since pus can drain out, water from the outside (that has germs in it) can also run into the middle ear easily. Therefore, you must be very careful that children with tubes do not get water in their ears. This usually means no swimming unless there are special earplugs and a doctor's permission.
- Watch for any sign of any hearing or speech problems.

Monilial (Candida) infections

What are they? Monilial infections are caused by a yeast (Candida albicans) and are very common in children in diapers. In the mouths of infected infants you will see white patches (called thrush) that look like milk curds, but cannot be wiped off. Babies rarely develop thrush after 3 to 4 months of age.

Diaper rashes caused by monilial infections look different and start as very red, raised, round spots. Often there will be a larger spot with surrounding smaller ones. Sometimes the spots will all run together and you will see large areas of beefy red, raised skin that are very sore and may even bleed. Occasionally, bacteria will invade this raw skin and set up a secondary infection with ooze or pustules.

Who gets them and how? These infections are particularly common in diapered children, but adults can get thrush in their mouths or a monilial rash in their groin or other moist areas. They are very mild infections in healthy people and almost everyone gets exposed. Yeast organisms that cause monilial infections are everywhere. Although they can be spread from one person to another, usually people catch it from themselves—the organisms are already on their body, waiting for the right conditions. When skin is wet and a little raw (such as in diaper and groin areas), the yeast can invade the skin and start spreading. Yeast infections can also occur after treatment with antibiotics.

How are they treated? The child's health care provider will prescribe medication (drops for the mouth, cream for the diaper area).

When should children with monilial infections be excluded and allowed to return? If children have diaper rashes that last more than 1 to 2 days, ask their parents to see health care providers for diagnosis and treatment. You do not need to exclude children with these infections.

Tick-borne diseases

What are they? These are several diseases, including Lyme disease and Rocky Mountain spotted fever, that are spread to people by the bite of an infected tick.

Lyme disease (LD) is caused by a form of bacteria and is spread to people by a tiny deer tick. In Lyme disease cases, symptoms can begin with a skin rash characterized by large, red, doughnut-shaped welts. Other symptoms are similar to those of flu and can include headache, fever, chills, muscle aches, and stiff neck. Symptoms generally appear from 1 to 3 weeks following a tick bite. Some patients, even if untreated, will recover from Lyme disease without complications. However, approximately half of all LD patients develop a chronic form of the disease and have repeated episodes of painful swelling in the joints. In rare cases, Lyme disease sufferers may develop facial paralysis or heart problems. Early diagnosis is important. If patients are treated early with appropriate antibiotics, this disease can be a mild illness and later complications can be avoided.

Rocky Mountain spotted fever is carried by a large and more readily seen tick called the dog tick. Symptoms usually begin with a rash appearing first on the wrists and ankles and spreading to other parts of the body. Other symptoms include a high fever, chills, and severe headache and usually appear 3 to 10 days after a tick bite. The disease can be effectively treated with antibiotics.

Who gets them and how? Anyone who is bitten by an infected tick can get them. Ticks are most commonly found in brushy, wooded, or tall grassy areas. They are **not** found on open sandy beaches. The deer tick is very small, no larger than the size of a period on a printed page. During the tick's life cycle it may feed on an infected animal, usually a mouse. In later stages of the cycle it clings to vegetation and is spread by direct contact to the skin of a passing animal or person. The bite of the tick can then spread the bacteria to the new host. The greatest chance of being infected is while walking barelegged through brush or tall grass, May through August. **It is important to remember that not all ticks carry Lyme disease or Rocky Mountain spotted fever. Thus, a tick bite does not necessarily mean that disease will follow, and prompt removal of a tick will lessen any chance of disease transmission.**

How are they diagnosed? Diagnosis of Lyme disease is based primarily on recognition of the typical symptoms of LD such as the characteristic skin rash. Atypical cases, or cases presenting with only later-stage complications of LD, are difficult to diagnose. In these people, a blood test looking for antibody to the bacteria is often helpful. The diagnosis of Rocky Mountain spotted fever is based on typical symptoms and can also be confirmed with a blood test.

How are they treated? Oral antibiotic treatment is helpful early in the illness and often prevents complications later.

When should people with tick-borne diseases be excluded and allowed to return? There is no need to exclude a child or adult.

Where to report it? Report a diagnosis of LD, Rocky Mountain spotted fever, or other tick-borne illness to your local board of health. Notify all parents and staff of a case of tick-borne illness so that parents will watch for ticks as well.

If any child is bitten by a tick during the day, notify the parents of that child so they can inform their health care provider. Tell them what the tick looked like. If the child develops the symptoms described, particularly the skin rash and/or flu-like symptoms, ask the parents to see a health care provider promptly for evaluation and treatment.

How to prevent tick-borne diseases. You should take these precautions during and after spending time in brushy, wooded, or tall-grass areas.

- Wear long-sleeved shirts and long pants. Keep shirttails tucked securely into pants and pant legs tucked tightly into socks. Wear sneakers or hiking boots instead of open sandals. Wear light-colored clothing. (Ticks are dark in color and will be easier to see against a light background.)
- Conduct daily tick checks. Ticks are most often found on the thigh, flank, arms, under-arms, and legs and are very small. Look for new "freckles."

- If you find a tick, remove it immediately. Deer ticks are very small and hard, about the size of a pin-head. They are orange-red or black, depending upon their stage of growth, and prefer to attach themselves to a human host under the hair. Dog ticks are larger, ranging from 1/10 to ¼" in length. They are brown and also prefer to attach themselves under the hair or on protected parts of the body. **To remove a tick,** use tweezers to grip the tick body firmly and pull it straight out. If using fingers, place a protective covering between your fingers and the tick, and wash your hands afterward. Wash the bitten area with soap and water.

Use of insect repellant

Insect repellents containing DEET can be effective against ticks but they should be used cautiously. A pesticide named permethrin is available as a clothing spray; it is *not* to be used on the skin. A combination of DEET and permethrin-treated clothes may provide the best protection against tick and mosquito bites.

- Use repellents no more than 1 to 2 times per day. Do not treat skin under clothing.
- Particularly with children, avoid using high concentrations of DEET products. Do NOT ever use on damaged skin.
- Avoid inhaling the product. Keep out of eyes, and do not apply to parts of children's hands that are likely to have contact with their eyes or mouth.
- After returning indoors, wash treated skin with soap and water.
- If you suspect that a child is reacting to an insect repellent, wash treated skin and call the child's doctor.

18
Care of the mildly ill child

The care of ill children in group programs generates controversy. This issue can be viewed from many perspectives, including the child's needs, the parent's need to work, the staff's ability to cope and to give the necessary attention, and the cost of serving ill children.

According to the American Academy of Pediatrics, as stated in *Health in Day Care*,

> The center should have a written policy concerning the management of sick children. It should be conveyed in writing at the time a child is registered. This policy, arrived at after consultation with health care providers, should take into consideration the physical facilities and the number and qualifications of the center's personnel. The decisions involved in developing policies are extremely difficult. It must be recognized that children do become ill at unpredictable times. Working parents often are not given leave for children's illnesses. Centers may not have sufficient space or personnel to care for sick children properly. Home care for sick children is expensive.

If an infant or child becomes ill during the hours she or he is in child care, the parent(s) should be notified. To keep the infant or child in the child care program even temporarily, there must be adequate quiet space separate from the rest of the children where the sick child can be watched and given appropriate care. Staffing levels must be adequate to care for the sick child. Personnel must have sufficient training to recognize the child who requires prompt medical attention. Most states have laws requiring reporting of specific communicable diseases when they occur in a public facility. Child care personnel should be familiar with these requirements and promptly report the designated diseases. Child care staff members becoming ill with gastrointestinal or skin infections or

Every case of caring for a mildly ill child is different and should be decided individually by staff and parents together using guidelines and procedures developed in consultation with health professionals.

who develop temperatures greater than 101° F. should be excused from child care as quickly as possible. Sick leave policy should be as liberal as possible to prevent personnel from exposing children to infection. (1987, pages 65–66)

This AAP standard provides a starting point for looking at the issue of group care of ill children.

Basic issues for decision making

Set a flexible policy
Many health policies concerning the care of ill children have been based upon common misunderstandings about contagion, risks to ill children, and risks to other children and staff. Current research clearly shows that certain ill children **do not** pose a health threat. Also, the research shows that keeping certain mildly ill children at home or isolated at the program **will not** prevent other children from becoming ill. Many children shed viruses before they are obviously sick and, for gastrointestinal infections, even after they seem perfectly well. For both respiratory and gastrointestinal infections, they can spread the illness before they develop symptoms. Children receiving antibiotics for a specific bacterial infection usually are not contagious after a day's treatment.

Obviously, seriously ill children should not be in a group. However, based on the above facts, there is no medical reason to exclude some children who are mildly ill or who are being treated. Except in special programs, children with active diarrhea should be cared for at home.

Appropriate reasons to exclude mildly ill children are
- the child's disease is highly communicable and previously unexposed; susceptible children might be exposed
- the child does not feel well enough to participate, and/or
- the staff is not able to adequately care for sick and well children

Decisions must be made on a case-by-case basis. There is no **medical** justification for a policy that sets arbitrary cutoffs such as, "Any child with a temperature higher than 100° F. may not remain at the center."

The basic question is can the child participate with **reasonable comfort** and receive adequate, appropriate care without interfering with the care of the other children? One child who has a low fever and cough may still have a high-energy level, good appetite, and good mood. Another child may be droopy, whiny, uninterested in any activity, and very unhappy. **Every case is different and should be decided individually by staff and parents together using guidelines and procedures developed in consultation with health professionals.** The focus of policies for all children should be on what conditions and symptoms the program can **include and manage.** All other conditions and symptoms should be excluded. Please refer to Figure 17.2 for exclusion guidelines.

Issues for programs to consider
When you need to decide whether to keep a mildly ill child at your facility, ask these questions:
- Are there sufficient staff (including volunteers) to change the program for a child who needs some modifications, such as quiet activities, staying inside, or extra liquids?
- Are staff willing and able to care for a sick child (wiping a runny nose, checking a fever, providing extra loving care) without neglecting the care of other children in the group?
- Is there a space where the mildly ill child can rest? Is there a space that might be used as a get well room so that several children could be cared for at once? Is the child familiar with the staff?
- Are parents able or willing to pay extra for sick care if other resources are not available, so that you can hire extra staff as needed?

Issues for parents to consider
When parents need to decide whether to send a child to the group program, they must weigh many facts, such as how the child feels (physically and emotionally), the program's ability to serve the needs of the mildly ill child, and income/work lost by staying home. Lost work in many cases means lost income, but it may also mean the loss of a job. For low-income families, this is a very difficult problem.

Although many parents may honestly try to consider all the facts and to decide what is best for the child, this is hard to do when the facts are fuzzy. A child may awaken cranky but show no signs of illness. Or the child may have vomited after dinner the night before but slept well and awakened cheerful. Or the child may have an unexplained low-grade fever but seem absolutely fine. In these situations parents need to use their best judgment very early in the morning. It is important to establish health policies that are reasonable and discussed with parents in advance. Be sure to keep the lines of communication open with parents daily. When an illness in a child arises, communication is key—discuss the issue with the parent sensitively, demonstrate concern about the health of the child and the situation for the parent, refer to the health policies, and demonstrate flexibility to make the situation work best for all of the parties involved.

Keeping the communication lines open

A child's parents should always talk with staff in the morning about any mild illness that occurred the night before. This process should include face-to-face contact when the child is dropped off. If there is no opportunity for personal contact, the parent should write a note or complete the symptom record (see Figure 18.1). When the child leaves, staff must let the family know what happened during that day—preferably in written form. Simple information about activity level, appetite and food intake, naptime, and bowel movements can be invaluable to the family and to the doctor who may be called for advice later in the evening. Written reports about a child's illness from child care staff help to overcome the parent's natural tendency to miss some of the details when picking up the child at the end of the day (see Figure 18.2).

Conduct a daily health check

When you greet the children in the morning (preferably before parents have left), give each child a quick health checkup. This does not have to be a big deal! Just as you would notice a new haircut or a new pair of sneakers, you can be attuned to

- general mood (happy, sad, cranky)
- activity level (sluggish, sleepy, or whatever)
- breathing difficulties, severe coughing
- discharge from nose, ears, or eyes
- skin color, itching, rashes, swelling, bruises, sores

If you have concerns about how a particular child looks or feels, discuss them with the parent right then. Perhaps the parent needs to take the child home. Perhaps you feel strongly that the child should leave. If you decide that the child will remain, be sure to discuss how you will manage the child and at what point you will call the parent.

Note that it is the program's decision, not the parent's, whether the program will accept responsibility for the ill child from the parent. If the child stays all day, make sure you let the parent know what happened during the day (see Figure 18.1).

Know what to do when a child appears ill

When you discover a seriously ill or injured child, use your emergency procedures.

Get medical help immediately

(This section is reprinted courtesy of the American Red Cross.)

For some conditions, you need to get medical help immediately. When this is necessary, and you can reach the parent without delay, tell the parent to come right away. You may also have to have the parent tell the doctor that you will be calling because you are with the child. If the parent or the child's doctor is not immediately available, contact the program's health consultant or EMS for immediate medical help.

Tell the parent to come right away and get medical help immediately when any of the following things happens:

- An infant under 4 months of age has an axillary temperature of 100° F. or higher or a rectal temperature of 101° F. or higher.
- A child over 4 months of age has a temperature of 105° F. or higher.
- An infant under 4 months of age has forceful vomiting (more than once) after eating.
- Any child looks or acts very ill or seems to be getting worse quickly.
- Any child has neck pain when the head is moved or touched.
- Any child has a stiff neck or severe headache.
- Any child has a seizure for the first time.
- Any child has a seizure that lasts more than 15 minutes.
- Any child acts unusually confused.
- Any child has uneven pupils (black centers of the eyes).
- Any child has a blood-red or purple rash made up of pinhead-size spots or bruises that are not associated with injury.
- Any child has a rash of hives or welts that appears quickly.

Figure 18.1. Symptom record

Child's name _____

Date _____ Symptom _____

When symptoms began, how long did they last, how severe, how often? _____

_____

Any change in child's behavior? _____

Child's temperature _____   ❑ axillary   ❑ oral   ❑ rectal   ❑ aural (ear)

Food and fluid taken in the past 12 hours _____

Urine, bowel movement, vomiting in the past 12 hours _____

Circle or write in other symptoms—

runny nose   sore throat   cough   vomiting   diarrhea   rash

trouble breathing   stiff neck   itching   trouble urinating   pain

Other symptoms _____

_____

Exposure to medications, animals, insects, soaps, new foods _____

_____

Exposure to other people who were sick? Who, and what sickness? _____

_____

Other problems that might affect this illness (asthma, anemia, diabetes, allergy, emotional trauma)

_____

What has been done so far? _____

_____

Health provider's advice for this illness _____

Name of person completing form _____

- Any child breathes so fast or hard that he or she cannot play, talk, cry, or drink.
- Any child has a severe stomachache that causes the child to double up and scream.
- Any child has a stomachache without vomiting or diarrhea after a recent injury, blow to the abdomen, or hard fall.
- Any child has stools that are black or have blood mixed through them.
- Any child has not urinated in more than 8 hours; the mouth and tongue look dry.
- Any child has continuous clear drainage from the nose after a hard blow to the head.

Note for programs that provide care for sick children: If any of these conditions appears after the child's care has been planned, medical advice must be obtained before continuing child care can be provided.

If a child appears **mildly** ill, take the child aside, encourage rest, and assess the situation. **Remember that you are not expected to diagnose illness.** Report the symptoms you have observed to the proper person(s)—the parent(s), the director, the health staff person (if any) or health consultant, and/or the child's health provider. When you report the symptoms, follow your program's procedures, be as specific as possible, and note the following:

- symptom(s)
- when it began/how long it has lasted
- how much
- how often
- behavior change (e.g., activity level, comfort level, crying or complaints, eating, sleeping)
- temperature
- other
  (See Figure 18.1 on page 262.)

Please see Chapter 9 for more information about health observations.

Take these general steps when a child becomes ill:

- keep the child comfortable
- observe the child and report and document the symptoms
- call the parent (or emergency contact)
- decide if the program can care for the child
  Each child's family should identify at least two

Figure 18.2. Daily health check instructions

Note: When you perform the health check, be at the child's level—kneel down if the child is sitting or standing, hold the child, or have the parent hold the child at your level.

- Look at how the child acts and looks.

1. Is the child's behavior normal for this time of day or is there some difference?

2. Is the child clinging to the parent, acting cranky, or acting normally?

3. Does the child look pale or flushed?

4. Do you see a rash?

5. Do the child's eyes look shiny or red?

6. Are there dark circles under the child's eyes?

7. Is the child's nose running?

8. Is the child coughing or having any difficulty breathing?

9. Does the child seem itchy?

- Listen to the child and to the parent. What do they tell you about how the child feels and acts? Does the child's voice sound normal?

1. If the child can talk, ask "How are you today? Is everything okay?" Listen to the child's voice. Is the child hoarse?

2. Ask the parent how the child has been feeling and acting:

- Did the child have a good night?
- Did the child eat normally?
- Did anything unusual happen?
- Touch the child's skin.

1. Gently run the back of your hand over the child's cheek, forehead, and the back of the child's neck. See if the child feels unusually warm to the touch or if the skin feels different (for example, bumpy) and should be looked at more closely.

2. Use your hand, not your lips, to touch children. Your lips could pick up germs from the child's body, and you might give your germs to the child.

- Sniff for unusual odors.

1. Children who have not eaten for many hours may have a fruity mouth odor.

2. Some children may arrive with stool in their diapers and need to be changed right away.

3. Parents may have used some medication with a distinctive odor that you will want to know about.

Figure 18.2 courtesy of the American Red Cross

emergency contact people who are usually available to take the child home when the parent cannot be reached or is not available. Be sure these two contacts are in the child's record, and test their telephone numbers occasionally to be sure they are current. Testing telephone numbers is most easily incorporated into the office routine if you divide the number of children in the program by the number of working days in 6 months (approximately 120) and test that number of telephone contacts every day.

Common minor illnesses

Most programs will need to provide at least **temporary** care of ill children even if their general policy is to send sick children home. If children become ill during the day, use the following guidelines to help you manage their illnesses and keep them comfortable.

Guidelines for fevers

Fever is a common symptom for young children. Many parents (and the public in general, including teachers) have unrealistic fears about fevers. In fact, fevers are rarely harmful and treatment is not always necessary. An above-average body temperature can be caused by many things including strenuous exercise, time of day (temperature rises in late afternoon), infection, environment (a hot room, a hot day, or being bundled up), or individual variations.

Fever is generally defined as a temperature of 100° F. or more whether taken orally, rectally, or in the armpit (axillary). A fever of 105° F. is considered high, although, in general, the height of the fever does not correlate to the seriousness of the illness. How sick a child acts and the cause and potential complications of the illness are the most important issues.

Fever is often the child's body's response to infection. Fever between 100° and 102° F. may help children fight off infections, and there is a growing trend to treat it less aggressively. It is a symptom, not a disease, and is not itself dangerous below 106° F. Some children with temperatures of 104° F. or even 105° F. may have infections that are basically not dangerous. Keep in mind that infants and young children tend to run higher fevers than adults. Whether or not the temperature

can be brought down with fever-reducing medicine does not relate to the severity of the illness. Some serious illnesses are associated with fevers that come down, and some mild illnesses are associated with high fevers that won't budge.

Because fever may be due to a communicable or serious illness, it is important that children with fevers of 102° F. or higher be evaluated by their health care provider for inclusion in the program. Ask a parent to come soon and to get medical advice within the next few hours when any of the following happens:

- A child 4 to 24 months of age has a rectal temperature of 102° F. or higher or an axillary temperature of 101° F. or higher.
- A child over 24 months of age has an oral or axillary temperature of 102° F. or higher.
- **Call (or have parents call) a doctor immediately when an infant 4 months of age or younger has an axillary temperature of 100° F. or higher or a rectal temperature of 101° F. or higher or a child over 4 months of age has a temperature of 105° F. or higher. This call is CRITICAL for any child younger than 2 months.**

Figure 18.3 provides instructions for taking children's temperatures. **Use disposable thermometer covers to make good sanitation easier. You may prefer digital thermometers that provide fast, accurate readings and are unbreakable, inexpensive, and readily available.**

When a child has a fever and is in your care even temporarily,
- Comfort the child.
- Offer small amounts of liquid often, but avoid citrus juice or milk which may upset the stomach. Clear liquids such as water, flat soda, gelatin, broth, and apple or grape juice are best. (Clear liquids are those you can see through when you hold them up to a light.) Children need to drink more as fevers rise.
- When the fever is 100° to 102° F., in general it is not necessary to bring down the child's temperature unless the child is very uncomfortable. Take off layers of clothing if the child is bundled or overdressed; however, cool the child off slowly as shivering will further increase the child's temperature.

- When the fever is higher than 103° F., strip the child down to underwear or diaper.
- When the fever is 104° F. or higher, give the child a **tepid to warm** (90° F.) sponge-down. (Water should be warm enough to be comfortable and to avoid shivering. As long as the water is cooler than the body, the heat of the child's body will go from the hot skin, taking body heat with it into the water, lowering the temperature.) Do **NOT** use alcohol wipes or rubs.
- You may give acetaminophen if the child's temperature is over 102° F. (e.g., Tylenol, Tempra, Panadol) **only** if you have a parent's authorization and a physician's order. This can be a standing order, written into your health policies with a consent form signed by the parent at enrollment. Never give a child aspirin because it can cause Reye's syndrome, a dangerous condition of the brain.
- Call (or have parents call) a doctor for fever in an infant 6 months of age or younger. This call is *critical* for any child younger than 2 months.
- Keep in mind that children who **DO** have serious infections act sick and may present one or more of these symptoms:
  —unusual drowsiness or excessive sleep
  —loss of alertness
  —fast or different breathing
  —very sick appearance
  —refusal to eat or drink
  —irritability
  —refusal to play
  —complaints about pain
  —excessive crying

The most significant sign of serious illness is a child who looks and acts very ill.

Febrile seizures. Approximately 4% of children who experience fevers will have a febrile (associated with fever) seizure. Because these seizures are rarely harmful and they are generally not preventable, they should not be cause for undue worry. Most febrile seizures occur as the temperature is rising, before you even realize the child has a fever. Febrile seizures are usually brief (less than 15 minutes) and stop by themselves. Children who are likely to have such seizures are those who have had one before the age of 3 years.

If a child has a history of febrile seizures and develops a fever, you should try to bring down the fever quickly by doing the following:

- Remove the child's clothing.
- Apply cool, thin cloths (such as dish towels or cloth diapers) to the face and neck. OR, sponge the body with warm water, cooler than the body temperature, in a tub.
- If the child is awake and can swallow medicine, give the appropriate dose of acetaminophen **if you have a standing order from the child's physician and parental permission.**

Febrile seizures are unusual and rarely have permanent effects. If a child has a seizure of any kind, it probably is a febrile seizure. You should follow your emergency procedures for seizures. All children who have a seizure for the first time should be seen by a physician as soon as possible.

Guidelines for colds

- Try to keep room temperature at or lower than 70° F.
- Use a cool mist humidifier (that has been properly cleaned/disinfected) to keep the air moist during winter. Do not add anything to it. Do **not** use steam vaporizers. The new ultrasonic humidifiers are better than previous types.
- Sit the child up so mucus will drain away from the child's ears.
- Raise the mattress or cot under the head and chest for sleeping. Do not use pillows because they tend to flex the head on the chest, making breathing more difficult. Put something under the mattress instead.
- Offer lots of clear liquids.
- Assist the child by helping to blow/wipe nose. **Wash your hands afterward.**
- Remove mucus from babies' noses before they eat. Use a soft, rubber bulb with a soft, narrow tip to suck out (aspirate) mucus for children who cannot blow their noses. Ask parents to send an individual aspirator, and use it only for the appropriate baby. (A 3-oz. ear syringe works very well for this purpose.)
- Let the child rest. She or he may need less strenuous activities or more sleep.
- Don't force the child to eat.
- Don't give cold medicine without parental consent *and* physician's order.

Figure 18.3. How to take a child's temperature

Preparation

- For mercury thermometers, shake the thermometer until the mercury line is below 95° F. To avoid breakage, shake it above something soft.
- Always use a new disposable thermometer cover, regardless of the method you choose.
- The person taking rectal temperatures should have specific health training.

Where to take the temperature

- In children younger than 6 months: axillary (armpit) temperature for screening; if axillary temperature is higher than 99° F., check with a rectal temperature.
- In children older than 2 years: oral (by mouth) temperature if possible. Otherwise, take rectal temperature.
- The new digital thermometers are easy to read and register quickly (within about 45 seconds), making it possible to take oral temperatures of children as young as 3 years old.

Taking axillary (armpit) temperatures

- Use an oral thermometer, if possible.
- Place the tip of the thermometer in a dry armpit.
- Close the armpit by holding the elbow against the chest for 5 minutes.
- If you're uncertain about the result, recheck it with a rectal temperature. *After the newborn period, axillary temperatures are not reliable. Use this method for screening purposes only.*

Taking rectal temperatures

- Use for children 6 months to 2 years old.
- Have the child lie stomach down.
- Lubricate the end of the thermometer and the child's anal opening with petroleum jelly.
- Carefully insert the thermometer about ¾" but never force it.
- Hold the child still while the thermometer is in and press the buttocks together.
- Leave the thermometer inside the rectum for 2 to 3 minutes. Never leave the child alone when a thermometer is in place.
- Never use an oral thermometer in the rectum.

Taking oral temperatures

- Be sure the child did not recently drink a very cold or warm drink. Wait 15 minutes, if so.
- Place the thermometer tip under the right side of the tongue.
- Have the child hold the thermometer in place with the lips and fingers (not the teeth).
- Have the child breathe through the nose with the mouth closed.
- Leave the thermometer inside the mouth for 3 minutes.
- If the child can't keep the mouth closed because the nose is blocked, take an axillary temperature. If the child cannot keep the bulb of the thermometer between the bottom of the tongue and the floor of the mouth, the reading will not be accurate.

Taking aural (ear canal) temperatures

- Follow the manufacturer's instructions.

Reading the thermometer

- For mercury thermometers, determine where the mercury line ends by turning the thermometer slightly until the line appears. If this is difficult for you, practice.
- For digital thermometers, note the number when the thermometer signals the reading is ready.

Cleaning the thermometer

- Wash the thermometer with cold water and soap. (Hot water will crack the glass or break the thermometer.) A cracked thermometer should be thrown away.
- Rinse the thermometer with cold water.
- Wipe it with rubbing alcohol or immerse it in the bleach solution. Then let it air dry.
- Shake down the thermometer and put it back in its case.
- Wash hands thoroughly afterward.

Adapted from Schmidt (1984).

Guidelines for vomiting and nausea

- Stop solid food.
- Offer clear liquids—water, flat cola or ginger ale (shake bottle or stir in glass to remove the bubbles), gelatin, broth. **Do not force child to drink,** but offer liquids often.
- Offer liquids in *very* small amounts: ½ to 1 oz. (1 to 2 tablespoons) every 5 to 15 minutes for 30 to 60 minutes. If a tablespoon of fluid is vomited, reduce the amount given each time to a teaspoon.
- Offer frozen juice or ice chips to help soothe the child.
- Advise parents to give only clear liquids for 24 hours and to go slowly on solids for the next day or until the child is completely recovered.
- Give plain, low-salt crackers; dry, plain cookies or toast; or rice cereal if the child asks for food and has not vomited recently.
- Call the parent.
- Ask the parent to call the doctor when a baby younger than 6 months is vomiting.
- If a child has vomited on clothing, remove the clothing and sponge the child with soap and water, if necessary. Dress the child in clean clothing or wrap in a blanket or towel. Place the soiled clothing in a leakproof plastic bag, label, and send home for the parent to wash.

Guidelines for diarrhea

One loose stool does not mean that a child has diarrhea. Some children get diarrhea when they take antibiotics. Others may have loose stools for a long time after recovering from an infectious gastrointestinal disease. However, you should carefully watch a child with even one loose stool and take precautions.

Diarrhea is

- an increase in the number of stools over what is normal for that person
  and
- stools that are unformed—loose/watery; take the shape of the container they are in. (Exception: Breast-fed babies have stools that are **normally loose.**)

Children with diarrhea that is easily contained in the diaper or toilet but no other symptoms **do not need to be sent home or excluded** if you can take appropriate precautions. A child with large, loose stools or both diarrhea and fever or another symptom of disease should be sent home (see section on infectious diarrheal diseases in Chapter 17 for details).

If the child with diarrhea stays or if the child is waiting to be picked up by parents, the following guidelines for care should be followed.

- Offer clear, dilute liquids (see vomiting section). Liquids high in sugar (colas, apple juice, grape juice) should be diluted.
  —**For infants:** 1 to 2 oz. at a time, every 15 minutes or so.
  —**For preschool children:** 2 to 4 oz. at a time, every 15 minutes or so.
- Avoid any milk except breast milk. (The sugar in full-strength juice and milk can make diarrhea worse.)
- If the child acts hungry, offer a binding, bland diet (e.g., rice, noodles, oatmeal, dry cereal, crackers, low-sugar gelatin, mashed banana, applesauce).
- If the baby is younger than 6 months, ask the parent to call the doctor.

Although vomiting and diarrhea are generally considered mild illnesses, they can sometimes lead to **dehydration,** a more serious condition. Dehydration—an excessive loss of water and nutrients from the body—is a special concern in infants. **Watch for these symptoms:**

- decreased frequency and amount of urinating
- concentrated (dark) urine
- few or no tears
- sunken eyes
- a sticky or dry mouth, and/or
- thirst
- loss of skin elasticity (i.e., skin does not spring back when pressed gently)

Call your health consultant if more than one child in the same group has diarrhea.

Guidelines for constipation

Constipation is present when a child has excessively hard bowel movements that cause pain or are accompanied by mucus or blood. A child who has infrequent bowel movements is not constipated if the stool appears normal when it is passed. Normal bowel patterns may vary from twice a day to once or twice a week. When the stool is hard it usually means the child is not drinking enough fluid to keep up with the body's needs or does not have enough roughage (fiber) in the diet. If a child is constipated be sure that you discuss the problem with the parents so that together you can decide what to do.

To help reduce the hardness of stools, begin by increasing fluid intake, especially juices. Have the child drink at least 32 oz. (four medium glasses) of fluid each day, divided into frequent, small amounts. Try to have the child eat fruits such as apricots, pears, peaches, and prunes—fresh, dried, or canned in their own juice—twice a day. Encourage the child to eat bran cereals; celery and carrots (because they have fiber that holds fluid in the intestine to keep stools soft); and leafy, green vegetables such as lettuce, spinach, greens, and green and yellow beans that provide roughage. Limit binding foods such as bananas, apples, and high-fat dairy products. If these measures do not work, consult a doctor.

Stomachache

A stomachache may have many causes. Ache or cramps may be caused by an infection, constipation, or a serious bowel problem. Some children have stomachaches when they are upset. Severe and constant pain may mean that stomachache is serious. If a child has any of the following, tell the parent to come right away and get medical help immediately.

- A child has a severe stomachache that causes the child to double up and scream.
- A child has a stomachache after vomiting.
- A child has a stomachache without vomiting or diarrhea after a recent injury, blow to the stomach, or hard fall.

If a child with a stomachache remains in your care, offer clear liquids and make the child comfortable in a quiet area.

Rashes

Although rashes are usually not symptoms of serious illness, people tend to worry about them because unusual skin conditions are so easily seen. While you will not diagnose or decide on treatment for rashes, you should supply parents with detailed information for them to report to their physician who will want to know the following:

- Is the rash itchy to the child?
- Is the rash red (blood colored) or pink?
- Is the skin warm to the touch?
- Is the rash raised or flat? Pinprick size or blotchy? Dry or blistery?
- Where on the body was the rash first noted? How has it changed since then?
- Has the child had a recent injury or exposure to infection, drugs, or chemicals?
- Does the child look or act sick in any other way?
- Has the child had this rash before?
- Has the child been in contact with someone who has this rash?

Solid red, warm areas that are spreading may be caused by infection. Many infections that affect the whole body are associated with rashes. (Please refer to Chapter 17 for details.)

Many rashes look alike; sometimes even the doctor cannot make a definite diagnosis. The best clues are provided by any other symptoms accompanying the rash and by knowing what's going around.

Although most rashes are more troublesome than dangerous, there is a group of rashes associated with severe and life-threatening illness. These rashes look like little blood spots or bruises under the skin. Children may develop little blood spots around their faces and necks from crying hard or vomiting; but when this type of rash appears elsewhere on the body, without being explained by trauma, a health professional should be called **immediately.** The rashes from spontaneous bleeding into the skin signal serious disturbances in the body's bleeding control systems. **Spontaneous blood-red or purple spots or bruises without trauma should be addressed as a medical emergency. Also, a rash of hives or welts that appears quickly should be evaluated immediately by a health professional.** Fortunately, these illnesses occur infrequently.

Use cold soaks with plain water to relieve itchy rashes. Do *not* use ointments, creams, powders, or lotions or give medicine unless you have both the doctor's instructions and parent consent.

Take these steps to promote good skin health:

- Rinse the skin with water to remove food and urine.

- Soap should be used only when you need to remove stubborn sticky or greasy material; follow with a thorough rinsing with plain water.
- Avoid prolonged exposure to wetness or stool.
- Wear the least amount of clothing needed to keep warm.

In general, you should avoid special skin products unless they have been requested by a health professional. Many products are heavily perfumed and, in fact, may create skin problems (e.g., dry skin or diaper rash). Some creams are very difficult to wipe off. Even the chemicals in premoistened, disposable wipes can cause trouble. The less you do to the skin, the better.

Diaper rash. Diaper rash is the result of a combination of irritation from rubbing of moist surfaces on the skin, chemical action of stool and urine on the skin, and wetness for prolonged periods. The ammonia odor in the diaper area comes when bacteria on the skin break down urine. To care for diaper rash you should take the following steps:

- Treat the irritated skin. When a rash is present
  —let the baby sleep without a diaper and plastic pants during naps
  —provide a cool sitz bath (at least 15 minutes to give time for deep cooling and contraction of blood vessels)
- Neutralize the ammonia, and make it hard for the bacteria on the skin to grow:
  —Put vinegar (2 to 3 tablespoons) in a sinkful of water for sitz baths, ½ cup in the bathtub. Vinegar is a mild acid that works against the ammonia and prevents bacterial growth. Bathing also cuts down the need for rubbing the child's sore bottom to clean off stool and urine.
  —Make the urine more acid by having the child drink acidic fruit juice—cranberry is good (citrus less effective).
  —Increase child's intake of liquid because bacteria do not grow well in diluted urine.
- Suggest to parents that if a diaper is used **at night,** they should do the following to keep the urine away from the skin:
  —Use a zinc oxide ointment (such as Desitin) or petroleum jelly as a barrier between the skin and stool and/or urine. Make sure the child is clean and dry before applying.

  —Use a "diaper doubler" insert inside a regular diaper or an extra-absorbent diaper at night.
- Keep stool away from the child's skin since stool contains broken down bile that is like a detergent and is irritating. Change the child right away and wash child's bottom well with a little soap and lukewarm water. For a small infant, this rinsing can be done easily over the sink. Do not run water from the tap directly onto an infant's skin because a sudden surge of hot water from the tap can scald the child. You must wash and disinfect the sink after this type of use.
- **Avoid talcum or baby powder. It can be inhaled into the lungs.**

Heat rash. Heat rash is also known as prickly heat. Small red bumps usually occur on the neck, upper chest, and back of the head. To help manage heat rash

- do not overdress child
- wash and dry the child's skin, especially between skin creases
- sponge and dry the area with cool tap water often
- **do not use baby powder**

Guidelines for teething

Teething can cause irritability, drooling, rubbing at the mouth, pulling at the ears, and slightly looser stools. Teething does not, however, cause fever in a child. If a child has a significant fever while teething, it is likely to be a sign of another illness, and medical evaluation may be recommended. Take these steps to comfort the child:

- Provide something hard and/or cold to bite on (a very cold, large carrot; a bagel; a teething biscuit; or a safe, teething-ring toy).
- Rub the child's gums with a **clean** finger or an ice cube. (Wash your hands before and after doing this.)

Guidelines for sunburn

Young children are more likely to get sunburned than adults, but everyone should avoid prolonged skin exposure to the sun. Sun causes aging and changes that can lead to skin cancer in later life. Certain areas such as the face, shoulders, and back of knees are more likely to burn than other areas. Protect these areas by using hats, long-sleeve shirts, and sunblock. **Ask the parents to provide**

the sunblock and written consent for its use. The number on the sunblock indicates how many times the normal exposure time the block will provide protection. Use sunblocks with number 15 or more. Do not apply suntan or sunscreen lotions to broken skin.

Because it takes several hours for a sunburn to show, watching for reddening of the skin is not a dependable way to tell when a child has been in the sun too long. **By the time you notice any change, it is too late.** The sun's rays are most intense from 11 a.m. to 2 p.m. Reflections of the sun's rays from water and sand increase sunburn dangers. Cloudy days can fool you; clouds won't stop the sun from burning. **It is a good idea on most summer days to plan for playtime in the shade, frequent fluid intake, and skin cooling.**

When a child has a sunburn, medications should not be applied to the skin without a doctor's recommendation. There is no **cure** for sunburn, but the pain and itching that accompany a burn can be treated with a cool bath or cold compresses applied three or four times a day for 10 to 15 minutes at a time. Severe burns may be accompanied by intense pain, blistering of the skin, nausea, chills, and fever. If a child has these symptoms, ask the parents to consult their physician.

Guidelines for heat exhaustion and dehydration

After prolonged exposure to high temperatures and high humidity, children may have one or more of these symptoms of heat exhaustion:

- pale and clammy skin
- heavy sweating
- fatigue
- weakness
- dizziness
- headache
- nausea
- muscle cramps
- vomiting
- fainting

Avoid heat exhaustion and dehydration by encouraging children to drink liquids and cool off frequently. Provide small amounts of clear liquids at least every 2 hours to help restore fluids that the body has lost through evaporation. Achieve quick and sanitary cooling by having children play under a sprinkler or by using cool water on paper towels to remove the perspiration and oil from their skin.

Thirst is **not** a good indicator of dehydration because a child can become dehydrated before becoming thirsty. Check a child's frequency of urination and urine color (concentration) to determine fluid needs. Normally, the urine of a child should be pale yellow or colorless, and urination should occur every 2 or 3 hours. Dark yellow (concentrated) urine is a sign the body is not well enough hydrated to be able to make dilute (light colored) urine.

When a child (or adult) has symptoms of heat exhaustion, the first thing to do is to move the person to a cool and shaded area. Then contact the parent and ask that the child's health care provider be called immediately.

How to give medication

Almost all children, at one time or another, need medication. It is reasonable to expect that parents will ask you to give medication either for a chronic problem, for a mild illness, or as needed for temporary discomfort. Implementing the Americans with Disabilities Act (ADA) may require providers to administer medications to children with chronic conditions or special health needs. You will want to know of any state regulations with respect to administering medication to children in your care. The American Academy of Pediatrics recommends that all child care providers be trained in how to safely administer medication.

It may be helpful to communicate with parents to enlist their help when children require medication. This might include setting up a schedule for giving medications only at home or consulting with the health care provider about prescribing medication in a different form (liquid, pill, capsule) and/ or varying the number of times a day a medication is required (e.g., morning and bedtime versus three times a day). If a parent works near your facility, you might ask the parent to come during the day to give the medication, if necessary.

If your program accepts responsibility for giving medications, make certain that you follow all applicable regulations. **Typical** regulations for administration of medication are

- Prescription or nonprescription medications will be administered to a child only with the written order of a physician that indicates the medication is for that specific child.
- No medication, whether prescription or nonprescription, will be administered to a child without written parental authorization (Figure 18.4).

All medicines must have proper labeling. For prescription medicines, the medicine container must have the original label and carry the following basic information:

- the name of the child who will be getting the medicine
- the name of the child's doctor
- the name of the medicine
- the issue date of the medicine
- the dosage
- how often to give the dosage
- how many days to give the medicine
- the route of administration (for example, oral)
- special precautions (e.g., taken with or apart from food)
- storage requirements (for example, refrigeration)
- expiration date

For nonprescription medicines, the medicine container must have the following:

- the name of the child who will be getting the medicine
- directions for safe use
- the date the medicine expires
- a list of active ingredients
- the name and address of the health care provider who made the recommendation

Remember, only use medicines that come in their original containers.

- Written records of the administration of prescribed medication to children will be kept and will include the time and date of each administration, the name of the staff member administering the medication, and the name of the child.
- All medicine will be stored in child-resistive safety containers, labeled with the child's name, the name of the drug, and the directions for its administration. Any unused medication will be disposed of or returned to the parent(s). Note: All prescribed medications must, by law, be dispensed in child-resistive packaging unless the purchaser specifically requests otherwise. Those who work with children should monitor compliance at the pharmacy so all medications are safely packaged.

Some additional practical guidelines for giving medications are

- Only trained staff should give a child medicine. Have a physician or nurse describe/demonstrate the specific procedures to be used.
- Have parents ask the pharmacist who fills the prescription to give them a small, extra **labeled** bottle to bring to your program.
- Keep a medicine log sheet posted at the spot where you give medication to the child (e.g., on refrigerator) so you won't forget to write down the exact time and date. Put this log sheet in the child's folder after the course of medication ends.
- Be sure you receive very specific instructions about how the medicine should be given (e.g., before or after meals, with a full glass of water after the medication, tilting head). Most prescription labels do not have this information.
- Learn the possible side effects of the medication and inform the parent immediately if you observe any. Do not give more medication without the approval of the parent or child's physician.
- Always read what the label says about storage; some drugs need to be refrigerated. Avoid storing medication in warm, wet, or lighted places.
- **ALWAYS READ THE LABEL CAREFULLY BEFORE YOU GIVE ANY MEDICINE; BOTTLES OFTEN LOOK THE SAME.** Be sure that the child's name is on the bottle because often several children may be taking the same medicine. As an extra precaution, put medication in a bag labeled with the child's name in large letters. Double-check the name of the child, dose, time, and method of administration.
- Keep medicines in a locked, cool, and dry place out of reach of children. Find a way to secure medicines that are kept in the refrigerator. Refrigerated medicines should be kept away from food.
- Be sure that you do not leave medicine out unless adult supervision is available. When you answer the telephone or leave the room, put the

Figure 18.4. Medication consent and log

PARENT COMPLETE THIS SECTION

I give permission to administer medication to my child as stated below:

Date	Parent's Signature	Child's Name	Name of Medication/ Possible Side Effects	Days & Times To Be Given	Amount Each Dose/By Mouth, Nose, Ear	Refrigeration?

STAFF COMPLETE THIS SECTION

Safety Check	Time Given	Staff Initials	Date	Reaction/Notes

Safety Check:
1. Child resistant container
2. Original prescription or manufacturer's label
3. Name of child on container
4. Current date on prescription/expiration label
5. Name and phone number of licensed health professional who ordered medication on container or on file

medication away first or take it with you. A child can take an overdose in seconds.

- Never refer to medicine as candy or something else children like. They may try to get more of it when unsupervised.

Tips for giving medicine safely

The American Red Cross offers these tips:

1. Wash your hands before giving any medicine.

2. Be gentle, yet firm, when giving a child medicine. He or she may not want to take it.

3. Medicines come in many forms. They can be given by mouth, sprayed in the nose, dropped into the ear, put into the rectum, or rubbed on the skin. Be sure to follow written instructions.

4. After administering medication by any route, wash your hands thoroughly.

To give medicine by mouth—

- Measure the exact amount of liquid the child must swallow. Shake the liquid medicine before pouring it if the label says to shake. Use a dropper or other special measuring device for liquids. Give liquids slowly and wait for the child to swallow each portion.

- Break large pills into smaller pieces if there is a line on the pill.

To give ear drops—

Ear drops go in more easily if you gently pull the ear toward the back of the head.

To give eye drops—

Eye drops go in more easily if you gently pull out the lower eyelid and put the drops in the "cup" the lower lid makes when pulled out.

To give nose drops—

Nose drops go in more easily if you lay the child on his or her back. For nose sprays, the child can stand or sit up.

To give a rectal suppository—

Before giving a rectal suppository, ask a doctor about the best way to insert it. (Be sure you know your program's health policy before giving a rectal suppository.)

19
Models for the care of mildly ill children

When young children become ill they need adequate rest, appropriate diet, medications as ordered, and appropriate physical and emotional support.

Because every child is bound to become sick at times, it is crucial that options for sick child care be discussed at the time a child is first enrolled in a group program. Many parents have not thought ahead about what they will do if the child becomes ill and cannot attend the group.

In some cases, employers will have personnel policies that allow a parent to provide care for a sick child at home. Paid time, within limits, can be given to the parent to support this option. Employers should be encouraged to develop flexible policies that consider the fact that family illness is unavoidable. However, when care by the parent is not possible, there are a variety of substitute child care models for mildly ill children.

General guidelines
There are some practices of care that relate to all models of programs for the care of mildly ill children. Consider these basic needs:
- training for providers in pediatric first aid including rescue breathing and first aid for choking, care for ill children, infectious diseases, child development, and CPR
- a suitable environment, including a sink and bathroom nearby
- a separate space to group children with diarrheal illnesses
- appropriate storage for medications
- careful hygiene of the sick care area
- emergency procedures established
- plans for contacting parents
- medical backup

- disposable towels and tissues
- materials for quiet activities for the child
- a cool air (preferably ultrasonic) vaporizer in winter
- a method for laundering items such as bedding

Care for mildly ill children in group programs
The issue of child care for mildly ill children is an emotionally charged one. It challenges some very basic notions about caring for children and the fine line between parent responsibilities versus staff responsibilities. While it may be difficult to handle even mildly ill children, you should consider some of these models as a way to meet this very real need for children and families.

Care at the child's own program
The advantage of both of the following options is that mildly ill children can be cared for in their familiar environment by adults they already know and trust.

Get well area of the classroom. This model requires use of a small area of the classroom where a child can rest or play quietly. It may be as simple as a cot in a quiet area. The area needs to be in view of an adult for supervision and frequent contact. The child may choose to participate in some group activities, while using the get well area as a home base. Ideally, a volunteer or floating adult will look after the child as needed, stay indoors when the others go outside, and provide additional physical and emotional support. This option is *not* appropriate for children with uncontrolled diarrhea.

Get well room. This model could be considered when children cannot manage in the classroom and when a small *separate* space is available. AAP/

APHA standards recommend that staffing, space, equipment, and all facilities be completely separate from the regular program and that children be separated by type of illness (intestinal, respiratory, etc.). At least one adult needs to be present at all times; an ideal ratio is one adult to no more than two or three sick children. The room should be equipped with a comfortable resting place; quiet activities (e.g., reading, playing records, and table toys); and easy means for providing food, liquid, and medication. You may want to have a regular volunteer or extra staff person on call. This person may be someone who also substitutes for staff. The individual should be teacher-qualified if she or he is alone with children and specifically trained to care for mildly ill children as outlined.

Care in specialized programs for ill children

This model requires a separate facility specifically designed for ill children. The facility may be independent, or, in some cases, sponsored by a regular program. Because the program for sick children is separate, the children may not be familiar with the staff, the environment, or other children. It is important, therefore, to have children visit before they become ill and intermittently so that each child can have a positive introduction to the staff and faculty.

This type of medical infirmary for ill and recovering children may serve the **physical** needs of children very well, but it is least likely to support children **emotionally** because both the environment and the staff are unfamiliar. The program may also be far from home which could mean a long, uncomfortable ride for the sick child.

Many states are developing licensing requirements for this model of specialized care. Refer to your licensing agency's regulations.

Care for mildly ill children in family child care programs

Care in the child's regular family child care program

Home-based child care is often more flexible and informal than larger group programs. A mildly ill child may be included if the provider is willing and able to handle minor illnesses.

Care by an independent specialized program for ill children

Some home-based child care is designed specifically to care for ill children. This home could be separate from any agency. While this setup could work very well, it is likely that no regulations or administrative support exists to monitor the care.

Care by satellite homes linked to a group program or agency

In this model, the program or agency (such as a hospital) is responsible for placement of children, training of providers, and payroll. The providers can be used as substitutes in the sponsoring agency when they are not giving sick care. Because of this linkage, children can become familiar with the providers before being cared for in the home environment. Because all of the children come from the same program, all the ill children come from the same germ pool and new illnesses are rarely passed around.

Sick care services at home

Care by known adults

Children may be cared for in their own homes by adults such as a family member, friend, or family baby-sitter. This situation is probably one of the most comfortable options for the child, both emotionally and physically. The adult should be informed about the nature of the illness and given complete instructions for care.

Informal network of caregivers

Some programs keep a list of all available adults who wish to care for ill children at the child's home. Especially good resources are students (in early childhood or health fields), substitute staff persons, and older or retired persons. These caregivers should be given detailed instructions for care.

Home health agencies/baby-sitting services

Home health agencies may have workers who care for ill children. This service tends to be quite expensive but has the advantage of providing reliable and trained staff. Some communities have developed specific child care programs for sick young children with the help of public funding or employer support to help pay the high fees.

References

Chapter 1

American Academy of Pediatrics. Committee on Early Childhood, Adoption, and Dependent Care. 1984, 1993. The pediatrician's role in promoting the health of a patient in day care. *Pediatrics, 74*(1), 157–158.

American Academy of Pediatrics. Committee on Early Childhood, Adoption and Dependent Care. 1987. Deitch, M.D., S.R. (Ed.). *Health in day care: A manual for health professionals.* Elk Grove Village, IL: Author.

American Academy of Pediatrics. 1995. Caring for our children. (Six 30-minute videotapes). Elk Grove Village, IL: NAEYC.

Aronson, S.S. 1983. Health policies and procedures. *Child Care Information Exchange,* (September 1983), 14–16.

Dixon, M.D., S.D. (1990). Talking to the child's physician: Thoughts for the child care provider. *Young Children, 45*(3), 36–37.

Pennsylvania Chapter of the American Academy of Pediatrics. 1993. *Model child care health policies.* PA: Author. (Available from the National Association for the Education of Young Children, 1509 16th Street N.W., Washington, DC 20036-1426.)

*Reinisch, E.H., & Minear, R.E., Jr. 1978. *Health of the preschool child.* New York: Wiley.

*U.S. Office of Human Development Services, Administration for Children, Youth and Families. *Head Start health services: Health coordination manual* (DHHS Publication No. [OHDS] 84-31190. Washington, DC: U.S. Government Printing Office.

Chapter 2

Aronson, S.S. 1991. *Health and safety in child care.* New York: HarperCollins.

Aronson, S.S. 1984. Health and safety training for child care workers. *Child Care Information Exchange,* (October 1984), 25–28.

Brown, M. 1974, 1994. *Stone soup.* New York: Macmillan.

*Miller, J. 1975. *Web of life: Health education activities for children.*

National Highway Traffic Safety Administration. 1984. *We love you—Buckle up!* Washington, DC: Author. (Available from National Association for the Education of Young Children, 1509 16th Street, N.W., Washington, DC 20036–1426)

Nelson, H.M., & Aronson, S.S. 1982. *Health power: A blueprint for improving the health of children.* New York: Westinghouse Health Systems.

*U.S. Office of Human Development Services. Administration for Children, Youth and Families. 1984. *Head Start health services: Health coordination manual* (DHHS Publication No. [OHDS] 84—31190). Washington, DC: U.S. Government Printing Office.

Whicker, P.H. 1983. *Aim for health.* Winston-Salem, NC: Kaplan Press.

Chapter 3

Noyes, D. 1987. Indoor pollutants: Environmental hazards to young children. *Young Children 42*(6), 57–65.

*out of print

Chapter 4

American Academy of Pediatrics. Committee on Early Childhood, Adoption and Dependent Care. 1987. Deitch, M.D., S.R. (Ed.). *Health in day care: A manual for health professionals.* Elk Grove Village, IL: Author.

National Association for the Education of Young Children. 1991. *Accreditation Criteria & procedures of the National Academy of Early Childhood Programs.* Washington, DC: Author.

Chapter 5

American Academy of Pediatrics, & American Public Health Association. 1992. *Caring for our children—National health and safety performance standards: Guidelines for out-of-home child care programs.* Washington, DC: Author.

*Granger, R.H. 1977. *Your child from one to six* (DHEW Publication No. [OHDS] 77—30026). Washington, DC: U.S. Government Printing Office.

Provence, S. 1967. *Guide for the care of infants in groups.* Washington, DC: Child Welfare League of America.

Chapter 6

American Society for Testing and Materials (ASTM). 1993. *Standard consumer safety performance specifications for playground equipment for public use.* (Designation F1487-93). PA: Author.

Briss, P.A., Sacks, J.J., Addiss, D.G., Kresvow, M. and O'Neil, J. 1994. A nationwide study of the risk of injury associated with day care center attendance. *Pediatrics, 93*(3), March 1994.

Esbensen, S. 1987. *The early childhood playground: An outdoor classroom.* Ypsilanti, MI: High/Scope.

Frost, J.L. 1986. Children's playgrounds: Research and practice. In G. Fein, & M. Rivkin (Eds.). *The young child at play: Reviews of research, Vol. 4* (pp. 195–211). Washington, DC: National Association for the Education of Young Children.

Frost, J.L. 1992. *Play and playscapes.* New York: Delmar Publishers, Inc.

Lovell, P., & Harms, T. 1985. How can playgrounds be improved? *Young Children, 40*(3), 3–8.

McCracken, J.B. 1990. "Playgrounds: safe and sound." Washington, DC: National Association for the Education of Young Children.

National Association for the Education of Young Children. 1985. "Toys: Tools for learning." Washington, DC: Author.

U.S. Consumer Products Safety Commission. 1993. *Handbook for public playground safety.* Washington, DC: Author.

U.S. Consumer Products Safety Commission. 1992. *Little Big Kids: Play happy, play safely.* (formerly titled *Play happy, play safe,* 1988). Washington, DC: Author.

U.S. Consumer Products Safety Commission. 1993. *The safe nursery.* (formerly titled *Nursery furniture and equipment can be dangerous, 1977*). Washington, DC: Author.

Wanamaker, N., Hearn, K., & Richarz, S. 1979. *More than graham crackers: Nutrition education and food preparation with young children.* Washington, DC: National Association for the Education of Young Children.

Chapter 7

Scott, D.K. 1985. Child safety seats—They work. *Young Children, 40*(4), 13–17.

National Highway Traffic Safety Administration. 1984. *We love you—Buckle up!* Washington, DC: Author. (Available from the National Association for the Education of Young Children, 1509 16th Street, N.W., Washington, DC 20036–1426)

Chapter 8

American Red Cross. 1990. *American Red Cross child care course.* (Available from local chapters.)

American Red Cross of Massachusetts Bay. 1986, 1989, 1993. *Health and safety for infants and children.* Boston, MA: American Red Cross.

Green, M. 1984. *A sigh of relief—The first aid handbook for childhood emergencies.* (2nd ed.). New York: Bantam.

National Safety Council. 1985, January–February. Home fire extinguishers. *Home Safety Newsletter.*

Schutz, C.E., & Belda, M. (Eds.). 1987. *Guidelines for good health in Illinois day care.* Chicago: Illinois Department of Public Health.

Williams, K. (in collaboration with the Preschool Enrichment Team, Inc.). 1985. *Childhood emergency sourcebook.* Holyoke, MA: Preschool Enrichment Team.

Chapter 9

Haggerty, R.J. 1984. Section II—Health promotion. In M. Green, & R.J. Haggerty (Eds.). *Ambulatory Pediatrics III* (pp. 27–37). New York: Saunders.

Meisels, S.J. 1989. *Developmental screening in early childhood: A guide.* Washington, DC: National Association for the Education of Young Children.

Nelson, H.M., & Aronson, S.S. 1982. *Health power: A blueprint for improving the health of children.* New York: Westinghouse Health Systems.

North, A.F., Jr. 1972. *Day care 6: Health services. A guide for project directors and health personnel.* (A Head Start paperbound book)

Preschool Enrichment Team. 1983. *Preschool vision screening: A reason to start young.* Holyoke, MA: Preschool Enrichment Team.

Reinisch, E.H., & Minear, R.E., Jr. 1978. *Health of the preschool child.* New York: Wiley.

Souweine, J.; Crimmins, S.; & Mazel, C. 1981. *Mainstreaming: Ideas for teaching young children.* Washington, DC: National Association for the Education of Young Children.

*U.S. Department of Health and Human Services. (1978). *Mainstreaming preschoolers.* Washington, DC: U.S. Government Printing Office.

Chapter 10

Aronson, S.S. 1984. Why is adult health an issue in day care? *Child Care Information Exchange,* (March 1984).

*Child Care Employee Project. *Health and safety resources for child care workers.*

*Child Care Employee Project. 1982. "Child Care Employee Project handout #9: Occupational health and safety for child care staff." Berkeley, CA: Author.

Pickering, L. & Reenes, R. 1990. Occupational risks for child-care providers and teachers. *Journal of the American Medical Association, 263*(15). Chicago: American Medical Association.

Chapter 11

American Dental Association. 1992. "Your child's teeth." (formerly titled "Care of children's teeth," 1976). Chicago: Author.

American Dental Association. 1983, 1988. "Nursing bottle mouth." Chicago: Author.

American Dental Association. 1992. *Your child's teeth.* Chicago, IL: Author.

Moss, S.J. 1977. *Your children's teeth.* New York: Brentano.

Chapter 12

American Dietetic Association. 1993. Position of the American Dietetic Association: Nutrition standards for child care programs. *Jounal of the American Dietetic Association, 94(3),* 323–328.

Birch, L.L., Johnson, S.L., & Fisher, J.A. 1995. Research in Review. Children's eating: The development of food-acceptance patterns. Young Children, *50*(2), 71.

Goodwin, M.T., & Pollen, G. 1980, 1990. *Creative food experiences for children.* Washington, DC: Center for Science in the Public Interest.

*Howard, R.B., & Herbold, N.H. 1982. *Nutrition in clinical care.* (2nd ed.). New York: McGraw–Hill.

*Howard, R.B., & Winter, H.S. 1984. *Nutrition and feeding of infants and toddlers.* Boston: Little, Brown.

Ivens, B.J., & Weil, W.B. 1984. *Teddy bears and bean sprouts—The infant and vegetarian nutrition.* Fremont, MI: Gerber Products.

Satter, F. 1983. *Child of mine—Feeding with love and good sense.* Palo Alto, CA: Bull Publishing.

Shapiro, S.(Comp.). 1990. *Nutrition resources for early childhood: A resource guide.* Washington, DC: National Center for education in Maternal and Child Health.

State of Washington, Department of Social and Health Services, Nutrition Education Training Program. 1981. *Food for the preschooler. Volumes I, II, III.* Olympia, WA: Author. (Available from Department of Health Materials Management, P.O. Box 47905, Olympia, WA 98504-7905).

*U.S. Department of Agriculture, Food and Nutrition Service. 1985. *A planning guide for food service in child care centers.* (FHS Publication No. 64). Washington, DC: U.S. Government Printing Office.

U.S. Department of Agriculture, & U.S. Department of Health and Human Services. 1985, 1990. *Nutrition and your health: Dietary guidelines for Americans.* (2nd ed.). (Home and Garden Bulletin No. 232). Washington, DC: U.S. Government Printing Office.

Vermont Department of Health, Nutrition Services. 1993. *Feeding your baby; Feeding your toddler; Feeding your preschool child.* (formerly titled *Guidelines for feeding infants and young children,* 1979). Burlington, VT: Department of Public Health, Division of Local Health.

Wanamaker, N., Hearn, K., & Richarz, S. 1979. *More than graham crackers: Nutrition education and food preparation with young children.* Washington, DC: National Association for the Education of Young Children.

Chapter 13

The Arc. 1993. *All kids count: Child care and the Americans with Disabilities Act (ADA).* Arlington, TX: Author.

Child Care Law Center. 1993. *Caring for children with special needs: The Americans with Disabilities Act and Child Care.* San Francisco, CA: Author.

Diamond, K.E., Hestenes, L.L., and O'Connor, C.E. 1994. Research in review. Integrating young children with disabilities in preschool: Problems and promise. *Young Childen, 49(2),* 68–75.

The Division for Early Childhood of the Council for Exceptional Children. 1993. *Position statement on inclusion.* Pittsburgh, PA: The Division for Early Childhood.

The Division for Early Childhood of the Council for Exceptional Children and the National Association for the Education of Young Children. 1993. *Understanding the Americans with Disabilities Act: Information for early childhood programs.* Washington, DC: National Association for the Education of Young Children.

Froschl, M., Colon, L., Rubin, E., & Sprung, B. 1984. *Including all of us: An early childhood curriculum about disability.* Educational Equity Concepts. (Available from Gryphon House, P.O. Box 207, Beltsville, MD 20704-0051).

Pickering, L. (Ed.). 1990. Infections in day care centers. *Seminars in Pediatric Infectious diseases.* Orlando, FL: W.B. Saunders.

Souweine, J., Crimmins, S., & Mazel, C. 1981. *Mainstreaming: Ideas for teaching young children.* Washington, DC: National Association for the Education of Young Children.

*U.S. Department of Health and Human Services. 1978. *Mainstreaming preschoolers.* Washington, DC: U.S. Government Printing Office.

Wolery, M., Holcombe, A., Venn, M., Brookfield, J., Huffman, K., Schroeder, C., Martin, C., & Fleming, L. 1993. Research report. Mainstreaming in early childhood programs: Current status and relevant issues. *Young Children, 49(1),* 78–84.

White, B.P., & Phair, M.A. 1986. "It'll be a challenge!" Managing emotional stress in teaching disabled children. *Young Children, 41(2),* 44–47. Washington, DC: National Association for the Education of Young Children.

Chapter 14

American Academy of Pediatrics. Task Force on Infant Positioning and SIDS. 1992. Positioning and SIDS. *Pediatrics, 89(6).*

Koblinsky, S., & Behana, N. 1984. Child sexual abuse: The educator's role in prevention, detection, and intervention. *Young Children, 39(6),* 3–15.

Meddin, B.J., & Rosen, A.L. 1986. Child abuse and neglect: Prevention and reporting. *Young Children, 41(4),* 26–30.

National Committee to Prevent Child Abuse (NCPCA). 1994. *Current trends in child abuse reporting and fatalities: The results of the 1993 annual fifty state survey.* Chicago, IL: Author.

Tower, C.T. 1992. *The role of the educators in the protection and treatment of child abuse and neglect.* Washington, DC: U.S. Department of Health and Human Services, Administration on Children, Youth, and Families, National Center on Child Abuse and Neglect.

Chapter 15

American Academy of Pediatrics. Committee on Environmental Health. July 1993. Lead poisoning. From screening to primary prevention. (formerly titled Lead Poisoning, 1987). *Pediatrics, 92(1).*

Chapter 16

Pamphlets, booklets, and information sheets from agencies such as those listed in Figure 13.2 (page 168–170).

*Black, E., & Nagel, D. (Eds.). 1982. *Physically handicapped children: A medical atlas for teachers* (2nd ed.). New York: Grune & Stratton.

*Booth, A., Donsbad, P., & Maykut, P. 1981. *Mainstreaming children with a handicap in day care and preschool: A manual of training activities*. Madison, WI: Wisconsin Council on Developmental Disabilities.

Boston Children's Medical Center, & Feinbloom, R. 1985, 1993. *Child health encyclopedia: The complete guide for parents*. New York: Bantam.

City of Boston. Mayor's Commission on the Handicapped/Boston Public Schools, Department of Student Support Services. 1982. *Chronic health problems: The special needs booklet series*. Boston: City of Boston.

Freudenberg, N., Feldman, C., Clark, N., Millman, E.J., Valle, I., & Wasilewski, Y. 1980. The impact of bronchial asthma on school attendance and performance. *Journal of School Health, 50*, 522–526.

Goldberg, E. 1994. Including children with chronic health conditions: Neubilizers in the classroom. *Young Children, 49*(2), 34–37.

*Healy, A., McAvearey, P., Von Huppel, C.S., & Jones, S.H. 1978. *Mainstreaming preschoolers: Children with health impairments*. (DHHS Publication No. [OHDS] 80-31111. Washington, DC: U.S. Government Printing Office.

Mazzocco, M.M. and O'Conner, R. A. 1993. Fragile X syndrome: A guide for teachers of young children. *Young Children, 49*(1).

Chapter 17

American Academy of Pediatrics. 1988, 1991, 1994. *Report of the Committee of Infectious Diseases*, (AAP "Red Book") (21st ed.). Elk Grove Village, IL: Author.

American Academy of Pediatrics, & American Public Health Association. 1992. *Caring for our children—National health and safety performance standards: Guidelines for out-of-home child care programs*. Washington, DC: Author.

Andersen, J., Bale, J., Jr., Blackman, J., & Murphy, J. 1986. *Infections in children. A sourcebook for educators and child care providers*. Frederick, MD: Aspen Publishers, Inc.

Child Care Law Center. 1993. *Caring for children with HIV and AIDS in child care*. San Francisco, CA: Author.

The Child Infectious Diseases Study Group. Centers for Disease Control. 1985. Considerations of infectious diseases in day care centers. *Pediatric Infectious Diseases, 4*(2).

Centers for Disease Control. 1985, August 30. *Morbidity and Mortality Weekly Report*. Atlanta: U.S. Department of Health and Human Services.

Donowitz, L.G. 1991. *Infection control in the child care center and preschool*. Baltimore, MD: Williams and Wilkins.

*Goodman, R., Osterholm, M., Granoff, D., & Pickering, L. 1984. Infectious diseases and child day care centers. *Pediatrics, 74*(1), 134–139.

Haskins, R., & Kotch, J. 1986. Day care and illness: Evidence, costs, and public policy. *Pediatrics, 77*(6), (Supplement, Part 2).

Meinking, T. 1986. Comparative efficacy of treatment for pediculosis capitis infestation. *Archives of Dermatology, 122*, 267–271.

National Association for the Education of Young Children. 1987. Lice aren't nice. *Young Children, 42*(3), 46.

National Pediatric HIV Resource Center. 1992. *Getting a head start on HIV: A resource manual for enhancing services to HIV-affected children in Head Start*. Newark, NJ: Author.

*Osterholm, M.T., Klein, J.O., Aronson, S.S., & Pickering, L.K. (Eds.). 1986. Infectious diseases in child day care: Management and prevention. *Reviews of Infectious Diseases, 8*(4).

Pickering, L. (Ed.). April 1990. Infections in day care centers. *Seminars in Pediatric Infectious Diseases, 1*(2). Philadelphia, PA: W.B.Saunders.

Ross Laboratories. 1985. *Day care: Report of the Sixteenth Ross Roundtable*. Columbus, OH: Author.

Watt, M.R., Roberts, J.E., & Zeisel, S. A. 1993. Ear infections in young children: The role of the early childhood educator. *Young Children, 49*(1). Washington, DC: National Association for the Education of Young Children.

Chapter 18

*American Academy of Pediatrics. Committee on Infant and Preschool Child. 1973. *Recommendations for day care centers for infants and children*. Elk Grove Village, IL: Author.

*American Academy of Pediatrics. 1971. *Standards for day care for infants and children under three years of age*. Elk Grove Village, IL: Author.

American Academy of Pediatrics. 1987. *Health in day care: A manual for health professionals*. Elk Grove Village, IL: Author.

American Red Cross. Child Care Course, Caring for Ill Children Unit. (Available through local chapters.)

Aronson, S.S. 1981. *Management of minor illness and injury*.

Aronson, S.S. 1984. Summer safety and first aid. *Child Care Information Exchange*, (August 1984), 13–15.

Aronson, S.S. 1985. What to do about rashes. *Child Care Information Exchange*. (May 1985), 26–28.

Aronson, S.S. 1985. Medication administration in child care. *Child Care Information Exchange*, (January 1985), 26–29.

Boston Children's Medical Center, & Feinbloom, R.I. 1985, 1993. *Child health encyclopedia: The complete guide for parents*. New York: Bantam.

Nelson, H.M., & Aronson, S.S. 1982. *Health power: A blueprint for improving the health of children*. New York: Westinghouse Health Systems.

Preschool Perspectives. 1984. Rx for administering medication. *Preschool Perspectives, 1*(1), 7–8.

Schmidt, B.B. 1984. Fever in childhood. *Pediatrics, 74* (Supplement), 929–936.

Chapter 19

American Academy of Pediatrics, & American Public Health Association. 1992. *Caring for our children—National health and safety performance standards: Guidelines for out-of-home child care programs*. Washington, DC: Author.

*Fredericks, B.; Hardman, B.; Morgan, G.; & Rogers, F. 1986. *A little bit under the weather*. Watertown, MA: Work/Family Directions.

Mohlabane, N. 1984, 1993. *Infants in day care centers: In sickness and in health*. Oakland, CA: BANANAS Child Care Information Referral and Parent Support.

*Parents in the Workplace. 1983. *Sick child care: A problem for working parents and employers*. Minneapolis, MN: Greater Minneapolis Day Care Association.

Rodgers, F.S., Morgan, G., & Fredericks, B.C. 1985. Caring for the ill child in day care. *Journal of School Health, 56,* 131–133.

Appendix 1
National resources for health and safety information

See also Figure 13.2 (page 168–170) for a list of resources for children with special needs.

National organizations
American Academy of Pediatrics, P.O. Box 927, 141 Northwest Point Blvd., Elk Grove Village, IL 60009 (also state chapters).

American Alliance for Health, Physical Education, Recreation and Dance, 1900 Association Drive, Reston, VA 22091.

American Automobile Association, 12600 Fairlakes Circle, Fairfax, VA 22033 (highway and pedestrian safety).

American Cancer Society, Inc. 1599 Clifton Road, N.E., Atlanta, GA 30329.

American Dietetic Association, 216 West Jackson Blvd., Suite 800, Chicago, IL 60606-6995.

American Heart Association, 7320 Greenville Avenue, Dallas, TX 75231.

American Medical Association, Department of Community Health and Health Education, 535 N. Dearborn Street, Chicago, IL 60610.

American Optometric Association, Department of Public Information, 243 N. Lindbergh Blvd., St. Louis, MO 63141.

American Public Health Association, 1015 15th Street, N.W., Washington, DC 20005.

American Red Cross, 17th and D Streets, N.W., Washington, DC 20006 (contact local chapter first).

American Society for Testing and Materials, 1916 Race Street, Philadelphia, PA 19103.

Association for the Care of Children's Health, 7910 Woodmont Avenue, Suite 300, Bethesda, MD 20814.

Centers for Disease Control, 1600 Clifton Road, N.E., Atlanta, GA 30333.

Child Care Employee Project, 6536 Telegraph Avenue, #A-201, Oakland, CA 94609-1114.

Child Care Health Project, 8374 Fresno Avenue, La Mesa, CA 92041.

Child Care Law Center, 22 Second Street, San Francisco, CA 94105.

Children's Defense Fund, 122 C Street, N.W., Washington, DC 20001.

Council for Exceptional Children, 1920 Association Drive, Reston, VA 22091.

Environmental Protection Agency (EPA), 401 M Street, S.W., Washington, DC 20406.

ERIC/EECE, Educational Resources Information Center, Elementary and Early Childhood Education, University of Illinois, 805 W. Pennsylvania Avenue, Urbana, IL 61801.

Health Insurance Council, 488 Madison Avenue, New York, NY 10022.

Heart Disease Control Program, Division of Special Health Services, United States Public Health Service, Department of Health and Human Services, Washington, DC 20025.

Johnson & Johnson Consumer Products, Grandview Road, Skillman, NJ 08558.

Metropolitan Life Insurance Company, School Health Bureau, Health and Welfare Division, 1 Madison Avenue, New York, NY 10010 (health, safety, and first aid).

National Academy of Sciences (NAS), National Research Council, 2101 Constitution Avenue, N.W., Washington, DC 20418 (food and nutrition).

National Association for the Education of Young Children, 1509 16th Street, N.W., Washington, DC 20036–1426.

National Association of Vision Professionals, 1775 Church Street, N.W., Washington, DC 20036.

National Board of Fire Underwriters, American Insurance Company, 85 John Street, New York, NY 10038 (fire prevention education).

National Center for Education in Maternal and Child Health, 38th and R Streets, N.W., Washington, DC 20057.

National Commission on Safety Education, National Education Association, 1201 16th Street, N.W., Washington, DC 20036.

National Dairy Council, 6300 N. River Road, Rosemont, IL 60018-4233.

National Drowning Prevention Network, P.O. Box 161661, Fort Worth, TX 76161.

National Health Council, 350 5th Avenue, Suite 1118, New York, NY 10118.

National Health Information Center, P.O. Box 1133, Washington, DC 20013-1133.

National Information Center for Handicapped Children and Youth, P.O. Box 1492, Washington, DC 20013.

National Institutes of Health (NIH), U.S. Public Health Service, Department of Health and Human Services, Bethesda, MD 20892.
Allergy and Infectious Diseases (NIAID)
Arthritis, Diabetes, Digestive and Kidney Diseases (NIADDK)
Cancer (NCI)
Child Health and Human Development (NICHHD)
Dental Research (NIDR)
Eyes/Blindness (NEI)
Heart, Lung and Blood (NHLBI)
Neurological Disorders and Stroke (NINDS)

National Institute of Mental Health (NIMH), 5600 Fishers Lane, Rockville, MD 20857.

National Organization for Rare Disorders, P.O. Box 8923, New Fairfield, CT 06812.

The National PTA, 700 N. Rush Street, Chicago, IL 60611 (child health and safety).

National Passenger Safety Association, 1050 17th Street, N.W., Suite 770, Washington, DC 20036.

National Pesticide Telecommunications Network, Texas Tech University, Thompson Hall, Room S-129, Lubbock, TX 79430.

National Safety Council, 444 N. Michigan Avenue, Chicago, IL 60611.

Nutrition Foundation, Inc., 1126 16th St., N.W., 3rd Floor, Washington, DC 20036.

Office of Child Development, U.S. Department of Health and Human Services, P.O. Box 1182, Washington, DC 20013.

Office of Special Education and Rehabilitative Services, 330 C Street, S.W., Switzer Building, Room 3006, Washington, DC 20202.

Public Health Service (PHS), Public Inquiries Branch, U.S. Department of Health and Human Services, Washington, DC 20201 (health and poison prevention).

School Health Education Study, 1507 M Street, N.W., Room 800, Washington, DC 20005.

Sex Information and Education Council of the United States, 130 W. 42nd Street, #2500, New York, NY 10036.

Society for Nutrition Education, 1700 Broadway Street, Oakland, CA 94612.

State Farm Insurance Companies, Public Relations Department, One State Farm Plaza, Bloomington, IL 61701 (first aid and safety).

United States Consumer Product Safety Commission (CPSC), Room 336-B, 5401 Westbard Avenue, Bethesda, MD 20207.

United States Department of Agriculture, Agricultural Research Administration, Bureau of Human Nutrition and Home Economics, Washington, DC 20250.

United States Department of Health and Human Services (DHHS), P.O. Box 1182, Washington, DC 20013.

United States Department of Labor, Occupational Safety and Health Administration, (OSHA), 200 Constitution Avenue, N.W., Washington, DC 20210.

United States Department of Transportation, 400 7th Street, S.W., Washington, DC 20590.

Periodicals

Child Care Information Exchange, P.O. Box 2890, Redmond, WA 98073. (Monthly magazine for directors with regular health update column written by Susan S. Aronson, M.D.)

Child Health Alert, P.O. Box 338, Newton Highlands, MA 02161. (A monthly newsletter with summaries and comments on recent health research and issues. Written in a clear and understandable format. A good resource.)

Child Health Talk, National Black Child Development Institute, 1023 15th Street NW, Suite 600, Washington, DC 20005. (Four issues per year.)

Daycare Health, Mathanna Publications, Box 5351, Bellingham, WA 98227-9970. (Five issues per year.)

Health Links, Pennsylvania Chapter of the American Academy of Pediatrics, The Dayton Building, Suite 220, Bryn Mawr, PA 19010 (Four issues per year.)

Pediatrics for Parents, P.O. Box 1069, Bangor, ME 04402-1069. (Excellent monthly newsletter with practical health information in an easy-to-read format. Includes summaries of research and helpful hints dealing with children; appropriate for parents and staff.)

Please refer to the list of organizations—nearly all of them have publications.

Health and Safety in child care
Health

American Academy of Pediatrics. Committee on Early Childhood, Adoption and Dependent Care. 1987. Deitch, M.D., S.R. (Ed.). *Health in day care: A manual for health professionals.* Elk Grove Village, IL: Author.

American Academy of Pediatrics. 1995. Caring for our children. (Six 30-minute videotapes). Elk Grove Village, IL: NAEYC.

*Child Care Employee Project. 1984. *Health and safety resources for child care workers.* Berkeley, CA: Author. (Available from Child Care Employee Project, P.O. Box 5603, Berkeley, CA 94705.)

*Greater Minneapolis Day Care Association. 1983. *Child health guidelines: Health, nutrition, infants, and toddlers.* Minneapolis, MN: Author. (Available from Greater Minneapolis Day Care Association, 1006 West Lake, Minneapolis, MN 55408.)

Gunzenhauser, N., & Caldwell, B. (Eds.). 1986. *Group care for young children: Considerations for child care workers and health professionals, pub-*

lic policy makers, and parents. Johnson & Johnson Baby Products Company, Pediatric Roundtable Series: 12. New Brunswick, NJ: Johnson & Johnson.

McCracken, J.B. (Ed.). 1992. Pediatricians, families and child care: An overview of the symposium on day care for children. *Johnson & Johnson Consumer Products, Inc., Pediatric Roundtable Series: 15*. New Brunswick, NJ: Johnson & Johnson.

*Schloesser, P. (Ed.). 1986. *Health of children in day care: Public health profiles*. (Available from Maternal and Child Health Clearinghouse, 38th and R Streets, N.W., Washington, DC 20057.)

King County Department of Health–Day Care Health Program. 1985. *Child day care health handbook*. Seattle, WA: Author.

National Association for the Education of Young Children. 1991. *Accreditation Criteria & procedures of the National Academy of Early Childhood Programs*. Washington, DC: Author. (Available from National Association for the Education of Young Children, 1509 16th Street, N.W., Washington, DC 20036–1426.)

Ross Laboratories. 1985. *Day care*. Report of the Sixteenth Ross Roundtable. Columbus, OH: Author.

Safety

Aronson, S.S. 1993. Smoke is poison and more on clean sand. *Child Care Information Exchange, July 1993*. Redmond, WA: Child Care Information Exchange.

Bergwall Video Productions. 1990. *Child care: Indoor safety* (3 videotapes). *Child care: Outdoor safety* (3 videotapes). Garden City, NJ: Author.

Juvenile Products Manufacturers Association (JPMA). 1993. *Safe and sound for baby*. Marlton, NJ: Author.

McCracken, J.B. 1990. *Playgrounds: Safe and sound*. Washington, DC: National Association for the Education of Young Children.

National Highway Traffic Safety Administration. 1992. *Consumer Information: Transporting your children safely*. Washington, DC: U.S. Department of Transportation, National Highway Traffic Safety Administration.

Toy Manufacturers of America, Inc. 1993. *Toys and play*. NY: Author.

U.S. Environmental Protection Agency. Office of Pesticide Programs. 1991. *Citizen's guide to pesticides*. (H7506C). Washington, DC: Author.

Infectious diseases

American Academy of Pediatrics. Committee on Early Childhood, Adoption and Dependent Care. 1987. Deitch, M.D., S.R. (Ed.). *Health in day care: A manual for health professionals*. Elk Grove Village, IL: Author.

American Academy of Pediatrics Committee on Infectious Diseases. 1988, 1991, 1994. *Report of the Committee on Infectious Diseases* ("Red Book") (21st ed.). Elk Grove Village, IL: Author.

Bananas Child Care Information and Referral and Parental Support. 1980. *Sick child care guide for parents and child care providers*. (Available from Bananas, Inc., 5232 Claremont Ave., Oakland, CA 94618.)

*Centers for Disease Control. 1984. *What you can do to stop disease in the child day care center*. (Stock #017-023-00172-8). Washington, DC: U.S. Government Printing Office.

*Fredericks, B., Hardman, R., Morgan, G., & Rodgers, F. 1986. *A little bit under the weather*. Boston, MA: Work/Family Directions. (Available from Work/Family Directions, Inc., 9 Galen Street, Suite 230, Watertown, MA 02172.)

Haskins, R., & Kotch, J. 1986. Day care and illness: Evidence, costs, and public policy. *Pediatrics*, 77(6). (Available from American Academy of Pediatrics, P.O. Box 927, Elk Grove Village, IL 60009.)

Osterholm, M., Klein, J., Aronson, S., & Pickering, L. 1986. Infectious diseases in child day care: Management and prevention. *Reviews of Infectious Diseases*, 8(4).

*Sleator, E. 1986. *Infectious diseases in day care*. Urbana, IL: ERIC Clearinghouse. (Available from ERIC Clearinghouse, University of Illinois, 805 W. Pennsylvania Avenue, Urbana, IL 61801.)

Child health

American Academy of Pediatrics. 1988. *Guidelines for health supervision* (2nd ed.). Elk Grove Village, IL: Author. (Available from American Academy of Pediatrics, Publications Department, P.O.

Box 927, Elk Grove Village, IL 60009.)

Boston Children's Medical Center, & Feinbloom, R.I. 1985, 1993. *Child health encyclopedia: The complete guide for parents.* New York: Bantam.

Marotz, L., Rush, J., & Cross, M. 1985, 1989, 1993. *Health, safety, and nutrition for the young child.* Albany, NY: Delmar. (Available from the Department of Human Development and Family Life, University of Kansas, Delmar Publishers, Inc., 2 Computer Drive, W., Box 15-015, Albany, NY 12212.)

Pantell, R.H., Fries, J.F., & Vikery, D.M. 1984, 1990. *Taking care of your children.* Reading, MA: Addison-Wesley.

Child health curriculum

Brevis Corporation, 3310 S. 2700 East, Salt Lake City, UT 84105. (Very clever and appealing materials on handwashing for children and adults.)

Hendricks, C., & Smith, C.J. 1982, 1991. *Here we go. Watch me grow.* (Available from ETR Associate Network Publishing Company, P.O. Box 1830, Santa Cruz, CA 95061-1830.)

*Miller, J. 1975. *Web of life: Health education activities for children.* (Available from Pennsylvania Dept. of Education, Bureau of Curriculum and Instruction, 8th Floor, 333 Market Street, P.O. Box 911, Harrisburg, PA 17108.)

National Dairy Council. 1979. *Chef combo.* Rosemont, IL: Author. (Available from your local dairy council.) (Nutrition curriculum kit that includes puppets, games, and other activities.)

National Highway Traffic Safety Administration. 1984. *We love you—Buckle up!* Washington, DC: Author. (Available from National Association for the Education of Young Children, 1509 16th Street, N.W., Washington, DC 20036–1426.) (A curriculum packet that contains a teacher's guide, a book for children, handouts to copy for parents, a poster, 36 stickers, and other information about child passenger safety.)

*Whicker, P. 1983. *Aim for health.* Lewisville, NC: Kaplan Press. (Available from Kaplan Press, P.O. Box 609, Lewisville, NC 27023.)

Children with special needs

Abbott, C.F. and Gold, S. 1991. Conferring with parents when you're concerned that their child needs special services. *Young Children, 46*(4), 10–14. Washington, DC: National Association for the Education of Young Children.

Baker, A.C. 1993. New frontiers in family day care: Integrating children with ADHD. *Young Children, 48*(5), 69–73. Washington, DC: National Association for the Education of Young Children.

*Black, E., & Nagel, D. (Eds.). 1982. *Physically handicapped children: A medical atlas for teachers* (2nd ed.). New York: Grune & Stratton.

*Brooth, A., Donebad, P., & Maykut, P. 1981. *Mainstreaming children with a handicap in day care and preschool: A manual of training activities.* Madison, WI: Wisconsin Council on Developmental Disabilities.

Chandler, P.A. 1994. *A place for me: Including children with special needs in early care and education settings.* Washington, DC: National Assocation for the Education of Young Children.

Fauvre, M. 1988. Including young children with "new" chronic illnesses in an early childhood setting. *Young Children, 43*(6), 71–77. Washington, DC: National Association for the Education of Young Children.

Froschl, M., Colon, L., Rubin, E., & Sprung, B. 1984. *Including all of us: An early childhood curriculum about disability.* Mt. Rainier, MD: Educational Equity Concepts. (Available from Gryphon House, Inc., P.O. Box 275, Mt. Rainier, MD 20712.)

Goldberg, E. 1994. Including children with chronic health conditions: Neubilizers in the classroom. *Young Children, 49*(2), 34–37. Washington, DC: National Association for the Education of Young Children.

Holder-Brown, L., and Parette, H.P., Jr. 1992. Children with disabilities who use assistive technology: Ethical considerations. *Young Children, 47*(6), 73–77. Washington, DC: National Assocation for the Education of Young Children.

*U.S. Department of Health and Human Services. 1978. *Mainstreaming preschoolers.* (Stock #017-092-00029-4.) Washington, DC: U.S. Government Printing Office.

First-aid resources

American Red Cross. 1990. Child Care Course. (Certified course with units on preventing childhood injuries, infant and child first aid, preventing infectious diseases, caring for ill children, learning about child development, communicating with children and parents, recognizing and reporting child abuse.) (Available from local chapters.)

Freeman, L. *What would you do if . . . A kid's guide to first aid.* 1983, 1993. Seattle, WA: Parenting Press. (Available from Parenting Press, 7750 31st Avenue, N.E., Seattle, WA 98115.) (Emphasizes discussion of prevention and first-aid information for children.)

*Green, M. 1984. *A sigh of relief—The first aid handbook for childhood emergencies* (2nd ed.). NY: Bantam.

Nutrition resources

American Academy of Pediatrics, the American Dietetic Association, and the Food Marketing Institute. 1990. *Healthy start . . . Food to grow on program.* (An information and education campaign of the AAP, the American Dietetic Association and the Food Marketing Institute to promote healthful food choices and eating habits for healthy children older than 2 years of age. Series of brochures). Chicago, IL: The American Dietetic Association.

Berman, C. & Fromer, J. 1991. *Teaching children about food.* Palo Alto, CA: Bull Publishing.

*Bershad, C., & Bernick, D. 1981. *Bodyworks: The kid's guide to food and physical fitness.* New York: Random House.

Massachusetts Department of Public Health. 1984. *Infant feeding policy.* Boston, MA: Author.

National Center for Nutrition and Dietetics of The American Dietetic Association. 1993. *Eat right america: The good nutrition reading list.* Chicago, IL: American Dietetic Association.

*Natow, A., & Heslin, J.A. 1984. *No-nonsense nutrition for kids.* New York: McGraw-Hill.

Satter, F. 1983, 1991. *Child of mine—Feeding with love and good sense.* Palo Alto, CA: Bull.

*U.S. Department of Agriculture, Food and Nutrition Service. 1985. *A planning guide for food service in child care centers.* (FNS Publication No. 64) Washington, DC: U.S. Government Printing Office.

U.S. Department of Agriculture, Food and Nutrition Service. 1992. *Building for the future: Nutrition guidance for the child nutrition programs.* (FNS-279). Available from state agency or VA: USDA/FNS.

U.S. Department of Agriculture, & U.S. Department of Health and Human Services. 1985, 1990. *Nutrition and your health: Dietary guidelines for Americans* (2nd ed.). (Home and Garden Bulletin No. 232.) Washington, DC: U.S. Government Printing Office.

Van Leuven, N. 1988. *Food to grow on: A parent's guide to nutrition.* Pownal, VT: Storey.

Wanamaker, N., Hearn, K., & Richarz, S. 1987. *More than graham crackers: Nutrition education & food preparation with young children.* Washington, DC: National Association for the Education of Young Children.

Resources for developmental and health screening

Developmental

Meisels, S.J. 1989. *Developmental screening in early childhood: A guide.* Washington, DC: National Association for the Education of Young Children.

Meisels, S. and Provence, S. 1989. *Screening and assessment: Guidelines for identifying young disabled and developmentally vulnerable children and their families.* Washington, DC: National Center for Clinical Infant Programs.

Vision

Broken Wheel Test. (Available from Bernell Corporation, 750 Lincolnway East, South Bend, IN 46634.)

Snellen E (Tumbling E). (Available from the National Society to Prevent Blindness, 500 E. Remington Road, Schaumburg, IL 60173.)

Speech and hearing

American Speech-Language-Hearing Association (ASHA). *How does your child hear and talk?* Rockville, MD: Author.

Appendix 2
Children's picture books about health, nutrition, and safety

Mary Renck Jalongo and Melissa Ann Renck—Compilers

Health care

Aliki. 1962. *My five senses.* New York: Harper & Row.

Berger, M. 1983. *Why I cough, sneeze, shiver, hiccup and yawn.* New York: Crowell/Harper & Row.

Berger, M. 1985. *Germs make me sick!* New York: Crowell/Harper & Row.

Brandenberg, F. 1978. *I wish I was sick, too!* New York: Puffin.

Brown, M. 1979. *Arthur's eyes.* Boston: Little, Brown.

Brown, T. 1984. *Someone special, just like you.* New York: Holt, Rhinehart & Winston.

Brenner, B. 1973. *Bodies.* New York: E.P. Dutton.

Cole, J. 1984. *How you were born.* New York: Morrow.

Cole, J. 1985. *Cuts, breaks, bruises and burns: How your body heals.* New York: Crowell/Harper & Row.

Cole, J. 1987. *The magic schoolbus at the waterworks.* New York: Scholastic.

DeSantis, K. 1985. *A doctor's tools.* New York: Dodd.

Howe, J. 1981. *The hospital book.* New York: Crown.

Isadora, R. 1985. *I hear.* New York: Greenwillow.

Isadora, R. 1985. *I see.* New York: Greenwillow.

Krementz, J. 1986. *Taryn goes to the dentist.* New York: Crown.

Marino, B.P. 1979. *Eric needs stitches.* New York: Reading, MA: Addison-Wesley.

Oxenbury, H. 1983. *The checkup.* New York: Dial.

Oxenbury, H. 1986. *I hear.* New York: Random House.

Oxenbury, H. 1986. *I see.* New York: Random House.

Oxenbury, H. 1986. *I touch.* New York: Random House.

Peterson, J. l977. *I have a sister, my sister is deaf.* New York: Harper & Row.

Rabe, B. 1981. *The balancing girl.* New York: Dutton.

Reit, S. 1985. *Some busy hospital!* New York: Golden Books.

Rockwell, A., & Rockwell, H. 1982. *Sick in bed.* New York: Macmillan.

Rockwell, A., & Rockwell, H. 1985. *The emergency room.* New York: Macmillan.

Rockwell, H. 1973. *My doctor.* New York: Macmillan.

Rockwell, H. 1975. *My dentist.* New York: Greenwillow.

Showers, P. 1975. *Hear your heart.* New York: Harper & Row.

Shower, P. 1980. *No measles, no mumps for me.* New York: Crowell/Harper & Row.

Silverstein, A. 1978. *Itch, sniffle and sneeze: All about asthma, hay fever and other allergies.* New York: Four Winds.

Steedman, J. 1974. *Emergency room: An ABC tour.* McLean, VA: Windy Hill Press.

Stein, S.B. 1974. *A hospital story: An open family book for parents and children together.* New York: Walker.

Trier, C.S. 1982. *Exercise: What it is, what it does.* New York: Greenwillow.

Wolf, B. 1980. *Michael and the dentist.* New York: Four Winds.

Zim, H.S. 1952. *What's inside me?* New York: Morrow.

Foods and nutrition

Aliki. 1976. *Corn is maize: The gift of the Indians.* New York: Crowell/Harper & Row.

Carle, E. 1969. *The very hungry caterpillar.* New York: Philomel Books.

Cauley, L.B. 1977. *Pease porridge hot: A Mother Goose cookbook.* New York: Putnam.

Cooper, J. 1977. *Love at first bite: Snacks and mealtime treats the easy way.* New York: Knopf.

Degan, B. 1983. *Jamberry.* New York: Harper & Row.

de Paola, T. 1978. *The popcorn book.* New York: Holiday House.

Ehlert, L. 1987. *Growing vegetable soup.* New York: Harcourt Brace Jovanovich.

Gibbons, G. 1985. *The milk makers.* New York: Macmillan.

Hoban, R. 1964. *Bread and jam for Frances.* New York: Harper.

Lynn, S. 1986. *Food.* New York: Macmillan/Aladdin.

Pluckrose, H. 1986. *Think about tasting.* New York: Watts.

Rockwell, A., & Rockwell, H. 1982. *How my garden grew.* New York: Macmillian.

Rylant, C. 1984. *This year's garden.* New York: Bradbury.

Seixas, J.S. 1984. *Junk food.* New York: Greenwillow.

Seixas, J.S. 1986. *Vitamins: What they are, what they do.* New York: Greenwillow.

Sharmat, M. 1980. *Gregory the terrible eater.* New York: Four Winds.

Showers, P. 1985. *What happens to a hamburger.* New York: Crowell/Harper & Row.

Smaridge, N. 1982. *What's on your plate?* Nashville, TN: Abingdon.

Spier, P. 1981. *The food market.* New York: Doubleday.

Safety

Brown, M., & Krensky, L. 1982. *Dinosaurs beware! A safety guide.* Boston: Little, Brown.

Gibbons, G. 1984. *Fire! Fire!* New York: Crowell/Harper & Row.

Girard, L.W. 1984. *My body is private.* Niles, IL: Whitman.

McLeod, E.W. 1975. *The bear's bicycle.* Boston: Little, Brown.

Schick, E. 1980. *Home alone.* New York: Dial Press.

Smaridge, N. 1965. *Watch out!* Nashville, TN: Abingdon.

Wachter, O. 1983. *No more secrets for me.* Boston: Little, Brown.

Index

Adult health
   assessment form, 124
   back protection, 122
   examinations, 121, 123
   infectious disease prevention, 123, 125
      for pregnant women, 125
      handwashing, 125
      immunization, 125
   plan, 121
   promoting, 121
Air conditioner, 23
Air quality, 22–23
Allergies, 189, 191 *See also* Food allergies and intolerances
   milk and lactose intolerance, 146
Americans with Disabilities Act (ADA), 161–164
Appetite, 140
Art materials
   poisons in, 61–62
Asbestos, 25
Asthma, 191–195
Back protection, 122
Bathrooms
   safety checklist, 52–53
Bleach solution, 17, 18, 26, 29
   concentration of, 17
   commercial alternatives to, 17
   for spraying versus soaking, 17, 26
Breast-feeding, 133
BURNS and SCALDS, 92
Calcium, 144
Campylobacter, 208, 212–213
Carpets, 25
Carriages, 72
Carriers (baby), 70, 71
Chicken pox (varicella), 222–224

Child abuse
   accusation of in program, 180
   characteristics of families at risk for, 177
   identification of abused children, 175–176
   emotional abuse, 176–177
   materials for young children, 182
   physical abuse, 176
   physical and emotional neglect, 177
   preventing, 179–181
   reporting, 178–179
   resources, 183
   screening staff, 180–181
   sexual abuse, 177
Choking
   CPSC rattle test, 73
   hazards, 60, 63
CHOKING/CPR
      for infants under 1 year, 90
      for children over 1 year, 91
Clean
   definition of, 30
Cleaning (handling)
   contaminated materials, 25–26
   guidelines, 30
   See also housekeeping
Clothes
   dress-up, 27
Colds, influenza, 219, 265
Community resources, 10
Conjunctivitis (pinkeye), 232, 235, 237
Constipation, 267–268
Consultant, health care, 7
   communicating with, 7
   qualifications and role of, 7
   where to find, 7–8
CONVULSIONS, 92

CPR
  for infants under 1 year, 90
  for children over 1 year, 91
Cribs, 71
Cytomegalovirus (CMV), 240, 243–244
Dehydration, 270
Dental health
  care, 128–129, 130
  education, 128
  referral criteria, 129
  See also teeth; tooth
Development, 101, 105
  feeding skills, 134–135
  health history, 102–104
  red flags, 106–111
    hearing, 110–111
    motor development, 108–109
    social-emotional development, 107
    speech and language development, 109–110
    vision, 111
Diabetes, 198–199
Diaper rash, 269
Diapering
  area, 37, 69
    poisons in, 63–64
  procedures, 39–41
Diapers
  cloth versus paper, 37–38
  diaper service, 38
  handling of, 26
Diarrhea. See also diseases
  267
Disabilities
  types of, 172–173
    autism, 172
    deaf-blindness, 172
    deafness, 172
    hearing impairment, 172
    mental retardation, 172
    multiple disabilities, 172
    orthopedic impairment, 172
    other health impairment, 172–173
    serious emotional disturbance, 173
    specific learning disability, 173
    speech or language impairment, 173
    traumatic brain injury, 173
    visual impairment including blindness, 173
Discipline, 179–180

Disease
  control, 203, 205–206
  contagious or communicable, 203
  infectious, 203
Diseases
  noncontagious, infectious, 255–257
    monilial (Candida) infections, 255, 256
    otitis media (middle ear infection), 255
    tick-borne diseases, 255, 256–257
  spread through blood, 247–251
    hepatitis B, 247–249
    HIV/AIDS, 247, 249–251
  spread through direct contact, 232–233, 235, 238
    conjunctivitis (pinkeye), 232, 235
    cytomegalovirus (CMV), 240, 243–244
    herpes simplex virus (HSV), 240, 244, 246
    impetigo, 232, 233
    pediculosis (head lice), 232, 238, 240
    ringworm (tinea), 232, 233, 235
    scabies, 232, 235, 238
    sexually transmitted diseases (STDs), 240, 245, 246
  spread through intestinal tract, 206, 208–209, 212–213, 215, 217
    Hand, foot, and mouth syndrome (coxsackievirus), 217
    hepatitis A, 213, 215, 217
    infectious diarrheal, 208–209
      Campylobacter, 208, 212–213
      Giardia, 208, 209
      Salmonella, 208, 212
      Shigella, 208, 209, 212
    pinworms, 213
  spread through respiratory tract, 217, 219–220, 222, 224, 226, 228–229, 231–232
    chicken pox, 222, 224
    colds, influenza, 219
    fifth disease (Erythema Infectosum), 224, 226
    Haemophilus influenzae type b illness (Hib disease), 228–229
    impetigo, 220
    meningococcal illnesses, 226, 228
    rheumatic fever, 220
    roseola (sixth disease), 219–220
    scarlet fever, 220
    shingles, 222, 224

strep throat, 220
tuberculosis, 229, 231–232
vaccine-preventable, 251–255
diphtheria, 251, 253–254
measles, 251, 252
mumps, 251, 252–253
pertussis (whooping cough), 251, 254–255
polio, 251, 252, 253
rubella (German measles), 251, 252, 253
tetanus, 251, 254
Diphtheria, 251, 253–254
Dishwashing, 34
Disinfect
definition of, 30
Disinfection, 17
of toys, 26
Drowning, 68
Ear tubes, 255
Emergencies
preparing for, 81
procedures for, 82
EMERGENCY CONDITIONS, 261
Emergency contact information, 84
Epilepsy/seizure disorder, 196–197
Evacuation
procedures, 86–88
Examinations, 119
Exclusion guidelines
for children and adults, 207
for staff, 125
Extermination. *See* pest control
EYE INJURIES, 92
FAINTING, 92
Feeding
children with special needs, 147–148
nutritional concerns, 147–148
infants, 133
beginning cow's milk, 137
food components for, 136
handling formula, 157
solid foods, 133, 137
toddlers, 138, 139
food components for, 139
FEVER, 92, 264–265
Field trips
safety, 67, 79–80
Fifth disease (Erythema Infectosum), 224, 225, 226

Fire
procedures in case of, 87–88
FIRST-AID
education
for children, 89
for parents, 89
for common situations
BURNS and SCALDS, 92
CHOKING/CPR
for infants under 1 year, 90
for children over 1 year, 91
CONVULSIONS, 92
EYE INJURIES, 92
FAINTING, 92
FEVER, 92
FRACTURES and SPRAINS, 92
HEAD INJURIES, 92
NOSEBLEEDS, 92
POISONS, 92
SKIN WOUNDS, 93
STINGS and BITES, 93
TEETH, 93
kits
supplies for, 82
procedures
injury assessment, 88–89
Fluoride, 127
Food
allergies and intolerances, 146
dietary guidelines, 148–149
Food Guide Pyramid, 148
groups, 140
habits, 141–142
handling, 25, 32
and hyperactivity, 146–147
nutritional concerns
fats, 142–143
milk, 144
salt, 143
sugar, 143
vegetarian diets, 143–144
nutritional problems
Failure-to-Thrive, 145
iron deficiency, 145
obesity, 144–145
preparation and handling, 157–158
purchasing, 153

safety, 142
storage, 153
See also kitchen
Forms
incident report, 82, 85
parental permission, 81
FRACTURES and SPRAINS, 92
Garbage, 34
Giardia, 208, 209
Gloves, disposable, 19
when to wear, 19, 26
Growth percentiles, 114–117
Haemophilus influenzae type b, 228–229, 230
Hand, foot, and mouth syndrome, 217, 218
Handwashing, 17, 20
policy for, 32
procedures
for adults, 33
for infants/toddlers, 33
for older children, 33
HEAD INJURIES, 92
Health assessment
diagnosis, 99, 101
form for children, 120
for for staff, 124
screening, 99, 105, 112–119
treatment, 101
Health education
for staff and parents, 12
topics, 12–13
how to include in program, 11
what to include, 11–12
Health histories. *See* health records
Health policies, 1, 3
topics to include in, 4–5
writing, 3
Health providers
children's, 8
communicating with, 7, 8–9
disagreement among, 9
Health records, 10, 101
confidentiality of, 10
contents of, 10
developmental history, 102–104
Health team members, 100
Heart problems, 195–196
Heat exhaustion, 270
Hepatitis A, 206, 213, 215, 215, 217

Herpes simplex virus (HSV), 240, 244, 246
High chairs, 70
Hepatitis B, 247–249
HIV/AIDS, 246, 247, 249–251
Housekeeping, 29
equipment, 29
Humidifier, 23
Immunity
evidence of, 251–252
Immunization
recommended schedule for, 204
Impetigo, 220, 232, 233, 234
Inclusion
benefits of, 164–165
emergency planning considerations, 200
how to carry out, 165–166
INSULIN REACTION, 199
Kitchen, 32, 59
safety checklist, 51–52
utensils, 63
Laundry, 34
Lead
environmental managment, 186
protecting children against, 186–187
See also screening, lead
sources of, 185
Letter to parents
chicken pox, 223
conjunctivitis, 237
diarrheal diseases, 210–211
fifth disease, 225
hand, foot, and mouth syndrome, 218
head lice, 241–242
hepatitis A, 216
Hib disease, 230
impetigo, 234
meningococcal illnesses, 227
pinworms, 214
ringworm, 236
scabies, 239
strep throat, 221
Lice, 27
Lyme disease, 256–257
Mainstreaming. *See* inclusion
Mantoux test, 229, 231, 232
Measles, 251, 252
Medication
consent and log, 272
how to give, 270–271, 273

Meningococcal illnesses, 226–228
Menus
 planning, 153, 154–155, 156
Microwave ovens, 63
Monilial (Candida) infections, 255, 256
Mumps, 251, 252–253
Nausea, 267
NOSEBLEEDS, 92
Nutrition
 community resources, 151–152
  Child and Adult Care Food Program, 151–152
  Expanded Food and Nutrition Education Program, 152
  Food Distribution Program, 152
  Food Stamp Program, 152
  Nutrition Education and Training Program, 152
  WIC, 152
 education, 148, 149–151
Observation, daily, 3, 6, 101, 261, 263
Otitis media (middle ear infection), 255
Parents. *See* Letters to parents
Pediculosis (head lice), 232, 238, 240, 241–242
Pertussis (whooping cough), 251, 254–255
Pest control, 31
Pesticides, 24, 158, 257
Pets, 31–32
Physician. *See* health provider
Pinworms, 206, 213, 214
Plants
 poisonous, 62, 63
Play
 outdoor, 22
 water (*see* water play)
Playground, 64–66
 safety checklist, 56–59
 safety guidelines
  climbing apparatus, 65
  horizontal ladders and bars, 65
  slides, 65
  seesaws, 65
  swings, 65
 surfacing materials, 64, 66
Playpens, 72
Plumbing, 35
POISONS, 92
 in programs, 61–64, 158
Polio, 251, 252, 253

Pollution, indoor, 23–25
 steps to reduce, 23–24
Pools, 27, 68
 safety checklist, 53
Potty-chairs, 26, 35, 42
Preventive health care
 goals for, 97
 recommendations for, 98
Radon, 24
Rashes, 268–269
Rattle test, 73
Reye's syndrome, 219, 222, 223
Rheumatic fever, 220
Ringworm (tinea), 232, 233, 235
Rocky Mountain spotted fever, 256–257
Roseola (sixth disease), 219–220
Rubella (German measles), 251, 252, 253
Safety
 checks, 47
 checklists, 48–59
 education, 74 (*see also* transportation safety education)
 for infants and toddlers, 69, 73–74
 indoor
  doors, 59
  electrical wiring, 59
  kitchen and cooking facilities, 59
  traffic and play areas, 47
 outdoor
  playgrounds, 64–66
 pedestrian, 67
 summer, 67–68
 winter, 69
Safety seats
 legal requirements, 75
 selecting, 75–76
 use of, 76, 77
Salmonella, 208, 212
Sandboxes, 27
Scabies, 232, 235, 238, 239
Scarlet fever, 220
Screening, 99, 105, 112
 anemia, 113, 118
 formal, 112
 hearing, 112–113
  acoustic reflex, 113
  pure tone audiometry, 113
  tympanometry, 113

height and weight, 113, 114–117
informal, 112
lead, 118–119, 185
urine, 118
vision, 112
Sexually transmitted diseases, 240, 245, 246
Shigella, 208, 209, 212
Sick child care
models for, 275–276
Sickle-cell anemia, 197–198
Sinks, 19
portable water alternatives, 19, 21–22
SKIN WOUNDS, 93
Smoking, 23
Snacks, 140–141
Snow, 69
Space, 22
Special needs. *See also* disabilities
modifying your program, 167, 171–172
resources for children with, 168–170
staff attitudes toward children with, 166–167
Sprinklers, 27
Staff
breaks, 126
responsibilities for health, 3
director or administrator, role of, 6–7
teaching staff, role of, 7
See also adult health; substitute coverage
turnover and health issues, 26
STINGS and BITES, 93
preventing, 68–69
Stomachache, 268
Strep throat, 220, 221
Strollers, 72
Sudden Infant Death Syndrome, 180
Substitute coverage, 125–126
Sunburn, 269–270
Swimming pools. *See* pools
Symptom record, 262
TEETH, 93
brushing, 127–128
healthy foods for, 127
See also dental health; tooth
Teething, 269
Telephone (emergency list), 83, 86
Temperature
how to take a child's, 266
room, 22

Tetanus, 251, 254
Thermometer, 266
Thumbsucking, 130
Tick-borne diseases, 255, 256–257
Toilet, 35. *See also* potty-chairs; bathrooms
Toilet learning, 38, 41–43
equipment needed for, 42
Toilet training. *See* toilet learning
Tooth. *See also* dental health; teeth
baby bottle tooth decay, 130, 137–138
bleeding around, 130
broken, 130
knocked out, 130
toothache, 130
Toy chests, 61
Toys
disinfecting, 26
gross-motor, 61
infant/toddler, 73
cleaning, 27
safety, 69, 73
riding, 66–67
safety checklist, 50
safety of, 60–61
Transportation
emergency procedures, 78, 79
of children with special needs, 76, 78
safety education
for children, 80
for parents, 80
safety rules, 76
Tuberculosis, 229, 231–232
Vaporizer, 23
Vehicles
safety checklist, 55–56
Ventilation, 35. *See also* air quality
Vomiting, 267
Walkers, 70
Water play, 26–27
Weaning, 138

Information about NAEYC

NAEYC is . . .

a membership-supported organization of people committed to fostering the growth and development of children from birth through age 8. Membership is open to all who share a desire to serve and act on behalf of the needs and rights of young children.

NAEYC provides . . .

educational services and resources to adults who work with and for children, including

- *Young Children, the* journal for early childhood educators
- **Books, posters, brochures,** and **videos** to expand your knowledge and commitment to young children, with topics including infants, curriculum, research, discipline, teacher education, and parent involvement
- An **Annual Conference** that brings people from all over the country to share their expertise and advocate on behalf of children and families
- **Week of the Young Child** celebrations sponsored by NAEYC Affiliate Groups across the nation to call public attention to the needs and rights of children and families

- **Insurance plans** for individuals and programs
- **Public affairs information** for knowledgeable advocacy efforts at all levels of government and through the media
- The **National Academy of Early Childhood Programs,** a voluntary accreditation system for high-quality programs for children
- The **National Institute for Early Childhood Professional Development,** providing resources and services to improve professional preparation and development of early childhood educators
- The **Information Service,** a centralized source of information sharing, distribution, and collaboration

For free information about membership, publications, or other NAEYC services . . .

- Call NAEYC at 202-232-8777 or 800-424-2460.
- Or write to the National Association for the Education of Young Children, 1509 16th Street, N.W., Washington, DC 20036-1426.